Oedipus Lex

Philosophy, Social Theory, and the Rule of Law

General Editors
Andrew Arato, Seyla Benhabib, Ferenc Fehér, William Forbath, Agnes Heller, Arthur Jacobson, and Michel Rosenfeld

1. William Rehg, *Insight and Solidarity: A Study in the Discourse Ethics of Jürgen Habermas*
2. Alan Brudner, *The Unity of the Common Law: Studies in Hegelian Jurisprudence*
3. Peter Goodrich, *Oedipus Lex: Psychoanalysis, History, Law*

Oedipus Lex

Psychoanalysis, History, Law

Peter Goodrich

UNIVERSITY OF CALIFORNIA PRESS
Berkeley Los Angeles London

University of California Press
Berkeley and Los Angeles, California

University of California Press
London, England

Library of Congress Cataloging-in-Publication Data
Goodrich, Peter, 1954–
Oedipus lex: psychoanalysis, history, law / Peter Goodrich.
p. cm. — (Philosophy, social theory, and the rule of law)
Includes bibliographical references and index.
ISBN 0–520–08990–1 (alk. paper)
1. Law—Psychology—History. 2. Jurisprudence—Psychological aspects—History. 3. Lawyers—Psychology—History. I. Title. II. Series.
K487.P75G66 1995
340'.01'9—dc20 95–10026
CIP

Printed in the United States of America

1 2 3 4 5 6 7 8 9

The paper used in this publication meets the minimum requirements of American National Standard for Information Sciences—Permanence of Paper for Printed Library Materials, ANSI Z39.48–1984 ♾

CONTENTS

PREFACE

The most ancient of the Western mythologies of the foundation of law, that of the decalogue, tells the story of an order of legal writing established against the disorder of images. The writing and rewriting of the law took place around the destruction of an idol. The idol in question, the golden calf or Osiris, has been variously interpreted as representing Egypt, plurality, or feminine deities and cults of creativity. The foundational story of the writing of law is predicated upon destroying or outlawing idols, the images of other laws, of different forms of representation and of gender. The story of foundation establishes an iconic order of legality as writing, speech, or text whose letters or *literae* will banish both the use and the meaning of images and the other idols or figures of thought. This study will pursue this narrative or trauma of social foundation primarily through the example of early modern discourses of foundation of common law. It will be argued that the inaugural doctrinal discourses or treatises of common law inherit or replicate the structures of classical Western patristic writings and their theological and latterly secular narratives of legality. The common law too can be studied in terms of an originary trauma or misrecognition of identity. The Anglican legal tradition was born of the Reformation and of the new form of letters, the printed text. In doctrinal terms it developed initially as an aspect of the protest against images and established itself through discourses against the distraction of images and the idols of the mind. It built its doctrine and identity against the ornaments of Rome and the sophistries of the Continentals. It also wrote itself against women, the living images which threatened to confuse the spirit or truth of law through mere appearance and "carnal pretence."

The following study will thus interpret the foundation of common law primarily through a historical analysis of Renaissance and Reformation debates on the history, uses, and laws governing images. In that respect it offers an analysis of those foundational debates within ecclesiastical and secular law that first spelled out the terms of the modern governance of perception, the direction of thought through control of the visual, the figures of law both internal and external to its subjects and its texts. The argument builds upon the historical enfolding of spiritual and temporal discourses concerned with the governance of the soul, with spiritual laws variously directed at idolatry and iconoclasm, image and figure, statue and law. The development of secular doctrines concerned with governance of text, interpretation and ethos in the reformed age of print established both the form and the meaning of law. The analysis thus suggests both a displacement and an incorporation of one law in the other: the secular law inherited or otherwise annexed or absorbed the earlier powers, techniques, and jurisdictions of the spiritual law and its "Courts of Conscience." The laws against images became protocols of reading or hermeneutic rules prohibiting images, figures or, in strict terms, harlots, "loose women," "the whore of Babel" in the lawful text. The argument uses history as a means of thinking the terms of a critical jurisprudence and may be addressed synoptically: the regulation of the visible was always in essence a determination of the licit forms and the proper references to the invisible or unseen. The regulation of exterior images was directed at control of interior images, mental idols, or unseen signs. In short, the visible was "a spectacle of things invisible," and the governance of visibility was in consequence a direction of things heard, remembered, desired, or imagined as the customs or precedents of common law.

The discourses against rhetoric, against images, and against women that this work traces and expounds are discourses of the foundation of law in the definition and capture of subjectivity. They spell out the laws or constraints of thought in the inaugural discourses of social being and its constitutive texts. It remains to be added that while law is always a governance of thought and so can perhaps be most radically rethought as such, it also constitutes itself upon an unthought—upon custom, repetition, and repression. Law, for Aristotle, was "wisdom without desire." In a literal sense that reference could be taken as meaning that law is a truth that represses desire, a text that negates its images and denies the figurations or fluidity of its texts. In a sense which will to many seem extreme, the analysis also suggests a logic of the supplement or return of the repressed. In this aspect this work seeks to represent some of the more obscure texts of the tradition, some of the forgotten themes and works of early legal doctrine, the other faces or "other scenes" of the institution. The critical analytic suggestion embodied in this text thus concerns a politics of recuperation, of recovery of the traumas that law cannot consider, of recollection of the repressed and failed images, figures, texts, and thoughts prohibited by the prose of doctrine, by the language of judgment, by the protocols of a wisdom without desire.

Some time after imagining the title *Oedipus Lex,* I was alerted to the existence of another use of the neologism in a jurisprudential context by the Canadian jurist Professor J. C. Smith in a book titled *The Psychoanalytic Roots of Patriarchy: The Neurotic Foundations of Social Order* (New York: New York University Press, 1990). My use of the term is, I believe, sufficiently incidental and certainly adequately displaced to excuse the unconscious borrowing. The signifier floats. So too I should apologize for my neologism "gynaetopia." It should, of course, be the phonetically more complex genitive, "gynaecotopia." I have simply preferred the bastard form. So also, for reasons that are self-evident, *ius interruptus* is preferred to the grammatical *ius interruptum.*

My thanks to the usual causes, women, men, and institutions. The British Academy, the Nuffield Foundation, and Birkbeck College all provided small research grants which greatly facilitated comparative and archival research. My thanks to those at Cardozo Law School, New York, who collectively tolerated my presence and sharpened my thought over a semester as visiting professor. Arthur Jacobson, David Carlson, Chuck Yablon, Marty Slaughter, Michel Rosenfeld, Jeanne Schroeder, and Richard Weisberg all politely and perspicuously challenged my cultural prejudices and my theoretical preconceptions. I hope to repeat the experience. At Lancaster University my thanks to my colleagues in opposition, to Peter Rush, Alison Young, Les Moran, and Piyel Haldar for their extremism and their scholarship. My disparate thanks to Renata Salecl, Peter Fitzpatrick, Neil Duxbury, Matthew Weait, and Tim Murphy, all of whom were at times either sufficiently direct or simply rude enough to say what they thought. For their peripatetic style of scholarship, for their voice, and for their imagination, my thanks to Tony Carty, Patrick Durkin, Linda Mills, Ronnie Warrington, David Walliker, and Costas Douzinas. For glimpses of an authentic augury of thought and for lessons in the sorcery of history and of writing, my thanks to Yifat Hachamovitch and to the birds.

THE

Reverſe or Back-face

OF THE

Engliſh JANUS.

TO-WIT,

All that is met with in STORY

Concerning the

COMMON

AND

STATUTE-LAW

OF

Engliſh Britanny.

From the firſt MEMOIRS of the two NATIONS, to the Deceaſe of King *HENRY* II. ſet down and tackt together ſuccinctly by way of Narrative.

Deſigned, Devoted and Dedicated to the moſt Illuſtrious the EARL of *SALISBURY*.

Written in *Latin* by *JOHN SELDEN* of *Salvinton*, Student of the *Inner-Temple* in *LONDON*; and Rendred into *Engliſh* by *REDMAN WESTCOT*, Gent.

Hæc faci-
es Populum
ſpectat; at
illa Larem.

London, Printed for *Thomas Baſſet*, and *Richard Chiſwell*. MDCLXXXII.

ONE

Introduction

Melancholia Juridica

The study of law has always traveled under the sign of Saturn, and the sages both of common and civil law have seldom paused to doubt the depressing character of legal study. The humanist reformer Hotman referred to the "abyss" of this study being such as to steal every waking hour, leaving no time either for scripture or other pursuits. The only fault greater than the "irritating and futile" flaws, the impostures or injustices of the interior matter or substance of the discipline was the vice which he perceived to be natural to its form: "What man of sense and judgment can read a single page of this word play [*badinage*] without suffering weariness of heart as at a foul smell."[1] Hotman also referred to the study of law as an endless, disputatious, and damaging pursuit of fragments, pieces, and patches (*lopins*) representing "uncertain conjectures and tenuous divinations."[2] The lawyer compulsively sought to reconstruct a law lost in antiquity, particularity, and incoherence. Even Baldus, the most learned of fourteenth-century Continental jurists, is reported to have remarked on his forty-seventh birthday that he was still an apprentice in the law, that he still knew only a little of the law and was "dazzled by the authorities," so much so that he was forced to judge as often by chance as by reference to assured, certain, or written rules.[3] Nor were the common lawyers more reticent in their condemnation of the discipline. Dr. John Cowell, the second holder of the chair of common law at Cambridge University, remarked in 1607 that the study of common law had yet to be embellished

1. François Hotman, *Anti-Tribonian ou discours d'un grand et renômmé jurisconsulte de nostre temps sur l'estude des loix* (Paris: Perrier, 1567, 1603 ed.) at 111. My translation.
2. Ibid. at 134.
3. Ibid. at 109.

by systematic or serious learning, that it had yet to acquire scholarship and a knowledge of Continental learning, that it had yet to gain "some comfortable lights and prospects toward the beautifying of this ancient palace, that has hitherto been but dark and melancholy."[4] His contemporary Sir John Doderidge referred to the study of law as being "*multorum annorum opus,* the work of many years, the attaining whereof will waste the greatest part of the verdour and vigour of our youth," and requiring not only constancy and endless hours but also the continence or chastity of an unrelenting discipline.[5] So too, even Sir Edward Coke, most usually an eulogist of the tradition and its perfections, was forced to admit that the student in the laws of the realm, "having *sedentariam vitam,* is not commonly long-lived; the study [is] abstruse and difficult, the occasion sudden, the practice dangerous."[6]

The examples of law's melancholia could easily be multiplied. The directions or preparatives for legal study required both physical and mental preparation for the dangers of the discipline. The demands of law were numerous and life-long, the discipline required the training of the body and the capture of the soul. Sir John Fortescue referred to law as a "forbidding" discipline, as a sacral pursuit which was to engender a "filial" fear in its students.[7] William Fulbecke talked of the pernicious and addictive character of legal study, and of the obscure, dull, and coldly prosaic style of its texts: "The books of law . . . are not pleasant to read, the words or terms are harsh and obscure, the style no whit delightful, the method none at all."[8] Abraham Fraunce similarly considered legal study to be "hard, harsh, unsavoury, unpleasant, rude and barbarous" and as if that were not enough he concluded with an olfactory reference to its "loathsome savour."[9] The discipline of law demanded everything of its student and sought, in the emblematic community of the Inns of Court, to regu-

4. Dr. John Cowell, *The Interpreter or Booke containing the Signification of Words* (Cambridge: Legat, 1607) at fol. 3a.

5. Sir John Doderidge, *The English Lawyer* (London: I. More, 1629, 1631 ed.) at 29.

6. Sir Edward Coke, *A Book of Entries containing perfect and approved presidents of Courts, Declarations . . . and all other matters and proceedings (in effect) concerning the pratick part of the laws of England* (London: Streeter, 1610, 1671 ed.) at fol. A 5 a.

7. Sir John Fortescue, *De Laudibus Legum Angliae* (London: Gosling, 1468–70, 1737 ed.) at 3.

8. William Fulbecke, *Direction or Preparative to the Study of the Law* (London: Clarke, 1599, 1829 ed.) at 51–52. The long subtitle to the book reads: *Wherein it is shewed what things ought to be observed and used of them that are addicted to the study of law.* Sir Edward Coke, *The Reports* (London: J. Rivington, 1611, 1777 ed.), pt. III at fol. C 7 b, also refers interestingly to a study whereby "thou shalt wholy addict thyself to the admirable sweetness of knowledge and understanding: *in lectione non verba sed veritas est amanda.*"

9. Abraham Fraunce, *The Lawiers Logike, exemplifying the praecepts of logike by the practice of the common lawe* (London: W. How, 1588) at sig. 3r.

late every detail of gesture, dress, diet, lifestyle, company, and behavior. The early legislation of the Inns explicitly required reverent behavior, a minimum of noise and forbade beards and long hair as well as colorful clothing, alcohol, tobacco, and games of shoffe-grotte. Lawyers should wear "sad colours," appear downcast, and generally be quiet in the limited sphere of their life outside of court.[10] In terms of principle Fulbecke, in the course of elaborating the proper regimen of the law student, stated "the next thing I require in a student is temperance . . . a restraint of mind from all voluptuousness and lust, as namely from covetousness, excess of diet, wantonness and all other unlawful delights."[11] Other authors agreed fully that the study of law, which required as its first art that of memory, necessitated that the "student keep a diet, and eschew surfeits, to sleep moderately, to accompany with women rarely, and last of all to exercise the wit with cunning of many things without book."[12] Other more pedantic and curious manuals of advice dictated that the student should rarely eat red meat, since its "vapours and fumes do cloud the mind and overshadow the clearness of the brain,"[13] and should rise early and not study too late. The need to begin study at dawn was in part a reflection of the demands of an unending pursuit, but it was also metaphysical: dawn was the friend of the muses (*aurora musis amica*), the air in the morning "was subtilized, and made thin, pure and free from all gross vapours but in the night time it is thickened, and corrupted with all contagious exhalations, which possessing the senses, do pierce into the brain."[14] The night, in a sense to which this study will frequently return, was the time of fantasy or imaginings, of images and women, and all were perceived as threats to the capacity, probity, and reason of law, for "night always comes on with the mind disturbed."[15]

10. On the early rules and legislation of the Inns of Court, see William Dugdale, *Origines Juridiciales or Historical Memorials of the English Laws, Courts of Justice, Forms of Tryal* (Savoy: T. Newcomb, 1666, 1671 ed.), especially 188–192. See further Peter Goodrich, "Eating Law: Commons, Common Land and Common Law" (1991) 12 *Journal of Legal History* 246.

11. Fulbecke, *Direction or Preparative* at fol. J 9 b.

12. Thomas Wilson, *The Arte of Rhetorique* (London: Garland, 1533, 1982 ed.) at 420.

13. W. Phillips, *Studii Legalis Ratio or Direction for the Study of the Laws* (London: F. Kirkman, 1667) at fol. k i a–b; William Fulbecke, *Direction or Preparative* at 48.

14. Fulbecke, *Direction or Preparative* at 46–47; similarly Phillips, *Studii Legalis Ratio* at fol. J 9 b, distinguishes the spirit at dawn and dusk: "For the spirits of our Bodies, following the dispositions of the air, which in the morning at sun rising is subtill and thus pure and free from all gross vapours and our minds being of the same condition, are quick and nimble . . . and after sleep the memory is moistened with the vapours arising out of the stomach, and so made fitter and better disposed to receive the figures of the matter conceived and apprehended."

15. Marsilio Ficino, *De Vita* (1480), translated by C. Boer as *Book of Life* (Dallas: Spring Publications, 1980) at 16. The other source of this fear is "the monster . . . the coitus of Venus" also discussed in ch. 7.

It is tempting to conclude that the study of law either attracts or produces unhappiness. It is tempting to surmise that wealth, status, and political influence, the rewards of law, can never be a full compensation for the risks of looking too long "upon ink and black buckram."[16] The fate of the law student is that of studying a discipline that Sir Roger North depicted not only as dangerous, difficult, and less pleasant than other disciplines but also as demanding the "whole man . . . [who] must not only read and talk, but eat, drink and sleep law . . . *nulla die sine linea.*"[17] In Fulbecke's view, lawyers were eventually consumed by law. They became "so full of law points that when they sweat it is nothing but law, when they breathe it is pure law, when they sneeze it is perfect law, when they dream it is profound law. The book of Littleton's *Tenures* is their breakfast, their dinner, their tea, their boier [supper] and their rare banquet."[18] Law, or legal addiction, consumes the subject from within until nothing but law is left—a façade, a face, a "winding cause," the melancholy of exploitation and nothing more. And, according to Burton's *Anatomie of Melancholy,* it was not simply the individual who would need to be saved from law's inevitable melancholic effects but equally the state or commonwealth which was prone to succumb to the same humor or condition of melancholy. In diagnosing the mental health of a population, in analyzing the unconscious of the institution, Burton does not hesitate to offer law and lawyers as a symptom of collective mental illness: "I undertook at first that Kingdoms, Provinces, Families, were melancholy as well as private men," and thus he adds "where [a population] be generally . . . contentious, where there be many discords, many laws, many law suits, many lawyers . . . it is a manifest sign of a distempered melancholy state."[19] For much of the first book of the *Anatomie,* law is virtually synonymous with the diagnosis of melancholy. The topic or theme is a common one in commentaries upon the state of the commonwealth. For Burton, law "is a general mischief in

16. Cyril Tourneur, *The Revenger's Tragedy* (London: Eld, 1607) at lines 49–53: *Lussorioso:* "Why, will that make a man melancholy?" *Vindice*: "Yes, to look long upon ink and black buckram—I went to law in *Anno Quadragesimo secundo,* and I waded out of it in *Anno setagesimo tertio.*" For another dramatic satire of law and lawyers, see George Ruggles, *Ignoramus or the English Lawyer* (London: n.p., 1621, 1736 ed.).

17. Sir Roger North, *A Discourse on the Study of the Laws* (London: T. White, 1650, 1824 ed.) at 7. He remarks a page later that "there are other studies more pleasant than law."

18. William Fulbecke, *A Parallele or Conference of the Civil Law, the Canon Law and the Common Law of this Realme of Englande* (London: Society of Stationers, 1602, 1618 ed.) at fol. B 2 a–b.

19. Robert Burton, *The Anatomie of Melancholy: What it is, with all the kinds, causes, symptomes, prognosticks, and severall cures of it by Democritus Junior* (Oxford: H. Cripps, 1628) at 39. For further views of melancholy, contemporaneous with Burton's, see T. Bright, *A Treatise of Melancholy* (London: Vautrollier, 1586); Nicholas Breton, *Melancholike Humours* (London: Scholartis Press, 1600, 1929 ed.).

our times, an unsensible plague, and never so many of them . . . and for the most part a supercilious, bad, covetous, litigious generation of men. . . . A purse milking nation, a clamorous company, gowned vultures, *qui ex iniuriam vivunt et sanguine civium,* thieves and seminaries of discord . . . irreligious Harpies, griping catchpoles . . . without art, without judgment."[20]

The nation, according to Thomas Wilson in 1601, was being consumed by common lawyers, a profession that had gained an unwarranted and uncivilized monopoly on disputing "since the practise of civil law has been as it were wholly banished and abrogated, and since the clergy has been trodden down by the taking away of Church livings."[21] The profession had expanded beyond reason and conscience, and some more compendious means of composing disputes had to be possible. As if the condition of seizure, addiction, or apprenticeship to law was not deterrence enough, the lawyer thus had also to face a constant stream of criticism precisely directed at the obscurity, superabundance, immorality, and greed of, and delays promulgated by, his profession. Early political commentators on the growth of the modern legal profession constantly talked of swarms of lawyers infecting the commonwealth like the plague.[22] Dramatists satirized the lawyer as a pettifogging fraud, as a hanger-on and parasite: "Without the least taste of university learning, they advance, swelled with presumption, and full of ignorance and impudence to the Bar."[23] They were brave and ludicrous "magnificoes" who hid their ignorance of both law and custom behind the use of "inkhorn" terms, a nonsensical jargon composed of Greek, Latin, French, Dutch, Danish, and double Dutch—"if all men spoke such gibberish, 'twere a happiness to be deaf."[24] The lawyer was more popularly perceived as a wheedler and wrangler, a scrivener without a soul, an advocate of venal motive whose only cause was a barbarous self-interest in dirty lucre. The law was expensive and time-consuming, delay was piled upon delay, while incompetence or simple confusion would eventually

20. Ibid. at 49.

21. Thomas Wilson, *The State of England, A.D. 1600* (London: Camden Miscellany, 1601, 1936 ed.) at 25.

22. For further representative critiques of common lawyers, see: John Day, *Law Tricks* (Oxford: Malone Society Reprints, 1608, 1950 ed.); John Warr, *The Corruption and Deficiency of the Laws of England* (London: R. Dutton, 1649). Excellent secondary discussions are provided by J. H. Baker (ed.), *The Reports of John Spelman* (London: Selden Society, 1978); C. W. Brooks, *Pettyfoggers and Vipers of the Commonwealth: The Lower Branch of the Legal Profession in Early Modern England* (Cambridge: Cambridge University Press, 1986).

23. Richard Head, *Proteus Redivivus or the Art of Wheedling or Insinuation* (London: W. D. 1675) at 272.

24. Ruggles, *Ignoramus* at 8. See further, Sir Henry Spelman, *The Original of the Four Law Termes of the Year* (London: Gillyflower, 1614) at 99; see also Fraunce, *Lawiers Logike,* Preface. Burton, *Anatomie of Melancholy,* refers at 49 to the disease of *damnificos linguas,* a language of the damned.

ensure that the litigation almost always outlived the litigants. The melancholy engendered by the internal difficulty of legal study was thus frequently complemented by an extreme external lack of appreciation. To cap it all the lawyer was perceived as socially incompetent, emotionally inept and, more generally, as "impatient, sour . . . morose and incapable of conversation."[25]

The external condemnation of the profession of law no doubt contributed considerably to the unhappiness of the lawyer. More than that, however, it indelibly marked the character of the legal institution. In one sense it made the lawyer defensive and protective of his calling and its homosocial professional environment. In response to criticism the common law tradition was stated to be the most ancient and best of all systems of law, it was unique and "connatural to the nation": it was uninterrupted tradition, age-old usage, immemorial practice.[26] In the extravagant words of one eulogist, "the law of England is really to us who live under it, the Foundation of all our happiness; it secures to us our Estates, our liberties, and our lives, and all that is dear to us in this life, and not only so, but by securing our religion, it secures to us the means of attaining everlasting happiness too. By this law, we not only enjoy the pleasures of this world, but even God."[27] The law, according to Roger Coke, is embodied in the Crown, which has the role of a "nursing father" and is bound to care for its subjects in both their temporal and their "ghostly" or spiritual form.[28] In addition, extensive popular criticism forced the lawyer to reinvent and to rely heavily upon the architecture, theater, and other symbols of justice to identify the profession and to protect the tradition. Lawyers had to restate that this law was English law, that its ancient practice was both custom and constitution, and its rule the law of nature habituated to the manners of England. The essence of common law became the fantasm of its Englishness. It was a tradition that existed to protect those things that the English value and had always valued. Its constitution was domestic, its law unwritten, its creed a matter of good manners and of doing things as they had always been done.[29] At one level, I will suggest that if the legal tradi-

25. Judith Drake, *An Essay in Defence of the Female Sex* (London: Roper, 1696) at 140–141.

26. For a classic statement of this view, see Sir John Davies, *A Discourse of Law and Lawyers,* in *Le Primer Reports des Cases & Matters en Ley Resolves et Adjudges in Les Courts del Roy en Ireland* (Dublin: Franckton, 1614, 1615 ed.).

27. J. Fortescue-Aland, "Preface," in Sir John Fortescue, *The Difference between an Absolute and a Limited Monarchy, as it more particularly regards the English Constitution* (London: private distribution, 1475, 1714 ed.) at iv.

28. Roger Coke, *Justice Vindicated, from the False Fucus put upon it, by Thomas White Gent., Mr Thomas Hobbes, and Hugo Grotius* (London: T. Newcomb, 1660) at 21 and 98.

29. The most influential discussion of this theme is in Richard Hooker, *Of the Lawes of Ecclesiastical Politie* (London: R. Scott, 1593, 1676 ed.). Specifically on manners, see Calybute

tion seems melancholic, if it appears historically as insular, slow, and obscure, this is no more than an expression of the fact that such is the character of the English. The legal tradition embodies the melancholic soul of a private nation afraid not simply of others but, in analytic terms, primarily of itself and of its emptiness, its stupidity or lack of thought.

It would be easy to suppose that in consequence of such existential and emotional inadequacy, thinly veiled by the façade of legal reason, some inner compensation would be needed as a palliative for those that risk studying a discipline so dangerous to both individual and collective well-being or institutional health. The first and recurrent theme of the present study is thus the analysis of legal melancholia in terms of that which is mourned or has been lost in the course of a monastic legal training. This aspect of study was constantly remarked by the wives of lawyers and by early feminists as leaving the law student unfitted for ordinary conversation and the legal husband emotionally incompetent to deal with the demands of an extralegal or nonadversarial life. In Freud's terms, melancholia is the morbid internalization of the loss either of a loved person or "of some abstraction which has taken the place of one, such as a fatherland, liberty, an ideal, and so on."[30] Melancholia is distinguished from mourning by the unconscious character of the lost love-object, and it is thus the first task of a jurisprudence of melancholia to reconstruct the lost objects of legal life: for the individual these would probably be youth, vigor, manners, emotions, the English tongue, and the various bodily hedonisms associated with a life beyond the library and its dusty aura of the texts of law. For the institution the losses are more complicated but would undoubtedly include the loss of its authentic sources, the pristine immemorial law which preceded the inventions of statute, the native common law in the Celtic and later Anglo-Saxon tongues that existed prior to the Danish, Roman, and Norman invasions, the true unwritten constitution which represented an "honest" England that preexisted Europe and its increasingly vocal call to a written law. The Oedipus myth should also, however, alert us to the fact that the negative dimension of loss inevitably has a positive representation. Oedipus marries his mother as part of a search to evoke, to restore, or to become the dead or lost father—the king, an imaginary patriarch whom Oedipus had never known.[31] In more technical language

---

Downing, *A Discourse of the State Ecclesiasticall of this Kingdome, in relation to the Civill* (Oxford: W. Turner, 1586, 1632 ed.).

30. Sigmund Freud, "Mourning and Melancholia," in Sigmund Freud, *Collected Papers,* IV (London: Hogarth Press, 1948) at 154.

31. For discussion of this theme, see Paul Ricoeur, *Freud and Philosophy: An Essay on Interpretation* (New Haven: Yale University Press, 1977); Jean-Joseph Goux, *Oedipe Philosophe* (Paris: Éditions Aubier, 1990); Gananath Obeyesekere, *The Work of Culture: Symbolic Transformation in Psychoanalysis and Anthropology* (Chicago: Chicago University Press, 1990).

Freud termed this process that of a "hallucinatory wish-psychosis" with which the melancholic replaces a reality that has caused pain and grief: every dream, for Freud, fulfills a wish. Is it possible, in other words, that the positive imagery of law, the dreams of order, science, reason, and justice, are simply the melancholic lawyer's projection to cover the lack of reason, system, and justice in a common law composed of infinite particulars, of precedents, customs, statutes, and other contingent and specific rules?

I do not suppose that a psychoanalytic diagnosis of the institutional condition of law will make either lawyers or law happy enterprises—after all they have their dinners, costumes, words, (emotional) distance, and money for that—but it does suggest that it might be intelligible to treat the study of law as both more and less than the systematizing analysis of a technical order and practice of rules. The corollary of the argument for a study of law's melancholia, of its unconscious losses and fictive gains, is an assertion of the value of a critical legal theory or of a jurisprudence that understands and analyzes the law not simply for professional ends but also as a specific genre of human relationship and as an activity or form of life. The *agon* and the agony of learning legal rules is to the legal mind only one aspect of law's dominion. The apparent evil hides a deeper good, the conscious delay and disorder of law an unconscious order and grace, the visible spectacle an invisible reference. The apparent world of the law, like the ecclesiastical order of images from which it devolved, is only ever an *indicium,* a symptom or sign of the value of law and of that metaphysical or invisible order that extends beyond or underpins the tangible surface realm of legal instruments and judgments. One simple illustration from an early fourteenth-century legal ruling on contempt of court should suffice to illustrate the point.

In the case of *William de Thorp* v *Mackerel and another,* the plaintiff, the "king's sworn clerk," was walking from the Inns of Court to the Court at Westminster in the company of sundry other "men of law."[32] While proceeding along Fleet Street, William was attacked by Thomas Mackerel and others, who assaulted William with "force and arms and beat, wounded and ill-treated him and inflicted other outrages on him, that is to say pissed on him [*urinam super ipsum*] and trampled him underfoot." The writ of trespass later issued by the plaintiff, a *venire facias,* stated that the defendant was in contempt of the King and his court and further that this contempt had been committed *in presencia curie* or in the presence of the court. Judgment was for the plaintiff, and the court simply accepted as un-

32. *William de Thorp* v *Mackerel and another* (1318), Coram Rege Roll no. 233, in Sayles (ed.) (1955) 74 Selden Society 79. For another example, see *Henry of Naburn* v *Walter le Flemyng, Richard of Duffield and others* (1316) 74 Selden Society 72.

problematic that although the contempt had been committed some two miles from the Court at Westminster, it was nonetheless committed in the presence of the court. It was, in short, a contempt or scandalizing of the court which was to be treated by the common law according to the geographical fiction that what took place some two miles from the court occurred in the court, in the presence of, or in contemporary terms, in the face of the court. William de Thorp was awarded 100 shillings in damages and later became Lord Chief Justice.[33]

Aside from its immediate expression of animosity toward a scandalous irreverence to a particular officer of the court, the decision in *Thorp* v *Mackerel* can be interpreted most directly as indicating, if only momentarily, the dependence of the visible order of law upon an unseen and unconscious mapping of a nonphysical legal territory. The relationship can be posed in many different ways. In medieval terms the visible and natural body of law was subordinate to the mystic body or *corpus mysticum* of the realm. Just as the canon law held that the church did not inhabit a territory (*ecclesia non habet territorium*), the law of the land was also conceived as extending from the realm of appearance and of corporeal presence to a territory and space of the mind. When William de Thorp was attacked it was only coincidentally a natural person who was injured. The real subject of the contempt was the dignity, the imaginary peripatetic place, symbolic presence, or office of law. What was attacked was not a simple body but rather an image or sign of law's other body, the other scene of its presence and place. Historically the law always traveled with the person of the King,[34] and by the time and extension, the court and the judges, the itinerant delegates of the King's justice, were similarly to be deemed as traveling by simulation or *as if* they were part of the law or of the Crown's mystic presence or "other scene." And thus, according to William Lambard, "it must be true, that the king and his council are not to be tyed to any one place, seeing that the place itself neither addeth nor derogateth to, or from their authoritie."[35]

The institution, in short, constantly spills from the court and the text into life, and to trace that quiet and imperceptible crossing of boundaries requires a jurisprudence that is attentive to the little slips, repetitions and compulsions, melancholic moods or hysterical outbursts, that hint at the transgressive movement from one order to another, from conscious to unconscious law. More than that, the law depends upon a geography of

33. Dugdale, *Origines Juridiciales* at sig. 99r.

34. By legislation of 1300, the Court cannot be "divorced from the person of the King" but was always to be deemed as traveling with him. See *Statutes of the Realm*, i 139 [*Articuli Super Cartas*, cap. 5].

35. William Lambard, *Archeion or Discourse upon the High Courts of Justice in England* (London: H. Seile, 1591, 1635 ed.) at 148.

mental spaces, which cannot be reduced to its physical presences, its texts (*lex scripta*), or its apparent rules. The appearance of law is only ever an index or sign, a vestige or relic of anterior and hidden causes. A structural principle is operative in legal dogmatics, which attributes causes strictly to an invisible or unconscious order, to the imagination of the senses (*formae imaginariae*) and in doctrinal terms to the spirit of law. The order of this spirit or meaning, text or truth, is a positive unconscious within which are stored the originary and repeated themes of institutional life. They constitute a historical *a priori*, the patterns and forms of an itinerant law, those memories of the tradition which by virtue of their foundational or structural quality are no longer represented but simply are lived without the need for further representation: "The mask is the true subject of repetition. Such is the case because the nature of repetition differs from that of representation, because the repeated cannot be represented, but must always be signified, while masking at the same time that it signifies."[36] A canonic geography or mapping of law institutes a cartography of those structures, those forms of terror or manipulation that bind invisibly and from within, for they are the measure of that most complex and mixed of spiritual and temporal constructions, namely the presence of an "unwritten law." In one recent and intriguing depiction of the architecture of the Inns of Court the same point is made by reference to their topology: "Common law is *revealed*: . . . accordingly, the Inns function as a 'threshold' between the physical world and the invisible principles of law. If the body claims truth from metaphor, then the Inns hide behind the face of the city, the street, creating an insubstantiality out of an imposing gaze, the expression of law that, having once appeared, always struggles against the hazard of chance which would erase it. Hence, the mask of the Inns is articulated less with architectural ornament than with the slipping away of what is deflected by the mask . . . the final and ultimate teleology of law; an authentic source."[37]

The second theme of the present study is to pursue the deflections or screenings instituted by the mask, façade, or image of law. The law is in psychoanalytic terms a symbolic permutation or point of passage between one order and another and it is variously depicted as hinge, pleat, or gate, Mercury or Janus, name or text. It is the point of splitting or moving from one order to another, an intangible folding or exchange between differ-

36. Gilles Deleuze, *Différence et répétition* (Paris: Presses Universitaires de France, 1968) at 29.

37. David Evans, "The Inns of Court: Speculations on the Body of Law" (1993) 1 *Arch-Text* 5, at 11. See, for a discussion of the body as mask, Peter Goodrich, "Specula Laws: Image, Aesthetic and Common Law" (1991) 2 *Law and Critique* 233.

ent realms, a changing of places.[38] The specific strategy of this study is that of thinking historically of psychoanalytic jurisprudence. Using the earliest theoretical discipline associated with law, namely rhetoric, the study progresses to a genealogy of the image in law through an analysis of Reformation and Renaissance discourses on images and their destruction, on idolatry and iconoclasm both as forms of thought and as expressions of law. The result of that analysis is, broadly, to trace the law's relation to the image and specifically to reconstruct the genealogy of law's laws of interpretation, its laws of thought and their exclusion of figuration within the evidential and expository traditions of legal dogmatics. Contemporary jurisprudence is thus here challenged through the practice of comparative history and through the reconstruction of a series of discourses of and upon law from the Renaissance and the Baroque, from the sixteenth and seventeenth centuries. The allusion to those specific historical periods is in part a reflection of a postmodern sense of the contemporary, namely, that things are not going well, and in part an attempt to rethink the institution and to rewrite the law in the terms of its failures, in the terms of the traditions and texts—the emotions, the lives—that have been suppressed or excluded from doctrine and its representations of institutional history.

In positive terms the analysis of early legal treatises examines two formative or constitutional repressions, namely those of the image and of woman. Common law jurisprudence adopted to varying degrees the Continental doctrines of iconomachy (of hostility toward images) and of the inferior condition of woman through the influence of the Reformation and the Renaissance, respectively. The present work traces that dual inheritance and endeavors to elaborate the influence and continuing, although displaced, effects of those two repressions. The discourse against images, technically the antirrhetic, it will be argued, became in the aftermath of print culture a discourse against textual figures, painted words, and imaginary signs. It was a discourse of denunciation, against the heresy or heterodoxy of what Tyndale terms "image-service,"[39] and subsequently a discourse against words, against the materiality or rhetoricity of language.

38. For a most extensive discussion of symbolic permutation, see Pierre Legendre, *L'Inestimable objet de la transmission: Étude sur le principe généalogique en occident* (Paris: Fayard, 1985), especially at 298 ff. In classical Freudian terms the important texts on permutation are: Sigmund Freud, *Totem and Taboo: Resemblances between the Psychic Lives of Savages and Neurotics* (Harmondsworth: Penguin Books, 1919); Sigmund Freud, *Civilization and its Discontents* (London: Hogarth Press, 1975); Sigmund Freud, *Moses and Monotheism* (London: Hogarth Press, 1939).

39. William Tyndale, *An Answer unto Thomas Mores Dialogue made by William Tyndale* (London: n.p., 1530) at fol. C xiii b: "When the images are no longer memorials only then they should be taken down for the abuse."

The antirrhetic was continuously presented in terms of the image as a woman or a harlot and the service or worship of images as fornication or adultery. Because it was law, one might say, the antirrhetic thought in terms of analogy, of metaphor or substitution, and so outlawed images because they did not seek to substitute but rather relied on contiguity or metonymy, upon a free association, a mobility that passed through the law but always also exceeded it. In short, the antirrhetic was also a means of establishing a law of gender division. The antirrhetic instituted a prose that was if not always resistant to the images of femininity, was nonetheless unremittingly hostile to the "other sex." Where the antirrhetic operated to institute a specific and singular order of iconic or "real" images, the displaced discourse of the antirrhetic, that which propelled the law against the political right or law and suffrage of women, operated to institute a particular order and law of thought consonant with the antique requirement of the *Decretals* that law be served with chaste eyes, *oculos castos servare.*[40] The denunciation of woman in the early doctrinal and constitutional writings of common law was the repression of a figure of femininity, of a metaphor or face which represented the plurality or creativity of thought, an other scene of reason, a genealogy of myths or histories of difference.

The final theme, although I am uncertain of its success, is that of the return of the repressed within the discourse of law. In strict Freudian theory the repressed constantly presses against the barrier of consciousness, "in order to impose its contents on consciousness. Yet the resistance offered by consciousness, on the one hand, and the pressure of desire, on the other, leads to a displacement and deformation of that which could otherwise be reconstituted unaltered. The dynamic of delirium recalls the constitution of the dream or the phantasm."[41] The repressed returns, in other words, and is repeated in displaced forms. I am less concerned, however, with the point of principle than with the politics of theory that it implies. The historical and rhetorical reconstruction of textual imagery and of feminine genealogies or *gynaetopias,* of the forms of repressed discourse within the jurisprudential tradition, suggests a specific and rigorous strategy of institutional politics, a strategy of legal difference. Repression is a

40. Gratian, *Decretum,* in *Corpus iuris canonici* (Leipzig: B. Tauchnitz, 1140) at C 6 q 1 c 13; discussed in Pierre Legendre, *L'Empire de la vérité* (Paris: Fayard, 1983) at 110–113.

41. Julia Kristeva, "Psychoanalysis and the Polis" in W. J. T. Mitchell (ed.), *The Politics of Interpretation* (Chicago: Chicago University Press, 1983) at 91–92; see also Luce Irigaray, *Marine Lover of Friedrich Nietzsche* (New York: Columbia University Press, 1991) at 5: "Here is the future, in that past which you never wanted." For an extended elaboration of this theme, see Pierre Legendre, *L'Amour du censeur: Essai sur l'ordre dogmatique* (Paris: Éditions du Seuil, 1974). For two striking statements of this view in Freud, see "Repression" in *Collected Papers IV* at 84–98; Sigmund Freud, *Beyond the Pleasure Principle* (London: Hogarth Press, 1961).

positive and internal act, it lays out a space within the institution; in the case of law the space is one of images, of flowers, ornaments, aesthetic judgments, tastes, emotions, lifestyles, and fantasies, a space consonant with all of those disciplines and discourses that doctrine and law conceived to be incidental, accessory, merely rhetorical, contingent or other to the tradition (*ius non scriptum*) or established practice of law. The recollection of institutional repression offers a positive politics, a wealth of resources, of fragments and contaminations of the science of doctrine, the purity of reason or the ideality of law. It offers the possibility of a criticism or critical legal studies that rereads and rewrites doctrinal scholarship and, by implication, the future of professional practice through the epistemological other of legal knowledge. In one sense, different forms of reading are aligned to different rhetorics of writing, and the challenge to the law or rhetoric of genre is a radical challenge because it threatens the founding principle of institutional transmission, its custody of meaning and text. In a more complex sense, the accepted literary or, more properly, grammatological forms of doctrinal scholarship are closely tied to appeals to laws of reason and reference, clarity and iteration, which necessarily deny—not least through visual metaphors of reason—the very existence of the object of critical scholarship, an unconscious or repressed tradition within the legal institution.

The threat of the repressed within the institution is in one significant sense the threat of the unknown or, more precisely, the intimation of that which has not yet been determined, which is not mapped in advance by law's *regula* or calculus in the institutional form of knowledge as recognition.[42] The positivized jurisprudence of common law, the epistemology of doctrine, is tied by precedent to a knowledge that is known in advance, to a prior determination of the forms, classifications, languages, and similitudes through which judgment will be repeated. The critical method of the present study aligns itself with the suspension of such prior judgment, with the bracketing of the established positivities of legal method, and in so doing it suspends also the preexistent audience of law's literary practice. Critical legal studies has as one of its goals that of rewriting the arts of law, that of writing differently and so also thinking the difference of law.[43]

42. This theme is lengthily elaborated in Gilles Deleuze, *Différence et répétition.* For an analysis of *aporia* or suspension of recognition or predetermination in legal analysis, see Jacques Derrida, "Force of Law: The 'Mystical Foundation of Authority'" (1990) 11 *Cardozo Law Review* 919; and more broadly, Jacques Derrida, *The Post Card: From Socrates to Freud and Beyond* (Chicago: University of Chicago Press, 1987), especially at 4–5.

43. While the present work is intended as a contribution to critical legal studies, and at least in a European sense is located within and by reference to that genre, it does not directly address the literature or topics of critical legal studies. It is my view that little would be added to this study by spelling out the negative implications of historical and comparative traditions

It addresses an audience that is either unknown or that does not yet exist, one that has yet to come into being. It is in that perhaps limited respect both institutionally creative and theoretically radical. Certainly it is the rhetorical character and experimental style of critique, rather than any substantive content, that occasions the greatest degree of institutional hostility and doctrinal denunciation. The academic institution is quite simply lost in the face of a literature whose audience is unknown, either long passed on or not yet in existence in institutional terms. It cannot police the disciplinary boundaries nor assert the institutional propriety of a rhetoric that displaces its audience. Nor can it legislate a politics of style in which poetry is law.

The recourse to rhetoric, aesthetics, and psychoanalysis as providing methodologies and terminologies for critical analyses of law is not simply an obscurantist or an elitist strategy. These disciplines are those that even liberal versions of doctrine would exclude and philosophy of law pronounce improper or in error. Without directly addressing the substantive implications of the opposition between dogmatic jurisprudence and its margins, the peripheries against which it defines its own sanctity and truth, it is possible to observe that law carries with it a history of advocacy, polemic, and denunciation. Even at the level of doctrine it cannot be denied that the dogmatic function has always been political in the sense of being gauged to institutional and didactic goals. It teaches the exemplary forms of citizenship, it fabricates or institutes subjectivity, it demarcates the principles and boundaries of social thought. The law as model, image, or icon of social presence is the site of social reproduction, of political love and collective desire. To offer an analysis of the law's relation to images it is necessary to retrace the relationships, the judgments or forms of living that the image masks, internalizes, or hides. The "real image" or icon is the point of attachment to law, and the analysis of the image therefore puts into play the stake of legality as such, the capture of subjectivity, the apprehension or seizure of thought in the institutions, texts, or judgments of law. The law, Coke's "nursing father,"[44] takes hold, it institutes subjectiv-

---

of critique for the scholarship of much of contemporary critical legal studies. At the same time, however, to the extent that this work attempts to evidence and think through a dissonant tradition of legal critique, the histories of forgotten texts and interpretations, and the failures and the repressions of doctrine, its motive of resistance to legal orthodoxy does not differ greatly from that of contemporary critical legal scholarship. The difference is rather one of method and of historical scholarship or of institutional and so also ethical responsibility. For discussion of these and related themes, see Peter Goodrich, "Critical Legal Studies in England: Prospective Histories" (1992) 12 *Oxford Journal of Legal Studies* 196; Peter Goodrich, "Sleeping with the Enemy: An Essay on the Politics of Critical Legal Studies in America" (1993) 68 *New York University Law Review* 389.

44. Roger Coke, *Justice Vindicated* at 43.

ity through and across the imagery of law and the rhetoricity of its texts. The following chapters pursue and analyze that imagery or montage of lawful being as the subjective content of institutional subjection, as what used to be termed the "humane" form of law: its justice, its style, its poetic sermons or judgments. To recollect and elaborate the plastic and textual forms of law's appearance is also to trace and analyze the signs of law's disappearance, the sites of its repressions, of its violences, and of its failures. It is in the recuperation of the "other scenes" of law, precisely in the recollection of its failures, its losses, and its repressions, that a critical jurisprudence can offer some elements of political radicalism. The other scenes of law—its images, its figures, its architecture, its rites, myths, and other emotions—are potentially the economies of resistance to law. They evidence, I will argue, the possibilities of a jurisprudence of difference, and specifically a genealogy of other forms of law, of plural jurisdictions and distinctive subjectivities, of other genders, ethnicities, and classes of legality and of writing. Such, it is to be hoped, will be the revenge of the image upon a law that over centuries has denied the value of vision.

TWO

History Becomes the Law

Mourning, Genealogy, and Legal Historiography

Historiographers disagree so much that most must be lies. . . .[1]

I will begin with an event. It takes the form of an emblem of that process of losing that constitutes and reconstitutes the past. Under the rubric of memory, a late Renaissance treatise on codes of conduct, *The Ladies Calling,* offered practical advice for widows in the following terms:

> The remains of her husband be of three sorts, his body, his memory and his children . . . The more valuable Kindness, is that to his Memory, endeavouring to embalm that, keep it from perishing, and by this innocent Magic . . . she may converse with the dead, [and] represent him so to her own thoughts, that his life may still be repeated to her; and as in a broken Mirror the refraction multiplies the Images, so by his dissolution every hour presents distinct ideas of him, so that she sees him the oftener, for his being hid from her Eyes.[2]

The widow's memory of her husband, her diffuse and frequent recollection of his various images, was somewhat disingenuously or at least inaccurately termed an "innocent magic." The advice or injunction to remember was followed by further instructions as to the proper character of her inner representations or recollections of loss: "She is not only to preserve, but to perfume his memory, render it fragrant as she can not only to herself, but to others."[3] To the extent that the widow was responsible for publicly attesting the life and memory of her husband, she was further exhorted to revive specifically the "remembrance of whatever was praiseworthy" in the life of the deceased, to vindicate his name and to stifle

1. Henry Cornelius Agrippa, *Of the Vanitie and Uncertaintie of Artes and Sciences* (London: H. Bynneman, 1575) at sig. 13v.

2. Richard Allestree, *The Ladies Calling* (London: n.p. 1677) at 68–69.

3. Ibid. at 69.

or allay all calumnies or accusations, even such as were true. Memory, in short, was a creative art that aimed not simply to preserve, register, or reinscribe the dying image of the husband but also to remember for posterity, to recollect so as to represent a fidelity that would outlast and embellish the passing of the husband and the transience of death.

The widow was enjoined to write and to rewrite and so to embody a specific history. Her task was that of a living narration, an invention of memory that would both honor the deceased and restore, rectify, or cure the future—the public image and lineage of his life. The widow must love and embody what remains of the past, its fantasm or meaning. In consequence she must love the past differently, not simply because of its disappearance but also because of the need to reconstruct its images or remains according to the protocols of present meaning. Through the image of that which has died, she was to embody, preserve, and represent the dead, not only symbolically, to others, but also emblematically as the other in herself. Such is properly the "ladies calling," or the woman's fate, which is explained elsewhere in Allestree's treatise in terms of the due observance of distance (modesty) and specifically the virtue of a movement from external to internal images as the method or therapy of incorporation of virtue or grace: "Why should they dote on the fictitious image, of a perhaps fictitious beauty, which their glass presents them when they need but look inward to see an infinitely fairer idea?"[4] For the widow, inward virtue or the "fair idea" lies in the fidelity that is actively expressed in the fantasmatic histories of an image. She is the bearer of the responsibility of a particular and peculiarly inventive or displaced series of memories. It is the argument of this chapter that the widow herself may act as the emblem of a form of historiography, that of a genealogy in which the multiple images of the past both represent the fate and disperse the identity of contemporary institutions or present lives. While the example of the widow's memory of her husband is already charged with resonances of genealogy and of law, legitimacy, and propriety, a number of specific elements of historiography can be grafted onto the process of mourning and memorializing that the widow undertakes in obedience to an unwritten or informal law.

HISTORY AS CURE

Memory remains as the trace of the other. Memory, however, is an active faculty, and it cannot be ignored that the subject which bears or incorporates the other, the absent object of memory, is the widow.[5] She does so, if

4. Ibid., Preface.

5. On the creative force of memory, a power well recognized in law, see, for example, Doderidge, *English Lawyer* at 12–13, depicting memory as "the chest of an inestimable treasure,

she observes her calling, because of a duty to the dead husband and so as to live on as his memory, as a widow, unmarried, chaste yet not a virgin.[6] The duty of mourning and of recollection of that which has passed should therefore be understood actively and therapeutically as instituting a type of being through a restrained although never passive rite of loss.[7] The purpose of recollection is not only to preserve and further the image of the departed but is equally to train the soul and to remind the widow or the friend of a separation that they too will experience. The widow is cautioned "not to be conformed to this world"[8] and further advised that death should remind her of the vanity, the folly, and the bitterness that are aspects of all temporality: "The time that's passed is vanished like a dream or shadow. . . . Already we are dead to all the years we have lived, and vain it is to expect to live them over again."[9] The act of mourning impresses upon the soul the intimation or shadow of mortality. It preaches the inevitability and constancy of death as such—not simply of the husband's death. It equally defines death, past and future, as something ordained by providence, signaled by Saturn, by law, and yet sent to cure or to relieve the husband and the widow alike of unhappiness. More than that, how-

given from God for the preservation of all kinds of knowledge: it is as Plutarch says, the store house of all our understanding; and as Plato says, *Mater Musarum,* the Mother of the Muses: as Aristotle says, it is the guide of our experience, and the ground-work of all wisdom." For more general studies, see Mary Carruthers, *The Book of Memory: A Study of Memory in Medieval Culture* (Cambridge: Cambridge University Press, 1990); Frances Yates, *The Art of Memory* (London: Routledge and Kegan Paul, 1966).

6. Allestree, *Ladies Calling* at 80, recommends that the widow not marry again. In ecclesiastical terms remarriage would be a concession to lust and sexual pleasure. For the patristic grounds of this view, see, for example, St. Ambrose, *De Viduis,* in *The Principal Works of St. Ambrose,* Select Library of Nicene and Post-Nicene Fathers, vol. 10 (Oxford: Parker and Co., 1896). Generally, see James A. Brundage, *Law, Sex and Christian Society in Medieval Europe* (Chicago: Chicago University Press, 1987); M. Ingram, *Church and Courts, Sex and Marriage in England, 1570–1640* (Cambridge: Cambridge University Press, 1987); A. Blamires (ed.), *Woman Defamed and Woman Defended* (Oxford: Oxford University Press, 1992); Madeleine Lazard, *Images littéraries de la femme à la renaissance* (Paris: Presses Universitaires de France, 1985).

7. That the widow's mourning should be restrained is a theme pursued in Thomas Allestree, *A Funeral Handkerchief* (London: for the author, 1671) at 8, forbidding "inordinate passion; not tears simply but their excess; not tears of sympathy . . . but despairing repining tears." Also on widows and melancholy, see Burton, *Anatomie of Melancholy* at 193. More broadly on femininity and melancholy, see Julia Kristeva, *Black Sun: Depression and Melancholia* (New York: Columbia University Press, 1989); Juliana Schiesari, *The Gendering of Melancholia: Feminism, Psychoanalysis, and the Symbolics of Loss in Renaissance Literature* (Ithaca: Cornell University Press, 1992); Anne Juranville, *La Femme et la mélancholie* (Paris: Presses Universitaires de France, 1993).

8. Richard Allestree, *Whole Duty of Mourning and the great concern of preparing ourselves for death practically considered* (London: J. Black, 1694) at 56.

9. Ibid. at 5.

ever, mourning prepares the widow. It works upon her soul. Memory is the technique that will cure her of her loss by instituting innumerable images of that which has passed, by providing a vision or reordering of the past that will include the absence of the husband and so detach the widow from her loss.

The model of such detachment is broadly that of the crucifixion, of an exemplary death which is both a sacrifice and a redemptive communication with the spirit. Mourning is classically depicted in doctrine as the requisite manner of recollection of the spirit. In the terms of one Reformation defense of the Catholic faith: "Preach [*docente*] so as to move the people [*ecclesia*] not to clamour but to mourning. Let the tears of the audience be your commendation."[10] Doctrine, like history or as history, thus mourns so as to recognize the reality of the past and to detach the faithful, or those that recognize their calling, from the form of the past, its absence or loss. It is in the latter respect that the treatises on bereavement represent the rituals of mourning as curative: consideration of the dead institutes a "house," a commonplace or "school of mortification."[11] Recollection of that which has passed at the time of its passing, remembrance or reflection upon the last periods of a life, will act "to make a deeper impression on the soul, and be retained in the memory more than all the memorials that have been rehearsed."[12] The realization of the vanity and the transience of the body will prepare the widow for a life of renunciation consoled only by the images preserved in memory and a knowledge of the advantages of death. In the modern and less poetic language of psychoanalysis, mourning, which is also almost a symptom of femininity,[13] is equally depicted as working upon the soul or, in the terms of the modern discipline, as freeing the subject from its attachment to the object it has lost. For Freud, the "work" of mourning is that of the subject's coming to terms with the reality of loss.[14] The process is depicted as being one of intense struggle through which the mourner slowly parts with a continued existence, the internal image or hallucination through which the lost

10. Thomas Stapleton, *A Fortresse of the Faith first planted amonge us englishmen, and continued by the Universal Church of Christ* (Antwerp: Ihon Laet, 1565) at sig. 138r.

11. Allestree, *Whole Duty of Mourning* at 55.

12. Ibid. at 57–58.

13. See Luce Irigary, *Speculum of the Other Woman* (Ithaca: Cornell University Press, 1985) at 66–70; Juranville, *La Femme et la mélancholie* particularly 77–107.

14. Freud, "Mourning and Melancholia" at 154: "Now in what consists the work which mourning performs? I do not think there is anything far-fetched in the following representation of it. The testing of reality, having shown that the loved object no longer exists, requires that all the libido shall be withdrawn from its attachments to this object. . . . Each single one of the memories and hopes which bound the libido to the object is brought up and hypercathected, and the detachment of the libido from it accomplished. . . . When the work of mourning is completed the ego becomes free and uninhibited again."

object lives on in the mind of the mourner.[15] The process is depicted by Freud as one of separation or distancing, a curious and painful "mental economics" of detachment. This process of detachment could also, however, be interpreted as a species of hermeneutics, an *analysis,* another series of histories of, let us say, woman, image, and law.[16]

It is initially and inevitably the case that mourning is not for the benefit of the dead, nor does it endeavor to change the past but only, although such is not an insignificant act, to multiply and ameliorate its images in the present. The function of mourning, like that of all historical writing, is expressive of a contemporary event and endeavors either to excise a past, a fantasm, which threatens the health of the mourner, or to manipulate the images of vanished time as a resource for the future or, in the most spurious of contemporary notions, for living well. In either event, the curative virtue of mourning shares many features with the institution of historical writing, which is itself inevitably also an interpretation and displacement of the past: "Modern medicine and historiography are born almost simultaneously from the rift between a subject that is supposedly literate, and an object that is supposedly written in an unknown language. The latter always remains to be decoded. These two 'heterologies' (discourses on the other) are built upon a division between the body of knowledge that utters a discourse and the mute body that nourishes it."[17] The object of history is most obviously and most directly the alien realm of loss: the passed is that which is foreign, obscure, inert, and irrecoverable. The past can only be deciphered, and the only reason for that decipherment is the interest, pleasure, crisis, or peril of the contemporary. The institution of history, like reflection upon our own senescence, is multiple, varying, and purposive; it is the most powerful and the most social of the

15. Ibid. at 154.

16. For a critical appraisal of Freud's thesis coinciding with the advice of the *Ladies Calling,* see Jean Laplanche, *Seduction, Translation, Drives* (London: ICA, 1992) at 172–173: "Everything rests here upon the notion of detachment (*Losung*) which Freud, in an entirely inadequate understanding, considers as the liberating severing of a bond with the object, and not as an *analysis.* Upon the fabric of my existence, woven with the web of the other (now lost), loss causes me to perform an unravelling, a painful meditation. But each thread, although I indeed separate it off from the whole, is not broken as Freud claimed. It is, on the contrary, over-invested, contemplated separately, reintegrated into its history and beyond this history in common, of the couple for instance, reintegrated into a more inclusive and much longer history."

17. Michel de Certeau, *The Writing of History* (New York: Columbia University Press, 1988) at 3. Both existential and psychoanalytic approaches to history repeat this point extensively. It was an important theme in Jean-Paul Sartre, *Critique of Dialectical Reason I, Theory of Practical Ensembles* (London: New Left Books, 1976) and may be traced more recently in another important critique, Peter Sloterdijk, *Critique of Cynical Reason* (Minneapolis: Minnesota University Press, 1987), as, for example, at 115: "History is always a secondary force that must be preceded by an impulse of the moment."

species of thought, it is unconscious in its effects and yet active as either therapy or domination of an invisible or lost cause.[18] Retrospection is a kind of sorcery that imagines, invents, and reinvents those losses that mark survival or that constitute, in its most ancient sense, the image of contemporary identity as person, institution, collectivity, or law. The curative power of remembrance or, in institutional terms, of historical memory, lies not in the accuracy of the recollection nor in the similitude of the image to the subject recollected but rather in the internal effects of the play of past, image, and imagination.

Mourning, in psychoanalytic terms, stands between the subject and melancholia[19] either by virtue of separating the subject from the object or by reinterpreting the history of the subject so as to incorporate the loss of the loved object. Memory thus cures by instituting innumerable images of that which has passed, by providing a vision or reordering of the past that will include the absence of the husband or the loss of some other abstraction or ideal. Time, in another Renaissance conception of such recollection, "must play the physitian," to which the anonymous author of *The Lawes Resolutions of Women's Rights* adds, "I will now help him a little: why mourn you so, you that be widows? Consider how long you have been in subjection under the predominance of parents, of your husbands, now you be free in liberty, and free *proprii iuris* at your own law."[20] The widow comes to reinterpret the past and eventually to inaugurate a novel present, not least by virtue of the legal recognition of her civil status, of her will, upon the death of the husband. The multiple images of the husband, the fragmented reflections of a previous life, the shattered specular remains, are the opposite of a classical fidelity to the image or death mask of the *paterfamilias*. The widow inherits a life; she may love again although it is recommended that such a love be of the church, of the spirit and not of the flesh. The fragmentation of the past acts finally as a spur either to the integration of the self or to a more wayward and idolatrous mobility, a flux and renewal of form, the becoming of the widow now separated from her former subjections.

Separation has also been the technique of the historian whose interpretations depend upon that breakage, rupture, or periodicity which places

18. On the fantasmatic character of individual and collective memory, see Sigmund Freud, *Psychopathology of Everyday Life* (Harmondsworth: Pelican, 1942), especially ch. 4; also Sigmund Freud, "Screen Memories" in *Standard Edition of the Complete Psychological Works of Sigmund Freud* (London: Hogarth Press, 1953), vol. 3 at 303–322.

19. In the Freudian vocabulary, melancholia is an extended mourning which is differentiated from simple mourning not only by the pathological persistence of grief but by the unconscious character of the loss. See Freud, "Mourning and Melancholia" at 155.

20. Anonymous, *The Lawes Resolutions of Women's Rights or, the Lawes Provision for Woemen* (London: J. More, 1632) at 232.

the object of historical knowledge in the past. Against that breakage which constantly threatens to suggest the externality of both the past and of the event, the Baroque conception of plurality, of a past that constantly dissolves and reforms, is suggestive of an internality of the other or of its meaning, an internality toward which the history of mourning itself points. The truth of death, according to Allestree, was not privation but "permutation and change."[21] Death sent on—it was nothing less than the sign of all future possibility, the augur of an "impossible mourning," a distant "premonition of the other," the source of "a law which speaks to us through memory."[22] The other cannot ever be in us as a resurrected self, nor can the image of the other in any way accurately represent the reality of its remains. The image is the repetitive and numerous object of survival, it is the constant or occasional reminder of the dissolution of the subject, it is a fantasy that identifies both subject and death in the plural or dissipated reinterpretation of what has gone. The image as memory exists only in constant dissolution, in the corruption or deferral of presence, in the shattered unity of all identity over time. In similar terms the history of the institution or the history of law is subject to the same process of dissolution, it lives in the scriptural mirror or written remains of innumerable cases, diverse and fragmentary jurisdictions, in permutation and change obscured by the glass of reason or the distance of norms.

GENEALOGY

The object of the widow's memory was conceived explicitly as absence. The past was precisely nonpresence or discontinuity; the past was passed by virtue of absence, by dint of apparent disappearance, it was text or trace, image or fantasy, symptom or lack.[23] In this aspect the widow looks back upon her husband's fate, upon death as that which threatens to hide, render obscure, or remove from view. The first emblem of historical method

21. Allestree, *Whole Duty of Mourning* at 142.

22. Jacques Derrida, "Mnemosyne," in Jacques Derrida, *Memoires: For Paul de Man* (New York: Columbia University Press, 1986) at 6 and 8. For discussion of that text and the theme of memory, see D. Farrell-Krell, *Of Memory, Reminiscence, and Writing* (Indianapolis: Indiana University Press, 1990), especially 283–291.

23. See Paul Virilio, *The Aesthetics of Disappearance* (New York: Semiotexte, 1991); Jean Baudrillard, *The Evil Demon of Images* (Sydney: Power Institute, 1987) at 39: "The idea [is] that the disappearance of something is never objective, never final . . . it always involves a sort of challenge, a questioning, and consequently an act of seduction." That nothing disappears absolutely is, of course, the classic Christian response to death and is elaborated extensively, for example, in Allestree, *Funeral Handkerchief* at 23 ff.: "Death is a strict door-keeper, all that pass out that way, the door is shut on them, they shall never return to converse with us in this world. . . . All our groans, sighs, sobs, and pittiful cries cannot awaken them out of the sleep of death."

that this chapter invokes is thus that of the exteriority or silence of the past. The widow looks back upon a body now absent, she conjures a salutary image of that which was left behind, mute and beyond all objective recuperation. The object of memory and, by implication, the witing of history, is directed in this aspect to the creation of an internal exteriority: the historical care or concern is not so much with "what happened" but with the event of death and the silence or absence it engenders for those that live on. The object of memory is not, however, the corpse—which has in any event also disappeared or putrefied[24]—nor is it the state or the various signs of being dead or discontinued. The object of memory is the recollection of disappearance, the deciphering of the myths, emblems, and clues,[25] the relics, ruins, or remains of the passage of that which is passed on.[26] The mode of historical writing, in other words, is both cryptic and creative, it reminisces and it reinvents: "None of this, however, constitutes a reconstruction. Something has been lost that will not return. Historiography is a contemporary form of mourning. Its writing is based on absence and produces nothing but simulacra. . . . It offers representation in the place of bereavement."[27] So too, to take another example, *The Anatomie of Melancholy* places memory among the "inner senses" and observes that its objects are things "past, absent, such as were before in the sense."[28] In theological terms, memory is thus the conceit of images (*imaginaria visionis est indigna*), a sight of what no longer exists, an unhappy recollection

24. Although it should be noted that there is a discourse of putrefaction which reminds the widow or the friend of the "horrors of death." See Allestree, *Whole Duty of Mourning* at 49–50: "And in such degree hath corruption prevailed, that some bodies hath been forced to be buried very deep, in the earth. So noysome have they been, and soon putrefied, but they are not to be looked upon with the Eye, yet are they more to be thought upon, and our fading estate to be reflected upon." On the representation of the dead, or more precisely of dead bodies, see [Tribonian et al.] *The Digest of Justinian*, ed. Alan Watson. (Philadelphia: Pennsylvania University Press, 535, 1985 ed.) 11.7.44, discussed in Pierre Legendre, *Le Désir politique de Dieu: Étude sur les montages de l'état et du droit* (Paris: Fayard, 1989) at 37–38; see also Anonymous, "Of the Variety and Antiquity of Tombes and Monuments of Persons Deceased in Englande" (1598), in Thomas Hearne (ed.), *A Collection of Curious Discourses* (London: J. Richardson, 1771). More generally, see Nigel Llewellyn, *The Art of Death: Visual Culture in the English Death Ritual c. 1500–c. 1800* (London: Reaktion Books, 1991).

25. On decipherment and historical method, see Carlo Ginsburg, "Clues: Roots of an Evidential Paradigm," in Carlo Ginsburg, *Myths, Emblems and Clues* (London: Radius, 1990). See also de Certeau, *Writing of History* at 85: "The past is first of all a means of *representing a difference* . . . the figure of the past keeps its primary value of representing *what is lacking*."

26. On the theme of passage, see Walter Benjamin, *The Origin of German Tragic Drama* (London: New Left Books, 1976); see also the excellent discussion in Susan Buck-Morss, *The Dialectics of Seeing: Walter Benjamin and the Arcades Project* (Boston: MIT, 1989) at 159–201.

27. Michel de Certeau, *The Mystic Fable, Volume One: The Sixteenth and Seventeenth Centuries* (Chicago: Chicago University Press, 1992) at 10.

28. Burton, *Anatomie of Melancholy* at 23.

(*infoelix memoria*).[29] What is left, according to the *Digest,* is no more than a likeness, the image made from what has gone.[30]

Unable to restore the past as physical presence, the widow must engage in a pathological reflection upon the signs and, more strongly, the symptoms of an absence and so recuperate her own health by means of multiple and momentary refractions of her loss. She sees her husband more often by virtue of his dissolution and so, in a curiously Freudian turn, she remembers him so as to put him to rest, so as to forget his actual past. While the widow's relation to the past is quite explicitly imaginary, it would be wrong to suppose that the reinterpretation of the past differentiated personal mourning from historiography. Both endeavor to interpret or give meaning to loss. The exteriority of the past, its existence only in texts, ruins, and other sedimented or imaginary remains, is the site of the power of historical writing, namely that it gives speech, a language, to that which is silent; it deciphers an other that would not otherwise be read. One might thus note that on any model or by any method, the writing of history is engaged, either therapeutically or politically, both with its subject, the widow who remembers or the historian who writes, and with its object, the departed husband or the imagined past. Whatever the means of the relation between interior and exterior, presence and absence, life and its relics, the evocation of dissolution, of absence and silence, necessarily involves elements of a dialectic or play between image and subject, fantasm and reason, and finally, one might add, between repetition and reproduction. Where the widow fills the space of absence with multiple images, with partial and distortive reflections of the lost object, the history of institutions similarly traces the varied elements of discourse and structure, relic and fragment that compose the identity—the legitimacy—of cultural forms. The widow preserves the name of her husband not simply so as to relieve herself of a certain sorrow or sense of bereavement, but also for purposes of reproduction: the widow protects the memory of the dead man, but she also tends thereby to her children and to the law of succession, which passes on from father to son in an unbroken line:[31] whoever has seen me has seen the father.[32] In short, mourning institutionalizes the widow's loss and emblematizes that which has vanished as the prototype of

29. James Calfhill, *An Answere to the Treatise of the Cross* (London: H. Denham, 1565) at sig. 173v.

30. *Digest* 11.7.44. What is important in determining the sanctity of burials is where the head is buried, *cuius imago fit,* from which images are made.

31. On succession and specifically dower—the third of the husband's property held by the widow for her life—see, particularly, Anonymous, *Lawes Resolutions* at 231–360.

32. Through the image, the father becomes an emblem. For discussion of Athanasius, see Legendre, *L'Inestimable objet de la transmission* at 61–64.

that which will follow. The husband becomes a real image, an institution, a history to which the son adapts.

The fantasmatic character of adaptation is not directly the issue. The widow reflects upon an absence, she mourns by means of certain signs, symptoms, or effigies of that which has disappeared. Whatever the labor of adaptation or of resistance in which the widow in fact engages, the figure of the widow may act as an emblem of a species of historiographical method, that of genealogy. To the extent that she acts as host and guarantee of reproduction, the widow becomes an institution, she repeats. The institution may similarly be depicted as a widow. The institution or, more simply, the law, requires its own effigy, its own paternity, its own forms of legitimacy or familial identity and role. In this respect it acquires an unconscious or, in more pragmatic terms, it writes so as to have a past, it writes so as to lay claim to an identity. Against that historiographical tradition and its institutional texts, against the grain of identification, unification, and establishment, against the law of transmission through precedent, scripture, and patristic norm, the genealogical method turns rather to the multiple images of the broken mirror, to a past that is both fecund and fluid in its imaginary representations of loss. Genealogical method suggests nothing less than a history of law as a history of institutional imagination, a history of the unconscious of a human science, a history of the multiple images of justice, of person, thing, and action which form the work, the symptoms, of legal culture.[33]

In positive terms the genealogy of an institution takes the form of the expression of a series of partial histories. The genealogical method looks to the plurality of institutional histories and not only to its legitimate forms. Either as supplement or as excess, genealogical method traces equally the various unconscious forms of institutional transmission. It provides a reading of custody and succession, permutation and repetition through the symbols, the icons, idols and failures, the deaths and the survivals, the singularities and the repetitions embedded in the *longue durée* of all institutional forms: "I imagine a history of imperious or sovereign exceptions, a history which would develop a counter-subject . . . *a history of symptomatic intensities* . . . of fecund moments, of the power of the fantasm . . . a history of the limits of representation and perhaps at the same time a representation of these limits."[34] While the symptomatic intensities referred to are

33. On the notion of the work of culture adapted from psychoanalysis to social anthropological use, see particularly Obeyesekere, *The Work of Culture.* In terms of legal culture see Drucilla Cornell, "What Takes Place in the Dark" (1992) 4 *differences: A Journal of Cultural Studies* 45; Luce Irigaray, *Le Temps de la différence* (Paris: Livre de Poche, 1989).

34. Georges Didi-Huberman, *Devant l'image: Question posée aux fins d'une histoire de l'art* (Paris: Éditions de Minuit, 1990) at 231.

those of the history of art, there is no reason in principle why they should not be those of the art of law, of a tradition that claims to be the art of the good and the equal, the art of justice and of its representations before the law. The present study, however, will limit its analysis of these juristic arts to the genealogy of the image itself within the law. Its concern is therefore with a history or mourning peculiar to law, the history of the positivization of an institution, the history of its lost objects as revealed through its symptoms, its repetitions, the detritus of institutional survival, of the costs of a wisdom without desire.

The concerns of a genealogy of law are thus disparate and often contradictory. They require a rethinking of the institution in terms of the history of its failures and its exclusions as well as of its successful custody of the law over the indefinite time of institutional duration. It is a question, in short, of a most detailed reading of fragments and texts, of the forms and the margins of representation, of lost projects and peripheral interpretations over the antique and structural times of the law, for "antiquity has no bounds, no limits, it signifies the age of indefinite time."[35] It is in this sense that a genealogical history develops a somewhat different and nonlinear conception of time as imaginary distribution and as indefinite or oneiric sequence and cycle: the time of the institution is that of numina, of clouds, and not of sequence or chronography for "*religionis authoritas non est tempore aestimando, sed numine.*"[36] The reading of intensities as symptoms of events, as repressions, takes place within an institutional time characterized more by rhythm than succession. In the terms of legal historicism and of common law, it is a time already designated as immemorial and unbroken, the time of nature in culture and of virtue in law. It is marked precisely by the episodic duration of dreams, by the varying permanence of symbols or affectivities that answer to the logic of events and of thoughts and not to that of succession. In more formal terms the genealogical analysis of the institution may thus be depicted as concerned not with an origin or continuity of descent but rather with the "accidents, the minute deviations—or conversely the complete reversals—the errors, the false appraisals, and the faulty calculations that gave birth to those

35. John Favour, *Antiquitie Triumphing over Noveltie: Whereby it is proved that Antiquity is a true and certaine note of the Christian Catholicke Church* (London: Richard Field, 1619) at 35.

36. John Jewel, *A Defence of the Apologie of the Churche of England* (London: Fleetstreet, 1567) at 491 (the authority of religion should not be estimated in terms of time but of the Gods or of clouds). For a philosophical analysis of the same issue, see Yifat Hachamovitch, "In Emulation of the Clouds: An Essay on the Obscure Object of Judgement," in Costas Douzinas, Peter Goodrich and Yifat Hachamovitch (eds.), *Politics, Postmodernity and Critical Legal Studies: The Legality of the Contingent* (London: Routledge, 1994).

things that continue to exist and have value for us."[37] Genealogy suggests the study of the dispersed traditions of common law, its disparate sources and its several languages, its forms of delirium, its imaginary objects. There is, in other words, no real object of legal science but only that fantasm of unity necessary for the maintenance of the profession itself.[38] At one level, the fantasm has been recognized by the critics of common law jurisprudence in terms of the negative depiction of the sources of law. Thus the law is represented as being based upon what John Selden termed "dulling custom,"[39] upon a "poor illiterate reason,"[40] upon legally discovered precedent and the transmission of narrow repetitions which Mary Astell, to use proleptically a feminine genealogy, somewhat later designated as the "foundation of vice . . . a merciless torrent that carries all before it," including prudence and virtue.[41] In this sense the basis of law in custom is itself a species of ignorance or of forgetting, a form of unconsciousness or dream, a series of repressions, represented in the multiple and differing languages of separate jurisdictions and distinct historical eras of law. More technically, recourse to custom is a form of stupidity or idiocy, an appeal to the people (*idiota*) and to opinion (*doxa*), neither of which are guides to anything other than the irrationality of precedent or the unconsciousness of past causes.[42]

A genealogy that pays regard to the unconscious, to the intensities and the symptoms of the institution, suggests that custom has to be challenged on the one hand by the reason and virtue of plural principles and on the other by a history that predates or otherwise circumvents the narratives of legal custom, the self-evident and false truths lauded by Coke, Davies, and other "sages of the common law."[43] In both cases the classical form of

37. Michel Foucault, *Language, Counter-Memory, Practice* (Ithaca: Cornell University Press, 1977) at 146.

38. On the notion of a delirious profession, taken originally from the poet Paul Valéry, see Jean-Claude Milner, *For the Love of Language* (London: Macmillan, 1990) at 77–78.

39. John Selden, *The Historie of Tithes* (London: private circulation, 1618) at vi.

40. Sir Robert Wiseman, *The Law of Laws or the Excellency of the Civil Law above all other humane laws* (London: Royston, 1656, 1666 ed.) at 147.

41. Mary Astell, *A Serious Proposal to the Ladies for the Advancement of their True and Greatest Interest* (London: R. Wilkin, 1694, 1698 ed.) at 30, 49, 81–82.

42. I take the term *idiota* in this context from Thomas Stapleton, *A Returne of Untruthes upon M. Jewell* (Antwerp: Latius, 1566) at sig. 69r. See, for discussion of this theme in earlier legal history, M. T. Clanchy, *From Memory to Written Record* (Oxford: Blackwell, 1979, 1992 ed.). On the irrationality of precedent see Wiseman, *Law of Laws* at 36–45, at 45: "We conclude that the way of judging by precedents is as erroneous a guide to walk by, and as little satisfactory to the people, as a law or custom that is void of all Equity and Reason, and therefore by no means to be entertained or admitted."

43. On the historical sense of Coke, Davies, and others in the doctrinal tradition, see J. G. A. Pocock, *The Ancient Constitution and the Feudal Law* (Cambridge: Cambridge University

argument is to resort to a mythology of origins or of the "originals" of common law which are mystical precisely because the human source of law can never be directly represented. While it may be noted that common law has always resorted to mythical and often transparently feminine categories of origin in "time immemorial" or some other indistinct *corpus mysticum* at the dawn or border of law, the explicit invocation of origins tends to take the rhetorical form of an opposition between history and tradition, past and precedent as primary or first sources of law.[44] That origin and reproduction are best figured by the image of women is of considerable significance within the present work. It expresses not least the need to recognize that the opposition between different species of historical narrative is a principal stake in the politics of institutional forms. The play of history and myth, of symptom and fantasm is as much a feature of common law doctrine and its theory of sources as it is of the repressed genealogies of plural or other jurisdictions, let us say those of the feminine, of the *gynaeceum,* of the soul or of the spiritual courts, of localities, of language, of thought. "True 'mourning' seems to dictate only a tendency: the tendency to accept incomprehension, to leave a place for it, and to enumerate coldly, almost like death itself, those modes of language which, in short, deny the whole rhetoricity of the true. . . . In doing so, they also deny, paradoxically the truth of mourning, which consists in a certain rhetoricity."[45] The rhetoric, allegory, or figuration of retrospection multiplies the images of the past which can neither be wholly internalized nor fully comprehended as an externality. Genealogy in its turn is a method of such incomprehension and, like "true mourning," seeks no more than to provide a gently uncomprehending account of the multiple forms of the past, a poetics or at least plurality of historic absences or former laws.

In a more obviously institutional sense, the genealogy of common law may well reflect a sense of mourning for the passing of precedent, the loss of the unwritten, the positivization of judgment—and there are few who would imagine that things are going well. More broadly, the genealogical sense of the legal institution requires an expanded conception of its history. To understand the plenitude of law, to understand also what has been lost, involves the admission, which is intrinsic to genealogical study,

---

Press, 1987); also Gerald Postema, *Bentham and the Common Law Tradition* (Oxford: Clarendon Press, 1989). See also Peter Goodrich, "Ars Bablativa: Ramism, Rhetoric and the Genealogy of English Jurisprudence," in G. Leyh (ed.), *Legal Hermeneutics: History, Theory, Practice* (Berkeley and Los Angeles: University of California Press, 1992); and also, Peter Goodrich, *Languages of Law: From Logics of Memory to Nomadic Masks* (London: Weidenfeld and Nicolson, 1990) at 63–111.

44. On the concept of antiquity and origin, see, for legal examples, Spelman, *Original of the Four Law Termes*; Dugdale, *Origines Juridiciales.*

45. Derrida, "Mnemosyne" at 31.

that the institution internalizes its losses, that it carries a past obliquely on its surface, that it repeats, and that like all subjects it may be analyzed symptomatically in terms of the cultural work that its repetitions, its rites, and its symbols perform. To read the unconscious of an institution, the unconscious of law, over the surface of its texts and other forms of presence entails a strict attention to those signs of intensity or condensation which Freud articulated to the life history and which a hermeneutic of institutions will attach to the persistence or *longue durée* of collective forms and their symbolic expressions. Such an entry into the private life, the delirium or desire,[46] of the institution first requires a recognition of unconscious patterns, the projections—the incomprehensions—of the present in relation to the past: "One has then to concede that there does exist, at some distance, a social unconscious. And concede, too, that this unconscious might well be thought more rich, scientifically speaking, than the glittering surface to which our eyes are accustomed."[47] As to the referent of such an unconscious, it may variously be described as a "vanishing antiquitie," an "imaginarie thing," a "fantastical power," a myth, a desire, or some other image that will cover the void of a deathbound subjectivity.[48] However visible, the identity of the institution, of the law, is inevitably a feature of structures, of what used to be termed traditions and, equally inevitably, genealogy deconstructs, as all psychoanalytic thought deconstructs, the unities, the beliefs, the spiritual constraints of the current age and its emblems of collective subjectivity—order, identity, and norm.[49] A genealogy is in this respect a critical enterprise. To analyze the unconscious of law is to read the institution against itself, to read it paradoxically or against its common sense: in the form of repression, although not without a certain narcissism, the institution internalizes as its own form of unhappy consciousness the failures upon which its successes were built. To read the institution against itself is to read the history of institutional repression as a history of incorporations, a pathology of failures,

46. The expression is taken from Pierre Legendre, *Jouir du pouvoir: Traité sur le bureaucratie patriote* (Paris: Éditions de Minuit, 1976).

47. Fernand Braudel, *On History* (Chicago: Chicago University Press, 1980) at 39.

48. Such expressions are taken from the presciently titled *Of the Vanitie and Uncertaintie of Artes and Sciences* at sig. 52v–53v (Of the Interpretation of Dreams; *onirocritica*) by Henry Cornelius Agrippa.

49. Such is not of course to claim that there are not staggering continuities over the time of structures but rather that the unconscious inevitably works to undo the conscious life. For a powerful if historically vague analysis of the institutional unconscious, see Régis Debray, *Critique of Political Reason* (London: Verso, 1983). Most recently in Legendre's massive project on occidental structures, see Pierre Legendre, *Les Enfants du texte: Etude sur la fonction parentale de états* (Paris: Fayard, 1992). For an imaginative critique of conceptions of continuity and structure, see Giorgio Agamben, *The Coming Community* (Minneapolis: Minnesota University Press, 1993).

exclusions, losses, traumas, and their symbolic recollection. It is a question of reproducing a theology of law, a science of spirit, a history of the fates, not because these are desirable or recuperable forms but because the repressed returns and the injunctions of these unconscious structures are the law of law or, in secular terms, the law of thought. It is a question of genealogy when criticism uses history, and pragmatically that means that a method should be developed that is cognizant of a poetics repressed within institutional prose, of an affectivity harbored in its science, a power in its reason, an image in its logic, a justice in its law.

IMAGE AND UNCONSCIOUS

What is the history of law if not the history of institutional trauma or the history of collective encounters with the real?[50] In the mythology of common law, the argument may be taken further: from where are its rules drawn if not from the unconscious of its subjects, from the patterns of their repeated practices, from their habits, habituations, and other pathological or incorporeal forms? The laws, on this model, are explicitly dead letters (*literae mortua*) requiring the *anima legis* of the Crown or judge.[51] The law itself is variously depicted as a silent judge (*lex est mutus magistratus*), an inanimate justice (*lex est iustitia inanimata*),[52] a second nature (*usus altera fit natura*),[53] a tacit and illiterate consensus of men.[54] Such are all unconscious or sleeping forms, repeated practices that express repression by virtue of repeating rather than inventing, thinking, or judging anew: "I do not repeat because I repress, I repress because I repeat, I forget be-

50. Jacques Lacan, *The Four Fundamental Concepts of Psychoanalysis* (London: Pelican, 1978) at 54–55: "The real [presents] itself in the form of that which is inaccessible in it—in the form of the trauma, determining all that follows, and imposing on it an apparently incidental origin." Alternatively, Lacan is reported by Sherry Turkle, *Psychoanalytic Politics* (New York: Basic Books, 1978) at 243, as remarking (while in America) that "when we bang our heads against a stone wall we are struggling with the real," and its effect, one might speculatively add, is to daze, to render unconscious, to block, or to damage.

51. Francis Bacon, *The Elements of the Common Lawes of England* (London: J. More, 1630) at fol. A 2 a.

52. The first two classical maxims are taken from Davies, *A Discourse of Law and Lawyers* at 275–278. For another example, see John Selden, *The Duello or Single Combat: From antiquitie derived into this kingdome of England, with several kindes, and ceremonious formes thereof from good authority described* (London: I. Helme, 1610) at 23, who discusses trial by ordeal as trial by "mute judges."

53. Sir John Fortescue, *De Laudibus Legum Angliae* (London: Gosling, 1468–70, 1737 ed.) at 14.

54. William Blackstone, *Commentaries on the Laws of England* (Oxford: Clarendon Press, 1765), vol. 1 at 63–64 (*tacito et illiterato hominium consensu et moribus expressum*). On the sense of custom see Peter Goodrich, "Poor Illiterate Reason: History, Nationalism and Common Law" (1992) 1 *Social and Legal Studies* 7.

cause I repeat. I repress because, at first, I cannot live certain things or certain experiences except in the mode of repetition."[55] The common lawyer saw law as an archaism older than any other, as a speech without tongue, an unwritten scripture of the heart, an image (an idol) which Mercury must bring to life.[56] The source of law was a "vanishing imagination," it was variously internal decree, Druidical, feministic, divine, or prescribed by immemorial use.[57] Even without such obvious emblems of an imaginary source and imagined identities, the classical definition of law as a knowledge of things both divine and human betrays the juristic belief that law is a mixed discourse, a training both of the body and soul, a governance of the secular and the spiritual.[58] And further still, it would be hard not to recognize that sense of "another scene" or imaginary source in the principal rule of legal method both in common law and civil law for which the pontiff or lawyer or judge must know both the words of the law and the force of the law. They must act as "*interpositae personae*," as interpreters and legislators who will find behind, between, or beyond the *literae* or words of law its truth (*vera judicia*),[59] its force and power (*vim ac potestatem*), its other—in short, its legal meaning.[60] It is not the surface but the depth, not the apparent but the hidden, not the obvious but the arcane that prescribes the meanings and indeed the loves of a law that is paradoxically

55. See Gilles Deleuze, *Différence et répétition* (Paris: Presses Universitaires de France, 1968) at 158. See also Pierre Legendre, *L'Inestimable objet de la transmission* at 90: "We repeat even when we invent, we repeat. . . . It is the most interesting question we can raise: how, in the reproduction of the species, do institutions fabricate subjects who repeat, new subjects who repeat even in their creativity."

56. Davies, *Discourse of Law and Lawyers* at 276, provides the imagery of Jupiter as legislator and Mercury as interpreter. For a brief discussion of these metaphors, see Donald Kelley, *The Human Measure: Social Thought in the Western Legal Tradition* (Cambridge, Mass.: Harvard University Press, 1990). From a very different, although not incommensurate perspective, see Irigaray, *Le Temps de la différence,* ch. 4.

57. The figures of sources of law do not merit further detailed elaboration here. I have surveyed the principal figures in Goodrich, "Eating Law" at 256–260.

58. Doderidge, *English Lawyer* at 28, citing the classical maxim "*iuris prudentia est rerum divinarum humanarumque scientia.*"

59. On *vera judicia* or legal truth see the extended discussion in Wiseman, *The Law of Laws* at 65–70, discussing the civilian conception of *vera judicia*: "No words, forms, niceties, or propriety of language is of any regard in the Civil Law, in comparison of truth, faithfulness and integrity. For *verba menti, non mens verbis servire debet,* words are made as instruments to serve and express the mind, and not to command or control it."

60. Thus *Digest* 1.3.17 (Celsus) Scire leges non hoc est verba earum tenere, sed vim ac potestatem (to know the law is not to know the words of the law, but its force and power); *Digest* 50.16.6.1 (Ulpian) Verbum "ex legis" sic accipiendum est, tam ex legum sententia quam ex verbis (the expression "from the law" is to be taken to mean as much from its true sense as from its literal meaning). For a scrupulously scholarly discussion of this theme within Renaissance legal treatises, see Ian Maclean, *Interpretation and Meaning in the Renaissance: The Case of Law* (Cambridge: Cambridge University Press, 1992), especially 158–178.

without desire: "In reading it is not the words but the truth which ought to be loved (*est amanda*)."[61]

The key to reading the lawyer's love, the institutional design, the force, power, or violence of the text has always been conceived in terms of escaping the letter and discovering the spirit—the soul or *anima*—of law. From the perspective of historical criticism or genealogy it is a question of taking up again the figures of legal interpretation as symptoms of this excess, this love beyond the letter, this spirit or intensity which betrays another scene of law, a law of thought. While the tradition has named such a scene of interpretation variously as equity, justice, truth, or power, there is no reason not to pursue these internal images—that equity, for example, which the judge is to have always before his eyes as one appointed *semper aequitatem ante oculus habere.* There is no binding reason why doctrine should always speak in a language that denies the unconscious significance of this "work" of law, as if Freud had never written, as if the unconscious, once ignored enough or denied sufficiently often, will simply go away. For the widow depicted in the *Ladies Calling* it was a matter of shattering the mirror and so moving beyond the singular image to multiple reflections of the dead. The truth of mourning lay in an elegiac or poetic trace of the other, it lay in an allegory or dissimulation, a fantasm, which allowed the widow to love differently, to love plurally through multiple images now that the husband had departed. For the institution, for the law, it is not so different a matter: interpretation recognizes a "labile *ratio*" or mobile meaning, a spirit, soul, or force, a "ghostly form," that lies behind the shattered words or, rhetorically, the borrowed or broken figures, the images of the text. Renaissance lawyers indeed happily defined such meanings as signs of the soul (*notae animi*) or as "symbols of things [*notae rerum*] which express the passions and movements of the mind and will."[62] There is, in short, much more to legal interpretation than reading the simple surface of the text; there is a constant movement that creates and recreates a text that will conform to or express the love or force that comes as law: "the law 'always speaks,' and its force is derived from the fact that it speaks to us, although it is couched in written form."[63] Interpretation supplements, it adds a surplus and it replaces: for good or ill, it is commentary, another text; it brings art to law, equity to rules, images to words, spirit to

61. Coke, *Reports,* pt. III at fol. C 7 b (*in lectione non verba sed veritas est amanda*).

62. Goddaeus, *Commentarius repetitae praelectionis in titulum xvi libri I Pandectarum de verborum et rerum significatione* (Nassau: n.p., 1569, 1614 ed.) at 6, discussed in Maclean, *Interpretation and Meaning* at 160–161.

63. Maclean, *Interpretation and Meaning* at 173. This hermeneutic theme of the constant reinterpretation of the past, the alien or written, as if it were present is pursued with relentless rigor by Jacques Derrida, *Of Grammatology* (Baltimore: Johns Hopkins University Press, 1976) at 144–157, 269 ff.

letters, meaning to texts. Two questions emerge. On the one hand, there is the issue of how the law speaks, a question of interpretation or hermeneutics, a question also of symptoms and their analysis. On the other hand, the question is that of from where the law speaks, a matter of power, of the other scene or unconscious of the legal institution and of the subtext, motive, or desire that drives forward the languages of law, the rules of speaking, the institutions of life that are slowly internalized as the limits of thought.

At the level of interpretation, a symptomatic reading needs simply to pursue the path of the legal supplement, the histories of the instabilities of legal meaning and hence also of the inventions, creativities, traumas, and defenses of the interpretative art. Again drawing upon the Renaissance treatises on the meaning of words, the speech of law is itself never complete, the *oratio* or the *verba* require further extension, and these implications, amplifications, or corrections are termed *subauditio* or *subintellectio,*[64] terms which, however transcribed, admirably imply a sense beyond, beneath, below, to the side of, or near to what is heard or what is thought. The meaning that is transmitted *subauditio* is explicitly a rumored meaning, hearsay, a fragment, something internal to the intellect or understanding, an intuition, an image, an unconscious form.[65] To which I may add, at the risk of superfluity, that access to the unconscious is defined precisely as being by way of such fragments and slips, by way of that which is beneath the surface, underneath what is heard, below what is understood. More specifically still, it comes via the oneiric narrative of images: "Dreams think essentially in images."[66] Whether this ontological affinity between the subject's unconscious and the representation of the institution allows for any closer analogy of reading or interpretation will depend upon the cultural work which the law is seen to perform, upon whether the unconscious can be made to make a difference to our understanding of law.

Images in the text and in the other verbal and plastic representations of law are distortive forms both of recollection and of representation; they are the affects, the symptoms, the intensities or condensations of the desire that law hides or conceals behind the reason of rules. Subsequent chapters will review the juridical history of the image (*ius imaginum*) so as

64. See the divisions presented by Stephanus de Fredericis, *De iuris interpretatione,* in *Tractatus iuris universis* (Venice, 1574) at i.208–225; Jerome Sapcote, *Ad primas leges Digestorum de verborum et rerum significatione* (Venice, 1579) at 56.

65. On the significance of *subauditio* and *subintellectio,* see Maclean, *Interpretation and Meaning* at 166. On a similar theme in common law, see J. H. Baker, "Introduction," in J. H. Baker (ed.), *The Reports of John Spelman* (London: Selden Society, 1978), vol. 2 at 159–163.

66. Sigmund Freud, *The Interpretation of Dreams* (New York, Avon Books, 1965) at 82.

to read the images within the law. The present discussion of legal historiography will simply reiterate that such recourse to images in the history of legal interpretation, in both its difference and its repetition, is suggestive not only of law's uncertain desires, its traumas and repressions as well as its other affects, but also of their intrinsic or internal character, of the incorporation of such affectivities. If it is again a question of from where the law speaks, the image is the point of fracture or of divide, the screen or, in Kafka's parable, the door or gate that demarcates the boundary between the outside and the inside of law. The image is both inside and outside, both law and desire, sign and sentence, symptom and word. The image represents what did not previously exist, it provides a species of unity or form for what was otherwise fragmentary, shapeless, and inchoate, prior to thought or not yet institutionalized. The image "says the other,"[67] it screens its absence, it indicates that which has become separate from the institution or which cannot be seen but only figured: the images of law—the figures, the monuments, the fictions, signs, and texts—institute social desire, its obligations, its subjectivities, its sense of identity and, in the Occident, its sovereign power. The image enters under the skin, it is the institution, it is the law—if by law we mean the sign that moves, the motive, drive, or force that compels the subject to act.

The image, finally, is a false truth: it is *veritas falsa* because it can never be that which it represents. It is a mark of the soul, an emblem of spirit, a visible sign of that which cannot be seen.[68] Yet what is law in genealogical sensibility if not just such a series of images, a history written and rewritten innumerable times? Again returning to the historicism of the Renaissance, the art of law is both explicitly an addiction, a reverie, *fiat,* or disputatious whim as well as being dogma, truth, and sovereign will. For François Hotman we thus find over time a law that can never be known in its entirety, a law so complex and confused as to require both reason and chance, rule and fortune, fiction and norm in each act of recollection: "Even their judges admit to being dazzled by the authorities and to judging more by chance than by reference to assured and certain law."[69] Here again, the law is a chimerical thing, an impermanent institution, a collection and

67. De Certeau, *Mystic Fable* at 11. For an extended and frequently brilliant analysis of the image in these terms, see Legendre, *Le Désir politique de Dieu* at 33–42.

68. The definition: What is an image? A false truth (Quid est pictura? Veritas falsa), is from A. Alciatus, *De Notitia Dignitatem* (Paris: Cramoisy, 1651 ed.) at 190. For discussion of that definition, see Goodrich, "Specula Laws"; and most recently, Pierre Legendre, *Dieu au miroir* (Paris: Fayard, 1994), pt. I.

69. Hotman, *Anti-Tribonian* at 110–111: "Such a vast literature grows up on the books [of the *Corpus Iuris Civilis*] that Baldus, at forty-seven comments that he is still an apprentice; even the judges admit to being dazzled by the authorities and to judging more by chance than by reference to assured and certain law."

codification of disparate practices, a "discipline [which] is disputatious because it rests on nothing more complete than a collection of fragments, reports, pieces [*lopins*], themselves representing no more than uncertain conjectures and tenuous divinations."[70] Similar sentiments were regularly although less eloquently expressed by humanistic critics of English law: it was *aulae vanitatem*—a tapestry of vanities[71]—a "dark and melancholy science,"[72] it existed only in the recollection of particular cases, half-heard reports of antecedent judgments,[73] in the "dreams of serjeants and counsellors,"[74] in "digressions and imaginations,"[75] in a law "in vast volumes confusedly scattered and utterly undigested."[76]

Like the widow's memory of her husband depicted in the *Ladies Calling,* legal retrospection multiplies the images of the past. The broken mirror both multiplies and disperses, it is a visual Babel, an internal Baroque *folie du voir,*[77] it deconstructs, it supplements, it tears apart so as to set one past against another. Recollection, and particularly a recollection that recalls the multiplicity of the past, threatens the institution by indicating not only its contingency but also its disorder, its polemics, and its agonistic relations to other jurisdictions: historiography in its genealogical guise denies the unity of law and its culture through the exemplification of the disparate histories and numerous forms that laws may take. Legal humanism, historicism, or simply the law's recollection of its past deconstructs and has always deconstructed professional pretensions to universality and to positivization, to science or to truth. The common law may be intrinsically or essentially a historicist discipline—a system of precedent would seem to suppose as much—but such a characterization would attribute too great a degree of self-consciousness to a tradition that basks in "indefinite time," that denies the validity or the need for history,[78] and that believes,

70. Hotman, *Anti-Tribonian* at 131.

71. Burton, *Anatomie of Melancholy* at 3.

72. Cowell, *The Interpreter* at sig. 3r.

73. Baker (ed.), *Reports of John Spelman,* vol. II at 159–161.

74. Fraunce, *Lawiers Logike* at sig. 89v.

75. Ibid. at sig. 119r.

76. Ibid. at vi.

77. The expression is taken from Christine Buci-Glucksmann, *La Folie du voir: De l'esthétique baroque* (Paris: Galilée, 1986). See also her extended discussion of historical writing in Christine Buci-Glucksmann, *La Raison baroque: De Baudelaire à Benjamin* (Paris: Galilée, 1984).

78. Most famously, see Coke, *Reports* at pt. III fol. B v a: "To the grave and learned writers of histories, my advice is, that they meddle not with any point or secret of any art or science, especially with the laws of the realm, before they confer with some learned in their profession"; and at pt. VIII at sig. L 3 a (of legal records): "They are of that authority that they need not the aid of any historian." For another pertinent example, see Edward Stillingfleet, *Ecclesiastical Cases Relating to the Duties and Rights of the Parochial Clergy, Stated and Resolved according to principles of conscience and law* (London: Henry Mortlock, 1698) at 329: "Littleton

semantically rather than explicitly, in the continuity or presence, the positivized and permanent form of contemporary law.[79] To love the common law in either its Anglican or its American manifestation is to believe in the recollection of precedent, to value and to multiply the remains of common law, to recall endlessly the past and the precedents, the plural jurisdictions and the many substantive forms of oral memory and other inscriptions of unwritten law. To love the common law is to believe not in its reason or science, but in its capacity to change, its historic ability to become other, to pass on. It is this conception of the power of common law and of the plurality of its reasons that allows for the distinction between positivized and dynamic jurisprudences. At a more mundane level it allows the practical assertion of a labile *ratio* of common law, of a logic of the supplement, of an unconscious of law that is transmitted *subauditio,* underneath, next to, or along with every legal text as its image, its underside, its backface, or its law of law.

REWRITING LAW

The task of reassembling the diverse fragments, the histories and multiple images of common law has not gone entirely unheeded, nor is the tradition entirely free of histories that resist the dominant and almost unremittingly laudatory historicism.[80] The *Ladies Calling* required that the widow rethink her relation to her husband, that she appropriate or encompass his death and thereby learn to live differently, *proprii iuris,* according to her own law. Similarly and not without certain sentiments of mourning, advocates of alternative forms of legal governance, of feminine rule, of legal poetics, or of less ambitious species of legal reform have turned to the past of common law to recall images and precedents of other laws and of its possible subjects or its subjection of difference. The most striking example is undoubtedly John Selden's work *Jani Anglorum Facies Altera,* translated as *The Reverse or Back-face of the English Janus* and dedicated to the re-

---

says that time out of memory of man, is said to give right because no proof can be brought beyond it. And this he calls prescription at common law." See also, for a strikingly comparable French example, Antoine Hotman, *Traité de la Loy Salique,* in *Opuscules Francoises des Hotmans* (Paris: Mathieu Guilleme, 1611).

79. Hooker, *Of the Lawes of Ecclesiastical Politie* is the most important English exponent of this view.

80. On the specific issue of psychoanalysis and law see the useful review by David Caudill, "Freud and Critical Legal Studies: Contours of a Radical Socio-Legal Psychoanalysis" (1991) 66 *Indiana Law Review* 651. The most remarkable study is still Legendre, *L'amour du censeur.* For a case study utilizing psychoanalysis, see Pierre Legendre, *Le Crime du Caporal Lortie: Traité sur le père* (Paris: Fayard, 1989). See also the commentary in Renata Salecl, "Crime as a Mode of Subjectivization: Lacan and the Law" (1993) 4 *Law and Critique* 3.

cuperation of feminine genealogies of common law.[81] Selden's work collected all the surviving scraps and fragments, stories, customs, relics and myths of antique law that could be used in some way to evidence feminine genealogies and thereby support or install a prehistory of female rule, of women deities, of feminine sovereigns, of women as legislators and as illustrious or erudite subjects. The details, the images, of that work will be analyzed subsequently. The work itself had on its title page an emblem of Janus and a motto which read: "One face looks upon the people, the other upon the Gods (*haec facies Populum spectat; at illa Larem*)." One law, it might be argued, is conscious, the other unconscious—or, in Irigaray's terminology, one masculine, one feminine.[82] The back-face, the reverse side or retrospect, could hardly be bettered as an image of an institutional unconscious and it is in many senses the task of critical historiography to multiply the other faces or indeed the faces of the other in common law.

In a contemporary idiom the other faces of common law would coalesce around its histories of repression and its narratives of failure. They would include the faces of the vernacular, of nature, of equity, of justice, of women, of aliens, of ethics, of subjectivities, and more distantly and darkly of violence, desire, and the failures or miscarriages of law.[83] Such histories may appear to approximate a Baroque conception of the past as allegory or ruin, they may equally be taken as the narratives of legal fantasms or juristic imaginations. Further still, they might be taken to form an archaeology of law's appearances and its disappearances, of its contexts and of its fates. With whatever form and whichever objects such undesirable histories will take up, their political significance lies in their challenge to the closures of law.[84] If nothing else, they suggest the fecund possibilities of thinking law otherwise or thinking law differently. In such a context the emblem of the widow takes on another and perhaps peculiar connotation. The widow is a woman and at least for a time—even if not by legal definition—she is a woman in mourning. As I will later argue more extensively, woman is an image in law, she is the specter of creativity as also of death because femininity is, by tradition, nature: inexorable, material, passionate, and unconscious. The feminine, the image, it will be argued, is

81. John Selden, *Jani Anglorum Facies Altera* (London: T. Bassett, 1610, 1683 ed.), more accurately translated as *The Other Face of the English Janus.*

82. See Luce Irigaray, *J'aime à toi: Equisse d'une félicité dans l'histoire* (Paris: Grasset, 1992); and also my review of that work, "Writing Legal Difference" (1993) 6 *Women: A Cultural Journal* 173.

83. See Goodrich, "Critical Legal Studies in England" at 201; see also Costas Douzinas and Ronnie Warrington, *Justice MisCarried: Ethics and Aesthetics in Law* (Hemel Hempstead: Harvester, 1994).

84. For recent discussions of law, critique, and closure, see Alan Norrie (ed.), *Closure and Critique in Contemporary Legal Theory* (Edinburgh: Edinburgh University Press, 1993).

literally the repressed, she is in analytic terms the only wholly appropriate social expression of repression because she cannot be excluded but can only be exiled or excluded within. The feminine, the image, is the outside within, she is an internalized exteriority, a desire within wisdom, a fate or seduction within the present, either ignored or denied yet nonetheless inevitable and no less a law for being repeated without being recognized: "Repression, not forgetting; repression, not exclusion. Repression as Freud says, neither repels, nor flees, nor excludes an exterior force; it contains an interior representation, laying out within itself a space of repression"[85] or what to consciousness is an image, a woman, a mystery, or an enchanting void. She is the emblem of another law or law of law, of the contingency and thus fracture of such doctrine, dogma, or jurisprudence that claims the singularity, unity, or closure of legal forms. Woman is in the history of law a figure of uncertainty, of doubt or desire, foresight or faith, idolatry or immaculate conception; she is many and she is none, both matter and void. The interdiction of the image, in spiritual and latterly in secular law was, I will argue, a prohibition of the feminine, of the sensual and of imagination in the long process of positivization of common law.

In a paradoxical sense, the widow claims the future by multiplying the images of the past. The object of memory is difference in the sense that the widow is charged with loving *in memoriam* not the husband but the image, something else, something multiple and dispersed, a lost object or fractured presence, a series of masks or legitimate hallucinations. Death, which as an event is the metaphor through which history takes place, is heteronomous, it cannot have meaning, it can only have meanings in the same sense that humans have purposes and thereby engage and repress the contingency that obsesses memory and obscures the productive force of meaning: "Historiography tends to prove that the site of its production can encompass the past: it is an odd procedure that posits death, a breakage everywhere reiterated in discourse, and that yet denies loss by appropriating to the present the privilege of recapitulating the past as a form of knowledge."[86] The widow is in this sense potentially a figure of power, as is the image, because both threaten law with the violence of plurality, with the slippage of sensuality or, in a secular form, with the dangers, the pleasures, and the pains of idolatry, if not of a more rigorous rethinking of law. "To begin (writing, living) we must have death. . . . We must have death, but young, present, ferocious, fresh death . . . today's death,"[87] a death

85. Jacques Derrida, *Writing and Difference* (London: Routledge, 1978) at 196. For a feminist elaboration of this position in terms of bodies and sexes, see Judith Butler, *Bodies that Matter: On the Discursive Limits of Sex* (New York: Routledge, 1993).

86. De Certeau, *Writing of History* at 5.

87. Hélène Cixous, *Three Steps on the Ladder of Writing* (New York: Columbia University Press, 1993) at 7.

that will remind us of the body and of its future, the trace of the other, of finitude, of the resistance to closure that writing may yet represent.

When it returns to questions of law, the writing that mourns remembers the loss of one that was loved. As in mourning, which is of the essence of memory, so too in historiography writing institutes images that pass between the public and the private, between reason and imagination, spirit and materiality. Writing does not only inscribe, as memory does not merely recapture—it could not; rather, it reminds the soul of the body, the reason of another and more material law. The historiography of the image in law must play upon a series of differences and upon the multiple senses of the image in the unconscious of law. It must move in a profane and dissolute manner between jurisdictions and classificatory systems, between the archive and its institutions, between scripture and law so as to offer elements for a history of an extended present: "Genealogy does not pretend to go back in time to restore an unbroken continuity that operates beyond the dispersion of forgotten things . . . [nor] is it concerned with the erecting of foundations: on the contrary, it disturbs what was previously considered immobile; it fragments what was thought unified; it shows the heterogeneity of what was imagined consistent with itself."[88] It may be remarked in conclusion that while such a methodology is hardly novel it is nonetheless politically charged in institutional terms. After all, what is the legitimacy, the lineage, of the institution if not the written reason, the incontestable logic, the irrefragable truth of its law? What is that law if not text, the history, the writing, the thought that lays claim to found institutional identity?

In that mourning, and specifically the images of the other through which mourning internalizes loss, marks a certain desire, it marks the limit and, in a sense, the failure of law. It does so not only through its denial of the fixity of the meaning of loss but also in its creative representation of the past through a constant movement or flux between subject and object, and between past, present, and future. The law in a sense has always been a creative form of historical writing, it was in practice always a glossatorial and so philological tradition, it was at certain times synonymous with historical writing—the jurist was an epigone, a classicist[89]—and yet, ironically, its history was a history of the denial of history, a history of repetition, of

88. Foucault, *Language, Counter-Memory, Practice* (Ithaca: Cornell University Press, 1977) at 146–147.

89. On which correlation see Friedrich Nietzsche, "We Philologists," in Friedrich Nietzsche, *The Case of Wagner* (Edinburgh: T. N. Foulis, 1911) at 117–118, 126, 139–140, and Friedrich Nietzsche, "Homer and Classical Philology," in Friedrich Nietzsche, *On the Future of Our Educational Institutions* (Edinburgh: Foulis, 1909) at 147. For an important theoretical discussion of this correlation between history and law, see Gillian Rose, *Dialectic of Nihilism: Post-Structuralism and Law* (Oxford: Blackwell, 1984) at 131–170.

truths that take the form of repression.[90] For the common law tradition, historical sense and the mythologies of memory were in practice primary sources of legal decision, and doctrine has frequently recognized the subversive quality of such historical reflection. History frequently becomes the law, but it has tended to do so apologetically and in the doctrinal guise of truth, as *ratio scripta* (written reason) or some other concept of scriptural or universal law. Against such dogmatic contentions, even a strictly scholastic conception of the motives of recollection or the play of memory would offer a subtle deconstruction or gentle incomprehension and productivity within an overwhelmingly antiquarian and increasingly positivized legal historiography. In classical terms, the English lawyer and judge Sir John Doderidge suggested that the "memory intellective" has a double operation. The one is called "*actus memorandi,* the other *actus reminiscendi.* The first of these is the representation of things past, as if they were present, representing the image of things forepassed in the same manner as if they were now actually and really present. *Actus reminiscendi* is as it were the discourse of memory . . . out of one thing remembered [memory] discovereth another thing in manner lost and forgotten."[91] In each form, either as memory or as reminiscence, recollection both simulates and invents, it disturbs and pursues images, or, in Aristotle's terms, affections harbored within the soul. In that recollection suggests a certain passion, either nostalgic or visionary, to historical sensibility, it also suggests a desire that comes with the historical wisdom of the law. The image is the sign of such desire, and it is to the history and hermeneutics of the image in law that subsequent chapters will turn.

90. For an influential exposition of this thesis, see Donald Kelley, *Foundations of Modern Historical Scholarship: Language, Law, and History in the French Renaissance* (New York: Columbia University Press, 1970). For theoretical discussion of history and law, see Mark Cousins, "The Practice of Historical Investigation" in D. Attridge et al. (eds.), *Poststructuralism and the Question of History* (Cambridge: Cambridge University Press, 1987); W. T. Murphy, "Memorising Politics of Ancient History" (1989) 50 *Modern Law Review* 384.

91. Doderidge, *English Lawyer* at 16–17. In terms of sources, see Aristotle, *De Memoria et Reminiscentia,* in R. Sorabji (trans. and ed.), *On Memory* (London: Duckworth, 1970).

THREE

Apology and Antirrhetic

Icon, Idol, Image, and the Forms of Law

He begins [his book] with these words, "I cannot see." And verily if he had there left it and gone no further it had been well enough. For as for the thing that he speaks of, it appears by his words he cannot see very well indeed.[1]

The power of law has always been tied to the history and ambiguous status of images. Contemporary scholarship has frequently played with the paradoxical foundation of the Western legal institution both in and against images.[2] The decalogue was presented in the forbidding and erased form of commandments inscribed in stone and also pitched dramatically against idols, false images, or other gods. The image not only represented the law, as father, justice, or truth, but it also represented the stake or substance of law that lay not in external, visible, or merely temporal things but in the invisible or internal governance of the soul. The image could either save or destroy, it could turn the inward eye toward reason, truth, and law, or it could seduce and hold vision upon the nothingness of the image itself as a

1. Sir Thomas More, *The Debellacyon of Salem and Bizance* (London: W. Rastell, 1533) at fol. i. 1. a. This from a Lord Chancellor, commenting on the work of the barrister Christopher St. German, *Salem and Bizance* (London: Berthelti, 1533), a work which had the temerity to challenge a number of "defaults of the spirituality" and to question some of the "ex officio" procedures used by spiritual judges in bringing charges of heresy under the statute *De Haeretico Comburendo.* On the history of such challenges to the ecclesiastical jurisdiction see Robert Cosin, *An Apologie for Sundrie Proceedings by Jurisdiction Ecclesiastical, of late times by some challenged* (London: n.p., 1591).

2. For recent general studies, see Legendre, *Désir politique de Dieu*; Régis Debray, *Vie et mort de l'image: Une histoire du regard en occident* (Paris: Gallimard, 1992); Louis Marin, *Des pouvoirs de l'image* (Paris: Éditions du Seuil, 1993). Specifically on the foundation of law, see Jacques Derrida, "Force of Law: The 'Mystical Foundations of Authority'" (1990) 11 *Cardozo Law Review* 919; Arthur Jacobson, "The Idolatry of Rules: Writing Law According to Moses, with Reference to Other Jurisprudences" (1990) 11 *Cardozo Law Review* 1079; and more broadly, Jean-Joseph Goux, *Les Iconoclastes* (Paris: Éditions du Seuil, 1976); Serge Gruzinski, *La Guerre des images* (Paris: Fayard, 1990); David Freedberg, *The Power of Images* (Chicago: Chicago University Press, 1990); Jean Wirth, *L'Image médiévale* (Paris: Méridiens Klincksieck, 1989); Douzinas and Warrington, *Justice MisCarried*, especially ch. 8.

spurious surface, a face, an idol, vanity, or lie. Whichever form the image took, either licit or illicit, iconic or idolatrous, its function was structural, it established the order of meaning and of law, it governed the soul by dictating what the heart could see or the mind portray of itself. In the striking words of one Reformation polemic on the cross, debating whether the crucifix was a legitimate image or admissible sign of divinity, "the world itself is a certain spectacle of things invisible." More than that, although less eloquently, "the order and frame of it, is a glass to behold the secret working and hidden grace of God. The heavenly creatures and spheres above, have a greater mark of his divinity, more evident to the world's eye, than either can be unknown or dissembled."[3] In short, the world of appearance, of images, was either the sign or the dissimulation of an unseen, "aereall" or ghostly realm. It was for the law to determine the truth of the sign, its efficacy or force, and in doing so it would necessarily institute a governance of perception, a licit hierarchy of visible references, variously words, figures, signs, symbols, or statues that recalled or referred to the invisible order of true being.

The image played the law, either as the word, the inner sign of a dual nature, or as a figurative representation. In either case, whether it was the text alone, word, sacrament (*verba visibilia*), or statuary figure that governed the direction of vision, the law had to dictate the terms of legitimate signification so as to command the mystery, faith, grace, or meaning that escapes and will always escape the dead letter of prose. The law, both spiritual and positive, had to distinguish the orders of unseen or absent causes: false imagining from true reference, fantasy from prophecy, vestige from image, spiritual essence from diabolic appearance. In each case or instance the definition of an order of true reference, a doctrine or creed, required the designation of an order of signs through which the faithful, the believers or subjects of law, could be ordered to imagine, perceive, understand, or know the invisible truth. While reformist movements have tended to be iconoclastic, their doctrines do not escape the dialectic of true and false images, the orthodoxy and heterodoxy of the sign, but rather they shift the boundaries of visible and invisible and redefine the legitimate signs of internal direction. The text or word is no less a sign than the graven image or statue, it is different, as is a Eucharist predicated upon the metaphoric presence of divinity or a church without incense, vestments, or ornaments.

3. Calfhill, *An Answere to the Treatise of the Cross* at sig. 169v. The *Answere* was a response to John Martiall's *A Treatyse of the Crosse gathred out of the Scriptures, Councelles and Auncient Fathers of the Primitive Church, by John Martiall Bachelor of Lawe and Student in Divinitie* (Antwerp: I. Latius, 1564). For an excellent history of English iconoclasm, see Margaret Aston, *England's Iconoclasts I: Laws Against Images* (Oxford: Clarendon Press, 1988); see also Carlos Eire, *War Against the Idols: The Reformation of Worship from Erasmus to Calvin* (Cambridge: Cambridge University Press, 1986).

The differences of doctrine or jurisprudence cannot conceal the common terrain or problematic of such difference. The question of law remains that of which mechanisms of reference or which visual insignia, external images, memories, or internal phantasms best mark and remind the subject of its obligations or best hold it to law. Such is a question of visual and linguistic rhetorics, a question of persuasion or fascination, of bending and moving the will so as to order the subject according to an image, a spiritual or inner law.[4]

The significance and the danger, the stake or threat of the war of images may often be most apparent in the means of their denial. It is an old trope that the claim to represent an unadorned or literal truth is the most persuasive style of scientific or juridical argument. It is similarly an oratorical commonplace that silence will often refute an opponent much more effectively than the attention that comes with direct rebuttal. The image of objectivity is neither less combative nor any less imagistic for concealing its polemical force behind the assertion or figures of demonstrable truth.[5] These are simply the figures of law, of a rhetoric that exists to deny rhetoric, of an imagery that functions to efface itself by excluding, exiling, or repressing its imagistic nature or quality. While a history of law and images must labor extensively to evidence convincingly the imagistic quality of modern law and its coldly prosaic texts, such difficulty or resistance signals the crucial motive force or power of the image of a legal science or modern and technical profession of law. The imagery that surrounds and subtends the normative, yet still quite particular, text of modern law does not escape the antagonistic context of its historical repression, nor does it escape the antinomic structural role that image and figure have played in law. Law was always, in terms of oratorical method, a specific and distinctively sophistic genre.[6] While in certain formulations, associated

4. The classic study of linguistic and visual rhetorics was Christian Metz, *Psychoanalysis and Cinema: The Imaginary Signifier* (London: Macmillan, 1982). Most recently, see Martin Jay, *Downcast Eyes: The Denigration of Vision in Twentieth-Century French Thought* (Los Angeles and Berkeley: University of California Press, 1993); Yifat Hachamovitch, "In Emulation of the Clouds."

5. It is not without relevance that the scholastic conception of demonstrable truth is predicated upon a visual metaphor. To demonstrate, from the Latin *demonstrare*, means to show or figure a truth that cannot otherwise be known. More broadly on visual metaphors and truth, see Jacques Derrida, "The White Mythology," in Jacques Derrida, *Margins of Philosophy* (Brighton: Harvester Press, 1982); Peter Goodrich, "We Orators" (1990) 53 *Modern Law Review* 546.

6. Plato, *Theaetetus*, at 172 e–173 b argues that the legal orator, subject to the constraints of time and adversary circumstance, "is a slave disputing about a fellow slave before a master sitting in judgment with some definite plea in his hand." The rhetorician as lawyer "acquires a tense and bitter shrewdness . . . his mind is narrow and crooked. An apprenticeship in slavery has dwarfed and twisted his growth and robbed him of his free spirit." Tacitus, *Dialogue of*

particularly with Cicero and Vico, the method and ethos of rhetoric was deemed relevant to civic virtue and political stability or *sensus communis*, the practice of legal oratory was unambiguously associated not so much with the felicitous use of speech as with disputation, casuistry, apologetic, proof, and polemic. The ensuing analysis will retrace the history of that disputatious and polemical character of law to the early structure and jurisdictions of the institution, and more specifically to its doctrinal discourses on the image. These were antagonistic and combative in their rhetorical structure and practice, and while their concern was directly with the opposition between idolatry and iconolatry, iconoclasm and "image service," "*latria* and *dulia*,"[7] the structure of argument and the form of discourse became internalized within the rhetorical practices of law at the same time that the iconoclasm of the Reformation and the ascendancy of print forced the external image into its modern textual form as illicit figure or oratorical trope, metaphor, or "painted word" within the prose of law.[8]

The argument will proceed in three stages. I will argue first that doctrinal discourses, the forensic rhetorics of foundation and of law, have historically taken on a specific structure of defense (*apologia*) and denunciation (*antirrhesis*) and that this structure is evident as well in the antithetical and polemical substance of the legal tradition as a set of practices. Each tenet of doctrine is matched historically and rhetorically by a figure of heretical exclusion or excommunication; each affirmative value or force of law is counterposed to an enigma, evil, or antiportrait against which the law stands as order pitched against excess, reason against fantasy, antiquity against novelty, nature against artifice, and nation against barbarism. The discourse of doctrine is the armature of virtue, and it is explicitly imperialistic in its battle to convince, to convert, and to control those within its spiritual and territorial jurisdictions. The second stage of analysis will take up certain implicit themes within the language, imagery, and figuration of doctrinal discourse. Certain apparently extrinsic or insignificant features

---

Orators (London: Loeb Classical Library, 1911 ed.) at 127–131, also associates legal rhetoric with decadence and decay.

7. *Latria* was the honor due to God, to God's own divine substance and incomprehensible nature, and could not be represented in any artificial image—"latria debetur Deo." *Dulia* was honor that also belonged to God but "is not properly belonging to his substance but to his government and lordship," and hence the honor of *dulia* could be given to images as "signs of good and godly things," N. Sander, *A Treatise of the Images of Christ and of his Saints: And that it is unlawful to breake them, and lawfull to honour them* (Omers: J. Heigham, 1624) at 80–81, 86.

8. On print and image, see Elizabeth Eisenstein, *The Printing Press as an Agent of Change* (Cambridge: Cambridge University Press, 1980) at 66–70; Alain Boreau, "Les Livres d'emblèmes sur la scène publique," in R. Chartrier (ed.), *Les Usages de l'imprimerie* (Paris: Fayard, 1987).

of the structure and substance of doctrine will be put into play in the process of deconstructing the unitary images of systems of law. Specifically, the inexplicit yet repeated coincidence of image and femininity, vanity and void will be elaborated as a symptom of a certain structure of repression intrinsic to law. Finally, the stake and object of doctrinal forms of argument, of thesis and of treatise, of symbol and sign will be analyzed in terms of a semiotic structure or juridical form of discourse that works to bind the subjects of law to a series of unconscious dictates or laws of thought. The apology and antirrhetic will be measured successful—they will do their worst—when they capture, direct, and persuade the subject into the time and reason of institutional being.[9] Whatever the surface of the text or the image of reason, the play and power of law rest upon a meaning, force, or desire that is held and transmitted beyond the letters of law, *subauditio* or unconsciously, as a textuality inhabited by and constitutive of the legal subject. The polemical or antirrhetic capture of legal subjectivity, the simple persistence of the dogmatic forms of the legal institution, is the product of a rhetorical order of thought or division (disposition) of reality that subsists over the long term of ecclesiastical and common law history, in the images, languages, and categories of a legal reason that long outlives the impermanent and tendentious forms of merely positive laws. Without an appreciation of those essentially antithetic rhetorical structures and their persistent semiotic force, the critique of contemporary legal forms, whether in ethical, feminist, literary, or sociological terms, is doomed to the status of a repetitious and ineffective play upon institutional surfaces that history and dogma will soon consume and forget.

APOLOGIA, ANTIRRHESIS, AND THE FOUNDATIONS OF LAW

The defense of faith, of doctrine, creed or law, belongs in its positive formulation to the rhetorical genre of *apologia,* a Greek term "which signifies defence, not with arms, but with reason, answer in defence, excuse, purgation or clearing of that one is charged with."[10] The rhetorical style of apologetic argument is agonistic, it is explicitly that of trial and of judgment,

9. On the theme of capture by the institution, see Pierre Legendre, *Paroles poétiques échapées du texte* (Paris: Éditions du Seuil, 1982).

10. The definition comes from the exiled English recusant Thomas Harding, *A Confutation of a Booke Intituled an Apologie of the Church of England* (Antwerp: Ihon Laet, 1565) at sig. 1r. The apology referred to in the title and confuted in the text is John Jewel, *Apologia Ecclesiae Anglicanae* (London: n.p., 1562), translated as *An Apologie or Answere in Defence of the Churche of Englande* (London, n.p., 1564). The *Confutation* is in turn replied to in Jewel, *A Defence of the Apologie of the Churche of England,* and this in its turn is replied to in T. Harding, *An Answere to Mr Jewells Challenge* (Antwerp: Ihon Laet, 1565), and in T. Stapleton, *A Returne*

of combat and resolution: "In every Apology or excuse, three things meet together, the plaintiff or accuser, the defendant, the crime objected"; thus: "The Catholics and all good men complain and accuse . . . the new clergy of England answer in defence. . . . The thing objected is schism, heresy and breach of unity. They impugn the law by the words of the law. . . . So to overthrow the Church, they presume to take unto them the name of the Church."[11] The antagonistic and antithetical character of the apology is evident in the manner of its formulation as a style and genre of institutional discourse. Not only is law counterposed generically to the heterodoxies of schism, heresy, and breach of unity but the antagonist is accused of the most extreme or diabolical dissemblance, namely that which perverts law in the name of law. What is most to be feared and so most rigorously refuted is that argument which simulates the truth of doctrine, which uses the languages and terminologies of faith, the figures and, at times, the phantasms or miracles of doctrine, to prove a dissolute, new-fangled, evil, or erroneous form of faith. In more modern terms, the apology must establish and defend the boundaries of tradition and the limits of thought. The apologist must be most stringent where the threat is closest, most guarded where the antagonist attempts to steal the very terms of doctrine itself for false ends, where the opponent genuinely challenges, competes, or realistically threatens the established faith. It is in such circumstance that apology most directly pitches images of the inside against those of the outside, affection against horror, salvation—or at least propriety, good manners, and its norms of constraint—against the mysticism, disorder, and plurality of other forms of reason, other Gods.

The apology is a genre that seeks to establish and to defend the law. It is properly a foundational discourse, and so in its primary aspect it seeks to represent in images that object of faith, reason, or truth which escapes definition by virtue of being the first, originary, or creative moment or act. The apology is the defining discourse of community, and so its positive characteristics lie in identifying, most often in eulogistic terms, the authorities, axioms, and other unities and longevities of the tradition. In a rhetorical formulation the positivity of dogma or doctrine can be identified with a series of topics or commonplaces that indicate explicitly the foundational qualities of law to the community of its subjects. The apology first establishes lineage in the sense of legitimacy, the unbroken succession of bishops, of doctrines, or of authorities within—depending upon con-

of Untruthes upon M. Jewell (Antwerp: J. Latius, 1566). For an alternative etymology and elaboration of apology, see St. German, *Salem and Bizance* at fol. A iv b, deriving apology from the Latin *responsio/defentio* and proceeding to make "answer to some of his objections . . . whereby it appears that his objections proceed of little charity."

11. Harding, *Confutation* at sig. 1r–v.

viction—the established or reformist church. Thus "chronographies"[12] or "titles of antiquity"[13] are invoked to evidence the preexistence and continuity of the community and doctrine against all novelties (*novatores*) or newfangled thoughts.[14] The power of antiquity and tradition lay not simply in age but in absolute and unbounded age, in first principles coincident with the indefinite time of origins: "For we must not hold antiquity to be that which is old . . . but that which is oldest, that is first and primitive, without any mixture, or derivation, or mingling, or meddling with following ages, and after times. . . . Truth must be searched in the original, before it hath been strained through the multitude of men's wits."[15] Borrowing from patristic aphorisms, the truth is first and more ancient than men; all that follows the origin or comes afterward is by definition adulterous and merely human.[16]

The claim to antiquity is in many respects a claim to nature, to a truth that is visible in the world prior to human history, written acheiropoietically, by God and not by any interpolating or interposed human hand: "The natural image expresses and imitates the very substance of that thing, whose image it is."[17] Such inauguration, either in the "glass of the world" itself or in the heart, which knows the invisible scripture of law and which knows that all laws are written in the heart, founds an order of descent or of continuity, of an unbroken lineage from father to son.[18] It thus

12. Stapleton, *A Fortresse of the Faith* at sig. 139r–140r.

13. The term is taken from John Selden, *Titles of Honour* (London: W. Stansby, 1614) at fol. c i a. See also at fol. c 4 b: "The best or first I took always for *instar omnium.*"

14. Robert Parker, *A Scholasticall Discourse against Symbolizing with Antichrist in Ceremonies: Especially in the sign of the Crosse* (London: n.p., 1607) at pt. II, 120, arguing that the accusers (i.e., the Catholics) are "newfangelists." For an earlier example, see Bishop Aylmer, *An Harborowe for Faithfull and Trewe Subjectes against the late blowne blaste, concerning the government of women, wherein be confuted all such reasons as a stranger of alte made in that behalf, with a brief exhortation to obedience* (Strasborowe: n.p., 1559) at fol. E 4 b–F i a: "If men will decide weighty matters, hanging upon antiquity, they must not only counsel with the Bible, but exercise themself in ancient stories . . . for histories be the witness of time, the candle of truth, the life of memory . . . and the register of antiquity. Wherefore let no man disdain histories, or find fault with us though we travail in histories."

15. Favour, *Antiquitie Triumphing over Noveltie* at 33.

16. Ibid. at 39, citing Tertullian, "antiquior omnibus est veritas" and at 40, "id est verum quodcumque primum, id est adulterum quodcumque posterius."

17. Sander, *A Treatise of the Images* at 101. For an interesting parallel, a theory of an acheiropoietic text, see Dr. W. Fulke, *A Rejoinder to John Martials Reply against the Answere of Maister Calfhill* (London: H. Middleton, 1580) at 133 (on the word or spirit as judge): "The spirit by his own substance incomprehensible, is by his effects in the holy scriptures visible, revealed, known, and able to be gone unto, taking witness of the scriptures and bearing witness unto them. . . . The Law of God is judge, not priests."

18. Harding, *A Confutation* at 223: "The bishop of Rome, who is thought to have all laws in the chest of his breast (*iura omnia in scrinio pectoris sui*), by making the second law" simply executes or carries out the first.

founds community upon a genealogy of authorities, a legitimacy of sources, and a succession of images—of bishops, sovereigns, pontiffs, legislators, communities, or laws—which have represented antiquity in its historical progression. While it is in some senses obvious in the context of the Reformation that the Roman Catholic Church was likely to assert the antiquity of its tradition, it is a feature of reformist doctrine also that the community of the protesters equally invokes histories of a more pristine faith and an origin older than that claimed by the sophistic or wrangling Romans. Thus, in the words of a scholastic English reformer, "the protestants are returned to the ancient faith which was in this land before Augustine came from Rome, which was not so much good in planting faith where it was not, as in corrupting the sincerity of faith where it was before he came."[19] This antique or internal knowledge of law runs through the history of a community as an inner lineage, an identity of order and law derived through time and prescription: "For we have overthrown no kingdom, we have decayed no men's power or right, we have disordered no commonwealth. There continue in their own accustomed state and ancient dignity the kings of our country of England."[20]

The apology instances that which the subject should desire, imitate, and identify with as a sense of community, paternity, or *patria*. Rather than specify in detail the positivity, identity, or substance of specific doctrinal apologetics, it is more important to return to the questions of form. The apology aims to establish community, to found law either in the formative period of an institution or during a period of crisis.[21] The apology may simulate a certain didactic or dispositive structure of expression, but its rhetorical form is strongly antithetical. The exposition of institutions is necessarily predicated upon the rejection of their opposites: identity upon exclusion, desire upon fear or, going further, *eros* upon *thanatos*, affirmation upon negation, life upon death.[22] In the rhetorical canon, antithesis is a figure of comparison whose argumentative function is to amplify or diminish the *comparata*; it persuades reason "for the parts of the comparison being brought together, their likeness or unlikeness, their equality or inequality, is as plainly discerned."[23] Antithesis as a figure of expression of

19. Dr. W. Fulke, *T. Stapleton and Martiall (two popish heretics) confuted and their particular Heresies Detected* (London: Middleton, 1580) at 14.

20. Jewel, *An Apologie* at fol. G i b.

21. A classic and vehement example of the former is Tertullian, *Apologeticus*, in A. Roberts and J. Donaldson (eds.), *Ante-Nicene Christian Library, Vol. 10* (Edinburgh: T & T Clark, 1869).

22. On the play of *eros* and *thanatos* as unconscious drives, see Freud, *Beyond the Pleasure Principle.*

23. Henry Peacham, *The Garden of Eloquence conteining the most excellent Ornaments, Exornations, Lightes, Flowers and formes of Speech commonly called the figures of rhetorike* (London: H. Jackson, 1593) at fol. Y iii b. For other forensic discussions of antithesis, see Wilson, *Arte of*

passion is a theme to which the next chapter will return in examining the rhetorics of law. In terms of the apology as a discourse of foundation, identity is built against the image of other doctrines, against other gods and other laws, against an outsider that represents the other as the threat of the nomadic, the alien, peregrine, feminine, or strange. The apology paints the image of community against the other, it lists its virtues against the sacrileges of opponents, its coherence and familiarity against the pestilence and monstrosity of those outside the creed.[24] Doctrine depends upon an antiportrait or negative image, it proves doctrine by denouncing heresy, affirms jurisdiction by exclusion of illegitimate speech or by the power of excommunication. It conjures identity by showing the face, the plurality or void, of evil.

The generic rhetorical term that can be resurrected to describe the antithetical form of the apology is *antirrhesis*. It is defined uniquely by Peacham in the following manner: "Antirrhesis is a form of speech by which the orator rejecteth the authority, opinion or sentence of some person: for error or wickedness of it. . . . This form of speech doth especially belong to confutation and is most apt to repell errors and heresies, and to reject evil counsell and lewd perversions."[25] Peacham proceeds to give the examples of Christ against Satan, Paul against the Epicureans, Job against his wife. Such are obviously not simply discourses against evil, but discourses against extremity and against threat. The antirrhetic is the form of verbal violence, the language of enforcement and of sacrifice referred to earliest by Polybius in terms of discourses directed "against those that have betrayed their friends and kinsmen," and by Hermogenes as vehement speech directed against exiles.[26] In each case the definition of genre endeavors to capture the strength of aversion and the perilous stake of discourses against those that would destroy the identity of community, the

---

Rhetorique at 64–68, 201–207; George Puttenham, *The Arte of English Poesie* (London: Richard Field, 1589) at 175 (on antitheton); Thomas Farnaby, *Index Rhetoricus scholis et institutioni tenerioris aetatis accomodatus* (London: R. Allot, 1633) at 55–58; John Smith, *The Mysterie of Rhetorique Unveil'd* (London: E. Cotes, 1657) at fol. M 6 b.

24. Monstrosity refers to that which does not resemble its parents. On which, see Selden, *Titles of Honour* at fol. b 4 b. For a striking tabulation of those outside the faith, see John Godolphin, *Repertorium Canonicum or, an Abridgement of the Ecclesiastical Laws of this Realm consistent with the Temporal* (London: R. Atkins, 1678, 1687 ed.).

25. Peacham, *Garden of Eloquence* at fol. N iv b–N v a. For general introductions to antirrhesis, see Peter Goodrich, "Antirrhesis: Polemical Structures of Common Law Thought," in A. Sarat and T. Kearns (eds.), *Rhetoric and Law* (Ann Arbor: Michigan University Press, 1994); and Peter Goodrich, "The Continuance of the Antirrhetic" (1992) 4 *Cardozo Studies in Law and Literature* 207.

26. Polybius, *Histories* (Harmondsworth: Penguin, 1977 ed.) at 22.8; Hermogenes, *On Types of Style* (Chapel Hill: University of North Carolina Press, c. 181, 1987 ed.) at bk. 1.8.52 (on vehemence).

reason of faith, or the establishment of laws. The antirrhetic gives a face to evil, it marks the reality of fantasm or the slippage of foundation, the image, idol, or void that is harbored within and threatens all positive forms. The apology is necessarily tied, in structure and in substance, to the antirrhetic. Denunciation is the hidden essence of apology even though as an aspect of form it is not always the most apparent feature of doctrine in periods of relative stability.[27]

The antirrhetic, the genre of "words against," is not simply a stylized denunciation of those beyond the iconic boundaries of community or family, of those that "break the line," it is also a specific register of the passions and fears of doctrine and its institutions. The antirrhetic establishes doctrine upon a series of discourses against outsiders, heretics, iconoclasts, and radical critics. It builds the *apologia,* both doctrine and community, upon those passions that move the soul: upon hatred and denunciation, upon anger and disgust, upon fear and resentment. The earliest example is probably Tertullian, the patristic author of late second-century Carthage, whose *Apologeticus* was written explicitly against the threat of death. Even a synoptic account or tabulation of the surface figures of this inaugural Christian apology and its accompanying texts[28] give an intimation of the substance of the antirrhetical form. The Christian community is defined against the perversions and deceits of a series of antagonists; it exists against the Roman Emperor, against sects, against Jews, against pagans, against heretics, against all other Gods: "The dominant trait of this writing was that of anger: an anger in the image of Tertullian's God, a God which must be understood as always at war against evil, an incensed God avenging a fallen world. . . . This anger is a style . . . it lends the discourse a tone and even colours the most abstract concepts."[29] At all levels of Christian practice Tertullian advocated resistance to the behavior and norms of non-Christian communities. He wrote against the theater and public shows, against ornament, against images, against philosophy, against feminine enchantment, and against all forms of uncleanness and fornication. The list is a lengthy one, and it is only in the subsequent development of the tradition of apologetics that certain features of this "writing against" or antirrhesis become formulaic.

27. For the argument that heresy is intrinsic to doctrine, see Michel Foucault, "The Discourse on Language," reprinted as an appendix in Michel Foucault, *The Archaeology of Knowledge* (New York: Pantheon, 1982) at 220.

28. Specifically, *Adversus Marcionem* (Against Marcion), *De Spectaculis* (Of Theatre/Public Shows), *De Idolatria* (Of Idolatry), *De Cultu Feminarum* (Of Feminine Dress), *De Anima* (Of the Soul), *De Carne Christi* (Of the Body of Christ), all in A. Roberts and J. Donaldson (eds.), *Ante-Nicene Library,* Vols. 3, 11, 16.

29. Georges Didi-Huberman, "La Couleur de chair ou le paradoxe de Tertullien" (1987) 35 *Nouvelle Revue de Psychanalyse* 9, at 11–12.

Tertullian explicitly associated his apologetics or refutations with a statement of the law. The *Apologeticus* begins in the form of pleadings and asserts that the Romans have ignored the law and failed in all attempts to act justly.[30] The refutations and denunciations that follow are asserted in the context of the lawlessness of his opponents. Similarly, the celebrated first sentence of *De Idolatria* is the assertion that idolatry is the "greatest of all crimes" and the form of all crimes: idolatry is adultery, it is murder, lasciviousness, impurity, vanity, fornication, and lust.[31] Later antirrhetical discourses borrow many of the figures of outrage and of hate that Tertullian and other patristic writers developed. Speech against extremism became an extremist form of speech. The exemplary antirrhetic, however, and the neologistic use of the term derives from Nicephorus, author of the *Apologeticus Major* and three *Antirrhetici* against the iconoclast emperor Constantine V.[32] Written in response to questions posed by Constantine V, the *Antirrhetici* have the internal structure and logical form of a denunciation. While the object of denunciation is the reformist doctrine of iconoclasm, it should be observed briefly that the antirrhetic is also, as its etymology implies, an attack both in the sense of "words against" and "against words," specifically against "painted words," the verbal equivalent of the rhetoric of images.

In synoptic terms the *Antirrhetici* defend the icon as the model of an immediate relation between the visible and the invisible, the present and the absent, divinity and its manifest form: the icon represents the archetype, and it alone can direct the human eye from material forms to incorporeal truth. The icon is the imprint of divinity, the vestige, mark, or effigy of a spirituality that can be neither seen nor comprehended in its substance: "The icon is the counterpart [reflection] of the archetype, in it is found imprinted in visible form that of which it is the imprint. . . . It is not distinct from its model save for the essential difference of its substance."[33] The icon is enigmatic, it directs the eye from the symbolic to the imaginary, from symptom to cause, from creation to creator.[34] It is also

30. Tertullian, *Apologeticus* at 58–61.

31. Tertullian, *De Idolatria* at 1.1 and 1.3.

32. References are to the recent French edition of the texts, M-J. Mondzain-Baudinet (ed.), *Nicephorus, discours contre les iconoclastes* (Paris: Klincksieck, 1989). For further commentary on the *Antirrhetici*, see M-J. Mondzain-Baudinet (ed.), *Du visage* (Lille: Presse Universitaire de Lille, 1982); G. Ladner, *Images and Ideas in the Middle Ages* (Rome: Edizioni di Storia e Letteratura, 1983); G. Florovsky, "Origen, Eusebius and the Iconoclastic Controversy" (1950) 19 *Church History* 77; E. J. Martin, *A History of the Iconoclastic Controversy* (London: SPCK, 1930).

33. Mondzain-Baudinet (ed.), *Nicephorus, Antirrhetic I*, at 277 A.

34. The icon is enigmatic because its basis lies in Christ, in "the knowledge of the invisible and absolutely incomprehensible character of a unity of two natures." See *Antirrhetic I* at 309 C.

fundamental, it being the virtue of the icon to found the visible world. The icon makes nature possible—without circumscription and without icons "the universe in its entirety would disappear."[35] Without visible form, of which the icon is the primary evidence and nature is similarly the image, there would be neither world nor subjects in it. The icon founds nature, and those that would destroy the icon threaten, quite literally, to destroy the world, to cast the visibility of nature into the limitless and uncircumscribed void of formless matter. Little wonder that the *Antirrhetici* proceed then to spell out the abhorrent features, the madness, adultery, and idolatry of those iconomachs who would destroy the icons, the perfect, acheiropoietically imprinted, visible signs of a divine nature.

The iconoclasts are thus stated to be the enemies of nature, the perverters of reason, the destroyers of sanctity and of the institution in all its forms. These adversaries of the icon are not simply impious and ignorant, they are nihilists, idolaters of nothing, heretics who have severed all relation with the visible world and who are in consequence without civility, filiation, kinship, or legitimacy, without family and without God.[36] In frequent outbursts or exclamations within the *Antirrhetici* the opponents of the icon are depicted as mad, drunk, and bestial; they fornicate and pollute, they blaspheme and transgress the laws of nature and culture, reason and civility. In a strict sense they are no longer human, not simply because they are damned or in a spiritual sense "already dead," but because they have the souls of demons or in some instances "that of a dog, a pig or a savage beast."[37] The antirrhetic form or genre establishes a particular and enduring type of denunciation and of antiportrait that is repeated, most often unconsciously, in discourses of, or against, the foundation of law. In a somewhat extended form the key figures of the antiportrait may be listed from the *Antirrhetici* and from later works that follow its typology.

In doctrinal terms the antiportrait depicts the iconoclast or idolater as sacrilegious, she steals from the person of God and of the saints. The iconoclast mocks all that is venerable, all consecration and piety: "He transgresses the written and unwritten law, he destroys tradition and respects nothing."[38] There are two aspects to sacrilege, one positive, one negative. It is "a sin above all others," the sin of Satan, because it invades the person

35. Mondzain-Baudinet (ed.), *Antirrhetic I,* at 244 D.

36. For a contemporary analysis of filiation in these terms, see the texts collected in Pierre Legendre et al. (eds.), *Le Dossier occidental de la parenté: Textes juridiques indésirables sur la généalogie* (Paris: Fayard, 1988); A. Papageorgiou Legendre, *Filiation: Fondement généalogique du psychanalyse* (Paris: Fayard, 1990).

37. Mondzain-Baudinet (ed.), *Antirrhetic I,* at 276 B.

38. Mondzain-Baudinet, *Discours contre les iconoclastes* at 19. See further, Mondzain-Baudinet (ed.), *Antirrhetic I,* at 229 B, and *Antirrhetic III,* at 488 A et seq.

of the deity: in its positive formulation, sacrilege arrogates divine knowledge of good and evil to human beings. In destroying the visible world the powers of creation are transferred into the realm of darkness, of the formless and limitless substance of nothingness, of a world without sight or any direction of inner vision. In legal terms, we thus find sacrilege listed as a crime alongside "blasphemers, sorcerers, witches and inchanters," crimes that steal from the divinity so as to create other images and so other worlds.[39] In its negative variation, sacrilege is straightforwardly destructive: it pollutes and so destroys holy places, sacred books, relics, and other sacral objects. It destroys the sites and tools, the architecture, of tradition and transmission at the same time that it pollutes the aura that authorizes knowledge.[40] It is first and foremost unclean, and among the figures or emblems of that "shameless uncleanness" the most frequent and conventional is femininity: the sacrilegious image is variously a woman, an adulteress, a harlot, or a witch, and her polluted faith a nameless and "inchaunting void."[41]

The reason of the iconoclast is that of delirium and dream, it is unreason manifest, a private language without either logic or audience. The iconoclast speaks the language of Babylon, and precisely in placing his faith in language rather than icons, in "building a Name for himself on earth," his punishment is confusion, dispersion, babel, and noncommunication.[42] Without the power to communicate, deprived of all rules of logic and expression, locked in the private madness of analphabetic speech, "he ressembles an old illiterate and senile woman" with whom communication

39. Sir Henry Spelman, *The History and Fate of Sacrilege* (London: Hartley, 1632, 1698 ed.) at 2. On the detail of these crimes, see, for example, the writs of abjuration listed in William West, *The First Part of Symbolaeography* . . . (London: T. Wright, 1590, 1603 ed.); and in Godolphin, *Repertorium Canonicum* at 528, defining sacrilege as "the violation or usurpation of some thing that is sacred. . . . It may be committed in three several ways," in respect of a person, a place, or a thing. For relevant legislation, see William Rastall, *A Collection in English, of the Statutes now in Force, continued from the beginning of Magna Charta* . . . (London: T. Wright, 1603) at fol. 65 d: "Against Conjurations, Enchantments and Witchcraft" (5 Eliz. 1 cap 16, 1563). The crime is the worse for its effectivity: the dead are summoned (magic), new likenesses are formed (enchantment), the lost is found (divining), the future foretold (witchcraft), the unseen is seen (sorcery). The legislation referred to punishes according to the effects of the practises: where witchcraft killed or maimed the penalty was most severe. For a treatise that challenged these assumptions, see Reginald Scot, *Scots Discovery of Witchcraft: Proving the Common Opinions of Witches Contracting with Devils, Spirits, or Familiars . . . to be but erronious conceptions and novelties* (London: E. Cotes, 1586, 1654 ed.).

40. Mondzain-Baudinet (ed.), *Antirrhetic III*, at 480 C et seq. Spelman, *Sacrilege* 23.

41. Parker, *A Scholasticall Discourse against Symbolizing* at 7.

42. Spelman, *Sacrilege* at 10–11. The reference is to the Tower of Babel (Genesis 11.4). For commentary, see Jacques Derrida, "Des Tours de Babel," in Jacques Derrida, *Psyché* (Paris: Galilée, 1987).

is no longer possible.[43] Private language banishes all possibility of certainty, it threatens the institutions of meaning and denies any potential for agreement or commonality, respect or obedience. The demise of tradition and culture is also, finally, the death of nature: the iconoclast is a monster, a homosexual, an illegitimate being without similarity or resemblance to anything known. Antinature is in one sense simply that which lacks resemblance: in Selden's definition "one not like his parents is, in some sort monstrous, that is, not like him that got him, nor any other of the ascending or transverse line."[44] In a broader sense, the nihilistic unreason of the iconoclast brings with it a madness of nature, in which those who deny the relation of the icon to its model refuse all the fecundity of semblance and of similitude, they are sterile, obscene, and unproductive, "excluded from nature itself which lets loose earthquakes, famines, epidemics, cataclysms of all sorts, to express its suffering before such hatred towards God."[45] The conclusion of the *Antirrhetici* is thus the threat of perdition and damnation, of a world that is unknown and unknowable, a world populated by the damned, by nomads, lepers, nihilists, and other untouchables. There, in short, is what nature, reason, and law must be defended against.

Finally, and in more pragmatic rhetorical terms, there is the *ad hominem* vehemence of the antirrhetic to be accounted and the specific secular institutional correlates of its doctrinal exclusions to be tabulated. Moving to the example of the apologetics of the Anglican Church and its various defenses of its unitary ecclesiastical and secular polity, the strength of animadversion should again be noted. The antiportrait is here no less virulent, but it is more directed and closer in antinomy to the positive proposals of the apology. The antiquity of the tradition is opposed to the novelty of reform; the universality of the true church is counterposed to the local and particular character of its opponents; the reason of doctrine or creed is compared to the dreams and fantasies, tragedies, and delusions of heterodoxy; the unity of faith is contrasted to the diversity and dispersion of disbelief. Thus, to take a few limited examples, Jewel in his *Apologie* asks "what manner of men be they, and how is it meet to call them, which fear the judgment of the holy scriptures . . . and do prefer their own dreams, and full cold inventions: and do maintain their own traditions, have defaced and corrupted how these many hundred years the ordinances of Christ and of the apostles?"[46] In response, Harding depicts Jewel and others as being fit to be "likened to enchaunters, necromancers, and witches. . . . For as they say that they have their books and their mysteries

43. Mondzain-Baudinet, *Discours contre les iconoclastes* at 19.
44. Selden, *Titles of Honour* at fol. b 4 a.
45. Mondzain-Baudinet, *Discours contre les iconoclastes* at 20.
46. Jewel, *An Apologie* at fol. B vi b.

from those doctors, and first fathers . . . but can not show the delivery thereof by any succession from hand to hand."[47] Somewhat earlier in the same work, the defenders are "compared to a mad dog. . . . For as the mad dog runs up and down, here and there, and now bites one thing, and now another, snaps at man and beast and rests not in one place: so this Defender to deface the Church, shows himself to have a very unquiet head. He starts from one thing to another, and settles himself in no one matter, but in malice."[48] Jewel responds, unsurprisingly by again terming the Catholic recusant a harbinger of counterfeit traditions, vain images, empty names, a "tainted visage" and "pseudologia," or false rhetoric and painted words.[49] For a concluding example that also illustrates the directly antinomic character of the genre and its tendency to argue by inversion, Thomas Stapleton begins his attack upon Jewel's *Apologie* by stating that he is one who "calls evil good and good evil, he is one who in hypocrisy speaks lies, who has put his hope in lying and lies have been his safeguard . . . for what kind of authors has he not corrupted, misalledged, false translated and by one means or another abused?," to which it is added that his book is "dissemblance and dissimulation, hypocrisy, untruth, wilful and manifest falsifying, a lewd book."[50]

It may usefully be observed that the antirrhetic of the Reformation, even in the above synoptic sketch, differs or at least expands in important respects from the earlier forms. While the structure of antirrhesis is not manifestly different in doctrinal terms—the antagonist is still nihilistic, hypocritical and against nature, reason, and law—it nonetheless reflects the changing circumstances of the early modern world. In a generic sense, which will be taken up again in subsequent chapters, the antirrhetic became more nationalistic and particular. Its concern was with the portrait of England and of its national traditions, with the vernacular and with local customs, habits, and laws. Such an identity is not created *ex nihilo* but is forged in an antirrhetic fashion against the Roman Church and Roman laws. Moreover, it is developed against an image of the foreigner, the alien or other as that which exists just beyond the boundary of nation or the narrative of its laws. The other, *peregrina ceremonia* (foreign ceremony) or *ritus peregrinus* (alien rite), by definition disturbs and innovates; the other is unworldly and too worldly, immature, irrational and mendacious, he or she practices illusion and other "juggling deceits."[51] The danger associated with the other is that of disturbing the way things are, of intruding

47. Harding, *Confutation* at sig. 229v.
48. Ibid. at fol. 207 b.
49. Jewel, *A Defence of the Apologie* at 4 and 297.
50. Stapleton, *A Returne of Untruthes* at Epistle and Preface.
51. The terms are from Parker, *A Scholasticall Discourse against Symbolizing* at 79.

through discourse, criticism, or imagination upon the sleep of reason or the unconscious, complacent, and content establishment or habitude of common law. Such a theme will, however, take the analysis beyond the classification of the topics and forms of the antirrhetic. The current argument will thus return to the issue or stake of the antirrhetic in the relation of image to word and of word to law. Two specific arguments will be addressed, the one concerned with the status and fate of the image in relation to the text, the other with the role of both image and text in the governance not simply of perception or vision but of thought itself.

IMAGE, ICON, AND IDOL

That the vehemence and passion of the antirrhetic returned and returns so persistently to the evil or the power of images cannot be viewed as an accidental feature of doctrinal history.[52] The war of, or against, images was fought for control of what in the Renaissance and in postmodernity is reckoned as being the ultimate means of persuasion and conversion, of communication, knowledge, and power. For Tertullian all crimes were committed "within the sin of idolatry," for in idolatry "were all the concupiscences of the world."[53] The idol, which for Tertullian included all images or likenesses of things, both internal and external, detracted from or was interposed between the divine cause and its human subject: "Everything is worshipped by human error except the creator of everything himself. The images of these things are idols, the consecration of these images is idolatry."[54] Any form of imitation or mimesis was idolatrous because imitation interposed itself between the subject and an invisible truth as well as lying by claiming a resemblance or mimetic relation between the representation and the form. Two issues follow. The first is to observe Tertullian's preference for the word over the image, for prose over poetics and, in effect, for an internal governance inscribed directly by the divine or ghostly power rather than through the mechanisms of human representa-

52. In a strictly contemporary sense there is something of a revival in the condemnation of images. This new antirrhetic gains its most explicit voice in Jean Baudrillard, *La Transparence du mal* (Paris: Galilée, 1990) and in a vast array of occasional essays, as Jean Baudrillard, *Simulations* (New York: Semiotexte, 1983), and Baudrillard, *The Evil Demon of Images.* For brief but informed discussion of this attack upon the idols of postmodernity see Michael Camille, *The Gothic Idol: Ideology and Image Making in Medieval Art* (Cambridge: Cambridge University Press, 1989), Epilogue; Gruzinski, *La Guerre des images* at 309–336. See further, Régis Debray, *Cours de mediologie generale* (Paris: Gallimard, 1991). In a rather different vein, see Michèle le Doeuf, *The Philosophical Imaginary* (Stanford: Stanford University Press, 1989).

53. Tertullian, *De Idolatria* at 1.1 and 1.6. For discussion of the theory of acheiropoietic images, see Georges Didi-Huberman, *Devant l'image* at 218–231; E. Kitzinger, "The Cult of Images in the Age before Iconoclasm," 8 *Dumbarton Oaks Papers* 112–115.

54. Tertullian, *De Idolatria* at 4.2

tion: "For since without an idol, too, idolatry may be practised, certainly when an idol is present, it makes no difference of what nature it is."[55] The concern was to excise all forms of visual representation, whether idol, image, or phantasm. More than that, however, the image was associated by Tertullian with ceremonies and rites, with "pomp of dress and finery," with immodesty and fornication.[56] In condemning the theater, for example, Tertullian again associates it with pomp of dress and finery, with lust and idolatry: "At first the theatre was properly a temple of Venus . . . as well as the house of Bacchus. . . . That immodesty of gesture and attire which so specially and peculiarly characterises the stage are consecrated to them, the one deity wanton by her sex, the other by his drapery."[57]

Tertullian's concern to outlaw the image was directly correlated to a fear of the fascination of the visible, the temptation which comes through the eye and fascinates through excess or beauty, through pomp and circumstance, rite of dress or ornament, through immodesty or other shows of the body, gesture, and attire.[58] The disquisition on the veiling of the face of virgins concludes thus by censoriously recommending this blocking up of the pathway of temptation: "For who will have the audacity to intrude with his eyes upon a shrouded face? a face without feeling? a face, so to say, morose?"[59] The image, so desecrated as an idol and so lauded as an icon, was consistently defined, eulogized, or denounced in terms not only of its force but of its sensuality and of the concupiscence of the eye. Idolatry was adultery, the service of images a sin of the flesh. The image was perceived variously as a vanity, a nothing, a harlot, and a pollutant. In each instance the image was a material block or support of internal vision, it was *interpolator veritatis,* it was *mediante imagine,* imitation, relative presence, counterfeit, symbol, or simulacrum.[60] The initial point to be made is simply that the image is a body, a material presence, and also a reference to a body. For Tertullian "it is the same desire (*libidinis*) to see and to be seen."[61] Whereas for later authors the voluptuous quality of the image refers to the love that should be directed toward the divinity, the image is

55. Ibid. at 3.3

56. Ibid. at 1.6. More directly on this correlation, see Tertullian, *De Cultu Feminarum* at 314: "That salvation—and not of women only but likewise of men—consists in the exhibition principally of modesty," and at 317: "For that other, as soon as he has felt concupiscence after your beauty, and has mentally already committed [the deed] which his concupiscence pointed to, perishes."

57. Tertullian, *De Spectaculis* at 18.

58. See particularly *De Virginibus Velandis* (On the Veiling of Virgins), in *Ante-Nicene Library,* Vol. 18, at 177.

59. Ibid. at 179.

60. The classical aphorism is from Lactantius, "ut religio nulla sit, ubi simulachrum est," cited in Calfhill, *An Answere to the Treatise of the Cross* at sig. 6v.

61. Tertullian, *De Virginibus Velandis* at 178 (*eiusdem libidinis est videri et videre*).

nonetheless proximate to the body, the cross in one example being "given as a sign upon our foreheads, like as circumscision was to the Israelites: by this we Christian men differ and are discerned from infidels."[62] The sign of the cross on the forehead was effective also by virtue of being near to the imagination (*propter propinquitatem imaginationis*).[63] The sign was here self-evidently close to the mind, it was a reference to the body that bore it as well as to the body it bore.

The image, the face or mask, is at best an epistemic form, a sensible register of memory, an imprint of experience through which the subject learns and recollects.[64] The seventh Council of Nicea, translated by Martiall, thus defined the licit use of images as remembrance that would "lead the looker to desire the first samplers and patternes which they resemble. . . . Honour and reverence done to an image redoundeth to the glory of the first sampler and patterne, and he that adoreth and honoreth an ymage doth adore and honour that which is resembled by the image."[65] The image and the sacrament alike were modeled upon the conception of a visible sign which directed vision from external to internal, from sense to reference and from body to soul. For the reformers, however, the eye was too dangerous and powerful a medium: all images threatened to interpose between the spirit and its spiritual referent, to enchant, corrupt, or distract the concentration of the inward eye. The best medium of faith was the text and the word through which the subject could "hear" the truth without interposition or interpolation. Its archetype was not a visual sign or visible thing but rather an inner voice, an unconscious that spoke directly without the intercession of human voice or artificial words: "He that speaks with tongues, speaks not with men, but unto God, for no man hears him. . . . *Spiritus autem loquitur mysteria,* the spirit speaks mysterie, and *spiritu licet mysteria loquator,* in the spirit mysteries speak."[66] The word, in short, could take the place of the acheiropoietic image: relying only incidentally upon sense or vision, the word and hearing could act much more directly to control and direct the order of inward things, the governance of the soul.

The difference between image and word is a difference of substance and so also of organ, but not of referent. The image referred to the prototype, it was not the visible sign but the invisible grace or enigmatic referent that was the object of iconic direction. For the advocates of images and other symbols the iconic inscription had the advantage of being

62. Martiall, *A Treatyse of the Crosse* at fol. B 8 b.

63. Parker, *Scholasticall Discourse against Symbolizing* at 133.

64. In which context it is also proof, see Piyel Haldar, "The Evidencer's Eye: Representations of Truth in the Laws of Evidence" (1991) 2 *Law and Critique* 171.

65. Martiall, *A Treatyse of the Crosse* at fol. F 1 b–F 2 a.

66. Stapleton, *A Returne of Untruthes* at sig. 107v.

immediate—it was the inward imagination of the thing itself, a relative presence. It also had the advantage of being continuous over time and of addressing all people. The image was necessary and inevitable since "all knowledge comes by our senses, of which our eyes are the chief . . . and so often as the mind will either use or increase its knowledge, it always returns to these images and figures"[67] by and through which experience had recorded inwardly the evidence of the senses. The image would teach and it would direct, it would represent and it would persuade, it would "more styrre the mind's of men to vertue, than the bare lettre read in boke."[68] However powerful the image was, its proper power was natural: "The first and chief honour naturally belongs to the thing itself, the second to the inward image, the third to the reporter," namely the icon, symbol, sign, or "paincted table" which first moved the inward sense or imagination.[69] Provided that the thing itself left its vestige, imprint, or mark, the eye would move the soul to inquire of the substance of the outward form.

In later defenses of imagery, the affective and sensual quality of the image, its power to touch and to suggest, was emphasized as much as the heuristic value of sight. The visible form of God, according to one much debated defense of imagery, "carries off [*rapiamur*] our hearts to the contemplation of his invisible deity. . . . The pictures or images of his nativity, passion, resurrection and the like . . . serve to put us in mind of what he did and suffered for us."[70] The same point emphasizing the role of connection or analogy between representation and its object was repeated by means of a striking example: "Is there nothing then in a picture worthy of admiration, besides the painter or artificer? I dare avouch for the greater part of Ladies, who sit for their pictures, that they do it not purely to beget in beholders an admiration of the painter."[71] Similarly, while the soul may not be capable of visual representation, the representation of the body leads to contemplation of the soul, which gives the body sense. More than that, the defense of imagery suggested a relation between devotion and imagination, adoration and vision, thought and affection. The image pleased and moved the mind, it acted upon sense so as to direct the spirit and to reflect the passion and the pain, the awe and the fear, which lay at the heart of the Christian narrative. It was, however, precisely the affectivity and sensuality of the image, the pleasure it caused in stirring the mind, that the iconomachs and iconoclasts attacked in terms remarkable not only for their virulence but for the imagery of sense and of carnality, of

67. Sander, *A Treatise of the Images* at 76–77.

68. Martiall, *A Treatyse of the Crosse* at fol. P 7 b.

69. Sander, *A Treatise of the Images* at 160.

70. Thomas Godden, *Catholicks no Idolaters or a full Refutation of Dr. Stillingfleet's Unjust Charge of Idolatry against the Church of Rome* (London: n.p., 1672) at 79.

71. Ibid. at 86.

desire and sexuality, which pervaded the purportedly bare texts or plain English of reform.

The image was both "falseness and vision."[72] As falseness, the image was simultaneously confused and confusing, it mixed the orders of being and conflated the external and the internal. In epistemic terms the image was a species of error: the dual nature of divine visibility—of Christ as image of the Father—was an impossible and incomprehensible or ineffable union such that "no man ought to imagine, a division or confusion, contrary to the true sense and will not able to be expressed: and the same union being above reach of knowledge, of two natures agreeable in one person, so what a mad opinion is this of painters, who for filthy lucres sake, endeavour to make those things that cannot be made, and go about with their wicked hands to express counterfeits of those things, which are only with the heart and mouth acknowledged."[73] The image attempted an impossible representation and it was this impossibility which reformers deemed the falseness of representation. The image was hypocritical and mendacious, it abolished and defaced the majesty of divinity, it was a "doctor of lies . . . because as soon as Good is presented in an image, he is deprived of glory, and changed into a bodily, visible, circumscribed, and finite majesty. . . . We may not bind the presence of God, the operation of his spirit, and his hearing of us to any thing."[74] God is unbound and therefore those who would bind him to an image neither knew God nor remembered him but rather confused creature or artifact for the creator, and to this the reformer would add that "it is idolatry to worship God as *present* there, where he is not present."[75] In this aspect, idolatry was first and foremost nihilation, a false knowledge which in attributing presence to an image misunderstood the external for the internal, the inanimate for the animate, and so variously denigrated, denied, or destroyed the divinity within. Images might heighten affection, but if this was by "calling to mind that *Being* I am to worship, then they must be supposed some *likeness,* or *analogy,* or *union* between the object represented and the image, every one of which tends highly to dishonour of the Deity."[76] The idol was in this regard "a

72. William Wake, *A Discourse Concerning the Nature of Idolatry* (London: W. Rogers, 1685) at 55: "There is nothing but falseness and vision in all his notions and authorities," refuting Godden, *Catholicks no Idolaters.* The latter text in turn refuted Edward Stillingfleet, *A Discourse Concerning the Idolatry practised in the Church of Rome* (London: H. Mortlock, 1671). Parker, *Scholasticall Discourse against Symbolizing* at 133, offers a similar definition of idol in terms of images that work *inducere ad falsa.*

73. Calfhill, *An Answere to the Treatise of the Cross* at sig. 56v.

74. William Perkins, *A Warning against the Idolatrie of the last times* (Cambridge: Legat, 1601) at 24.

75. Parker, *Scholasticall Discourse against Symbolizing* at 3.

76. Stillingfleet, *A Discourse Concerning Idolatry* at 60.

nothing . . . but only that thing represented"; it was either pure surface, a "false show"[77] or it was "a nothing which has no being,"[78] a counterfeit, a shape without a soul in the strict sense that it bore neither resemblance nor relationship to the being it purported to depict: *idolum nihil representat, quod subsistat* (the idol represents nothing which endures). The impossibility of the image was that of an impossible likeness, it created a form without presence and as such it represented an illusion or fantasm, an incitement to sense without reference and, more broadly, to plurality and to other Gods.

The idol as nothing, void or nonknowledge might seem to need no further denunciation beyond such designation and proscription, yet even the figures of void and nothing carry a certain license and licentiousness.[79] Hammond lists seven forms of idolatry, and Selden lists no less than ten, beginning with other gods (*dii alii*) and ending with sacrifices to demons (*sacrificiarunt daemonis*).[80] As Tertullian had lengthily warned, the empty form or nonbeing of the image was an incitement not only to sensuality, a vision that rested on, rather than moving through and beyond the material form of the image, but it was also an invocation to other gods, to spirits, demons, aereall and ghostly forms which "by an influence equally obscure" might come to inhabit such objects and "breathe into the soul . . . with cruel lusts accompanied by various errors."[81] The secondary senses or definitions of the image were thus more complicated and extensive than the attribution of nonbeing would at first suggest. The image was a dream, a phantasm, a superstition of other Gods. More important, in terms of the imagery of this counterimagination, the image was a vanity that would

77. Sander, *A Treatise of the Images* at 106–109. The more detailed distinction offered by Sander was between false shows and wrongful appearances. The former referred to "a thing shown [which] neither was, nor is at all extant anywhere . . . nothing in this world . . . they are not," and the latter were "idols that are something in nature but nothing in faith. . . . Idols be also (or have a being in the world) but in respect of salvation they be nothing." For a much later version of the same argument, see Wake, *A Discourse Concerning,* especially at 16–21.

78. Henry Hammond, *Of Idolatry* (Oxford: H. Hall, 1646) at 1. See also Calfhill, *An Answere to the Treatise of the Cross* at sig. 185v: "Scimus quod idolum nihil est" (we know that an idol is nothing). Compare Baudrillard, *La Transparence du mal* at 25: "In the style of the baroque, we are the unrestrained creators of images, but secretly we are iconoclasts. We are not, however, those that destroy images but those that create a profusion of images in which there is nothing to be seen." For a polemical discussion of the aesthetic and philosophical context of that theme, see Luc Ferry, *Homo aestheticus: L'Invention du gout à l'age démocratique* (Paris: Grasset, 1990), especially ch. 5.

79. On which see Aston, *England's Iconoclasts* at 466–479; Brian Rotman, *Signifying Nothing: The Semiotics of Zero* (London: Macmillan, 1987).

80. Ibid. at 1–5; John Selden, *De Idolatrae,* in John Selden, *De Diis Syris* (London: G. Stansby, 1617) at 140–148.

81. Tertullian, *Apologeticus* at 97.

seduce or entice the onlooker into transgressions of the flesh. Hammond's third meaning of idol is most explicit: it is "pollution, filfth by which any man is contaminated. This is rendered sometimes as abomination, but more frequently as idol than anything else, which certainly refers not only to the pollution of the soul by the commission of that sin . . . nor only to that other notion of spiritual fornication, but principally to the abominable sins of uncleanness, and filthiness, which those idol worships were ordinarily guilty of."[82] The imagery which follows the Judaic definition of pollution and uncleanness is redolent of a sense of sin that goes beyond the merely imaginary: idol worship is "inversion of nature, disorder of marriage, adultery, and shameless uncleanness," it "inflames . . . with practices of fornication, whoring and the like . . . [with] lust, abominations, inordinate desire and naughtiness." Those that worshiped images were "those that rape and steal women or virgins," they were "wanton" and "lascivious," a theme and imagery of sensual excess to which the treatise returned again and again.[83]

The rhetoric or antirrhetic of iconoclasm is extraordinarily full of misogyny, of textual images, figures, and tropes which vitiate not only femininity but all ornament, vestment, and accident of appearance and of the senses. The image is an extravagant woman, a perpetual threat of excess, of plurality, and of transgression:

> We must compare the cross [i.e., image] with an harlot, say we then that the Cross is no idol now, because it hath no adoration, which is the soul of an idol, that is as if we should reason, this woman ceaseth to be an adulteress any longer, because now at present she is not actually in that copulation, which is the life, and the very soul of adulterous crime. No, an harlot remains an harlot though her sin be past: and so the sign of the cross an idol, though this idolatry be ceased among us.[84]

Elsewhere in his *Scholasticall Discourse* Parker offers innumerable further correlations between adultery, infidelity, sensuality, fornication, and images: "The image is an harlot, and man is no otherwise bent on worshipping it (if he may have it and see it) than he is bent to fornication in the company of a strumpet."[85] The image is not simply a void, a vagina, it is also a vanity: it is of no profit or use, it is vain, superfluous, needless, unbearably light, too playful, too merry, too histrionic, it is otiose rite, a vain

82. Hammond, *Of Idolatry* at 1. Compare Tertullian, *De Idolatria* at 2.3: "However, we already know clearly how much wider meaning the Lord assigns to these sins, since He already indicates adultery in desire, when namely somebody casts a lascivious glance and rouses a lecherous excitement in his soul."

83. Hammond, *Of Idolatry* at 8–9, 11, 12–15, 18.

84. Parker, *Scholasticall Discourse against Symbolizing* at 19–20.

85. Ibid. at 137.

thing, a miscarriage.[86] Following the miscarriage or the aborted character of images, it is noteworthy that the image is further termed not simply vanity, but incurable and bitter; its thigh rots and its belly swells, it is "an instrument of witchcraft, yea a very inchaunting void."[87] The latter attribution of witchcraft and sorcery to the image and to women should not detract from the simple correlation of image and woman, a correlation that long outlives the various wars of images and their explicit reference to plastic or painted representations. With print and with the fusion of church and state, of spiritual and temporal law, it can be argued—following the maxim *ut pictura poesis* (as in painting so also in poetry)—that the war against images moves from picture to text, from painting to prose, from statue to figure and trope.[88]

CAPTIVES OF THE SOUL

One final if curious example of the correlation of woman and image can be taken from a passage in Stillingfleet's *Discourse of Idolatry,* where he refutes the notion that because the image refers to the prototype, the image can be given a relative honor or *dulia* appropriate to something that resembles the prototype. Such, Stillingfleet argues, would be "just as if an unchaste wife should plead in her excuse to her husband, that the person she was too kind with, was extremely like him, and a near friend of his, and that it was out of respect to him that she gave him the honour of his bed."[89] Again, the image is a woman and idolatry a feminine vice in which sense and spirit become confused. The argument from the image and from likeness is equally hypocritical, a knowing deceit, a lie. Law is here confounded by the levity, mendacity, and carnality of femininity as an image and as the constant threat of contingency, of a sensuous materiality or surface upon which vision can all too easily terminate. Although this correlation will be taken up again in varied contexts in subsequent chapters, it may serve to illustrate here a certain baroque practicality to the discourse on images: while the textual images manipulated against imagery may indicate certain ironies and further contradictions or at least paradoxes, the underlying issue behind the movement against idolatry was not strictly theological or philosophical but rather concerned the institution of a particular type of writing, a prosaic law, a mode of institutional being and subjective restraint.

86. Ibid. at 134–136.

87. Ibid. at 10 and 7.

88. See Erich Auerbach, "Figura," in Erich Auerbach (ed.), *Scenes from the Drama of European Literature* (Minneapolis: University of Minnesota Press, 1984).

89. Stillingfleet, *Discourse Concerning Idolatry* at 88.

It is perhaps somewhat obvious that the attack upon imagery was a means of institutionalizing a specific mode or style of thinking as well as a particular regulation of behavior and restraint of desire.[90] Where Stillingfleet in effect preaches fidelity of sexual behavior, the antirrhetic was not slow to expand its objects from the images in the world to the images in the text and images in the mind. In terms of the former there is often a strange homology between the image in the world and the image in the mind, such that extinction of one was thought to lead to the destruction or cure of the other. The external image always threatened to fascinate or fixate, to delight or bemuse, but its ability to arrest or terminate vision upon the material object or painted surface has to be understood according to a phenomenological model in which the visible is only a metaphor for the invisible order. The spirit or mind was capable of an inner vision, and it was this internal perception that required the most stringent ordering. There is indeed a hierarchy of visibilities within which it is the eyes of the soul that can see all things both visible and invisible: "The eyes of the spirit (*oculi spiritus*) are able to see things, that be not seen, and have no being. . . . The eyes of the mind (*oculi anima*) will pass through all obstacles whereas the eyes of the body (*oculi corporales*), that see visible things, cannot do so much."[91] The eye of the mind was ideally to become the eye of faith and so to turn from things visible to things unseen. Truth lay not in visible signs but in the soul, and the soul could only be seen by "inward spiritual eyes."

The governance of perception or the banishing of external images from the ecclesiastical kingdom and jurisdiction was not an end in itself but simply one stage in the war against the idols of the mind.[92] It was the imagination, the spirit or heart, the poetry, imagery, or ornaments of prose that were ultimately the objects of direction. The church would act externally as pastoral watchtower (*specula pastoralis*) to govern the soul but had also to implant within, "for he made a temple to himself within the mind of man, living and clear."[93] For the reformers, the living truth or internal vision was to be directed singly and solely by the bare word, by the *litera* or text, and not by any idol of the soul or false mental image: "The right way

90. Michel Foucault, *The Order of Things: An Archaeology of the Human Sciences* (New York: Vintage Books, 1973), of course, develops just such an argument at the level of cultural forms of knowledge or epistemes.

91. Jewel, *A Defence of the Apologie* at 273.

92. For a lucid and provoking discussion, see Aston, *England's Iconoclasts* at 452–466. Such is also a significant theme in Freedberg, *Power of Images*, especially ch. 1 and ch. 12; see also Wirth, *L'Image médiévale*, pt. IV. The term "mental idol" comes from John Smyth, *Parallels: Censures: Observations* (1609) in John Smyth, *The Works of John Smyth*, ed. W. T. Whitley (Cambridge: Cambridge University Press, 1915) at ii. 348.

93. Calfhill, *An Answere to the Treatise of the Cross* at sig. 59v.

to conceive god, is not to conceive any form: but to conceive in mind his properties and proper effects. So soon as the mind frames unto itself any form of God an idol is set up in the mind. And the form of things internally conceived in mind, are never worshipped of us, as painted and carved images be."[94] In short, the imagination, unless strictly governed, would feign images and frame idols, it would pursue "tragical fantasies" and other improper thoughts, the vain pleasures of the surface and of the skin. Here then was the key to reform, it lay in the governance of thought, the control of men's minds through the expulsion of images from reason and figures from the texts of law. Whether outside or inside, the image was a woman and she represented the sorcery of thought, the possibility of imagining either through the figures of internal speech or through the tropes—the *energeia*—of the printed text.

That thought or internal images rather than external observance increasingly became the object of direction was at one level a logical corollary of the movement from images serving as the books of the illiterate or *idiota* to the vernacular translations and the printing of the Bible. It is in this context that the dispute as to the powers and dangers of rhetoric within doctrine gained considerable and altered emphasis. The new image was the visible word, not Christ but print, the "inke divinitie." Many of the reformers were aware of such a danger; Hammond even offered the view that "it is true that it hath been printed, that words in a book are images, and consequently to pray before a book, or use a book in prayer, is idolatry, or image worship."[95] The word, however, came to displace the image, to throw it within the text and so within the mind's eye as figure or rhetorical illustration. Rhetoric became a kind of law, a further object of antirrhetic against the visual insofar as "a simple eye is soon beguiled. It is very coarse wool, that will take no colour. It is a desperate cause, that with words, and eloquence may not be smoothed. Remember of what matters and adversaries thou has to deal. . . . Lay down all affection, and favour of parties. . . . Let reason lead thee: let authority move thee: let Truth enforce thee."[96] The text, in short, becomes the object of an ever more complex hermeneutics, its meanings or images now become subject to juridically precise protocols of reading and of inward direction, and the governance of perception becomes formalized in the displaced (textual) identity of reason, word, and icon. Similarly, the threat of iconoclasm or of reform moves from image to gloss, from statue to figure, from symbol to sign. The new form of persuasion is the book, the new heresy is rhetoric; indeed, according to the satirical comment of Cornelius Agrippa in *De*

94. Perkins, *A Warning against Idolatrie* at 108–109.
95. Hammond, *Of Idolatry* at 34.
96. Jewel, *A Defence of the Apologie* at fol. A iv b.

Incertitudine, "orators . . . defenders of idolatry . . . have seduced, rising up against Christ with most great colours of rhetoric, out of whose damnable and blasphemous eloquence, the heretics have taken many arguments or persuasions, which they put into simple mens ears, [and] have led them from the word of truth."[97]

One fantasm of truth replaces another and a new technology of fascination displaces its predecessor, but the structure or form of law evidences some remarkable continuities. The issue is that of how the law is best transmitted and retained, according to what passage of the image and by means of which form of custody. The image, like writing, served as an external mark or reminder not only of things past or absent but also of the affections or desires that were associated with absence, with the past, and with its histories. Images were "an inward book" to be read backward through memory and internal imagination. For the defenders of the image it was not difficult to argue both its greater power and also its many pragmatic advantages over the word. It was closer to its source and free of all need for interpretation: the image takes the place of the orator and forms a more direct inward picture than can be achieved through words, whether printed or spoken. Words require translation or "change of shape" from their textual or auditory form to an inward and visible form. At their most powerful, words are visible, they are images and can be seen, they are uttered to the eyes: "His words were not only heard but even visibly seen. . . . The whole people saw the words (*videbat voces*)."[98] For the same reason that the defender recognizes the peculiar power of the image, the reformer challenges and denounces the animation and the impiety of even those images that simply act as spurs of memory: they are corrupt and kindle affections or excitations of the flesh, they are artificial memories, fantasms which threaten to draw the eye of the spirit toward the corporeality or materiality of the visual object: "For the mind is rapt from heavenly consideration, to the earthly creature: from the soul to the substance, from the heart to the eye."[99]

The denunciation of the image becomes the model and form for the denunciation of rhetoric or oratory. The antirrhetic moves slowly from one species of attraction or of seduction to the next and it carries with it the same vehemence, a comparable fury—because both image and textual figure are visible forms—and a similar force of correction or of law. The antirrhetic seeks to secure the foundations of law and to expel those images which threaten the truth by imagination or superstition, by phantasms of

97. Agrippa, *De Incertitudine* at sig. 20r.

98. Sander, *A Treatise of the Images* at 162.

99. Calfhill, *An Answere to the Treatise of the Cross* at sig. 6r; see also William Perkins, *Art of Prophesying*, in William Perkins, *Work of William Perkins* (Abingdon: Sutton Courtenay Press, 1603, 1970 ed.) at 344.

the mind that have no foundation either in essence or in existence.[100] The antirrhetic moves on but it carries with it a hatred of the image in all its forms of appearance, it carries with it the misogyny that would endlessly seek to institutionalize contingency, to standardize particularity, and to subordinate the plurality and poetry of imagination to the uniformity and universality of reason.[101] Transmission is the form of law and it struggles constantly to control the direction and the termination, the destiny, of subjective vision or internal images. Its reason denies the worth of an interiority that does not conform to the laws of thought: where the image could be labeled idolatrous for confusing the medium or surface with the substance and for attributing significance to a thing without being or essence, the new antirrhetic of the post-Reformation era would similarly denounce "pseudologia," or false, even idolatrous words. Such language was imagistic in that it threatened reason and the laws of thought, it brought words of false doctrine which were as evil as images and indeed indistinguishable from images in their effects save that they came in the guise not of vision but of philosophy. Rhetoric and particularly a rhetoric that laid claim to truth was the new idolatry of the modern age. It was heresy in a secular form:

> Beware of him, that endeavours to prove his false doctrine *versutis disputationibus,* by subtle and crafty reasonings. . . . Beware that no man spoil [*depraedetur*] you through philosophy and vain deceit. . . . For these heretics put all the force of their poisons in logike, or dialectical disputation, which by the opinion of philosophers is defined to have power not to prove, but an earnest desire to destroy and disprove . . . by guileful logic.[102]

The antirrhetic not only endeavors to impose a law of thought, it aims to institute a being or reason of a highly specific kind. The subject of the antirrhetic, the legal subject, is defined by its antagonisms, identified by its exclusions, and fascinated—motivated—by the fantasm of a cold and enduring reason, a science, which forbids all images and so denies the power of all other laws. The subject of the antirrhetic is bound internally to law by an image of a univocal, singular, and literal reason, by the fantasy of a victory over "false imaginings," by a law of thought that begins from the knowledge that "idolatry is in a man's own thought, not in the opinion of another."[103]

100. Godden, *Catholicks no Idolaters* at 20.

101. Specifically on the theme of femininity and image over the *longue durée,* see J-J. Goux, *Les Iconoclastes* at 191 et seq.; Debray, *Vie et mort de l'image* at 77 et seq; Alice Jardine, *Gynesis: Configurations of Woman and Modernity* (Ithaca: Cornell University Press, 1985) at 31–49.

102. Harding, *Confutation* at sig. 32v–33r.

103. John Selden, *Table Talk* (London: E. Smith, 1689) at 23.

FOUR

Law Against Images

Antirrhetic and Polemic in Common Law

When Plato declares Diogenes to be raving mad, this betrays, besides contempt, a measure of self-defence.[1]

The veil of legality, the bare image of law, hides innumerable traumas of enforcement and of powerlessness. Law's rites, vestments, ceremonies, and texts depict the face or screen of a series of institutional violences. Juridical doctrines, precedents, and judgments are fabricated in the repetition and repression of antagonisms, in agonistic court procedures, and in adversarial and polemical oppositions. Law, as dogma, as a mode of thought, passes between subject and institution; it implicates, it speaks, it represses, and it binds. The antinomic attributes of legality, the antirrhetic in law, is an old theme and a hidden one. Doctrine has tended to conceal its conflictual roots both historically and conceptually even though the combative character of law is arguably its most ancient and theatrical or specular of features.[2] Law reflected violence and it instituted violence, its context or other surface of inscription was precisely that of the body, for the effect and purpose of trial "is not to decide or discuss, but to condemn or acquit."[3] Historically such purgation of differences was either *canonica* or *legalis*, by oath or by ordeal, linguistic or textual, a cure or condemna-

1. Peter Sloterdijk, *Critique of Cynical Reason* at 362 (translation modified).

2. On legal combat, see Sir John Davies, "Of the Antiquity of Lawful Combats in England" (1601) and Sir Robert Cotton, "Of the Antiquity, Use and Ceremony of Lawfull Combats in England" (1601), both collected in Thomas Hearne (ed.), *A Collection of Curious Discourses written by Eminent Antiquaries upon several Heads in our English Antiquities* (London: J. Richardson, 1771); Selden, *The Duello.* Some elements of a history, and a correlation of trial by jury, by combat, and by ordeal may be usefully found in Dugdale, *Origines Juridiciales* at chs. 25, 28, 29.

3. James Whitlocke, "Of the Antiquity of Lawful Combat in England" (1601), in Hearne (ed.), *Curious Discourses* at 190. More broadly see Costas Douzinas et al., *Postmodern Jurisprudence: The Law of Text in the Texts of Law* (London: Routledge, 1990), ch. 9.

tion excised or branded as occasion dictated upon the heart of the penitent or upon the skin of the convicted.

To trace the continuous supplement of legal violence, to follow the trajectory of antirrhetic and polemic, denunciation and polarity through which violence also speaks, it is necessary to understand a certain madness of law, and particularly the several jurisdictions of legal governance over the long term and practice of common law. Trial, condemnation, or acquittal by accident or by divinity was never and is never singular. Trial and law were historically mixed and thus actions could be simultaneously before the courts of conscience or before temporal jurisdictions, before spiritual ordinaries or before secular judges, according to both written and unwritten law. One law on the other, *utrumque ius*,[4] may refer classically to the relation of spiritual to temporal law, of Salem to Bizance,[5] but it refers equally to a fold within the institution and within the subject. It refers, one might argue, to two orders of defense, to two spaces of conflict, two repressions or forms of governance. One is of the citizen, one of the soul, public and private, conscious and unconscious, internal and external, each measured according to its own jurisdiction and its own "manners" but also according to an order or enfolding of laws: one before the other, one on the other, one in the other.[6] Ecclesiastical law indeed had already provided a model for the enfolding of different laws. The care of the soul and the judgment of the subject was depicted casuistically according to

4. On the concept of *utrumque ius*, see Pierre Legendre, "Le Droit romain, modèle et langage: De la signification de l'Utrumque Ius," in Pierre Legendre, *Écrits juridiques du Moyen Age occidental* (London: Variorum, 1988); and see also the extended review of that work in Yifat Hachamovitch, "One Law on the Other" (1990) 3 *International Journal for the Semiotics of Law* 187. For more detailed studies see Pierre Legendre, *La Pénétration du droit romain dans le droit canonique classique de Gratien à Innocent IV* (Paris: Imprimerie Jouve, 1964); Harold Berman, *Law and Revolution: The Formation of the Western Legal Tradition* (Cambridge, Mass.: Harvard University Press, 1983).

5. St. German, *Salem and Bizance* at fol. F xciiii a: "Salem and Bizance refer to Jerusalem and Constantinople which cities now be in thraldom and captivity of the cursed Turks." Figuratively, Jerusalem was the site of God's law, Constantinople of civil law. The reference to Salem or Jerusalem is reformist—it borrows from the Jews—whereas the Latinate tradition referred to the two Romes, those of the pontiff and the Emperor, of spiritual and secular government—*dua sunt genera christianorum*. See, for discussion, Legendre, *Le Désir politique de Dieu* at 105–114; Legendre, *Les Enfants du texte* at 103–122.

6. For a tabular depiction of the two laws, see Robert Cosin, "Ecclesiae Anglicanae Politeia," in *Tabulas Digesta* (London: n.p., 1604). See also on the relation of the two jurisdictions, Cosin, *An Apologie for Sundrie Proceedings*, particularly at fols. A 2 a–A 3 a, defending "government ecclesiastical" against disturbers, calumnies, indignities, clamors, and fancies; also Downing, *A Discourse of the State Ecclesiasticall* at 2, stating that religion is the ground of all law and manners, and at 5: "I conceive the aim of the best and wisest with us, is to preserve the Church and commonwealth together." On the relation of the two laws, see Sir Thomas Ridley, *A View of the Civille and Ecclesiasticall Law* (Oxford: H. Hall, 1607, 1676 ed.).

separate yet conjoined courts: judgment was first "parochial" and *in foro interiori,* in an interior court; it was second *in foro exteriori,* or by reference to external law; and was finally in *utroque simul,* or in both directions at the same time.[7] In short, many laws were needed to "curb and limit the exorbitances of licentious men. . . . For what idiot discerns not that manifold and deformed confusions of opinions, worships and manners have corrupted things both public and private?"[8] Even Sir Edward Coke, who was generally implacably opposed to the ecclesiastical law, was moved to recognize that "the temporal law and the ecclesiastical law have been so coupled together that they cannot exist the one without the other."[9]

The growth of common law may have appeared to be at the expense or to the exclusion of the ecclesiastical jurisdictions, but it was in the main an incorporation or absorption—either as repression or as displacement—of the spiritual powers within the temporality.[10] The antirrhetic, the attack upon images, upon painted words and "poor men's books" (*libri pauperum*),[11] was not abandoned with the fusion of the spirituality and temporality in the person of the Crown, it simply passed from one body to another. The state, the Crown, arrogated to itself the powers of the church, and in consequence and by right it had, according to Downing, both positive and spiritual supremacy, *iure positivo pontifico* and *iure divino Apostolica,* and hence it was supreme justice in both kingdoms, in conscience and in positive law, in *foro exteriori* as in *foro contentioso.*[12] The common law had long accepted that its legality was also a spirituality, its law a part of nature and truth, its judges priests and its study a knowledge of things both divine and human.[13] These were self-evident aspects of a tradition—"this heaven

7. Stillingfleet, *Ecclesiastical Cases* at 24–25.

8. Henry Consett, *The Practice of the Spiritual or Ecclesiastical Courts* (London: T. Bassett, 1685) at fol. A 2 b.

9. Cited in Brian Levack, *The Civil Lawyers in England, 1603–1641* (Oxford: Oxford University Press, 1973) at 126. See also Ralph Houlbrooke, *Church Courts and the People during the English Reformation, 1520–1570* (Oxford: Oxford University Press, 1979).

10. See Christopher St. German, *A Treatise Concerning the Division between the Spirituality and Temporality* (London: R. Redman, 1534) at sigs. 1v–2r (a discussion the state of the realm and "sorrow of heart" extant in the commonwealth because of the division). I develop this argument at length in *Languages of Law,* ch. 3. See also Ernst Kantorowicz, *The King's Two Bodies* (Princeton: Princeton University Press, 1957) on the dual nature of the Crown; also Gaines Post, *Studies in Medieval Legal Thought* (Princeton: Princeton University Press, 1964).

11. The notion that images are the books of the illiterate or "layman's books" (*sunt libri utiles laicorum*) is derived from Pope Gregory I. See Sander, *A Treatise of the Images* at 100. See Aston, *England's Iconoclasts I* at 124–132; Eire, *War Against the Idols* at 18–27.

12. Downing, *A Discourse of State Ecclesiasticall* at 72 (defining the Crown as *supremus iustitiarius totius Angliae*). See also, for another important discussion contemporary with much of the crisis of transition, Sir John Hayward, *Of Supremacie in Affairs of Religion* (London: J. Bilt, 1624).

13. Most famously, Sir John Fortescue, *De Laudibus Legum Angliae* at 4–5 (on judges as

that is Britain"—in which "religion, justice and law do stand together."[14] The antirrhetic thus became a part of the agon or trial of positive law, it joined the polemic of extant doctrine, it added its specific and substantive techniques of antithesis, antiportrait, and abhorrence of images to a tradition and rhetoric of law that was already marked deeply by the adversarial constraints and dialectical oppositions of a mixed and apologetic legal tradition.

LAW AND DISSIMULATION

It is a frequently neglected feature of forensic rhetoric that it has often been defined as an inappropriate and unethical genre, divorced alike from philosophy and from political civility. While such a definition is not a necessary one, it is a useful corrective to the repetitious and not infrequently historically ill-informed revivals of rhetoric as felicitous communication, eloquence, community, or ethics of speech.[15] Legal rhetoric, most

---

sacerdotes). On divine and human knowledge, see Doddridge, *English Lawyer* at 34–35; Henry Finch, *Law or a Discourse thereof in Foure Bookes* (London: Society of Stationers, 1627).

14. Fulbecke, *Direction or Preparative to the Study of Law* at Epistle and 3.

15. For Chaim Perelman, the pioneer of the new rhetorics of law, the function of the revival of the study of oratory was to facilitate communication, to identify specific messages, and to align legal orator and legal audience. Chaim Perelman and Obrechts Tyteca, *The New Rhetoric: A Treatise on Argumentation* (Notre Dame: Notre Dame University Press, 1969) formulates the goal of rhetorically successful speech in terms of "intellectual contact" which "establishes a sense of communion centred around particular values recognised by the audience" and held in common by them (14). See also Chaim Perelman, *Logique juridique, nouvelle rhetorique* (Paris: Dalloz, 1976) at 108, where the reciprocal desire of speech is formulated in terms of "a desire to realise and maintain contact of minds; a desire, in the head [*chef*] of the orator to persuade, and in that of the audience, a willingness to listen." For analysis of Perelman's work, see Peter Goodrich, "Rhetoric as Jurisprudence: An Introduction to the Politics of Legal Language" (1984) 4 *Oxford Journal of Legal Studies* 122. More recent studies vary little in their reformative goals. For Brian Vickers, *In Defence of Rhetoric* (Oxford: Oxford University Press, 1988), rhetoric will return language to nature, as for example at 296: "The lore of rhetorical figures [can] be seen as deriving originally from life. It is mimetic, an attempt to classify emotional states and their resulting speech forms. . . . The eloquence of rhetoric is merely a systematisation of natural eloquence." See my discussion of that view in "We Orators." Others have argued that oratory will return eloquence to the institution, and community to law, as, for example, James Boyd White, *Heracles' Bow* (Madison: Wisconsin University Press, 1985) at ch. 5; James Boyd White, *Justice as Translation* (Chicago: Chicago University Press, 1990) at 36: "To speak and act like a lawyer, as one learns at law school, is to commit oneself to a certain community and discourse, to enact a view of language and the world entails an ethics and politics of its own, even to give oneself a certain character." In its most extravagant view, rhetoric will undo the evil of theory, see Stanley Fish, "Denis Martinez and the Uses of Theory," in Stanley Fish, *Doing What Comes Naturally* (Durham: Duke University Press, 1990); Stanley Fish, "The Law Wishes to Have a Formal Existence," in A. Sarat and T. Kearns (eds.), *The Fate of Law* (Ann Arbor: Michigan University Press, 1991); or Gerry Frug, "Argument as Character" (1988) 40 *Stanford Law Review* 869, who argues that

famously in Plato's *Theaetetus,* was discounted as a specific and distinctively sophistic genre, and the legal orator, subject to the litigious constraints of time and adversarial circumstance, was depicted as "a slave disputing about a fellow slave before a master sitting in judgment with some definite plea in hand." The legal rhetorician "acquires a tense and bitter shrewdness . . . his mind is narrow and crooked. An apprenticeship in slavery has dwarfed and twisted his growth and robbed him of his free spirit."[16] The subsequent history of the legal profession provides no shortage of comparable critiques of forensic orators and oratory. Whereas Aristotle defined the appropriate style of legal representation and rhetoric as being one that was free of any and all material extraneous to proof of the facts or cause, the barrister and rhetorician Puttenham defined legal rhetoric in terms of the "figure of *allegoria,* which is the figure of false semblance (we speak one thing and mean another) common and indeed essential to public life—*qui nescit dissimulare nescit regnare* (he who knows how to dissimulate knows how to rule)."[17]

The art of legal rhetoric, the speech of the attorney or advocate, barrator, pettifogger, wheedler, or wrangler had always been in some measure socially and institutionally stigmatized as polemical and contrary to good faith. The legal profession, in the words of one satirist, had "made a feoffment of their souls, with livery and seisin to Satan, only taking a short lease back again."[18] From the most venal of motives they would argue any case and were trained—to the limited extent that a sojourn at the Inns of Court could count as training—to argue the most implausible or contrary of pleadings: "For him that would be a lawyer, after he has long listened at the bar, he must adventure to defend such a cause, as they that are most employed, refuse to maintain: thereby to make himself more apt and ready, against common pleaders in ordinary causes of process."[19] The training of

rhetoric will save law from that specter of nihilism which American critical legal studies associates somewhat arbitrarily with indeterminacies of interpretation, as at 871–872: "I reject the notion that the only alternative to finding a way to ground legal argument is nihilism. In my view, we should abandon the traditional search for the basis of legal argument because no such basis can be found, and we should replace such a search with a focus on legal argument's effects, in particular, on its attempts to persuade." For legal commentary, see Peter Goodrich, *Reading the Law* (Oxford: Blackwell, 1986), ch. 6. For philosophical critique, see Derrida, "The White Mythology."

16. Plato, *Theaetetus,* at 172 e–173 b. See also the denunciation of legal oratory in Tacitus, *Dialogue of Orators* at 127–133.

17. Aristotle, *Rhetoric* (London: Macmillan, 1886); Puttenham, *Arte of English Poesie* at 155.

18. Richard Head, *Proteus Redivivus or the Art of Wheedling or Insinuation* (London: W.D., 1675) at 284.

19. A. Munday, *The Defence of Contraries: Paradoxes against common opinion, debated in forme of declarations in place of publike censure: Only to exercise yong wittes in difficult matters* (London:

the legal orator was in seduction, in falsehood, and in polemic; it was a training not so much in speaking well but in preparation for verbal combat, a training in agonistics and antinomy. A striking example can be taken from the work of the French scholastic Bernard Lamy whose *De l'art de parler* went through three English editions in the last quarter of the seventeenth century.[20]

One of the principal questions posed in Lamy's treatise was that of the relation between speech and the body, and by attenuation between the text and law. How does the law descend into speech, how is the body to incorporate the law? Lamy addressed these questions in a discussion of postures of the body, remarking that just as animals know how to defend themselves and to keep what they acquire by force "without assistance of the soul," so also "we find in ourselves, that our Members (without direction from our Soul) dispose themselves into postures to avoid injury." That the body can dispose itself naturally "without reflexion or debate" to defend or invade is then made into a principle of speech. The soul may defend itself as well: "The figures imploy'd by her in discourse, do the same, as the postures in defence of the body. If postures be proper for defence, in corporal invasions; Figures are as necessary, in spiritual attacks. Words are the arms of the mind, which she uses, to disswade or perswade as occasion serves."[21] Speech, or more accurately the rhetorical art of effective speech, is the armory of the truth and the weapon of law, indeed only in discourse can a subject be present to itself.

The figures of speech, in Lamy's depiction, are explicitly the "Arms of the Soul" and the context of such agonistic imagery is further elaborated by way of illustration, or in rhetorical terms, *hypotyposis*: "To give it the deeper Impression upon our Mind, I will in this place describe a soldier fighting, his Sword in his hand; and an Orator speaking in a Cause, that he has undertaken to defend."[22] The metaphor of warfare is expanded at length. It is not uncommon to the tradition and it can be found usefully in certain earlier works both of rhetoric and of logic which came to be used extensively in the Inns of Court. Consider in this respect the introduction to one of the first vernacular logics, Dudley Fenner's *The Artes of Logike,* which begins by promising to "follow the precept of Solomon, to confute opponents by silence" and proceeds by explicitly summoning the

J. Winder, 1593) at fol. A 4 a. On the venal character of the profession, see the stringent critique in Thomas Powell, *The Attourney's Academy* (London: Fisher, 1610); and see also John Day, *Law Tricks* (Oxford: Malone Society Reprints, 1608, 1950 ed.). For discussion, see Brooks, *Pettyfoggers and Vipers*; Baker (ed.) *The Reports of Sir John Spelman.*

20. Bernard Lamy, *The Art of Speaking* (London: M. Pitt, 1676).

21. Lamy, *Art of Speaking* at 226.

22. Lamy, *Art of Speaking,* 240–242.

image of logic as a weapon, a sword in the hand of right reason.[23] So too, Ralph Lever's *The Arte of Reason, Rightly termed Witcraft* begins by defining reason as "a compound showsay, proving that which lyeth in controversie by knowne and graunted sayings."[24] Reason, in short, is not simply a weapon, an instrument of an antithetical art, it also operates in an ocular fashion so as to "show" or demonstrate the truth of that which is in dispute. To show or demonstrate is of course to figure that which cannot be directly expressed. The necessary argument, the argument that is presented as being "straightest," most probative, or least rhetorical is simply the most clearly figurative or powerfully persuasive, the most effective in achieving the desired bellicose end.

In this latter respect reason and law, authority and tradition are no more than variant representations of a similar set of combative themes or *comparata*. In pragmatic terms the lawyer is taught by the rhetor, and the lesson of forensic rhetoric is not simply that of obedience to authority or to the established sources, topics, and distribution of legal argument. It also seeks to persuade, it evokes emotion, that which will move, and so lists figures of speech that best arm or defend the lawyer's cause. It is again unsurprising that the figures listed are coded in binary opposition between signs of belonging and signs of exclusion, figures of affection and figures of denunciation, confession, and silence. It is useful to recall here the etymology of sign, *signum,* itself. The sign was the standard or flag of the military unit, it identified the unit and simultaneously, by being the emblem of the military community and the sign against which the enemy was marked, it was that for which the unit would die.[25] The legal sign is not dramatically different. It identifies both the community or captivity of legal subjectivity and simultaneously marks the silence or death of those outside the law, internal exiles, enemies within.

The lists of figures do not always wholly match the oppositional or antirrhetic thesis that is elaborated here, but neither do they greatly contradict it. For the barrister George Puttenham, the figures of legal speech can be grouped around the different forms of comparison, the like and unlike, similar and dissimilar, with the obvious although unconscious connotation that the former belong and the latter do not.[26] Similitude is op-

23. Dudley Fenner, *The Artes of Logike and Rhetorike, plainly set forth in the English Tongue, easie to be taught and remembered* (Middleburg: n.p., 1584) at Epistle and fol. A 2 b.

24. R. Lever, *The Arte of Reason, Rightly termed Witcraft, Teaching a Perfect way to Argue and Dispute* (London: Brynemman, 1573) at 99.

25. On which derivation and use, see the work of the barrister Gerard Legh, *The Accedens of Armory* (London: Tottill, 1562) at sig. 36r–38r; see also Sir John Ferne, *The Blazon of Gentrie* (London: J. Winder, 1586) at 2–4; William Wryley, *The True Use of Armorie* (London: I. Jackson, 1592) at 2–3.

26. Puttenham, *Arte of English Poesie* at 128–130, 189–191.

posed to dissimulation, the sign (the icon) that proves to the sign (the idol) that deceives or shows nothing.[27] On the one hand Puttenham indicates, not without a certain irony, that the exemplary figure of legal argument is that of *paranologia,* the figure of confession or admittance, "much used by English pleaders in Star Chamber and Chancery." It is the figure that, frequently with the aid of torture and so beyond all rhetoric and without mediation, unmasks the soul.[28] It is also the figure of admission, of an exemplary belonging instituted or reinstituted through a rite of purgation. On the other hand, the public life or political function of law is exemplified rhetorically, as was observed above, by the "figure of *Allegoria.*"[29] The mode of this dissimulation is termed perpetual metaphor, the constant use of improper or borrowed meanings, a speech "in sense translative and wrested from [its] owne signification."[30] It is speech that hides or defends itself from mundane view, an enigmatic, dark, or opaque speech that guards the truth from the vulgar and similarly marks the noble or "knower" as the bearer of law.

To the degree that law is the exemplary form of public speech, to the extent that it is normative of serious social speech, the antithetical character of its rhetoric deserves further elaboration. The rhetoric of foundation, the imagery and language of the earliest printed constitutional texts, the inaugural statements of legal doctrine associated particularly with John Fortescue, St. German, Thomas Smith, Edward Coke, and John Davies, and substantively with Littleton, Fitzherbert, Staunford, Compton, Lambard, and West, was grounded in an explicitly antirrhetic form. Its language, to take the most obvious indication, was the French and Latin of the law, and even where the vernacular was used for commentary or elaboration, the reports, the rolls, and the legislation remained in a tongue that would only serve the community of lawyers and not that of custom or populus.[31] On the one side, the antirrhetic must build an identity for national law, an image of community or constitution to which the subject can desire to belong. In this respect the realm of positive association, of an immemorial and monumental order of law, is built upon a rhetoric of affectivity, of icons that represent the people without their being of them. In the marginalia of the doctrinal texts we thus learn of the excellence of the English, the longevity of their laws, the honesty of their people, and the

27. See, for example, Richard Sherry, *A Treatise of Schemes and Tropes very profytable for the better understanding of good authors, gathered out of the best Grammarians and Orators* (London: J. Day, 1550) at fol. A vi b–A vii a.

28. Puttenham, *Arte of Poesie* at 190.

29. Ibid. at 155–156.

30. Ibid. at 156.

31. See Peter Goodrich, "Literacy and the Languages of the Early Common Law" (1987) 14 *Journal of Law and Society* 422; Goodrich, "Poor Illiterate Reason."

tranquility and obedience of their rustic and urban communities. In more substantive terms the English are marked as a race that is settled, united, and defended by their opposition to French and Roman customs and laws. Their law is in the Year Books and in Littleton, Fitzherbert, and Coke. It spells out a system of "unwritten" rules that date back to "time beyond memory," whose lineage is unbroken and unimpugnable, whose genealogy and forms of inheritance are the subject matter of the laws of property and succession, the *leges terrae.*[32]

Outside of the constitutional elaboration of an ideal community, the doctrinal rhetoric of legal identity attaches law to a series of figures of affection, metaphors of order, stability, and permanence—thus the extraordinary importance attached to the legal specification and emblems of sovereignty, of Crown, parliament, and courts. The subordinate figures of affection or inclusion are too numerous to endeavor to list, although certain ironies in the images of the freeborn Englishman and his rights deserve brief mention. From its very inception in common law, the freedom of the individual is a concession from the Crown and can be removed as the Crown wishes, *per speciale mandatum domini regis.*[33] In Thomas Smith's appropriate expression, no man is free save the sovereign, and further, "no man holds land simply free in England but he or she who holds the Crown of England: all others hold their land in *fee* . . . or *feoda* which is as much as to say in *fide* or *fiducia,* that is upon a faith or trust, that he shall be true to the Lord of whom he holds it."[34]

There is a faith or terror embedded in the territory whereby the *leges terrae* express a form of fealty or servitude that ties the subject to a tellurian nomos, to a corporeal reference, to *hominium* or *feu.* The irony or, more properly, the dissimulation of identity, of the imaginary community or constitution, is matched by a further series of identificatory figures. Just as the law must appear to guarantee the freedom of the subject, it will also protect the garden, the home, and the body of the subject, it will protect the ancestral rights enshrined in *Magna Carta,* it will defend the liberties established by the English Revolution. Insofar as the Crown, in making and interpreting law, is not subject to legal rule,[35] the metaphoric power of civil liberty, property right, or private immunity is so much the stronger. The common law develops indeed around precisely such points of affectivity, around clusters of legal affection by which the careful neighbor, the

32. On which term see John Selden, *Ad Fletam Dissertatio* (Cambridge: Cambridge University Press, 1647, 1925 ed.) at 141 and 173.

33. *Darnel's Case* (1627) 3 St. Tr. 1. For a more general consideration of this point, see Goodrich, *Languages of Law,* ch. 7.

34. Thomas Smith, *De Republica Anglorum* (London: H. Middleton, 1565, 1583 ed.) at 111.

35. Cowell, *The Interpreter*; William Noy, *A Treatise of the Rights of the Crown* (London: Lintoth, 1634, 1715 ed.).

reasonable man, the incompetent child, the fiduciary relation, charitable purpose, legitimate expectation, and the like figures of belonging are putatively or defeasibly protected by and definitive of common law, of its value, its purpose, and its end.

The power of metaphor in the service of law is well recognized by the early rhetoricians, and the sense of communal identity is in large measure a product of the imaginary similitude of a disparate populus and its symbolic or iconic political representations. The metaphor elicits the emotion necessary for political love and legal obedience. The metaphor, in marking similarity, also lays open the way to the distinction of groups or constitutions. To emphasize the emotional power of likeness is also to imply the need to exclude that which or those who are unlike. Puttenham lists figures of *aenigma* (riddle), *parimia* (proverb), *ironia* (deceit/dissemblance), *sarcasmus* (contemptuous irony), *asteismus* (mockery), *antiphrasis* (derisive contradiction), *hyperbole* (excess), *periphrasis* (indirection), and *synecdoche* (substitution) as the appropriate signs of political dissimulation or dissimilarity. Each figure deceives, dissembles, hides, or obscures in its own way, each is allegorical in the sense of saying one thing yet meaning another.[36] Lamy, to remain with an earlier example, differs in his classification of appropriate figures of exclusion but lays extraordinary emphasis upon the affective power of figures of contradiction, antithesis, paradox, and rejection. Thus "antitheses . . . are the effects of that strong impression made upon us by the Passion that animates us." Such figures of passion must be used "in the same manner to discover the Object of the Passion which we have in mind to inspire," and thus "if we declare against a Malefactor, who deserves the hatred of the Judges, we are not to be sparing of words. . . . We may compare him to Malefactors of former Ages, and declare his Cruelty to be greater than the Cruelty of the Tigres and Lions."[37] In structural terms the antithesis suggested is between "our" community and the theater of cruelty associated with the heathen, the Roman and the barbarian, the excluded, the stranger, and the beast.

DENUNCIATIONS

Forensic rhetoric reflects the structure of dogmatic discourse. It elaborates law's truth, it defends the causes of the profession against all adverse criticism or demand for reform, but it does not found the structural antagonism or antirrhetic that moves historically from ecclesiastical to civil polities, from theology to jurisprudence, from one law to the other. The

36. Puttenham, *Arte of Poesie* at 158–159.

37. Lamy, *Art of Speaking* at 232 and 247. See, for another example, Thomas Hobbes, *A Briefe of the Arte of Rhetorique: Containing in Substance all the Aristotle hath written in his three bookes of that Subject* (London: A. Crook, 1637).

symbol of such transition or of the dual nature of the polity, of its impossible unity of spiritual and temporal being, was a Crown to which all subjects owed allegiance and honor, from which all subjects held their land and other rights. The Crown was explicitly an icon of sociality, a metaphor to be defended and a cause to die for in either of its capacities, as head of the church or as head of the state. In historical terms it is worth observing briefly that the Crown established, or in the contemporary doctrinal idiom, reestablished, itself as spiritual sovereign through breach of its relation to Rome. It acquired its specific national identity *against* Rome, *against* the law of Rome, and *against* the jurisdiction of the Pontiff. In a similarly antithetical vein, the common law was represented as a reason of the people and of the land, a native, indigenous, vernacular reason which was distinctive by virtue of its polemical opposition to the heresy, the treachery, and the horror of papal sophistry and civilian glosses alike. Common law reason knew itself or less ambitiously established an identity *against* the French, *against* written law and its other civilian jurisdictions.[38] It claimed to be the natural reason of England, the scourge of foreign lucubrations and of the tyranny of other laws.[39] It resisted foreign, inkhorn, dishonorable, novel, and ill-mannered forms of legal reason as they existed abroad, without the "ligeance" of the English Crown. Following the terms of the antirrhetic, a synoptic account of foundational legal antiportraits can move from the categories of sanctity or authority to those of reason and nature.

From the Act of Supremacy[40] onward, the English constitution was an explicit marriage of ecclesiastical and secular, spiritual and temporal laws. The secular state had thus to defend itself against Rome, to justify its refusal of the universal authority of the Roman Catholic Church while at the same time establishing a distinctive constitution that rejected an equally universal Roman law. In terms of positive law, the defenses of common law against the logic and power of Rome took the form of a war of jurisdictions in which the ecclesiastical courts and civilian law were eventually subjugated to the prerogative and will of the king's courts.[41] In dialectical terms the defense of the legal authority and sacral prerogative of the Crown instituted a particular order and specific places of public or legal reason. In one sense, it established tradition, the "unwritten" authority of

38. I pursue this argument at length in "Critical Legal Studies in England."

39. In addition to authors and sources already cited, an interesting example of this phenomenon, from early in the tradition, can be found in Sir John Fortescue, *The Difference between an Absolute and Limited Monarchy, as it more particularly regards the English Constitution* (London: private distribution, 1475, 1714 ed.).

40. 28 Henry 8 cap. 1 (1534), in Rastall, *A Collection* at sig. 404r.

41. In addition to works by More and St. German already cited, see William Fulbecke, *A Parallele or Conference of the Civil Law, the Canon Law and the Common Law of this Realme of Englande* (London: Society of Stationers, 1602, 1618 ed.); Wiseman, *Law of Laws*; Sir Matthew Hale, *The Analysis of the Law: Being a Scheme, or Abstract of the Several Titles and Partitions of the Law of England, Digested into Method* (Chicago: Chicago University Press, 1650, 1971 ed.);

institutional sources of law, and judicially approved custom and opinion, as the ever-present mystery, the logic and truth, of an immemorial and invisible law. The judges take the role of custodians of a peculiar and antique "spirit of the law," of the *arcana iuris,* which is to be defended as axiom, maxim, and judicial declaration, against all secular, imperite, or vernacular forms of knowledge. Legal reason, in short, is conjoined with judicial power, tradition with authority, source with truth: "It is the great lesson of legal history that the power and authority of reason are one and the same."[42] The reason of law shares in the two natures of the ecclesiastical and civil polity, it became explicitly a knowledge of things divine and human, it was necessarily a language unto itself, it was incapable of error save through human failing or the interference of those unlearned in law.[43] To the other time and distinctive place of legal reason as the logic of an always already established law should be added certain observations as to the specific character of that reason as an expression of the genealogy of English institutions. The learned character of legal reason, its artificial quality, was a construction directed against all other possible forms of legal reason, be they of civil law, the scholarship of other disciplines, or the more popular logic of resistance to or reform of common law. What is staked out in the defense of legal reason is a legitimacy that belongs to the mythical antiquity of specifically English common law sources and forms, a lineage, a blood, a law whose rationality belongs to the immemorial authority of its source. Its logic is thus that of inheritance,[44] its order is that of succession,[45] its power and virtue is that of the fathers.[46]

Bacon, *Elements of the Common Lawes of England*; Dr. John Cowell, *The Institutes of the Lawes of England, Digested into the Method of the Civill or Imperiall Institutions* (London: Roycroft, 1605, 1651 ed.). For a good general discussion, see Levack, *Civil Lawyers in England.*

42. Legendre, *L'Inestimable objet de la transmission* at 38. See further Legendre, *L'Empire de la vérité.*

43. Thus, Coke, *Reports* at pt. II sig. A 5 a: "If you observe any diversities of opinions amongst the professors of the laws, content you, to be learned in your profession, and you will find, that is *hominis vitium non professionis.* And to say the truth, the greatest questions arise not upon any of the rules of the common law, but sometimes upon conveyances and instruments made by men unlearned, many times upon wills intricately, absurdly and repugnantly set down, by parsons, scriveners and other such imperites." See further, Davies, *A Discourse on Law and Lawyers.*

44. Sir Edward Coke, *Magna Charta with short but necessary observations by Lord Chief Justice Coke* (London: Atkins, 1680) at sig. A 2 a: "The best inheritance a subject has is the laws of the realm."

45. See particularly, Smith, *De Republica Anglorum* at 20, referring to the importance in royal succession of "the right and honour of the blood," for the "quietness and surety of the realm." See further, on the principle of succession, Ferne, *Blazon of Gentrie*; J. Bossewell, *Workes of Armorie* (London: Totell, 1572).

46. Thus Selden, *Titles of Honour* at sig. B 4 b. See further, Wryley, *The True Use of Armorie* at 3–4; Sir Henry Spelman, *Aspilogia* (London: Martin and Allestry, 1610, 1654 ed.) at 4–5;

Reason and nature join in the origin of a common law conceived to be "connaturall" with the people of England.[47] The time of the origin and of the ancestors of law is that of a natural governance instituted according to the model of a divine order of all visible forms. Nature is the zero point of the genealogical line; it is not only the first model of all subsequent reproduction but also the mediate historical source of positive law: "Among the learned in English law, this is called the law of reason, which natural reason has established among all men . . . a sign, possessed naturally, which is indicative of the right reason of God" and from which positive law "is derived as a thing which is necessarily and probably following of the law of reason and the law of God for the due end of human nature."[48] There are, in other words, two laws: one natural or "native," inscribed, "unchangeable and perpetual,"[49] without writing, in the heart of men; the other a replica of or derivation from the former. The relation between natural and positive law, between model and replica, primary and secondary, was not, however, simply a conceptual correlation, it was also a genealogical claim. The antiquity of the common law, its excessive age, was not only an argument directed against the claims of Roman law, it was also a positive statement of the historical proximity of England's unwritten law to nature itself: "This customary law is the most perfect, and most excellent, and without comparison the best, to make and preserve a commonwealth . . . as coming nearest to the law of nature, which is the root and touchstone of all good laws."[50] The immemorial and unwritten character of common law allowed its origin to be placed, beyond memory, in the realm of nature and not of man. The last defense of law was thus to be a natural law conceived as the order of things: "For by an order we are born, by an order we live and by an order we make our end. By an order one ruleth as head and others obey as members. By an order realms stand and laws take their force."[51]

The outline description provided above of a foundational order, of a common law tradition in which "reason, justice and law do stand together," should already indicate much of the likely content and form of the specific legal order that the Renaissance apologetics sought to institute and defend. At the somewhat recondite level of the theory of the

---

and the slightly later William Bird, *A Treatise of the Nobilitie of the Realme collected out of the body of the Common Law* (London: Walbanke, 1642) at 8–10.

47. Davies, *A Discourse* at 255.

48. Christopher St. German, *Doctor and Student* (London: Selden Society, 1528, 1974 ed.) at 13 and 27.

49. Finch, *Law or A Discourse Thereof* at sig. 2r. Finch explicitly distinguishes law of nature and law of reason as respectively primitive and secondary, *noeticum* and *dianoeticum.*

50. Davies, *A Discourse* at 252–253.

51. Wilson, *Arte of Rhetorique* at 17–18.

sources of law, the elements of antirrhetic and antiportrait are already evident: those that oppose or even simply question the order of common law and the professional or esoteric status of legal knowledge were not simply fools or "imperites" but were also, and by definition, likely to be accounted as harbingers and companions of the godless, the disordered, the irrational, the mad, and the unnatural. They were at the very least irreverent, unlearned, and prey to dreams, images, and other fantastical imaginings. The antithetic character of the statement and defense of common law can be rendered more explicit, however, by invoking elements of the substantive content of the definition of the new "old English order" of custom and judge-made law. While the examples that follow are illustrative, I believe, of a more general rhetorical form, they are not intended as anything approaching a comprehensive survey.

ANTITHETON: STRANGERS, FOREIGNERS, NOMADS, AND OTHERS

The first allegory or dissimulation of common law is that of its identity. The system of common law developed by the early doctrinal writers, Coke's sages, and the Renaissance treatises, is based upon the elaboration of a myth of an origin that precedes historical time and so lends an identity to a tradition that is otherwise and self-evidently polyglot, partial, and impermanent. The origin of common law is an obsessive object of doctrinal description, and the first law of England is variously depicted as being Samothean, Albion, Druidic, Spartan, Trojan, Roman, or Arthurian as well as being variously under the signs of Saturn, Jupiter, and Aries and associated with the mythic figures of Mercury, Neptune, and Janus.[52] What is sought in these repeated returns to the originary, to a past that was never present, is an emblem of ancestral identity, a character of Englishness, an insular nature that preexists and will outlive the crisis and criticism of an illogical and historically haphazard system of case-made law. As with any genealogy, the essential question is that of legitimacy, of the proper constitution of the social family, its image and its fate. If the depiction of family and familiarity, of legitimacy and line, is analyzed in terms of its explicit figures of antithesis, an antinomic structure can be elicited, one which opposes the myth of imagined community or of belonging to the histories of law, nation to alienation, antiquity to novelty, familiarity to strangeness,

52. For examples of these statements of origin of law, see Coke, *Reports,* referring variously to Brutus, the Trojans, Romulus and Remus, and King Arthur; Spelman, *Original of the Four Law Terms,* refers to Druids, Moses, and Lycurgus of Sparta; W. Lambard, *Archeion or Discourse upon the High Courts of Justice in England* (London: H. Seile, 1591, 1635 ed.) refers to Moses, the Greeks, and the Druids; Selden, *Jani Anglorum,* refers to the Samothes, as well as the Druids; Dugdale, *Origines Juridiciales,* refers to the Druids.

permanence to transience, and the halcyon Island of Ceres [53] to its Continental Gallic forebears.

The primary task of the reformation defenses of English law lay in finding some method of explaining the legitimacy of a newly united civil and ecclesiastical commonwealth that had left the universal church, the family of Rome, to become an independent constitution under the English Crown. The reformers, almost without exception, embarked upon the extreme endeavor of opposing truth to history. In its most extreme version, represented among others by Bishop Aylmer's "counterblast" against John Knox, we find a marginal note stating that "God is English," followed in panegyric form: "Oh England, England, thou knowest not thine own wealth: because thou seest not other countries penury . . . for first you have God, and all his army of angels on your side: you have right and truth, and seek not to do them wrong, but to defend your right. Think not that God will suffer you to be soiled at their hands, for your fall is his dishonour."[54] In words later cited unacknowledged by Edward Coke, Aylmer proceeds to depict a time of native origin and antiquity, of God's presence in England, which story is explicitly "the witness of time, the candle of truth, the life of memory, the Lady of life and the register of antiquity."[55]

In constitutional terms the legitimacy of papal authority in all matters of ecclesiastical law and government, consequent upon the historical conversion of England to Christianity by the pope's envoy Augustine,[56] was to be challenged by reference to royal rights of ecclesiastical government claimed to descend directly from God and so to precede and supercede the Roman presence in England. The reformers and proponents of the Anglican Church, the "neo-Church of England," all argued a basis for that faith in tradition and antiquity prior to Roman Catholicism: "We have planted no new religion, but only renewed the old . . . which by virtue of your traditions, and vanities, hath been drowned," to which Jewel adds,

53. William Camden, *Britannia sive florentissimorum regnorum, Angliae, Scotiae, Hiberniae chorographica descriptio* (London: Collins, 1586, 1695 ed.) at iii–iv.

54. Aylmer, *Harborowe for Faithfull and Trewe Subjectes* at sig. P iii a and P iv b. Aylmer's text counters John Knox, *The First Blast of the Trumpet against the Monstrous Regiment of Women* (1558) in *The Political Writings of John Knox* (Washington, D.C.: Associated University Press, 1985). The theme of Englishness is also important in rhetorical and explicitly educational terms, the movement for the vernacular in all the disciplines was couched in terms of the craft and the excellence of English. See, for examples, Richard Mulcaster, *The First Part of the Elementary* (Menston: Scolar Press, 1582, 1970 ed.), particularly at 254–260; Richard Verstegan (pseud.), *A Restitution of Decayed Intelligence in Antiquities: Concerning the most Noble and renowned English nation* (Antwerp: Robert Bruney, 1605) at 188–240.

55. Ibid. at sig. E iv b; Coke, *Reports* at pt. I sig. A 4 a, pt. III sig. B 1 a and B 5 a (the citation is originally from Cicero, *De Oratore,* lib. 2).

56. Bede, *The History of the Church of England,* translated and introduced in T. Stapleton, *A Fortresse of the Faith* (Antwerp: I Laet, 1565) at pt. II.

"your new fantasies, which you have painted with the colour of antiquity are vain and naught."[57] Each faith claimed a lineage and endeavored to show an authority and mystery that passed from the indefinite time of "the first fathers" and from them "the delivery thereof by . . . succession from hand to hand."[58] It was thus necessary to show that the source and authority of contemporary law was bound historically and by unbroken passage with the "primitive faith" and its origin in England; that the Crown, the "civill magistrate," had supreme authority over all persons and causes ecclesiastical because it had anciently possessed and asserted such rights.[59] It was, in short, an axiom of both theologies, of both constitutional theories, that there was "lawful succession" from a distant and indistinct source, that "the Pontiffs, or the Bishops . . . follow one another, without interruption either in their seats or their doctrines."[60] Henry VIII, in declaring the supremacy of the Crown, "resumed the ecclesiastical power of the King . . . and so the statutes [of supremacy] . . . are not laws inductory of a new, but declaratory of the ancient authority of our prince, with the solemn signification of their reassumption."[61] The English family had returned to its own, the natural law of *patria potestas* was to be complemented again by *regia potestas*—"the extension of the former to many families"—and the power of the Crown could thus be conceived as the constitutional equivalent in natural and civil law of the absolute power of the father.[62]

Such paternity was not simply an aspiration to Biblical authority but was also at its most powerful when formulated in terms of an inner lineage, in terms of an unwritten inscription that placed common law both outside the norms of historical evidence and against Rome and written law. The barrister and systematizer of the law of "blazoning," of heraldry and arms, John Ferne, refers English law to that which passed from God to Adam and secondarily from God to Moses, "after whom, whatsoever prosperity has done in the holy sanction of laws, they have but as apes, by imitation borrowed the semblable form of laws from him."[63] This was a law that mimed or mimicked an older law, a law that preceded and superceded that of the Romans and of the Continentals. The proof of this distinction lay not only

57. Jewel, *A Defence of the Apologie* at 491. A further statement of this position can be found forcefully elaborated in Fulke, *T. Stapleton and Martiall* at 14.

58. In this instance the source is Harding, *Confutation* at sig. 22v.

59. Fulke, *T. Stapleton and Martiall Confuted* at 13. See, for further examples, Jewell, *A Defence of the Apologie* at fol. A iii a–A iv b; Downing, *A Discourse* at 63–69. See also Selden, *Jani Anglorum* at 72.

60. J-B. Bossuet, *Politique tirée des propres paroles de l'écriture sainte* (Paris: Cot, 1709) at 20.

61. Downing, *A Discourse* at 66.

62. Ibid. at 64. The temporal theory of such paternal authority comes in Sir Robert Filmer, *Patriarcha or the Natural Power of Kings* (London: W. Davis, 1680), as, for example, at 18: "Paternal government may be traced by manifest footsteps" to Adam.

63. Ferne, *Blazon of Gentrie* at 40–41.

in the assertion of a lineage from first times or originals but also in the form of law and its uniquely "unwritten" character. According to a remarkable passage from the Renaissance antiquarian Henry Spelman, English law was unwritten because it was pre-Roman:

> We find among the Saxons, the example and reason why our common law was an unwritten law. They were originally a Grecian colony coming out of Lacedaemon and the territory of Sparta; where Lycurgus, among other of his decrees . . . ordained this for one, that their laws should not be written, because he would have every man to fix them in his memory; and for that purpose made them short and summary, after the manner of maxims.[64]

This counterfactual or polemical attribution of origin allowed the crucial passage from history to myth and simultaneously facilitated the transmission of law from the dispersion of Europe to the identity and peculiarity of the English. It was a tradition, learned from tradition and not merely from books.[65]

While the major force of Anglican ecclesiastical polemic was directed against the sophistries, lies and errors, the idolatry and false doctrine of the papal anti-Christ, the more secular legal treatises developed a comparable rhetoric against the threat and treachery of foreign law. If the English Crown was the authorizing source of national custom, and as such of all tradition, it followed naturally that English law was a secondary derivation or replica of that native sovereign power.[66] Leaving aside the specific question of the legal form of the *regia potestas,* and the indicative irony of its Latin title and Roman law sources, constitutional theory had first to depict a uniquely English populace whose character would find expression in England's antique customary law, that law which from *Fleta* to Fortescue and to Coke and Davies was described by apologists as connatural with the land.[67] The lawyer needed some image or emblem of the Englishness of common law that would both support the assertion of its antiquity and repel the threat of reformation by evidencing a unity to the tradition, a

64. Spelman, *Original of the Four Law Terms* at 102. On the importance of maxims, see Bacon, *Elements of the Common Lawes of England*; William Noy, *The Grounds and Maxims of the English Law* (London: H. Lintot, 1641, 1757 ed.). The theme of maxims as both the experience and the divine reason of common law can be traced back without difficulty to Fortescue, *De Laudibus* at 13–14; and St. German, *Doctor and Student.*

65. See particularly Davies, *A Discourse* at 254.

66. While Coke and others on occasion challenged the power of Crown and Parliament, they did so only on the basis that such power absolute should be vested in the judiciary, and not on the basis of the illegitimacy of that power as such. See further on this point P. Allott, "The Courts and Parliament: Who Whom?" (1979) 38 *Cambridge Law Journal* 79; Goodrich, "Critical Legal Studies in England," and references thereto.

67. For a recent variation on this theme, see Costas Douzinas and Ronnie Warrington, "The Most Perfect Beauty in the Most Perfect State: Sir Joshua Reynolds and an Aesthetic of the Spirit of Law," in Douzinas and Warrington, *Justice MisCarried.*

coherence and particularism that could override the history of foreign conquest, alien monarchs, Continental languages, and borrowed laws.

Who then are the English? or, by their generic name, the Britains? The received wisdom on the Continent was that the British were Gauls, the island having been once occupied and once conquered by France. Worse than that, according to Bodin and Hotman, English law was in both procedure and institution a borrowing from local French customary law.[68] According to the English historian William Harrison, Britain received from the Gauls "some use of logike and rhetorike, such as it was which our lawiers practised in their pleas and common causes. . . . Howbeit as they taught us logike and rhetorike, so we had also some sophistrie from them; but in the worst sense: for from France is all kind of forgerie, corruption of manners, and crafty behaviour not so often transported into England."[69] In an exhaustive survey of theories of origin, William Camden could find nothing more distinctive as a national characteristic of the British than a philological slip or phonetic synecdoche which applied the ancient British custom of painting the body with woad to the island itself:

> It was the general custom of all nations, to apply to themselves such names as had a respect to something wherein they either excelled, or were distinguished from the rest. . . . What, then, if I should suppose, that our Britons took that denomination from their painted bodies; for the word Brith, in the ancient language of this island, signifies any thing that is painted and coloured over. . . . Nor can any man in reason censure this, as either an absurd or over-strained etymology . . . the name (which is as it were the picture of the thing) expresses the thing itself.[70]

As Camden recognized, and as the legal antiquarians John Selden and Henry Spelman confirmed, there was very little distinctive about antique England: its people, its language, and its laws were all of foreign provenance and the latter in particular could well be greatly reformed and improved by conceptual systematization or codification according to the logic of their sources.[71]

68. Jean Bodin, *De Republica* (London: Knollers, 1580, 1606 ed.) at 559; François Hotman, *Franco-Gallia or, an Account of the Ancient Free State of France* (London: Goodwin, 1574, 1711 ed.).

69. William Harrison, *An Historicall Description of the Island of Britaine, with a brief rehersall of the nature and qualities of the people of England* (London: n.p., 1586), sig. 20r–20v.

70. Camden, *Britannia* at xxix.

71. On the need for systematization and for romanization or codification, see Thomas Starkey (ed.), *A Dialogue between Reginald Pole and Thomas Lupset* (London: Chatto & Windus, 1535, 1948 ed.) at ch. 4; Fraunce, *The Lawiers Logike* at iii–vi; Bacon, *Elements of the Common Lawes* at fol. B 2 b; Cowell, *Institutes* at sig. 2r–3v; Fulbecke, *Parallele or Conference* at sig. 2r: "The common law cannot otherwise be divided from the civil and canon laws than the flower from the root and stalk." See further Wiseman, *Law of Laws*; Dr. A. Duck, *De Usu et Autoritate Juris Civilis Romanorum in Dominiis Principum Christianorum* (London: n.p., 1679).

It is a principle of apologetics that the most vehement and antagonistic defense is reserved for the weakest arguments. In exemplary style, Coke determines that the historical and philological questioning of the origins of English law defames the self-evidence of legal truth, profanes the due reverence owed to common law, and is in constitutional terms as seditious and treacherous as consorting with the enemy and with Rome. The answer to such "seditious cavilling" is to keep historians and philologists away from the study of law and simultaneously to reassert the national peculiarity, excellence, and antiquity of the common law and of its lawyers. The national distinctiveness of common law extended beyond the reach of any other national history, while the correlative excellence of that law identified it closely with a populace that was itself not simply pure in its lineage—the island was inhabited before all others[72]—but superior in its quality: "I am convinced that the laws of England eminently excel all other countries," and particularly those of the Romans and of the French.[73] The laws of England were "of great antiquity. . . . Neither the laws of the Romans which are cried up beyond all others for their antiquity, nor yet the laws of the Venetians, however famous in this respect" could compete either for longevity or for excellence.[74] A slightly later commentary on Fortescue links the age of law to a deeper ethical foundation:

> Nothing but infinite wisdom itself, can comprehend that law, by which the infinitely wise architect at first created, and now directs and governs the whole universe. By this law, every thing lives, and moves, and has its being. By this law, every thing is beautifully produced, in number, weight, and measure. . . . Now of all the laws by which the kingdoms of Earth are governed, no law comes so near to the law of Nature and the divine pattern, as the law of England.[75]

Simple denunciation of those other and inferior laws was not sufficient; a more insidious and general antagonism toward all aspects of things foreign, strange, or unfamiliar remains to be described.

Despite the title of Inns of Court (*hospitii curiae*),[76] the first rule of ap-

72. See Fortescue, *De Laudibus* at 32–33; Coke, *Reports* at pt. 6 at fol. Z 2 a–b; Davies, *A Discourse* at 253–254; Finch, *Law* at 75.

73. Fortescue, *De Laudibus* at 89; Davies, *A Discourse* at 278: "Doth she [the profession] not register and keep in memory the best antiquities of our nation? Doth she not preserve our ancient customs and forms of government, wherein the wisdom of our ancestors doth shine above the policy of other kingdoms?" Coke, *Reports* at pt. 3 at sig. B 3 b: "Hereby as I think it is sufficiently proved that the laws of England are of much greater antiquity than they are reported to be, and than any constitutions or laws imperial of Roman emperors."

74. Fortescue, *De Laudibus* at 32–33.

75. Fortescue-Aland, "Preface" at i and iii.

76. See Cowell, *The Interpreter* at fol. Q 3 a; Sir George Buc, *The Third Universitie of England* (London: Society of Stationers, 1615), sig. 969v (defining the Inns as Hostelries or *Diversoria*).

prenticeship to the law was that of the exclusion of all outsiders, a bar on the introduction "of foraigners, discontinuers, strangers or other not of the society . . . nor common attorney or sollicitor."[77] Like any family, these Inns of "ancient amity," "seminaries or nurseries" were to nurture a legal profession that defined itself by blood and an exclusory membership: "It is an error to think that the sons of Graziers, farmers, merchants, tradesmen, and artificers can be made a gentleman by their attendance or matriculation . . . at an Inne of Court, for no man can be made a gentleman but by his father . . . because it is a matter of race, and of blood and descent," and in consequence the ungentle were to be excluded or weeded out.[78] What was true of the legal community and of the Inns as the training place or nursery of lawyers, of *apprenticii nobiliores*,[79] was equally the case on a broader political or constitutional stage. It was not enough simply to exclude foreigners and strangers: in over twenty enactments of the sixteenth century, it was legislated that no one was to appear like a foreigner or stranger. In legislation of 1509,[80] for example, it was forbidden for any subject to the realm to "weare in any part of his apparell any wollen cloth made out of this realme of Englande," and by legislation of 1511 it was ordered that "there be no cappes or hats made and readie wrought in any part beyond the sea."[81] Further legislation was directed against strangers, against Egyptians, and against vagabonds in any part of the realm, including native dwellers who took up with or appeared to be traveling "in fellowship of vagabonds . . . or calling themselves Egyptians, or counterfeiting, transporting, or disguising themselves by their apparell, speech or other behaviour, like unto such vagabonds."[82] Foreign colors and materials, which, according to Harrison, transformed the populace into "monsters," were a constant object of legislation and vilification, as too were French fashions of dress.

The Englishman was to be known by "his cloth . . . without any such cuts and garrish colours as are worn . . . by the French."[83] The Inns of Court introduced additional legislation to ban French dress and styles: "For, even as his apparell doth show him to be, even so shall he be esteemed among them."[84] Idolatrous dress would threaten the identity of

77. Legislation from the Middle Temple, cited in Dugdale, *Origines Juridiciales* at sig. 192r.

78. Buc, *Third Universitie* at 968–969; see also Ferne, *Blazon of Gentrie* at 58–59.

79. Dugdale, *Origines Juridiciales* at fol. 142 a.

80. *For Reformation of apparell* (1 Hen. VIII cap. 14), in Rastall, *A Collection* at sig. 13r.

81. 3 Hen. VIII cap. 15.

82. By 1 & 2 P. & M. cap. 4. By 22 Hen. VIII cap. 10: Outlawing "divers and outlandish people . . . using no craft nor seat of merchandise [who] by great subtlety and crafty means do deceive the people, bearing them in hand that they by palmistry could tell men's and women's fortunes."

83. Harrison, *An Historicall Description* at sig. 172v.

84. Dugdale, *Origines Juridiciales* at sig. 144r–149v, 192r–193v.

the citizen and encourage a foreign presence within the realm. Judging by the extent and scope of the legislation, foreign clothes would betray a foreigner within, the external model would reveal an internal decadence, the image an alien or extrinsic faith, another law. The historian William Harrison remarked in the latter quarter of the sixteenth century that "nothing is more constant in England than our inconstancy of attire. Oh how much cost is bestowed nowadays upon our bodies and how little upon our souls." It was "the phantasticall folly of our nation," it was excess, vanity, pomp, and novelty, it was change, variety, and sickliness; it betrayed the worst species of diversion and levity, a kind of monstrosity outside the inward grace of a singular and constant tradition and its laws.[85] It was always held by the tradition that external signs were but marks of internal states, that the visible encoded the invisible and should do so according to a legitimate order of icons or not at all. Legal concern with dress was a concern both with the indigenous, with a vernacular civility free of the stranger (*extraneum*)[86] and with all other cults that were suggestive of traditions and forces extrinsic to the native soil. It was also and more specifically a concern with the internal ordering of the realm and specifically the coding of status in dress. Not only did early legislation dictate the relevant cloths and colors for the different ranks of citizen, but a very specific rigor of law was determined for the dress, the colors, styles, and cloths of legal vestments.

Aside from the specific rules relating to legal ceremonies, the general dictate was that dress on all occasions, both inside and outside the Inns, should be in gowns "of a sad color." The profession, and it is exemplary, was forbidden beards, foreign fashions in clothes, colored doublets or hose, the wearing of ruffs, hats, cloaks, boots, spurs, swords, or daggers, or long hair, and more broadly it was stated that "they have no order for their Apparell; but every man may go as he listeth, so that his Apparell pretend no lightness, or wantonness in the wearer."[87] Inward virtue would be signaled through outward restraint and even a certain melancholia as befitted the profession of so consuming and antique a discipline and knowledge. Dress, by its severity, would show the lawyer's Englishness as against Rome, but it would also distinguish the lawyer over laymen, indicating his "eminence over the layman," an authority, it might be said, over both external and internal jurisdictions.[88] In the classical expression, which the common lawyers were not slow to borrow, the institution—the law—was to be conceived through the image of the sovereign as a "nurs-

85. Harrison, *An Historicall Description* at sig. 172r–173v.

86. Bracton, *De Legibus et Consuetudinibus Angliae,* translated as *On the Laws and Customs of England,* ed. S. Thorne (Cambridge, Mass.: Harvard University Press, 1968) at Vol. II, 387.

87. Dugdale, *Origines Juridiciales* at sig. 197r.

88. Ibid. at sig. 144r.

ing father" (King) or "nursing mother" (Queen) in both internal and external forms. The institution was to institute, nurse, and protect the subject from threats devised either by external or "ghostly" powers.[89] The institution was to take possession of the subject, to seize or apprehend its subjectivity, to inscribe the laws of thought as of expression and dress, to populate the imaginary with the delirium of a life lived in the law: "Reproduction is never reproduction of the same, but rather of kinship determined by blood (*cognacionis vinculo*). . . . It is a question of fiction and of texts, of making myth live, of creating the effects of interpretation and so of instituting the words and the force of law (*vis nominis et verbi per interpretationem*)."[90] The institution apprehends or seizes subjectivity, it is "a mother that nourishes not those who want but those who follow her rule; such an allegiance already supposes an apprenticeship, the entry into the imaginary space of the institution whose subjects are infants. . . . The centralized organisation works toward the production of infants."[91]

PARADOXON: PUBLIC LAWS AND PRIVATE REASONS

In many respects the enemy without the polity—the foreigner, the alien, the Frenchman, the Roman, and the Egyptian—is matched by the enemy within. The construction of a negative national identity, of an English character that only exists by virtue of its definition against an external threat, is replicated at an internal level by the formulation of a constitution defined against the subject and the subjectivity of reason. The Crown's arrogation of supreme authority over the ecclesiastical realm succeeded, in external terms, in constituting an independent kingdom, an imaginary community, as against the former position in which England was a province of the papal jurisdiction.[92] In internal terms, the expansion of the monarchical jurisdiction or *regia potestas* was to transfer the "government of the soul" to the civil magistrate. In place of the confused idolatry of earlier times and authorities—the purported sophistry, glosses, and barbarisms of Roman law—the civil subject was now properly reflected in the mirror of the constitution. The icon of the Crown and the spiritual unity of secular authority formed a model in which the subject could narcissistically see his own face, a law in which he was himself mystically present and so could only ever obey. Such presence was structured by a logic of transubstantial representation which denied the possibility of any disjunction between appearance and substance: the social body, the icon and model

89. Coke, *Justice Vindicated* at 98, 43, and 21, respectively.

90. Legendre, *L'Inestimable objet de la transmission* at 158–159, and see also 320–330. On the children of the text, see Legendre, *Les Enfants du texte.*

91. Legendre, *Jouir du pouvoir* at 190.

92. Downing, *A Discourse* at 6–7.

of civility, included and annexed the subject. Its art, the art of law, held the subject fascinated, magnetized, or bound to an already established law from which the only escape was into madness: it was the logic of the mirror, of mimetic duplication, of the mask or image, which is to say, of the Father in the Son.

The establishment of an identity, the constitution of a community, and the capture of subjectivity are first a matter of establishing a collective or national identity whose virtue will be matched only by the evil of those who do not belong to it. In the same sense that the church is the spouse of Christ, the civil polity is a marriage—the most holy and exemplary of unions—between the individual families that make up the populace[93] and the Crown that heads them. In accordance with the spiritual character of any marriage, the social family is joined in a mystical union in which the relation between the elements of the union is subject to the transcendental imperative of the union as such. It is a relation that breaks the boundaries of the individual will and specifically subordinates the weaker party to the desire of the stronger: Christian marriage is defined legally by *patria potestas* and socially by the subordination of women and children. The absolute dominion of the father of the social and political realm, *regia potestas,* is the logical extension and correlate of the metaphor of marriage. The prerogative power is variously described as *sacra sacrorum, sacra regni, iura sublimia,* and *majestatem potestatem.*[94] The common lawyers directly applied the Roman definition of royal sovereignty[95] to the English Crown and thus identified the polity with the absolute will of its head: "What pleases the prince, has the force of law," his will being "an absolute and perpetual power, to exercise the highest actions in some certain state."[96] The Crown is the icon of social presence and the subjects of the realm are the elements of that presence or mystic body. In constitutional terms the dual nature of the Crown, as both natural and political (mystic) body, is the explicit model for the dual nature of legal being, for an impossible subjectivity: "One and the same multitude may in such sort be both [spiritual and secular], and is so with us, that no person appertaining to the one can be denied to be also of the other."[97] Such membership of the spiritual or mys-

93. See Hooker, *Ecclesiastical Politie* at 441–443; also Downing, *A Discourse* at 9–13, 64–65.

94. For striking examples, see Hooker, *Ecclesiastical Politie* at 443–445; Sir John Hayward, *Of Supremacie in Affairs of Religion* (London: J. Bilt, 1624) at 9–11; Downing, *A Discourse* at 91–92.

95. The earliest source of such a borrowing is Ranulph Glanvill, *Tractatus de Legibus et Consuetudinibus Regni Angliae qui Glanvilla Vocatur* (Treatise on the Laws and Customs of the Kingdom of England) (London: T. Nelson, 1187, 1965 ed.) at 1 (citing *Justinian's Institutes* 1.1.).

96. *Digest* 1.4.1 (*quod principi placuit, habet vigorem legis*) in *Fleta (Commentarii Juris Anglicani),* cited in Dugdale, *Origines* at sig. 3v. Similarly, W. Staunford, *An Exposition of the King's Prerogative* (London: Society of Stationers, 1607) at sig. 5r; Noy, *A Treatise* at 54.

97. Hooker, *Ecclesiastical Politie* at 438.

tic realm, either as predestination or as fate, binds the subject of law to an absolute and foreign will of which he or she is inescapably an element or part.

The Crown is the icon or model of political and legal subjectivity, but it is not its representation: its subjects are not like it nor is it their similitude. The prerogative of the Crown asserts an absolute power whose social representation or symbolic presence is found in the unity of three elements that make up the legal sovereign. Here again the people are married to a higher order, authority, and reason which both defines and annexes them. Parliament represents the polity, and thus in Sir Thomas Smith's definition, "Parliament represents and has the power of the whole realm both the head and the body. For every Englishman is entended to be there present, either in person or by procuration and attornies. . . . And the consent of Parliament is taken to be every man's consent."[98] Selden adds a musical metaphor by way of explanation of this definition of subjective consent, suggesting that the Parliament of *Pananglium* (all England) resembles a composition: "So of the highest, middlemost and lowermost states shuffled together, like different sounds, by fair proportion doth a city agree by the consent of persons most unlike [and unlikely]; and that which by musicians in singing is called harmony; that in a city is called concord, the straightest and surest bond of safety in every commonwealth."[99] For Hooker, the appropriate metaphor for the power and dual presence of "the body of the whole realm" was an image, that of a triangle: "As in a figure of a triangle, the base doth differ from the sides thereof, and yet one and the self same line is both base and also a side; a side simply, a base if it chance to be the bottom and under-ly the rest."[100] A somewhat later critic of this Anglicanism makes the obvious point that such a depiction *is* an image and observes further that "the Church of England liturgy is prefaced by a picture representing God as a three cornered light casting out radiant beams on all sides of it; at a little distance a resplendent cloud of glory in a circular form encompassing the light. . . . Would such a depiction be an infinite disparagement of God? If so, what becomes of the Church of England?"[101] Conceptual images, abstract representations, and demonstrative reasonings are all variations in style and in genre, but they do not escape the law or power of images, their textual character does not render them less figurative nor does their marginal status make them any less visual.

98. Smith, *De Republica Anglorum* at 35.

99. Selden, *Jani Anglorum* at 94.

100. Hooker, *Ecclesiastical Politie* at 438. The same metaphor is used in Bodin, *De Republica* at 757.

101. Godden, *Catholicks no Idolaters* at 59.

Among the qualities of the realm stressed by such metaphors, by figures of perfection, are those of unity, exclusivity, and an irreal and so natural or perfect presence. The trinity of estates represented in Parliament is not only deemed to contain the whole realm but also to constitute a site of annunciation: it is the sacred place of law and when the whole realm speaks it must necessarily do so as the authoritative public voice of a unitary reason. In short it speaks for "us" and it speaks as "us," that is as the oracular and incontestable voice of the whole. There is an absolute force to the word of the law as the expression of the totality, a marriage of authority and reason that precludes from the very start the possibility of any member challenging or even legitimately questioning the reason of the whole. Public reason defines a private being which only has a legitimate existence within the public sphere of its representation. In short, public reason envelops and determines or possesses private reason: there is no private reason outside of that which is always already incorporated in the public sphere and acts as a part or *representamen* of the whole. In Hooker's depiction, the impossibility of any disjunction between the whole and its parts, between representative and represented, is spelled out at two levels. At a conceptual level the unity of the whole binds the part or member both temporally and logically: "Although we be not personally ourselves present, notwithstanding our assent is by reason of other agents there in our behalf. And what we do by others, no reason but it should stand as our Deed, no less effectually to bind us, than if our selves had done it in person. In many things assent is given, they that give it, not imagining they do so, because the manner of their assenting is not apparent."[102] At a pragmatic level, what is essential for Hooker is faith in authority, "in him whom he hath sent," not least because "easier a great deal it is for men by law, to be taught what they ought to do, than instructed how to judge as they should do of law; the one being a thing which belongs generally unto all, the other, such as none but the wiser and more judicious sort can perform."[103]

In rhetorical terms, the image or icon is a figure that represents likeness through portrait. It is a figure of sentence, a form of words that will "paint out the image of a person or thing by comparing form with form, quality with quality, and one likeness with another."[104] In the examples given, reason is represented as the figure of the whole; it embraces the

102. Hooker, *Ecclesiastical Politie* at 87.

103. Ibid. at 94 and 100.

104. Peacham, *Garden of Eloquence* at sig. x ir. See, for other examples, the definition in Sherry, *Treatise of Schemes and Tropes* at fol. F vi b; Puttenham, *Arte of English Poesie* at 201; Johannes Susenbrotus, *Epitome Troporum ac Schematum et Grammaticorum & Rhetorum* (London: G. Dewes, 1562) at fol. G 6 b.

unity of public and private, and specifically of a private fixated or held in the gaze of the whole. It remains, however, to be observed that the unity of reason is antithetically directed against the possibility of its fracture or fragmentation. The concept of a totality cannot avoid the implication of an outside, of a space of the unfaithful, disordered, seditious, or satanic. That space is occupied in legal doctrine by those who would judge for themselves or who "would follow the law of private reason, where the law of public should take place."[105] Thomas More, Richard Hooker, and Edward Coke are the most vehement exponents of the view that the authority of law in general, and of the judges in particular, is predicated upon a concept of law as the proper form of a public reason which is paradoxically neither accessible to the public nor open to public dispute.[106] Hooker is again most expansive in his delineation of the errors of unlearned judgments of law. Law is a matter for our "Directors" and not for the "vulgar sort." Those that challenge the institutions of public reason, even if only by means of discourse, are variously referred to as contentious, divisive, juvenile, academic, tedious, opinionated, perverse, strange, disturbing, superstitious, phantastical, zealous, diseased, foreign, extreme, overconfident, and dissolute.[107] "The Priest's lips should preserve knowledge . . . and other men should seek the truth at his mouth, because he is the messenger of the Lord of Hosts."[108] To think otherwise or to think differently would challenge the peace and quiet, the manners and establishment, of existing authority and its ways. For Sir Edward Coke those that criticize Littleton are ignorant, superficial, and stupid, "and I will not sharpen the nib of my pen against them."[109] More than that, however, legal knowledge, like biblical reason, is no ordinary or bare writing "such as every scrivener's boy writes in his master's shop,"[110] it is writing that binds and in which the reader must believe, for not only is it *vocabula artis,* the language of truth, but it is also a writing that only the learned should read "lest the unlearned by bare reading without right understanding, might suck out

105. Hooker, *Ecclesiastical Politie* at 102.

106. On the mystery of truth, opaque language, and inaccessible technicality of common law, see Sir Thomas More, *The Confutacyon of Tyndales Answere made by Syr Thomas More Knyght lorde Chancellour of England,* in *Complete Works of Thomas More* (New Haven: Yale University Press, 1534, 1973 ed.) at 272; More, *Debellacyon of Salem and Bizance* at fol. F ii b, M vi a–b, U ii a; Sir Edward Coke, *The First Part of the Institutes of the Laws of England; or, a Commentary upon Littleton, not the name of a Lawyer only, but of the Law it selfe* (London: I. More, 1629) at fol. C 6 a; Coke, *Reports* at pt. 3 at fol. C 6 b.

107. Exemplary passages can be found in Hooker, *Ecclesiastical Politie* at 54, 55, 57, 87, 193.

108. Ibid. at 49.

109. Coke, *Reports* at pt. 10 at fol. A a 1 b.

110. More, *Confutacyon of Tyndales Answere* at 272.

errors, and trusting to their own conceit, might endamage themselves, and sometimes fall into destruction."[111]

The order of public reason is an institutional one connoting temporal obedience and spiritual observance: "Power is of divine institution . . . [and] the subjection which we owe unto lawful powers, doth not only import that we should be under them by order of our state, but that we show all submission towards them both by honour and obedience. He that resists them resists God: and resisted they be if the authority itself which they exercise be denied."[112] External or visible conformity should be matched by a discursive submission, an inner tranquillity and compliance, for "they that seek a reason in all things, do utterly overthrow reason."[113] The legal person, in other words, is a member of two polities, subject to two laws and to the hierarchy which appertains between them. The body is prisoner of the soul: "The soul then ought to conduct the body, and the spirit of our minds the soul. This, therefore, is the first law."[114] The logic of such a dual law is that of inheritance and possession, tradition and compliance, belonging and identification. It establishes a constitution, a public order of lawful reason that can admit only a binary and antithetically defined classification of those that belong and those that are excluded, those that listen and those that speak back. It is an institutional reason, a logic of communal membership, an isomorphism of truth and power. Its antiportrait depicts an obverse or outside of reason in specifically denunciatory and exclusory terms, those that do not belong to reason and the institution exist in the twilight and spectral zone of idols, phantasies, and dreams: the outsider inhabits a world of the half-living and of the dead, she is both a nihilist and an augur of an apocalyptic fate.

Reason is an expression of belonging to the institution. Its figures and tropes are those of legitimacy, of family membership and purity of origin and line. In terms of origin and source, the most explicit correlation between rationality and group membership is found in the earliest depictions of lawful foundation in sacrifice or oedipal killing. For the common lawyers the first signs of law were those of common sacrifice and communal eating: "Our table as oft as we come to it, is the memorial of our mortality. . . . We feed upon death itself."[115] Eating terms (dining formally) so as to qualify at the Inns of Court was traditionally the first requirement of legal education and remains a prerequisite of qualification. It allows a cer-

111. Coke, *Reports* at fol. C 6 b.

112. Hooker, *Ecclesiastical Politie* at 469–470.

113. Ibid. at 82.

114. Ibid. at 81.

115. Allestree, *Whole Duty of Mourning* at 5. On the significance of food and sacrifice, see G. Bataille, *The Accursed Share* (New York: Zone Books, 1988); and on legal rites, see Goodrich, "Eating Law."

tain interpretation of the persistence within discourses on origins of common law, of the druidic past of the British polity. These first judges reserved the punishment of exclusion from sacrifice and common food for the worst offences: "Whosoever he is, that obeys not their sentence, they forbid him their sacrifices, which is amongst them the most grievous of punishments; for they who are thus interdicted, are accounted in the number of the most impious and wicked, all people shunning them, and refusing their conversation, lest they should receive damage by the infection [*contagione*] thereby."[116] Exclusion from the ceremony of sacrifice (*sacrificiis interdicunt*) deprived the interdicted both of membership of the abstract community of those that through sacrifice communicate with God, and deprived the expelled subject of all speech. With the demise of the druidic religion, the sacrificial interdiction became incorporated into ecclesiastical excommunication and secular writs of outlawry. As regards the latter, Bracton's definition of outlawry replicates the earlier form:

> He forfeits his country and the realm [*patriam et regnum*], and he is made an exile, and the English call such a person an outlaw, and of ancient time he was accustomed to be called a friendless man, and so it seems he forfeits his friends, and hence if anyone has knowingly fed such a person after his outlawry and expulsion, and received and held communication with him in any way, or harboured or concealed him, he ought to be punished with the same punishment.[117]

The outlaw is deprived of legitimacy, of social family, and community, including that of food and speech. The emblem of reason is that of a community bonded by blood in the dual sense of inheritance or succession and of sacrifice, the one being natural and the other ceremonial. The sacrifice transports social collectivity into natural order and its antithesis must be both antinature and destruction. The opponent of such an order is a person doubly unclean, an antiportrait of subjectivity, someone lost, a man or more probably a woman unattached to the institution or to law.

APORIA: CONTINGENCY AND THE GOVERNMENT OF WOMEN

The metaphoric use of femininity as a synonym of uncleanness and of the void or of nothing is one of the most common elements of Reformation

116. Dugdale, *Origines Juridiciales* at sig. 96v–97r. Dugdale's source is Caesar and is found as well in Fortescue, *De Laudibus* at 29–33; Lambard, *Archeion* at 5–7; Harrison, *An Historicall Description* at sig. 24r–24v.

117. Bracton, *De Legibus*, Vol. 2 at 321. See further, John Rastell, *An Exposition of Certaine Difficult and Obscure Words, and Termes of the Lawes of this Realme* (London: T. Wright, 1526, 1602 ed.) at sig. 193v–194r; Cowell, *The Interpreter* under *utlagaria*. For a specimen of a bull of excommunication, see Ridley, *Civille and Ecclesiasticall Law* at 245–249.

polemics and more broadly of the antirrhetic.[118] Woman as image stood as an obstacle in the path of internal vision, either as seduction or as revulsion, an object of lust or, in the figure of an illiterate and senile old woman in the *Antirrhetici,* of impurity and antinature. The rhetorical figure of woman represented first the sins of the flesh and of lust as against the law of the spirit. Sacrilege, the first sin of theft from the deity, was the sin of "a weak woman,"[119] and all subsequent or lesser sins of appearance, contact, and infidelity, respectively idolatry, fornication, or adultery and superstition, were depicted as being essentially feminine in character. In short, femininity is a sin or crime of contingency—of *contingencia,* of contact or touch—and where the cross, images, vestments, or ceremonies are attacked as heretical, their fault, like that of the harlot or the witch, is that of diverting the spirit from the incorporeal nature of truth. At one level, the sins of contact and of the flesh are literally aligned to feminine pollution, shame, uncleanness, vanity, and hypocrisy, to a "soul confused with sense."[120] At a deeper level, women, like idolaters, serve other Gods: the femininity of false (material) signs of divinity lies not only in their power to distract but also in their reference to a monstrous world "of nothing, that has no being," a world of fantasms and imaginations.[121]

In philosophical terms the legal conception of community was founded upon an antithetical relation between mind and matter, spirit and body, form and substance, in which the former abstract categories were correlated with truth and with the perfect community or emblematic society established by sacrifice, sacrament, or judgment. Precisely as flesh, as contingency, contact, or touch, the feminine would destabilize the universality of law and the abstract character of homosocial community as a relation of certainty paradoxically predicated upon the incertitude of paternity. At a jurisprudential level, the metaphysical character of truth and the abstraction of lawful community were instituted in concepts of familial and social legitimacy which derived from a patristic form of power: the father was present in the son or else the son was monstrous. The two laws, spiritual and temporal, were reflected in two families, domestic and social, in two "iconomies," those of the father in the son and of the spirit in the word, and in two powers, the paternal and the monarchical.[122] More than that,

118. See particularly Parker, *A Scholasticall Discourse,* especially at 7–8, 91–93; Henry Hammond, *Of Idolatry* (Oxford: H. Hall, 1646) at 1–3; Hammond, *Of Conscience, Scandall, Will-Worship and Superstition* (Oxford: H. Hall, 1644) at 13.

119. Spelman, *History and Fate of Sacrilege* at 3.

120. Parker, *Scholasticall Discourse* at 138.

121. Hammond, *Of Idolatry* at 1.

122. For the derivation and use of "iconomy" or *ikonomia,* see M-J. Baudinet, "The Face of Christ, the Form of the Church," in M. Feher (ed.), *Fragments for a History of the Human Body: Part One* (New York: Zone Books, 1989).

the reason of law obeyed a principle of legitimacy that was inseparable from the foundation of its authority: so long as the logic and validity of law was to be constructed genealogically, according to origin and inheritance, sources and their repetition, it would necessarily replicate a model of patristic power and paternal forms of judgment. The law was dependent upon a principle of blood mythologically rooted in the soil of England and expressed in purely abstract terms in the law of the land, a law of succession or inheritance of legitimacy in which the resemblance of father to son, of imitation or *imitatio dei,* was always already a principle of exclusion of feminine right.

For the Reformation theology of Anglican community and constitution, femininity represented another sense of blood, namely that of the contingency and materiality of flesh, the immediacy of contact as flesh and as blood, as a pollutant of the purity of the line. Conceived by the reformers as image, materiality, or body, the feminine was not simply a distraction or lure away from the abstraction and invisibility of the object of faith, it was a potent threat in the form of the image or counterfeit representation of other worlds and supra-human powers. Where for Tertullian there could be no doubt that "spiritual essences," demons, or ghosts existed and worked spiritual wickedness, corruption, and destruction, the reformer William Perkins was similarly convinced that the power of the feminine was evident in the reality of their creations: "That witches may and do work wonders, is evidently proved . . . and the wonders wrought by them are not properly and simply miracles, but works of wonder, because they exceed the ordinary powers and capacity of men, especially such as are ignorant of Satan's hability, and the hidden causes in nature, whereby things are brought to pass."[123] The work of the feminine witch is not damnable for being unreal, "they were works truly done and effected," but for being immoral. Works of wonder, of divination and soothsaying, are "lying wonders," but they are deceitful only by virtue of the "evil end and purpose in working them, which is to lie unto men" as to the hidden nature of their causes; they were "mere satanical wonders, serving to maintain idolatry and superstition."[124] It should be noted finally that such diversions or strange and monstrous occurrences are uniformly depicted in terms of the visibility of hidden things. They are another species of idolatry and are depicted, in rhetoric and substance, by reference to the language of images and the laws that appertain to perception. An illusion is defined technically as a

123. William Perkins, *A Discourse of the Damnable Art of Witchcraft; so farre forth as it is revealed in the Scripture, and manifest by true experience* (Cambridge: Legge, 1610) at sig. 6r–7v. The reference to Tertullian is to the *Apologeticus,* in A. Roberts and J. Donaldson (eds.), *Ante-Nicene Christian Library* (Edinburgh: T. Clark, 1869) at Vol. xi, 96–98.

124. Ibid. at 27–28.

satanically inspired deception or delusion, and "it is twofold; either of the outward senses, or of the mind."[125] The former, of outward sense, involves seeing, hearing, or touching things that are not present or that cannot be touched. Such involves delusion in the sense that Satan "casts mist before the eyes (as it were) to dazzle them," it deceives either by corrupting the instruments of sense, "as the humour of the eye . . . or by altering and changing the air, which is the means whereby we see."[126] Again it is the eye that must be directed, it is perception that is deceived and abandons the law by creating or dreaming of other beings, by letting imagination pass to illicit ends or through imagery invoke invisible or impossible things.

The idolatry depicted by Perkins in terms of witchcraft is not simply dependence upon or faith in the surface of things, in illusions and wonders, fantasms and imaginations, it also involves a corruption of the divine order in the sense of arrogating the power of creation to contingent things, to novelties, to images of an invisibility that is not God. More than that, it is of considerable significance that the exhaustive listing of the attributes of witchcraft are both formally and substantively analogous to what was conceived and repeatedly stated to be the powers of femininity. Witches were to be understood to be of the feminine gender, first, because Moses used a word of that gender, woman witch—*mecashephah*—in setting down the law against witches and also because women "as the weaker sex, is sooner entangled by the devil's illusions with this damnable art, than the man."[127] There is also, for Perkins, the testimony of experience which indicates, aphoristically, that the more women there are, the more witches. More than that, however, it is worth observing also that the characteristics of the witch consistently repeat the correlation of image and illusion with femininity, imagination with contingency, illegality with idolatry, credulity with melancholia or evil humor.[128] The witch creates, and that is her sin. In divination she reveals "strange things, either past, present or to come."[129] She is able to foretell and predict; she is able to read dreams; she can converse with the "living dead"; she can charm or enchant nature, raise strange passions, work diabolical wonders with words; through imagination, "a strong conceit of the mind,"[130] she is able to communicate or touch things of the soul. The list of powers and deceits available through the imaginings of witchcraft could be lengthily expanded; they are forms of harlotry and of lust, of sensuality and visual as well as tactile pleasure. The witch is

125. Ibid. at 24.
126. Ibid. at 25.
127. Ibid. at 169.
128. Scot, *Scots Discovery* at 11.
129. Perkins, *Damnable Art* at 57.
130. Ibid. at 138–139.

an antitype of femininity, the images of her art constitute an intrinsic form of illegality, her being is otherness. The forms of the art, its imaginations and delusions, are definitive of that which escapes the law and its cold prose, that which abandons or transcends the institution, that which thinks for itself.

It should be briefly noted that the denunciation of witchcraft was not without its opponents and, ironically, Sir Robert Filmer, contemporarily notorious as author of *Patriarcha,* was also author of a short response to Perkins's treatise on witchcraft, arguing that the cumulative methods of evidencing witchcraft suggested by Perkins fell far short of adequate legal proof.[131] It should further be noted that the theological debate on witchcraft and on imagery did not pass immediately into common law. Perkins, to stick with the same example, in his *Warning Against Idolatrie of the Last Times,* had no objection to the use of images in temporal affairs: these could be of three types, symbolical or political, historical, and finally architectural.[132] The point, however, is not to engage in the detail of theological debate nor to trace the immediate or journalistic transferences of political or spiritual desire. The next chapters will elaborate in detail the ambivalent and varied places of image and woman in common law; both repression and resistance will be tabulated. The present analysis is concerned rather with questions of rhetorical or discursive structure, with the figures of the legal antirrhetic and specifically with the displacement and incorporation of the war against images into the text and doctrines of an emerging vernacular and apparently secular law.

A law which borrowed substantially from the Anglican conception of a dual polity could not avoid confronting and denouncing the place of femininity in antirrhetical terms. The feminine was representative not simply of another blood opposed to the invisible lineage of legal legitimacy; rather, its purposes were immoral and its reality defective. The feminine existed positively as nonbeing. She was the obverse of a person, a figure of deceit and of illusion, she existed only as an antiportrait, as a sign of the misappropriation of divine power and as such had to be excised continuously from the public realm and from its texts, its words, its laws. This antagonism reflected structural constraints upon the constitution and the rhetorical forms of a foundation of law that could not conceive of contact or contingency precisely because its conception of legitimacy depended upon an indefinite time of origin, an originary presence that was never present and so could be neither sensed nor touched. The exemplary denunciation, in terms both of vehemence and of sources, is probably that

131. Sir Robert Filmer, *An Advertisement to the Jury-Man of England Touching Witches* (London: Royston, 1653).

132. Perkins, *A Warning Against Idolatrie* at 106.

of John Knox, *The First Blast of the Trumpet against the Monstrous Regiment of Women.*[133] In a striking reprise of the antirrhetic, Knox denounces women as images and their governance or political office as idolatry. The woman ruler would be an idol, an image not of God but of the Devil, a monster because, unlike any man, "an idol I call that which hath the form and appearance but lacketh the virtue and strength which the name and proportion do resemble and promise . . . and such I say, is every realm and nation where a woman beareth dominion . . . she has the appearance but not the powers": she is "monstriferous," a "counterfeit," destruction, Jezebel.[134] The latter topic is a common one and will be pursued in detail later in this work. Synoptically women were not to be taken as the image of God. Their faces were to be covered, they were to be *nupta,* or veiled, not primarily because of the dangers of lust or sins of the eye, of seeing or being seen in a certain way, but because it was man who was made in the image of God.[135] Law, for Knox, had always subordinated the feminine sex, man was head and woman member of both private and public "iconomies."

The *First Blast* established much of the tone and most of the terms of the *aporia* of woman—the dissembling figure of femininity—within common law. It made full use of all the elements of the denunciation of images: the woman ruler was against nature, against reason, and against God, she was a stranger and she was madness, carnality, and contingency: "A woman promoted to sit in the seat of God, that is, to teach, to judge, or to reign above man, is a monster in nature, contumely to God, and a thing most repugnant to his will and ordinance."[136] The details need not detain, nor is it necessary here to tie the patristic denunciation to the literary *querelle des femmes.* The positions established were to be important in legal terms and indeed were based on the position of women in civil law as well as on the writings of the church fathers. Knox relies initially and heavily upon Roman law and cites in the early stages of his work seven titles from the *Digest* and one from the *Institutes.* The theme is, however, in essence scholastic as well as civilian, and when common lawyers take up the topic they rely, not without irony, upon civil law, upon Aristotle, and upon Roman tradition. Sir John Fortescue, in a treatise on whether a woman can succeed to a kingdom, relies in judgment upon civil law and upon St. Augustine in deciding that nature, order, and law decided against any such claim: "The woman ought to be subject to the man, as the flesh to the spirit. . . . The pre-eminence of the man over the woman seems to be compared to that of the reasoning faculties over the sensual appetites, or

133. Knox, *First Blast of the Trumpet.*
134. Ibid. at 56.
135. Ibid. at 49–51.
136. Ibid. at 48.

of the soul (*anima*) over the flesh."[137] The law returns, in other words, to the woman as an image. Nature, reason, and the hierarchy of divine decree all combine in condemning the political claim of women: "Order is the proper nature of natural things. . . . The good of the universe consists in order. . . . There is nothing virtuous and good which does not observe the law of order. . . . And what is order but a disposition of equal and unequal things assigning to each its proper place?" Fortescue then adds that the race is divided twofold by means of two sexes and the hierarchy that exists by nature and divine law between them.[138] Sir Thomas Smith, in a foundational work of constitutional theory written somewhat over a century later, was to concur: "In which consideration also we do reject women, as those whom nature hath made to keep home and nourish their family and children, and not to meddle with matters abroad, nor to bear office in a city or commonwealth no more than children and infants."[139] The details of such argument will be pursued in the next chapter. In terms of the antirrhetic of law it is sufficient and significant to note the homology between image and woman and specifically to note the correlations adverted to above between femininity and disorder, between idol and face, between idolatry and the governance of women.

CONCLUSION: PENITUS AMPUTARE, INNER INCISIONS

The rhetoric of foundation, of origins and sources, of constitution and community, is in large measure a discourse of symptoms. The plastic image, the tropes or textual figures of the antirrhetic are alike signs for the direction of vision both in a literal sense and also in an anagogic or internal sense: the "mind's eye" or inward image is to be directed toward a hidden grace, an invisible and imaginary source. The symbol is in Reformation terms always a monument, it moves the mind (*movet mentum*), legitimately or falsely, from form to substance, sense to spirit, and from body to soul. The symbolic is therefore no more than the medium that evokes or refers to the imaginary, the perfect community or model of relation, of which the symbol (image or word) is a distant replica. In this respect it is interesting to consider the disputed status of "aereall," or vanishing signs. The question posed was whether the sign of the cross made on the forehead, in the air, or with water could be idolatrous. Such signs vanished almost immediately, their materiality was transient in the extreme and it would in many senses be hard to conceive of such spectral signs as being

137. Sir John Fortescue, *De Natura Legis Naturae* (1466) in *The Works of Sir John Fortescue* (London: private distribution, 1869) at 326.

138. Ibid. at 322–323.

139. Smith, *De Republica Anglorum* at 19.

in themselves objects of false worship or *latria.* For the reformers, however, the vanishing sign was the exemplary idol by virtue of being that much closer to the model it replicated: "But if there be any odds between the material and the mystical [aereall] cross, it is the mystical that hath the start . . . for the cross aereall hath more need to be abolished than the material. . . . As in the mother, so in the daughter. Provided that the cross aereall be acknowledged the mother of the material."[140] The material sign is in this logic a monument of the mystical, the more evanescent or the less material the form of signification, "so much the quicker is the passage *ab imagine ad rem significatem.*"[141]

The dispute as to vanishing signs is a dispute as to the permissible forms of the signs of the invisible. In the reformer's argument the proper form of signification of invisibility or perfection was the word, and in its purest form that word was spoken: God was heard but never seen, his voice was known but not his face. The word was the "image of the soul" and a faith which was heard came consequently by the word, by tradition, and by text.[142] The emphasis upon the scriptures was thus secondary to the conception of an oratorical word that was in its strictest sense the presence of the Father in the Son: writing was in this respect artificial memory, a visual image—although a permitted one—of a precedent sound or speech.[143] The dual nature of all signs was thus transmitted from the visual to verbal, from the imagistic to the rhetorical and graphic, but the structure of seeing and reading was analogous. The inversion or reversal that took place was not at the level of the structure or hierarchy of reference but rather at that of the lawfulness of specific types of sign: whereas the image had previously been the mark of memory, the book of the illiterate, the symptom or model of presence, that role was now to be taken by the word, and the image was, by the same process of inversion or reversal, to be subordinated to the word. Allowing that in the age of print the text was the principal type of the word, scripture the first source of faith, it follows that the image became an aspect of, and internal to, the text. Where in civil law the image previously took the place of knowing how to read (*pro lectione pictura est*), the text now took the place of knowing how to see: "We have not images of their bodies, but of their souls, for those things which are

140. Parker, *A Scholasticall Discourse* at 47–48.

141. Ibid. at 49 (from the image to the thing signified). See also Calfhill, *An Answere* at sig. 24r, 29r–29v, on the power of the air.

142. Calfhill, *An Answere* at sig. 64v, also 22r–24v.

143. It is this structure of priority and reference that contemporary philosophy, and Derrida in particular, has so consistently endeavored to deconstruct. See particularly Derrida, *Of Grammatology.* See further Derrida, *The Post Card*; also my commentary on this theme in Peter Goodrich, "Contractions," in Anthony Carty (ed.), *Post-Modern Law* (Edinburgh: Edinburgh University Press, 1990).

spoken . . . are images of their souls [and] the written lives of holy men are printed unto us, as certain lively images."[144] Rhetoric became an art of seeing well or vividly through words, through graphic signs and oral disputations, through texts and speech. In a work on the *ars dictaminis,* or art of writing letters, Angel Day opines most explicitly that "the excellency of the writer, and the painter concur in one, who the more that each of them studies by perfection, to touch all things to the quick, by so much the more nearer do they both aspire to that exquisite kind of cunning, that in each of these differences, is absolutely to be required." Successful painting will "present many things to the eye, the conceit whereof is marvellous" and so also will excellent writing visually provoke desire and depict situations upon which a "man may gaze . . . as a thing in *present* life, and most certain view."[145]

The assertion of the word as the primary legitimate form of knowing became the basic method of science in the age of print.[146] It displaced rhetoric but did not alter its object or function, namely that of construing a truth of which language was only ever the model, figure, or replica. The image had come to be perceived as too worldly, too sensual, too contingent, or too close and was replaced by the word: the image was a false model, it represented nothing, it was transparent, a simulacrum.[147] This transference was not without its cost. By the same token that the text became the principal form for the direction of vision, it became a dissimulation, an image that forgot (repressed) that it was an image, a sign that hid its dual function in the abstract linguistic claim that it was no more than a medium, a transparent means of reference. It is possible to cite a double cost, two moments of repression. The first reduced the image to language, while the second associated imagistic or figurative language with rhetoric

144. Calfhill, *An Answere* at sig. 65r.

145. Angel Day, *The English Secretorie or Methode of Writing of Epistles and Letters with a Declaration of such Tropes, Figures and Schemes, as either usually or for ornament sake are therein required* (London: Cuthbert Burby, 1586, 1607 ed.) at 23.

146. The conventional wisdom is that print inaugurated the restraint, if not the death, of rhetoric. Thus, most notably, Roland Barthes, "L'Ancienne rhetorique" (1970) 16 *Communications* 172; and G. Genette, "La Rhetorique restreinte" (1970) 16 *Communications* 158; T. Todorov, *Theories of the Symbol* (Oxford: Basil Blackwell, 1982). The same argument is expounded somewhat repetitively in Vickers, *In Defence of Rhetoric,* chs. 3 and 4. On the visual character of print see W. Ong, *Ramus: Method and the Decay of Dialogue* (Cambridge: Harvard University Press, 1958); Elizabeth Eisenstein, *The Printing Press as an Agent of Change* (Cambridge: Cambridge University Press, 1980); Petrus Ramus, *The Logike* (London: Vautroullier, 1574) (emphasizing logical schemata as aids to memory); H-J. Martin, *Histoire et pouvoirs de l'écrit* (Paris: Perrin, 1988); R. Chartrier and H.-J. Martin (eds.), *Histoire de l'edition Francais* (Paris: Fayard, 1989).

147. The relevant reforming maxim is taken from Lactantius, *ut religio nulla sit, ubi simulachrum est* (there is no religion where there is an image).

and for that reason subordinated rhetoric to logic as the proper method of science and of law.[148] In short, the rhetorical, figurative, and imagistic levels of the text became the "positive unconscious" of the sign, the marks of language's long term, the history (trauma) that tradition and its associated forms of repetition endeavored—indeed existed—to forget.[149]

The full implications of the repression of rhetoric as a discipline associated with images, with the signs of nothing, cannot be investigated here. It remains, however, to link the repression of the discipline to the rhetorical or antirrhetic structure of legal argument. The antirrhetic was explicitly a discourse of foundations, its stake was the delineation of a reality that would exist against or overcome all others. Its unity was thus forged against dispersion, its nature against human artifice, its reason against sophistry and feminine deceit, its authority against irreverence or illegitimate signs. The antirrhetic, as genre, thus established a specific structure of antagonism, of prosecution or threat, a rhetorical structure that was most evident and accessible through its characteristically antithetic figures of diction, its tropes and other incidents or accidents of expression. The semiotic force of rhetorical study lies precisely in the ability of rhetoric to read critically against such figures, to reconstruct the accidents or intentions of the text in terms of a discursive structure that transcends the apparent significance of textual image and verbal diction and so allows a comprehension of the stake and force of the antirrhetic as genre. Two concluding remarks seem appropriate.

The first observation is hermeneutic. Contemporary revivals of legal or forensic rhetoric have tended to concentrate upon that aspect of the classical discipline which promotes argument or dialectic as the appropriate or ethical means of institutional action. Rhetoric will found community upon probable reasons, upon a communitarian dialogue or dialectic

148. The development of this repression can be traced in terms of the use of rhetorical categories and divisions in the vernacular logics of the reformation period. Ramus published a rhetoric to accompany the logic and organized the *Logike* itself rhetorically, according to dialectic (argument) and disposition (judgment), see Ramus, *Logike* at 17–18, 71–72. Lever, *Arte of Reason,* organized his "witcraft" according to topics (commonplaces), invention, figures, and memory; Fenner, *Artes of Logike and Rhetorike,* divides logic into invention and judgment; Thomas Wilson, *The Rule of Reason, conteyning the Arte of Logique* (London: John Kingsten, 1584), divides reason into topics, invention, division, style, and disputation. For a similar development in legal logics, see Fraunce, *Lawiers Logike*; Doderidge, *English Lawyer,* 148 ff. It was, in a sense, rhetoric's finest post-classical hour. For elements of this view, set out in philosophical rather than historical terms, see Friedrich Nietzsche, *On Language and Rhetoric* (Oxford: Oxford University Press, 1873, 1989 ed.) at 21–27.

149. This sense of positive unconscious is taken from Foucault, *The Order of Things* at ix. On the historical significance of the unconscious in history or in the *longue durée,* see L. Febvre, *A New Kind of History* (Princeton: Princeton University Press, 1978) at 38–42; Braudel, *On History,* pt. 2.

in which the force or felicity of argument will determine appropriate legal outcomes. The opposite is more likely to be the case. Understood historically, the antirrhetic character of oratory aligned rhetoric with the adversarial fate or defense of institutions: although the discipline certainly had a function in guarding the great theological, legal, and political orthodoxies of the institution, it did so by dividing and opposing elements of community, by constituting hierarchies of belief, authority, and reason.[150] While the return to rhetoric may well have the advantage of translating antagonism into discourse, it cannot plausibly be viewed as anything other than a return to a fundamentally antithetic dispute as to the character, foundation, and reason of the institution. Its object is difference, whereas its figure, image, or emblem is most properly that of dispersion. Language, as the very term antirrhetic implies, is the sign of plurality and of confusion; it marks the difference of peoples and the separation or distance that is the object of law.

At a substantive level the lesson of rhetoric's history is that the institutional sites of oratorical and polemical practice are both theatrical and affective: it is the function of rhetoric to persuade and to possess. The recurrent crises of images, as well as of words, figures, and ornaments of speech and of law, are testimony to a dramatic institutional stake, that of reproduction. The history of rhetoric thus plays itself out in relation to the defense of institutional genealogies: the question of the authority of truth and of law is answered by establishing its lineage, by inventing or evoking a source that will resolve what truth is, by indicating whence it came. The legitimacy of institutions and offices, of persons and laws, is thus played out in relation to their lineage and their rights of succession: it is lineage or genealogy as the source of authority which is at stake in the questioning and defense, the antirrhetic, of legal forms or institutional traditions. When the antirrhetic figures of sanctity, nature, and reason are repeated in the discourse or defense of law, they mask and repress the restatement of truth as a question of blood, a question of a legitimacy that rests upon genealogical principles, upon lineage and its representation of a social filiation or legal constitution predicated upon a shared father or common origin and source. In a less technical vocabulary, it is myth, the fictions of truth and community, that rhetoric exists to dispute and defend. To challenge the form, authority, and reason of law is to question the order of reproduction to which they belong; it is also to invoke the antirrhetic, to invoke the discourse of foundations, to question the nature of rhetoric in the rhetoric of nature. It is for this reason, to take a contemporary example, that when critical legal studies and feminist legal theory question the character and

150. For an interesting, though perhaps unconscious exemplification of this argument, see Rose, *Dialectic of Nihilism* at 11–49.

legitimacy of legal judgment, they are met with the full, although unconscious, rhetorical force of the antirrhetic. The critics of doctrinal forms are nihilists,[151] they lack both decency and respect,[152] they are faithless and their reason is that of confusion and dispersion,[153] their fate is properly that of expulsion and their best expression would be silence. Critics of doctrine and of patriarchy have tended to avoid the terms and substance of this antirrhetical discourse of nature, belonging, and reason as irrational or mythological and thus inappropriate to the rational dialogue of civility and its constitutional forms. My analysis of the antirrhetic has suggested that such a position is repressive in the technical sense of constituting a legal unconscious, of driving the image of law's other or the thought of contingency within. The analysis has attempted also to suggest that far from being extrinsic or accidental, the figures of antirrhetic are the explicit and repeated signs of the discursive structure of foundation and of constitution. They are the deep or sedimented form which the institution takes over the long term. Criticism or eulogy that endeavors to engage questions of the history or the form of law cannot avoid directly addressing the nature, sanctity, and reason, and the unity, faith, and authority that is the stake of such discourse and the reality of its institution.

In more mundane jurisprudential terms, the history and recovery of the antirrhetic provides an important corrective to the rhetorical analysis of doctrinal discourse. The foundational character of doctrine and specifically of constitutional writings lies precisely in their polemical form. The treatise, the primary form of legal doctrinal writing that developed from Renaissance statements of the Anglican form of civil and ecclesiastical polity, does not escape the rhetorical marks of the antirrhetic. In its positive formulation, the treatise asserts an identity and community that is both fictitious (imaginary) and exclusory. In specifying the demonstrative character of its reasoning and the comprehensiveness of its jurisdiction, the treatise may not need to invoke explicitly the antiportrait of its opponents. In its modern positivized form the legal treatise is most usually content to "refute by silence." Its silence, however, is not without the traces of

151. The contemporary aspersion of nihilism dates back to responses to American legal realism and is generally utilized in a pejorative rather than a philosophical sense. See, for discussion, M. Kramer, *Legal Theory, Political Theory and Deconstruction* at 23–25, 240–241; Goodrich, *Reading the Law* at ch. 7; Neil Duxbury, "Some Radicalism about Realism?" (1990) 10 *Oxford Journal of Legal Studies* 11. For a much cited example, see P. Carrington, "Of Law and the River" (1984) 34 *Journal of Legal Education* 222.

152. As, for example, C. Fried, "Jurisprudential Responses to Realism" (1988) 73 *Cornell Law Review* 331; P. S. Atiyah, "Correspondence" (1987) 50 *Modern Law Review* 227; R. Post, "Post-Modernism and the Law," *London Review of Books* (February 1991).

153. As, for example, White, *Justice as Translation* at 263–264, 267. Also on closure rules, see Fish, *Doing What Comes Naturally* at 392–398. D. N. MacCormick, "Reconstruction after Deconstruction: A Response to CLS" (1990) 10 *Oxford Journal of Legal Studies* 539.

its polemical motives or origins. In one sense the pure or normative character of the treatise as a statement of a system of positive rules of law is necessarily iconic: its normativity expresses its distance from the sociality which it both constitutes and regulates. In this respect, its iconic character opposes it to the diversity and contingency of social relations: the unity of the normative order is purchased at the price of dissimulation, its coherence is the mask of the diversity of its object. It is constituted against the social and against the historical particularity of the subjects of law. In more classical terms, it defines itself against contingency (antinature), private reason, and imagination. A demonstrative style is in this sense no more than a figure or image of proof, and a treatise, in being the exemplary work of demonstration, is also the strongest form of figuration: it represents or imagines a purity of reason—an ideal which legal practice can never achieve. In a secondary sense, the treatise can be read symptomatically in terms of the explicit traces of the antirrhetic which reside in the inessential and marginal characteristics of the treatise. Refutation by silence or the demonstration that proves or "shows"[154] the truth of that which lies in controversy cannot escape the polemical necessity of policing the boundaries of the treatise. Precisely as doctrine, as teaching, it has to persuade, and that persuasion, in its own terms, transmits a language and forms of argument that developed over the long term of an agonistic and adversarial legal practice. The polemical form of that practice gains expression at a higher level of abstraction in terms of categorical distinctions in which doctrinal writing separates itself from questions of political and ethical judgment, from questions of justice and of social change as well as from any explicit expression of its own epistemic properties or rhetorical style.

154. Lever, *Arte of Reason* at 99.

FIVE

Haec Imago

This Mask, This Man, This Law

What else do maskes, but maskers show
and maskers can both daunce and play
our masking dames can sport you know.[1]

The seventeenth-century moralist Matthew Griffith devoted an extensive chapter of a treatise on household government to the conditions and desiderata of choosing a wife. In discussing looks as a criterion of choice he observes unexceptionally that the face or "visage is for the most part a prognostication of virtue and vice." He proceeds then, however, to warn that "thou may not trust too much to thine eyes (which are many times but a false pair of spectacles). . . . Some women are like painted cloth, look on the one side, and thou seest Virgins, Virtues and Queens; but on the other, nothing but patches and rags."[2] The painted cloth or face is an artifice or likeness, capable of deceiving an eye that rests too long upon the surface of things. The image allures and dissembles, it is the veil or screen, the mark of an absence. While its power is potentially divine, it is so only when the image observes the genealogical order of causes, when it represents the legitimacy and law of an invisible governance of the soul. The painted cloth, the face, and other forms of feminine beauty threaten alike to distract and divert from the word, from the prose of law and, in

1. Anonymous, *A Glasse to view the Pride of Vainglorious Women: Containing: A pleasant invective against the fantastical foreigne Toyes, daylie used in Womens Apparell* (London: Richard Ihones, 1595) at fol. A 4 b. On the power of masks and images see, most notoriously, Leon Battista Alberti, *On Painting* (New Haven: Yale University Press, 1436, 1956 ed.) at 63: "Painting contains a divine force which not only makes absent men present, as friendship is said to do, but moreover makes the dead seem almost alive. Even after many centuries they are recognised with great pleasure." For a discussion of that text see Louis Marin, *Des pouvoirs de l'image* (Paris: Seuil, 1993).

2. Matthew Griffith, *Bethel or, a Forme for Families: In which all sorts, of both sexes, are so squared, and framed by the word of God, as they may best serve in their several places, for usefull pieces in God's Building* (London: Jacob Bloome, 1633) at 255.

consequence, they in their turn face the force of the antirrhetic. The image of law should never be seen as an image but must rather disguise its own form; it must be an effigy or icon of an absent order, it must be a sign, mark, or vestige of an absolute reference or origin.

The antirrhetic served and serves to distinguish two orders of representation. It separated icon from idol, *imago* from image, and life—or more precisely the *longue durée* of the soul—from death. The antirrhetic opposes the two orders of being in a metaphysical antagonism within which the face or image of femininity has consistently been placed outside the order and system of law, *in signum subjectionis* or in subjection to the *imago* or law of real, as opposed to merely contingent, images. The law of images as it was inherited and adapted by the Anglican constitution was dependent upon a complex mixture of civilian influence and indigenous practice. Following Roman exemplars, the image was immediately a sign of degree and lineage and mediately the mark of the father. The image was, according to Selden's *Titles of Honour*, a badge, trophy, or effigy of paternity, of the "virtues of the fathers," of that continuance and resemblance which constituted the unity of "the Lady Common Law."[3] Borrowing directly from the Roman *ius imaginum*, Selden defined the image of legitimacy as that of origin, of the first or *instar omnium*, as sign of the unity of nature and of law.[4] The *imago* was the symbol of noble parentage, of name, ancestry, and dignity or office, and from it flowed virtue and the social worth or value of the present man "as from a pure spring continues genuine and like the first head."[5]

In Roman custom, the *imago* was the death mask, a wax impress of the face and shoulders of the Emperor. It was part of the Emperor's body and it functioned in ceremonies in the same way as the whole body, it *was* what it represented. The *imago* was both *ossa* and *nomen* and it was due all the honor and reverence that its prototype deserved: "What are these prototypes? Very specifically, they are again images (God, the Virgin; the persons of the saints whom humans should resemble); I could equally well say: they are names. Images and names, towards which are directed ritual gestures of love (kissing), of respect (baring the head), of fear (genuflection), formulations which are themselves legally classified and which, by virtue of this fact, raise a problem of sanction. The criminal law of images was an important issue."[6] The real image or *imago* founded reference, it

3. Selden, *Titles of Honour* at fol. a 3 b.

4. Ibid. at fol. C 4 a.

5. Ibid. at fol. B 4 b.

6. Legendre, *Le Désir politique de Dieu* at 228. For commentary on this text, see Yifat Hachamovitch, "The Ideal Object of Transmission: An Essay on the Faith which Attaches to Instruments" (1991) 2 *Law and Critique* 85.

inaugurated the social and established the law through the mouth or face of its interpreter as emperor, pontiff, or jurist. The accessory followed the origin, the image its principal or source, and so too the subject was made in the image, in the name of the father.[7] The image thus stood for the law, it was the place of its appearance in the social, it was the site of its inscription, the mark or emblem of the inaugural cause or source that made the law legitimate, both rational and powerful:

> Since the emperor cannot be present to all persons, it is necessary to set up the statue of the Emperor in law courts, marketplaces, public assemblies and theaters—in every place, in fact, in which an official acts, the imperial effigy must be present, so that the Emperor may thus confirm what takes place, for the Emperor is only a human being and he cannot be everywhere.[8]

The effigy, statue, or emblem represented and incorporated the reason of law, it was iconic in the specific sense of establishing the place—the theater, *ecclesia,* court, or site of enunciation—of legality.

The *imago* embodied the sanctity of its origin, and hence the places that were marked by images were to be understood as sacred, as due the honor of the prototype. In this respect the image established the place and the power of law as an imaginary site of reference: the image inaugurated the reason of law and such reason was a reference to further images, those of God or Virgin or sovereign. The *ius imaginum* conferred a comparable right on Roman nobility. For the sake of memory and posterity they were entitled to have and display the *imagines* of their ancestors. In contradistinction to later theories of images as chimerical or insubstantial things, classical Roman law attributed the *imago* an independent and real status, the *imago* was a part object, a body which *was* what it represented: it was both signifier and signified, mask and substance, a figure—a *synecdoche*—of the whole body and hence the augur of whence it came.[9] The *imago* was a reality in itself and was to be venerated as such in public and in the household. The real image or icon was a passage to the thing, it was to be honored because, in the Nicean doctrine, the honor shown to the image referred to the prototype (*honos qui eis exhibetur, refurtur ad prototypa*). The

7. *Justinian's Institutes,* trans. Peter Birks and Grant McLeod (London: Duckworth, 536, 1987 ed.) at 2.1.34.

8. Kenneth M. Setton, *Christian Attitudes Towards the Emperor in the Fourth Century* (New York: Columbia University Press, 1941) at 196; discussed in Yifat Hachamovitch, "One Law on the Other." See further Louis Marin, *Portrait of the King* (London: Macmillan, 1988) at 9: "The king is only truly king, that is, monarch, in images. They are his *real presence.*"

9. On the *imago,* see T. G. Watkin, "Tabula Picta: Images and Icons" (1984) 50 *Studia et Documenta Historiae et Iuris* 383; Florence Dupont, "The Emperor God's Other Body" in M. Feher (ed.), *Fragments for a History of the Human Body, Part Three* (New York: Zone Books, 1989). On the *ius imaginum,* see Selden, *Titles of Honour* at fol. C 2 a *et seq.*; Freedberg, *The Power of Images* at 212–224; Legendre, *Le Désir politique de Dieu* at 221–234.

icon, as a part object, as a relic of the prototype or source, was infected with divinity and death, it *was* the father in the son, and through that lineage or apparition the law lived, the text spoke, and truth—as reference to hidden sources, to rational causes—was put in place. In that the iconic image bound the subject to sovereignty, to the representation of social power and to its legitimacy, the image was the emblem of the conjunction of ancestry and antiquity, paternity and divinity, reason and law: "It is essential to register the extraordinary political significance of the classical controversies relating to the legal status of images."[10]

It was political sacrilege (*crimen maiestatis*) to deface or harm the image of the emperor; obedience to the *paterfamilias* and to the power inherited through the domestic *imagines* was equally and absolutely ordained by law.[11] Such obedience was attached to the image while the image itself was modeled upon the *sacrae imagines* of the Roman emperors.[12] Suffice it to remark that in its proper form the image—as effigy, mask, icon, or emblem—was the manner of custody and transmission of social power both as *patria* and *regia potestas.* It was both objectively and subjectively the site of power, and it was in relation to the image that the subject was bound to law. The image founded the order of reference and the paternity, which is to say the legitimacy, of the institution. It founded a specific order of succession and instituted subjectivity through the myriad of marks or notes of office, status, and public function that constituted the political order and public sphere.[13] The icon was the augur of public space and of its political affiliations. It was stringently protected by laws not only of *crimen maiestatis* but also of innumerable specific offences of *crimen falsi, crimen iniuriae, scandalum magnatum,* and *actio iniuriam,* all of which could be brought against any who challenged or desecrated images either by words (*sermonis*) or by deeds (*facti*).[14]

10. See Legendre, *Le Désir politique de Dieu* at 232, also at 234–235. "The distinction between image and idol fixes classification. In classical dogmatic theory, the idol is not an image . . . it is a reflection tied to a lie. A popular expression gives an exact account of the etymology (*eidolon*): something is thrown into full view. That is the idol, a false product of pure appearances."

11. See *Digest* 48.4 (*Ad legem Iuliam maiestatis*). The sanctity of majesty expressed in images is a feature of the "very long term [*très longue durée*] of western political structures." See the discussion of *crimen maiestatis* in Yan Thomas, "L'Institution de la majesté" (1991) 112 *Revue de synthèse* 331.

12. Discussed in André Grabar, *Christian Iconography: A Study of its Origins* (Princeton: Princeton University Press, 1968) at 78–80. More broadly on royal portraiture, see Louis Marin, *Portrait of the King.*

13. See A. Alciatus, *De Notitia Dignitatem*; A. Alciatus, *Emblemata* (Lug.: M. Bonhomme, 1550), for depictions of status and image in the public sphere.

14. On the available actions, see Bartolus de Saxoferrato, *Tractatus de Insigniis et Armis* (Venice: n.p., 1358, 1485 ed.) at fol. 2 b; see also the extended discussion of actions in Ferne,

The real image or icon instituted a particular form of governance, a specific kind of distance, a power of reason and of law predicated upon a singular order of reference, upon an order of legitimate images as the guides of exterior and interior vision alike. Polity, family, and person all shared in the hierarchy of causes and in the imitation of reason, each was in turn an image, a resemblance, a likeness of its cause: "The images of the Christian world are forms of fealty, forms of faith in an originary reference, in the originary writ of the Incarnation, the dogma that God himself had assumed human nature and could be reproduced in his humanity: great, strong father, sweet, sweet mother: Pantokrator, Glykophilusa, come and look."[15] Here then, in the icons, can be found a faith in reason that is also an expression of legitimate love, a political desire, an Augustinian *structura caritatis*. The genealogy of the political and legal realms institutes an order of images, of images backed by other images, of signs that refer to further signs—painted words, if you like—with a face both at the front and the back. Yet against this image (*haec imago*), this emperor or law, there is also to be found the principle of the idol, the image that refers to nothing, the painted cloth which is rag at the back or which makes no reference beyond its surface, which "like a woman or like writing, passes itself off for what it passes itself off for."[16] Here then is the paradox: the idol is nothing *because of* its contingency, it is no more than an image, a void, precisely because of its materiality, because it does not claim to be anything more than it is: a surface, an image, a skin. The idol is pure appearance, it is exteriority without a unitary or legitimate cause, it is multiplicity and not law.

The image has sides and takes sides, it inaugurates or institutes and simultaneously it represses, exiles, or dissolves those whose attachment to its orders are not sufficiently apparent, those whose reason does not explicitly conform to the power or faith of law. Two issues deserve attention in this respect. The first is simply to note the historical and conceptual correlation of image to word. In theological terms the word was the visible sign

Blazon of Gentrie at 266–271; John Logan, *Analogia Honorum* (London: Thomas Roycroft, 1677) at fol. 42 a. In theological terms, see Tertullian, *De Spectaculis*, in A. Roberts and J. Donaldson (eds.), *Ante-Nicene Christian Library, Vol. 11* (Edinburgh: T & T Clark, 1869), denouncing pagan images at the entrance to the theater. See also, on idols of the theater, Francis Bacon, *Novum Organum* (1620) in T. Spedding (ed.), *Works* (London: Longman, 1859) at IV, 53–63.

15. Hachamovich, "One Law on the Other" at 195. See further G. Ladner, "The Origin and Significance of the Byzantine Iconoclastic Controversy," in G. Ladner, *Images and Ideas in the Middle Ages: Selected Studies in History and Art* (Roma: Edizioni di Storia e Letteratura, 1983), Vol. 1.

16. Jacques Derrida, *Spurs: Nietzsche's Styles* (Chicago: Chicago University Press, 1979) at 127–128.

of an invisible presence; it had a dual nature, it was traditionally an image, a visual form or painted letter. The word, as *logos,* as Christ and as God, was the "substantial ground upon which we are to build our religion" and further, "we have the word, the ordinary mean, to lead us into all truth: we must not beside the word, seek signs and tokens. We have the bodies, what grope we after shadows?"[17] While such an exposition might seem to sever the image from law, even reformers admitted the word to be a most complex figure of judgment: "The *word* of God has different meanings according to its various properties and effects: where it multiplies it is *seed,* where it cuts the heart it is *sword* and divides flesh from spirit; where it binds together it is called *net,* where it washes us clean it is called *water,* where it enflames, it is called *fire*; where it feeds—*bread*; where it opens and gives entry—the *key*."[18] There could hardly be a more figurative or less prosaic definition of word or scripture. The word was a sign that was to displace the image; in its true form the word was to be read as a figure, as the prototype or exemplar of divine causes, as *verba visibilia,* as sensible image, as light or sign of an absent truth. The sacraments were explicitly figures or "outward tokens" to be read and understood as tropes: *ad tropicam intelligentiam sermo referatur.*[19] The word called an image to mind, and more explicitly, the words of the Eucharist, *hoc est corpus meum,* referred to a sign of sacrifice: "Eat my body and drink my blood is an allegory, a figure: he must be devoured by hearing: he must be chewed by understanding; he must be digested by faith."[20] The foundation of the institution upon the word, the textual basis of faith and of law, did not suppose any ordinary or singular prose: the classical maxim *ut pictura poesis* (as in painting so in poetry) might equally be extended to prose.

In legal terms text and law had always been synonyms, *ratio scripta* was *lex,* writing was power, and in consequence the theory of the image, of visual meaning and so of legitimate reference, became assimilated to theories of the text and of *ratio iuris*:

> The twelfth century Renaissance of Roman law . . . brought with it a movement to homogenize the theory of meaning—in medieval canonical terms, it was necessary to develop a theory of the *ratio,* of Reason, which would be equally applicable to both painting and writing. In schematic terms, I would formulate it as follows: for the west-European tradition, assimilating the image to the written—and it is hardly necessary to recollect the canonic maxim: *pro lectione pictura est*—the written (*écrit*) and the painted were both

17. Calfhill, *An Answere* at fol. 52 a.

18. Jewel, *A Defence of the Apologie* at 144.

19. Ibid. at 205 (the word refers to a figurative meaning).

20. Ibid. at 274. For further accounts of the semiotics of the Eucharist, see the remarkable analyses in Samuel Johnson, *The Absolute Impossibility of Transubstantiation Demonstrated* (London: William Rogers, 1687).

> to be understood by reference to a general theory of the text, there were two species of text, the written text and the painted text.[21]

The text institutes certain laws of thought, it establishes an order of succession, of paternity, and in consequence must be understood as a way of life or, in the Roman formulation, as instituting life (*institutere vitam*). This chapter will pose the question of what "this image" means as a law and as life. It will address particularly the question of what "this image" means for those that live as its idols, its women, its bare images, its chimeras or nothings. Whereas the present chapter will concentrate upon the histories of the repression of women and images, the next chapter, concerning the figure of *gynaetopia,* will invoke the return of the repressed, the images of other laws.

SOURCES OF LAW AND STATUSES OF WOMEN IN THE ANCIENT CONSTITUTION

While it doubtless needs little emphasis, it is as well to begin by restating in some detail the diverse subordinate statuses of women within the various historical domains of common law. One dimension of such an analysis is the manner in which it illustrates forcefully the interdependence of the diverse laws governing the civil and ecclesiastical polity and is still implicit, if frequently unrecognized, in contemporary law. At the level of structure or of what was endlessly termed "universal law," the civil position of women was dictated by their inferiority, their subordinate and accessory place in opposition to men. The first source historically and conceptually is invariably the *Corpus Iuris* itself, and there is little scope for feminist argument in the great Roman compilation. The *Digest* provides no definition of woman as such, nor does it recognize woman as a distinct juridical species or legal personality: the woman lacked power and could never be the subject of an image. What the *Digest* does provide is an extensive although scarcely coherent medley of prohibitions, incapacities, and denigrations of women as persons *alieni iuris,* subject to another's control.[22]

21. Legendre, *Désir politique de Dieu* at 231. For a more technical discussion, see Hubert Damisch, *Théorie du nuage: Pour une histoire de la peinture* (Paris: Seuil, 1972), particularly at 62–90 (on *iconmystica*).

22. Curiously, the most extensive discussion of the civil law on women is to be found in Knox, *First Blast of the Trumpet* at 44–48. For a general outline of the Roman law relating to women, see Jane Gardner, *Women in Roman Law and Society* (London: Croom Helm, 1986); and Olivia Robinson, "The Historical Background," in S. McLean and N. Burrows (eds.), *The Legal Relevance of Gender* (London: Macmillan, 1988); Brundage, *Law, Sex, and Christian Society.* With regard to the Renaissance reception of this law, see the excellent Ian Maclean, *The Renaissance Notion of Women* (Cambridge: Cambridge University Press, 1980), ch. 5. For a broader discussion and invaluable bibliographic guidance, see Ian Maclean, *Woman Trium-*

General statements of principle are to be found in D.1.9.1 (Ulpian)—"greater dignity inheres in the male sex" (*sexu virili*)—and in D.1.5.9. (Papinian)—"there are many points in our law in which the condition of females is inferior to that of males" (*deterior est condicio feminarum quam masculorum*). While it is not feasible to provide any comprehensive account of specific disabilities, the most obvious incapacities are comprehensively disabling. Most broadly, by D.50.17.2 (Ulpian): "Women are debarred from all civil and public functions and therefore cannot be judges or hold a magistracy or bring a lawsuit or intervene on behalf of anyone else or act as procurators." By D.16.1.1 it is reiterated that women, like children, cannot perform any civil functions (*civilia officia*), they cannot undertake obligations, and by D.16.2.5 women are prohibited from acting as anyone's *defensor,* concluding that "a woman is not allowed to act in defence either of her husband, her son or her father." The doctrinal logic underlying these and other incapacities stems from the obverse of women's inferior condition, namely the *potestas* or power of men. All authority in the family, including in early Roman law the power of life and death over the children (*ius vitae necisque*), lay with the male head of the family, the *paterfamilias.* The woman was thus either under the power of her own family or, after marriage *cum manu,* would become the daughter of her husband (*filiae loco*). Finally, if an adult woman became independent on the death of her father or husband, she was forced into tutelage, into having a tutor assigned.[23] By D.1.9.8 (Ulpian) husbands confered their dignity or status on their wives, while by the *Institutes* 1.1.11.10, "Women cannot adopt. They do not hold family authority even over their real children."

The positioning of women in permanent guardianship reflects an astringent scholastic view of feminine capability. Sex and disability (*sexum et casum*) are cognate with femininity, and it is reiterated throughout the law that women cannot perform the functions of men.[24] As to the logic underlying these restraints in Roman law, the texts give certain definite indications. The law *De Postulando* (D.3.1.5), which debars women from making applications to the magistracy, is stated to date back to "a shameless woman [*improbissima femina*] Carfania who by brazenly making applications and annoying the magistrature gave rise to the edict." Elsewhere, in D.16.2.2 women were said to be prone to seduction and to deceiving as well as being deceived. Their sex was characterized by weakness (*imbecillitas*), by vulnerability (*infirmitas*), cunning (*calliditas*), and deception. Other

---

phant: Feminism in French Literature 1610–1652 (Oxford, Clarendon Press, 1977). Most recently, see Yan Thomas, "The Division of the Sexes in Roman Law," in P. S. Pantel (ed.), *A History of Women in the West I* (Cambridge, Mass.: Harvard University Press, 1992).

23. See *Digest* 15.1.1.2-3 (Ulpian); D.23.3.24 (Pomponius); D.15.1.27 (Gaius).

24. See, for example, *Digest* 3.1.5 (*De Postulando*).

terms that recur are frivolity (*levitas*) and frailty (*fragilitas*). While such qualifications or adjectival additions are not properly law, they form part of the force and intention, the *vim et potestatem* or *veritas*, the *legis mentum*, of the primary texts of European legal development. By the time of the early Renaissance, these terms were forensic *topoi* or commonplaces to be expanded on the one hand by reference to divine law and on the other by returning to the earlier scholastic sources of the patristic tradition.

With the apocryphal exception of the daughter of Accursius, who is said by John Leslie to have "professed the Civil law openly,"[25] neither the glossatorial nor the postglossatorial tradition on the Continent offered much by way of reform of the position of women. The strongly antifeminist arguments of Jean Bodin's *De Republica*[26] were influential in England and typical of humanist constitutional doctrine and of its later reception. His refutation of gynocracy proceeded in three stages. First, he argues that "a monarchy ought to descend unto the heirs male, considering that the rule and government of women is directly against the law of nature . . . which hath given unto man wisdom, strength, courage, and power, to command; and taken the same from women."[27] The law of God, and specifically Genesis 3, ordains that women should be subject to man both in "Kingdoms and Empires" and in "every particular man's house and family." Proceeding to repeat the prohibition of feminine office from the *Digest*, Bodin moves secondarily to outline a history of the ill effects of those immodest or unchaste women who from the time of the Emperor Heliogabulus to the Renaissance had forced a reluctant humanity to endure their governance. In an interesting digression, Bodin next elaborates the problems of succession engendered by feminine government. If the Queen marries, there is the very real danger of the state passing to a stranger; if she does not marry, then there are no heirs of the blood.[28] More broadly, Bodin reiterates that the duty of woman, according to the civil law and the law of nations, "wherein all lawyers and Divines agree," precludes that sovereign government should ever pass to a woman, who ought principally to devote herself to "reverence of her husband."[29] It was in short "absurd and inconvenient"[30] for women to govern, to which he adds finally that

25. John Leslie, *A Defence of the Honour of the Right Highe, Mightye and Noble Princesse Marie Queene of Scotlande and Dowager of France with a declaration as well of her right, title and interest to the succession of the Crowne of Englande, as that the regimente of women ys conformable to the lawe of God and nature* (London: E. Dicaeophile, 1569) at fol. 139 a.

26. Jean Bodin, *De Republica.*

27. Ibid. at 746.

28. Ibid. at 748–749.

29. Ibid. at 752.

30. Ibid. at 753.

France by lucky virtue of the "Law Salique cuts the mother short and expressly forbids that a woman should by any means succeed into any fee."[31]

It would be possible to elaborate indefinitely the humanist views of the "effeminate and cowardly"[32] arguments that could be used to support female succession. Alciatus, in a dialogue in *De Notitia Dignitatem,* responds to the question "what is a woman (*quid est mulier*)?" by stating that she is a confused man, an insatiable beast, continual disquiet and unlimited disturbance.[33] Alciatus does argue elsewhere that women are not monsters,[34] but otherwise repeats the civilian definitions of feminine subordination, defining male and female sexes by mutual exclusion.[35] He does not, however, go to the extremes of later humanists such as Jacques Cujas who, more in the tradition of the *querelle des femmes* (the formulaic debate as to the place, social and natural status, education, and deportment of women) than that of law,[36] argues that women are not "properly speaking" human beings.[37] Such an argument is probably ironic and is certainly much refuted by his contemporaries, but it does serve to indicate the diverse sources and the range of disciplines to which law was prepared to resort in the topical and extensively debated issue of feminine right and female succession. Nor, finally, were civilian law, law of nature, and *ius gentium* or law of nations sufficient legal authority for an age of vernacular languages and reformed, or at least systematized, legal jurisdictions. The further legal source requiring elaboration is, precisely, local custom: in the case of France the Salic law, in the case of England a more confused and multinational inheritance.

Bodin's reference to Salic law is made in the context of a work that also

31. Ibid. at 753. The law states: "*De terra vero sallica nullo portio haereditatis mulieri veniat; sed ad virilem sexum tota terra haereditas perveneat*" (no portion of the land of France shall be inherited by a woman; but all the inheritance of the land shall come unto the male sex).

32. Ibid. at 754.

33. Alciatus, *De Notitia Dignitatem* at 190.

34. A. Alciatus, *De Verborum Significatione libri quatuor* (Luguduni: Gryphius, 1530 ed.) at 113, col. 1.

35. Alciatus, *De Verborum* at 105, col. 1.

36. One element in the *querelle* was traditionally the argument that women were not wholly human, and the question "is woman a human being?" was the subject of the anonymous treatise *Disputatio nova contra Mulieres qua probatur eas hominas non esse (A New Disputation against Women which proves that they are not human beings)* (Hague: Burchornius, 1595, 1641 ed.). For a succinct introduction to the *querelle* see Baldesar Castiglione, *The Book of the Courtier* (Harmondsworth: Penguin, 1527, 1967 ed.), bk. III; see also Joan Kelly, "Early Feminist Theory and the Querelle des Femmes," in *Women, History, and Theory: The Essays of Joan Kelly* (Chicago: Chicago University Press, 1984); Constance Jordan, *Renaissance Feminism: Literary Texts and Political Models* (Ithaca: Cornell University Press, 1990), chs. 1 and 2.

37. "Foemina item non est proprie homo," Jacques Cujas, *Opera Omnia* (Lyons: n.p., 1567, 1606 ed.) at 34–35.

states that English common law is simply a borrowing from French local law. François Hotman in his influential *Franco-Gallia* also asserts the primary role of the Salic exclusion of women but interestingly adds a reference to Tacitus to the effect that in Britain there was "no distinction of sexes in Government."[38] Hotman's general conclusion with regard to the state of French law stemmed from the civil law disability of women which was referred to "their weakness of judgment." On the other hand Hotman was sufficiently competent a historian to recognize that history and comparative law provide numerous instances of feminine sovereignty. Specifically in relation to Francogallia he acknowledges that the "kingdom has in the past been administered by Queens, especially by widows and Queen mothers. . . . In disputatious argument this would argue against their right in that this is accidental and not of their own right."[39] He also remarks that feminine rule has in the past been the occasion of "wonderful tragedies."[40] In terms that would sound well in the language of common lawyers, Antoine Hotman authored a treatise on the subject, *Traité de la loy Salique,* which argued that the exclusion of women in France depended upon antique custom, upon unwritten law, upon antiquity of the greatest weight and authority, "as being of uncertain origin, more august and venerable for being collected out of inviolably guarded and uninterrupted usage."[41] The exclusion could not be proved but could only be referred by conjecture to "the most ancient memory . . . *et sunt haec arcana imperii* [and these are the mysteries of government] which we would better reverence rather than research."[42] It remained to be argued that this immemorial French custom was of such age and validity as to be best considered as a part of nature "honouring France above all other nations in the world."[43]

In ecclesiastical, civil, and local law, the ambiguous place of women as the vehicles of biological and cultural transmission whose sex nevertheless overwhelmingly excluded them *de iure* from participation in political office, institutional function, or real property right, was evidently a significant issue. It was recognized that all human beings passed through the maternity and tutelage of the *gynaeceum* and yet, despite this crucial place and pedagogy of the feminine, civil law continued to deny it any direct association with the polity or public sphere. The Continental debate within legal doctrine indicates that women were a significant constitutional prob-

38. Hotman, *Franco-Gallia* at 115.

39. Ibid. at 126.

40. Ibid. at 127.

41. Hotman, *Traité de la Loy Salique* at 267.

42. Ibid. at 268. For a striking contrary view, see Marie de Gournay, *Égalité des hommes et des femmes* (1622), reprinted in E. Dezon-Jones (ed.), *Fragments d'un discours féminin* (Paris: Corti, 1988).

43. Ibid. at 269.

lem and simultaneously that lawyers could not ignore wider theological and literary debates as to the place of women. Within French literary culture the tradition of advocacy of feminine causes dated back to Christine de Pisan's *La Cité des femmes,* a *gynaetopia* descriptive of an imaginary city universally sheltering women. Written in 1404, *La Cité* was translated into English in 1521 and joined a wider postclassical tradition of defenses and laudatory works.[44] While the praise of illustrious women belonged to a classical literature stemming from Plutarch's *De Mulierum Virtutibus,* orators, educationalists, and ecclesiastics of the Renaissance and the Reformation saw the place, personality, and political role of women as a topic of immediate and threatening proportions. It was precisely because women were politically suspect and legally of uncertain status within the newly vernacularized jurisdictions across Europe that the *querelle des femmes* emerged in law. So too secular law emerged as an issue in theology and in literary discourse. Protestant bishops defended an English common law that was perceived to permit feminine succession, while Calvinist ecclesiastics argued for the application of Roman law to disable female sovereignty. Protestant theologians developed stringently antifeminist evidential rules for the prosecution of witches, an antiquarian lawyer methodized the history of sacrilege and collated its feminine origin in the sin of Eve,[45] while the first histories of the English constitution denounced the extravagance and the uncertainty of women and doubted the need for any legal reform of female status.[46]

The immediate common law background to the first treatise directly addressing women in law, John Fortescue's *De Natura Legis Naturae,*[47] is to be found in the various unsystematic rules relating to the diverse legal capacities and functions of women (*mulier*) in Glanvill, Bracton, and *Fleta.*[48] The source of the rules is fairly uniformly that of Roman law, and

44. Christine de Pisan, *The Boke of the Citye of Ladys* (London: H. Pepwell, 1521). This work is well discussed in Kelly, *Women, History and Theory,* ch. 3. Particularly influential in Britain were Juan Luis Vives, *De Institutione Foeminae Christianae,* translated as *A Very Fruteful and Pleasant Boke Called the Instruction of a Christen Woman* (London: H. Wykes, 1523, 1557 ed.); Henry Cornelius Agrippa, *De Nobilitate et Precellentia Foeminei Sexus,* translated as *Female Pre-eminence or the Dignity and Excellency of that Sex, above the Male* (London: Million, 1529, 1670 ed.). See also Sir Thomas Elyot, *The Defence of Good Women* (London: T. Berthelet, 1534, 1545 ed.).

45. Spelman, *The History and Fate of Sacrilege* at 2–3.

46. See particularly Harrison, *An Historicall Description.* See also Smith, *De Republica Anglorum*; Camden, *Britannia.*

47. Fortescue, *De Natura.*

48. D. G. Hall (ed.), *Tractatus de Legibus et Consuetudinibus Regni Angliae qui Glanvilla Vocatur* (London: Nelson, 1187–89, 1965 ed.); S. Thorne (ed.), *Bracton on the Laws and customs of England* (Cambridge, Mass.: Harvard University Press, 1968); H. G. Richardson and G. O. Sayle (eds.), *Fleta* (London: Selden Society, 1955).

the variations occasioned by medieval forms of homage, lordship, and kingship are consonant with the underlying structure of civil law. Thus Glanvill states the law of English inheritance as being that "if anyone has a son and heir and also a daughter or daughters, the son succeeds to everything . . . the general rule [being] that a woman [*mulier*] never shares in an inheritance with a man."[49] The most significant legal status of women is of course marriage, and Glanvill states that "legally a woman is completely in the power of her husband" (*mulier plene in potestate viri*), a civilian rule that is elaborated in terms of the complete loss of the wife's power over any property, including present or future dower, with the sole partial exception of an inheritance acquired prior to marriage. All her property is otherwise deemed to be at the disposal of her husband, for him "to give, alienate or sell in whatever way he pleases . . . and his wife is bound to consent to this as to all other acts of his which do not offend against God."[50] Glanvill further adopts Roman law in asserting that a married woman cannot make a will without her husband's consent,[51] and subsequently, under the title *de iure mulierem heredum,* states that if a woman or women are left as heirs of anyone, they stay in ward of their lords and "even if they are of full age . . . they remain in ward [*in custodia dominorum*] until they are married on the Lord's advice and direction."[52]

In Bracton the first classification of persons, following Gaius, is between slave and free.[53] The second division of persons is between male, female, and hermaphrodite, to which it is added that "women [*feminae*] differ in many respects from men [*masculis*], for their position is inferior [*detior*] to that of men."[54] Bracton is dependent upon Roman law in his depiction of women and is even more direct in asserting the inferiority of their status. Women are not simply in the *potestas* of others, in the wardship or tutelage of Lords, "some are under the rod [*sub virga*], as wives."[55] In terms of property, Bracton coins an appropriately circular legal maxim, "everything that is the wife's is the husband's," for the traditional reason that the wife does not have *potestatem.*[56] While many of the more detailed rules relating to women, such as that pertaining to women married to men attainted of felony or outlawed, have a local character,[57] the more general and exhaus-

49. Glanvill, *De Legibus* at 77.
50. Ibid. at 59.
51. Ibid. at 80.
52. Ibid. at 85.
53. F. de Zulueta (ed.), *The Institutes of Gaius, Part I* (Oxford: Clarendon Press, 1946) at 5, "quod omnes homines aut liberi sunt aut servi."
54. Bracton, *De Legibus* at vol. II, 31.
55. Bracton, *De Legibus* at vol. 2, 36.
56. Ibid. at vol. 2, 105.
57. Ibid. at vol. 2, 367; vol. 3, 360.

tive account of marital status and the incapacities that result from the woman's loss of will, remain and are acknowledged as civilian. So too Bracton recognizes certain of the forms of protection that the civil law offers women. Gifts made to concubines (*concubinae*) are to be recognized as valid, and a concubine may enfeoff her children. Gifts between husband and wife are invalid for fear of duress or beguilement or improper cause (*alias causas*) such as lust.[58] Nor may the husband commit fraud against "the constitution of dower" by making gifts to strangers with a view to the stranger transferring the property to the wife during the husband's lifetime or after his death.[59] Although the common law developed from the civil, it was not always politic to recollect that descent, and in consequence the status of women in municipal law, could at least on occasion be argued.[60] The legal context of Fortescue's *De Natura Legis Naturae,* the earliest text to be encountered in the common law *querrelle des femmes,* is undoubtedly that of Roman law and of Continental custom. For all Fortescue's concern in *De Laudibus Legum Angliae* or in *Governance of England* to assert the historical priority and the national distinction of common law, both the method and the substantive content of those treatises are drawn closely from the European law.[61] The context of the discussion is the law of succession and it is largely governed by civil and ecclesiastical rules.[62]

OF FATE, FORTUNE, JUSTICE, AND OTHER ILLUSTRIOUS WOMEN

In the context of a legal structure so markedly geared to institution of a male image and succession and so also to the restraint of female right, it seems remarkable that there was space at all for the assertion of contrary

58. Ibid. at vol. 2, 98–99. Mary Astell, *Some Reflections upon Marriage Occasioned by the Duke and Duchess of Mazarine's Case* (London: J. Nutt, 1700) at 38–39, interestingly picks up on this rule and remarks that "covenants between husband and wife, like laws in an arbitrary government, are of little force, the will of the sovereign is all in all."

59. Ibid. at vol. 2, 54–55.

60. Fortescue, *De Laudibus Legum Angliae* at chs. 39–45, provides the most considered account of differences between common law and civil law, particularly with regard to legitimacy and guardianship. For later discussion see St. German, *Doctor and Student.*

61. For recent discussions of Roman influence see F. de Zulueta and P. Stein, *The Teaching of Roman Law in England around 1200* (London: Selden Society, 1990); Kelley, *The Human Measure*; Goodrich, "Poor Illiterate Reason." The classic study is still Selden, *Ad Fletam Dissertatio.*

62. For an extensive discussion, see Henry Swinburne, *A Brief Treatise of Testaments and Last Wills, very profitable to be understood of all the Subjects of the Realme of England* (London: Society of Stationers, 1590, 1711 ed.) at fol. B i b, depicting "as in a glass those Civill and Ecclesiasticall lawes testementary now in force, and to be observed and executed in the Ecclesiasticall Courts within this realm of England." See also John Godolphin, *The Orphan's Legacy or A Testementary Abridgement in three Parts* (London: C. Wilkinson, 1677).

argument. Deprived of access to public office and defined most usually by the "civil death" (*civiliter mortua*) of marriage, namely by the loss of will that accompanied the transfer of the daughter to the husband, the representation of feminine right was necessarily a polemical activity and closer in style to myth than to constitutional doctrine. The specific question debated in the two books of *De Natura Legis Naturae* is that of succession in supreme kingdoms: "A King, acknowledging no superior in things temporal, has a daughter and a brother. The King dies without sons. The question is whether the Kingdom . . . descends to the daughter, the daughter's son, or the brother."[63] A variety of answers are available to this question. By some local English law it was possible that the daughter inherit, the law of gavelkind allowing succession to sons and daughters equally.[64] By Roman law the inheritance would pass by the male line to the king's brother, whereas in ecclesiastical law the same would hold with even more stringent prohibitions upon the possibility of feminine office. The issue raised in legal terms by the question of feminine succession is not simply that of whether women can hold office as a matter of indigenous law. It is a broader ontological question of transmission and so of the status, of the being of women. The question of what the mother can transfer (*transfundo*), carry across (*transduco*), or transmit is not only a question of the relation of mother to son, but also of the place of reproduction and so of women within the institution.[65] It is this question of the being of women that must be canvassed first in terms of the relevant applicable law and second in terms of the appropriate or most just interpretation of such law.

What is surprising about Fortescue's *De Natura* is that it devotes an entire treatise of two books to the question of woman and specifically her right to succession. Taking the form of a dialogue and latterly in the second book of a mock trial, the issue initially is that of *quid iuris,* of what law is to govern the debate. The resolution to this question is more complex than is immediately apparent. All vernacular law claims antique or immemorial status, as also it claims the benefaction of divine decree. Thus Antoine Hotman depicted the vernacular Salic law as customary practice so old as to be the uncorrupted law of nature expressive of a pristine sacred will: "We can say that this rule is a chief work of nature with which she wished to honour France above all other nations of the world. . . . France has this advantage, that of never having loosened the natural order

63. Fortescue, *De Natura* at 192.

64. This issue is debated at some length in Thomas Wood, *Some Thoughts Concerning the Study of the Laws of England* (London: J. Stagg, 1727 ed.). For details, see Sir Edward Coke, *The First Part of the Institutes of the Laws of England, or, A Commentary on Littleton, not the name of a lawyer only, but of the law itself* (London: I. More, 1629).

65. Fortescue, *De Natura* at 261–262. For commentary on this issue of transmission, see Legendre, *L'Inestimable objet de la transmission* at 38–43.

of their Realm."[66] Similarly, Fortescue depicts English custom as prior to and necessarily consonant with the divine law as well as the law of nature and nations. The question of which legal forum and which law is to decide the issue of feminine sovereignty raises questions of theology, nature, and positive law, of written and unwritten prescription, of regal and political dominion. A series of laws are traced to an origin, sacred pinnacle, or *hieros*: "Thus also have we proved that the rules of the political law, and the sanctions of customs and constitutions ought to be made null and void, so often as they depart from the institutes of nature's laws. . . . This law of nature sprang from God alone, is subject to his law alone, and under him and with him, governs the whole world."[67]

No one law can resolve an issue as fundamental as that of the constitution and being of women, but rather one law must be folded into another according to the sacred hierarchy of normative orders: "For the Civil Laws say that the offspring is a portion of the mother's entrails [*portio est viscerum muteruarum*]."[68] Despite this certainty of maternity, this ineradicable origin and visceral transmission, the mother is not the image of the child, nor is her order that of succession—it is simply that of facilitation of the paternal line. The offspring refers not to corporal progeny but to that metaphor which in the annunciation established Christ as Son of the Father by means of the Holy Ghost. Such pure transmission establishes the principle of relationship between the various laws. The figure of maternity or generation can at best refer only to a certain plurality which lawyers would from time to time confirm in defining the term *polity* as being derived from *policia*, "so called from plurality,"[69] from its many jurisdictions, its several laws, and its dual body in the political and regal dominions of the realm.[70] This plurality—this fluidity or contingency—of polities is potentially subversive of the hierarchy of laws, and this subversion is in a sense unconsciously figured in Fortescue's text in his use of metaphors of feminine succession and of feminine historical and philosophical office in the course of his lengthy depiction of the order of laws.

The order of law begins with man's abandonment of original justice (*iustitia originalis*) and state of grace. This means that the origin or originary law is unknowable: its past presence cannot any longer be recollected, it cannot be other than the immemorial and inconstant representation, *simulacrum* or *vestigium* of a prelapsarian state. It is termed divine providence

66. Hotman, *La Loy Salique* at 268–269.

67. Fortescue, *De Natura* at 221.

68. Fortescue, *De Natura* at 240.

69. Ibid. at 212.

70. Ibid. 205–211 on the distinction between "dominium regale et dominium politicum." For further discussion see Kantorowicz, *The King's Two Bodies*; Legendre, *Le Désir politique de Dieu.*

(*Divinum providentiam*), fate, law or will, and it is the mother of natural law: "Law of nature is daughter of Divine Law."[71] This Christian *amor matris,* or love of an ineffable mother, of incertitude as the feminine source of the descent of all law, is expressed more directly in the figure of justice herself. The maternal line that runs from Divine law to natural law, the feminine thread upon which both laws precariously hang, is justice depicted first as truth: "The truth of justice [*iustitiae veritas*], which is capable of being revealed by right reason" is the law of Nature. Secondly, however, the truth of justice is termed Phronesis "and is comely of face and lovely of aspect [*decora est facie et venusta aspectu*]."[72] The feminine face or decor of justice is no accident.[73] In one genealogy of the iconography of justice, the fates are daughters of the Parcae who are in turn the daughters of necessity. Dike is similarly a feminine God.[74] Fortescue provides a literal expression of this iconography or imagery in indicating at the beginning of the second book that "justice is also a judge [*iudex quoque justitia est*]," she who assigns to everyone her right, for a judge is so named from pronouncing judgment "and she pronounces judgment, since, as the laws say generally, judgment is given by her; she is indeed herself the judge of all human actions."[75]

One possible and essentially modern interpretation of Fortescue's use of feminine imagery is simply to deny that it has any political or legal significance: it is, like rhetoric and like art or plastic representation—like woman—merely decorative, ornamental, accessory, or accidental. The femininity of justice is simply its materiality, its contingency, and not its essence: it is as it is represented for the reason that its representation is merely an image, no more than a reminder or ephemeral sign of its cause. Surprisingly, Fortescue argues directly to this effect: "Nor is it any obstacle to her power that women are by law excluded from the judicial office; for although the word justice be of the feminine gender, she herself is not a woman nor of the female sex; for sex hath no place in virtues any more than in spirits."[76] While this statement might appear to deny the expres-

71. Fortescue, *De Natura* at 239.

72. Ibid. at 224.

73. Maclean, *Woman Triumphant,* ch. 7. See also D. Curtis and J. Resnik, "Images of Justice" (1986) 96 *Yale Law Journal* 1727.

74. See Thomas Heywood, *Tunaikeion or Nine Bookes of Various History concerninge Women* (London: Adam Islip, 1624) at 27; for an interesting depiction of the imagery of justice, see also John Selden, *De Diis Syris Syntagmata II* (Lipsiae: L. S. Corneri, 1617, 1672 ed.). For a theoretical discussion, see Peter Goodrich, "Fate as Seduction: The Other Scene of Legal Judgment," in Alan Norrie (ed.), *Closure and Critique in Contemporary Legal Theory* (Edinburgh: Edinburgh University Press, 1993).

75. Fortescue, *De Natura* at 249.

76. Ibid. at 250. (nam licet nomen *justicia* generis sit femini . . . ipsa non est femina neque sexus feminini).

sion of any feminine cause or sentiment in the actual representation of judgment, it is nonetheless the case that the femininity of the image, of the material, the present and the person of positive law and of its insular forms (*insulares sunt*), does at least institute certain anomalies and suggest separate orders and genders of the common law. Like Janus, the common law has at least two faces. Like the widow's memory of her husband depicted in the *Ladies Calling*, legal retrospection multiplies the images of the past.[77]

The civil law dictates that the law (*ius*) takes its name from justice (*iustitia*). This derivation of the name of law instructs the lawyer through a grammatical method which "makes known to us some natures both of laws and other virtues by force of etymologies."[78] That *ius* takes its name from *Justitia* obliges Fortescue to conjecture that "from the same it hath derived the origin of its generation, and is thus entitled to be distinguished by the name of its parent . . . but as the lustre from the light, the heat from the fire, the gushing stream from its spring, so doth the law of nature come from justice . . . justice begets law."[79] The generation of natural law, of "Dame Nature" as source of law, involves a complex principle of inner lineage or *harmartia*, a principle of ruin or of relics. The femininity of justice is not only the representation of a material and so contingent form of judgment, justice is memory as reminiscence and as legitimacy, the memory of generation, of maternity, of the certitude of the only begetting to the only begotten. Justice survives in the temporal law by means of vestiges and similitudes (*vestigiis et similitudinibus*). Justice is a temporal yet internal image (*ymaginem*) which triggers recollection of who we are by virtue of reminding us whence we came. The femininity of justice is the cunning of memory as reminiscence, as the mirror of the plurality of experience; it is the reason of likeness, the ultimate law which Fortescue admits can never produce a true image or pure visibility for "although in the footprints and similitudes [*vestigiis et similitudinibus*] of creatures there be no true likenesses whereby the creature may be truly assimilated to its Creator, no more than the shadow to the body, the footprint to the foot, or the image to the real thing, yet in all things some likeness is discovered to their creators."[80] The paradox that confronts the common law—"our Lady the common law"—is thus resident in the dual nature of the image and the two faces of justice. The image is both memory and the recollection or relic (footprint) of divine reason. It is the deceptive form of experience, the fragile symptom or sign of accident, and yet it is also the vehicle or

77. Allestree, *The Ladies Calling* at 68–69.
78. Fortescue, *De Natura* at 231, citing Isidore of Seville.
79. Ibid. at 232.
80. Ibid. at 233–234.

bearer of essence, it is the footprint of God (*Dei vestigia*) and so too the only surviving sign of the generation of law. And justice itself is paradoxically a woman. It is not a woman in terms of Christian or natural law essence, because neither spirit nor soul have a sex—the truth is precisely the proper form of the incorporeal. Justice is like a woman because even the law has a body and it is in bodies that sex exists (*in corporibus est sexum*). It is feminine because if it is a question of the application of law, a question of experience and judgment, of likenesses and their material inscriptions, then justice requires that the law acknowledge the ethical and contingent logic, the fluidity, of the event. Fortescue admits such contingency as one face of the common law but denies that such feminine attributes are ever anything other than secondary to the speculative logic of law. He admits the figure of woman as an accident in the development of common law and as a symbol that purveys a likeness of law but not its essence, which is God. To adopt even a very simplified psychoanalytic reading of Fortescue's denial of the significance of the female form of justice, it would have to be said that the denial, or more properly the negation, precisely confirms that the plural figure of woman is inseparable from that of law.

The second book of *De Natura* introduces the *querelle des femmes* into common law. The king's daughter may lose her plea comprehensively, she may indeed be silenced by the time of final pleadings, she may receive only roughly one twentieth of the space of argument, and yet the very fact of her pleading the feminine cause signals an important advance in the theory and constitutional practice of common law, both in its sources and in its method. The first law is divine will, and the daughter thus begins by citing divine law, the decision of the Lord with respect to the daughters of Zelophehad. The daughters of Zelophehad came to Moses after their father had died without male issue. They asked "why should the name of our father be done away from among his family, because he hath no son?"[81] Moses brought their cause before the Lord, who determined that "thou shalt cause the inheritance of their father to pass unto them. And thou shalt speak unto the children of Israel, saying, If a man die, and have no son, then ye shall cause his inheritance to pass unto his daughter."[82] While questions of succession are decided *iure divino,* the biblical decision as a precedent would appear to be directly binding only upon the children of Israel. The general principle promulgated is challenged by the other litigants in the much lengthier and more extravagant terms of the theological, natural, and civil status of women.

The first rebuttal of the daughter's argument comes from the grand-

81. Numbers 27.4–5.
82. Ibid. at 7–9.

son, who makes his plea by way of arguments from nature and civil law. The king's brother enters scholastic arguments as to the place and nature of women but also adds specific arguments from English common law. The general tenor of argument is unremarkable: the law should distinguish the right of succession to kingdoms from the right of succession to private estates. Nature subjects the female sex (*muliebri sexui*) to the male in both social and domestic circumstance while the civil law reflects this subjection by excluding women from public office and most particularly that of king. The sources and the content of the argument against women range far wider than is legally necessary: old testament history, Aristotle, St. Thomas Aquinas, the *Decretals,* civil law, and common law are all marshalled against the transmission of office to a woman by right of her parents (*iure parentum*). More than that, the *querelle* is invoked to specify with unnecessary or at least nonprobative detail female characteristics of simplicity (*simplicitas*), subservience (*adjutorium*), physical inferiority, lesser virtue, deformity (*mas occasionatus*), irrationality, slenderness of understanding (*tenuitate intellectus*), lack of heat, deficiency of construction, heedlessness, timidity, fear of death, and the proclivity to domesticity (*yconomia*).[83] The range of argument is adduced simply to indicate the uncertainty of the issue, on which common law has little to add save certain incidental rules of property law. A grant of land to a man and the male issue of his body reverts to the donor if that man dies without male issue. As this would appear to be implicit in the specific terms of the gift, it says little.[84] Together with a similar example of inheritance *per formam doni,* in respect of an entailed gift (*donum talliatum*), the vagaries of Anglo-Norman property law are said to indicate "the certainty of the law in these matters . . . so that in the sentences (*sententiis*) of judges that certainty is very constantly made known."[85]

The range and extremity of the argument against women forces the king's daughter to take up and contradict certain of the themes of her antagonists. The issue becomes straightforwardly historical and political. If inferior strength or courage precluded women (*foeminae*) from government, it would similarly exclude the young, the old, and the infirm. If the strongest should rule, one could add that the supreme authority might as well be given to an ox, a horse, or a gorilla. "A woman [*femina*] is capable of acting well in the regal state and dignity" nor does royal office "require the King to fight battles or give judicial sentences, in person."[86] The regency is a symbolic as well as a practical political office and can be exercised wisely by women. To prove such an assertion the daughter resorts to

83. Ibid. at 251–259.
84. Coke, *On Littleton* at I. c 2, s 24, affirms this rule.
85. Fortescue, *De Natura* at 261.
86. Ibid. at 266–267.

the history of noble women (*mulierum nobilium*) who governed wisely "with vigour and great justice" and of whom the daughter states "assuredly this parchment [*membrana*] would not suffice to contain the names, were they recorded." She lists Deborah of Israel, Tomyris of the Massagetae, "and who hath ever subjugated with the sword more strenuously than Semiramis. . . . Doth not the kingdom of the Amazons also, which is always ruled by women [*feminis*] defend itself against all the lords of the world?"[87] In terms of Anglican doctrine, such histories have the status of precedent if not immediately of immemorial law. Such precedents have to be confronted if not necessarily confuted inasmuch as it was enough to provide evidence of an older—and so more natural and more indigenous—law: "Did the law which permitted so many women to reign ever exclude me therefrom?"[88]

The replications and the duplications conform, in detail and in range of argument, to the broader *querelle des femmes*. What is exceptional is the scope of legal sources drawn upon to substantiate the disassociation of the feminine imagery and grammatical gender of nature, justice, virtue, and law from the dignity or civil office of women. Standard arguments from the name (*virago* is a diminutive of *vir*), from creation (man was created first), from original sin (Eve was first tempted), and divine judgment (God sentenced Eve to bring forth children in sorrow and to be in the power of her husband) are all adduced to support the morality of both laws, civil and canon, in relation to women. The only further point that bears brief description is that from the notion of "*ymago Dei*." It is man who is made in the image of God and after his likeness, for the Bible states, "*faciamus hominem ad ymaginem et similitudinem nostram.*" The canon law[89] reiterates that woman was not made in the image of God and adds that "the woman veils her head, because she is not the image of God." It would be against fate (*Divinae Providentiae*), against the nature of things (*nec de natura rerum*) and contrary to "the principle of Being" (*non esse de ratione entis*)[90] to grant women the right of succession. Both laws encapsulate and formulate as rules the previously existing and divinely ordained disability of women.

The duplication of the daughter reverses the assumptions of the replications. It is the form of the *querelle* to contradict in polemical fashion and the daughter does not disappoint. Suffice it to relate that her argument hinges on a history or antiquity that is older than that presented by the male litigants. If divine judgment punished feminine sin by subordinating

87. Ibid. at 267.

88. Ibid. at 268. On the status of antiquity as law, see, most famously, Coke, *Reports*, vol. ii, pt. iii, sig. B 5 a. For a superb analysis, see Favour, *Antiquitie Triumphing over Noveltie.*

89. *Causa* 33, Quaest. 5. cap. *Haec Imago.*

90. Fortescue, *De Natura* at 287.

women to their husbands, then logically and historically women were originally—and so by nature and inclination—free of subordination. In the law of nature the male argument is void: subjugation was a penalty and not a property of feminine being. Secondly, subordination was the sentence of married women only (*solam conjugatam*). It would be profane and against all principles of penal law to extend the punishment to unmarried women (*mulieres solutas*).[91] Yet there was never any question but that the judge in *De Natura,* Fortescue, Lord Chief Justice and subsequently Lord Chancellor, would affirm Bracton and the civil law. However old and however English the customs that Fortescue lauds in his other works, it transpires that it is only the method of analogical argument from particulars and the stress upon the development of law "by hearing"[92] that is distinctively indigenous.

The judgment itself is taken directly from patristic texts, specifically from Augustine's *Civitate Dei,* and asserts an ordained or providential order of being in which the original disposition of priorities or prelacies favored the male and subordinated the female sex (*femininum sexum*). The woman ought to be subject to the man, "as the flesh to the spirit. . . . The pre-eminence of the man over the woman seems to be [comparable] to the pre-eminence of the reasoning faculties over sensual appetites, or of the soul over the body."[93] Neither history nor counterexample nor evidence of feminine virtue could in any way transmute or by length of time prescribe a woman's right to office. The inferiority of women within the hierarchy of "proper nature" was a facet of the originary, of the state of innocence, and so an incontestable law of nature coincident with the spirit that preceded the generation of the sexes. And there the judgment stands: concerned in essence with the law governing the transmission of secular power, concerned with the difference between those that have *dignitas* and those that are *indigni* (unworthy of succession). So as to establish the legitimate order through which power is passed, the judgment itself becomes a precedent, an inheritance, a thing transmitted. Here, for Fortescue and the other *sacerdotes* of the Inns of Court, is the common law found and declared. It is in both senses of the term a male will or masculine testament, it is both handed down and sent on. What is established as a principle of being or asserted as providence or fate, as *imago,* is not amenable to change any more than could immemorial custom, practice time out of mind, or any other of the "rubbish of antiquity" fall either by reason or by desuetude from the common law.

91. Ibid. at 300–302.

92. Ibid. at 330.

93. Ibid. at 326.

YCONOMIA AND DOMESTIC SUBJECTION

The importance of Fortescue's depiction of the exclusion of women from inheritance of political office (*dignitas*) or sovereign succession lies not so much in the mooted point concerning feminine sovereignty but rather in the exemplary status of the arguments and the implications of this reason or legal *ratio* for both public law and private life. Public law instituted a reason, a mode of thought, a rhetoric that was also the limit or definition of subjectivity. That subjectivity, or one might say personality, was evidently iconic, it dealt with real images and real men, but although it recognized two sexes, it relayed only one form of personality, one gender, a singular mask. In discussing semblance and likeness, Fortescue follows the second Council of Nicea in defining the real image as a vestige of divinity or trace of its source. Semblance was an attribute of the prototype, it was a relative feature of the icon, of the visible marking of presence and most archetypically of the acheiropoietic sign. The *imago,* then, belongs to one order and represents one source, it produces a singular testimony of reason, one lineage and one law. Fortescue's treatise, for all that it equivocates as to the imagery of governance, does not hesitate to announce that "justice and law of nature are proved to be of one substance . . . of one quality and nature, and therefore *one*. . . . We are most surely instructed that the law of nature was created in one and the instant together with man; whence we are compelled to say that law and man are coeval, as were the first man, his reason, his will and his memory."[94] Not only is there only one law, but it is a law coincident with man, with the first man in the image of the father, with a reason and presence that was lost in the fall, with a father both absent and present in the image or in human form: "I am in the Father, and the Father is in me [*Ego in Patre et Pater in me est*]."[95]

In the genealogy of laws it is justice that is the law of nature, according to Fortescue's first treatise, it is an originary form from which man withdrew through sin or figuratively through feminine deceit. Justice was presence, the presence of God, the law of nature which assigns to each man his right (*jus*).[96] "The first man abandoned her . . . yet justice . . . which as the print of his footsteps we have likened to God, we speak of as absent from us, so often as we withdraw ourselves from her laws; and yet she herself does never desert us . . . and thus is ever present with us, punishing, directing, rewarding according as our deserts require," to which it is added slightly later "what does it take from the nature of chastity that

94. Ibid. at 234.

95. Fortescue, *De Natura* at 233.

96. That such is both justice and the impossibility of justice is a theme that is lengthily traveled in Derrida, "Force of Law."

chastity once spoiled is not virgin chastity?"[97] Order and law, in other words, can be continuously redeemed through the emulation or invocation of an ordained governance of the world (*mundi prelatia*), an origin and presence on the inside of things, known through inner sense or the vision of "downcast eyes." More than that, however, the hierarchy or enfolding of laws is not simply a question of an epistemic order, a way of knowing the cause or reason of civility and flesh, it is also an ontology, it institutes an order of being, it fabricates, it makes the soul.

Law stands on the boundary between knowing and being. Law—both in its spiritual and temporal uses, its psychoanalytic and positive forms—marks the hinge, the breakage, between inside and outside, power and truth. Law passes between exterior and interior, it is the hinge upon which the subject swings. In Roman terms it was the image or mask, for Kafka it was the gate, in Lacanian terms it is the swinging door—all metaphors of passage and thresholds, of Janus, and of the folding of one order into another. Law screens and mirrors, it appears outside but goes inside, it is text but it is also flesh, it institutes the subject. It enfolds the object in the subject, one law on the other, in a Baroque succession. One could go further, law is the productivity of the institution, it is the principle of reproduction within the institution:

> The problem is not how to finish a fold, but how to continue it, to have it go through the ceiling, how to bring it to infinity . . . the infinite fold separates or moves between matter and soul, the facade and the closed room, the outside and the inside. Because it is a virtuality that never stops dividing itself the line of inflection is actualized in the soul but realized in matter, each on its own side. Such is the Baroque trait: an exterior always on the outside, an interior always on the inside.[98]

Here, however, the argument exceeds itself for the Baroque teaches the subject to play the law whereas the profession teaches only the lawyer, the *imago,* to dare to embody such a fearful fluidity: "To fear God [*timere Deum*] is the effect of the law, which a man cannot attain to, unless he first know the will of God as it is written in the law. . . . This fear is as a son's for his father . . . this fear is promoted by the laws."[99] Fear is here predicated upon the principle of paternity, of a law that is of the Father and in the Son, a law more fearful for being inscribed twice, within and without; as

97. Fortescue, *De Natura* at 235.

98. On enfolding, see Gilles Deleuze, *The Fold: Liebniz and the Baroque* (Minneapolis: University of Minnesota Press, 1993) at 34–35. There is also the lengthy literary analysis of J. A. Maravall, *Culture of the Baroque: Analysis of a Historical Structure* (Minneapolis: Minnesota University Press, 1986). In specifically legal terms see Hachamovitch, "In Emulation of the Clouds."

99. Fortescue, *De Laudibus Legum Angliae* at 3.

conscience and as commandment it enfolds the law in the subject, it captures legal subjectivity. That capture is also termed fate, an alien or ancestral will, a place or *topos.* It is in terms of such an exteriority signaled within that law is to be understood as passage, communication, or transmission of one law on the other or, more graphically, as sacrifice or motion between realms that are simultaneously coupled and closed.

Fortescue, to use his example a final time, offers a remarkable metaphor of the relation of interior and exterior laws in depicting the basis of succession, of office and of land, from father to son in terms of an exchange between property and subject and by attenuation between text and law. The first cause of property is to supplement a lack, to compensate a loss: property is that minor fate which comes (as inheritance or succession) from the father as "efficient cause," as blood. Property

> ensues as a compensation for the sweat by which the body of the acquirer is enfeebled, the reason of the law [*legis naturae ratio*] has united it to its acquirer, so that the property gained might compensate the damage resulting from his loss of bodily wholeness [*integritatis*]: and thus property takes the place of the man's bodily integrity, which he has lost, and coheres as an accident to the toiler, and thenceforth accompanies his blood. . . . This is the source of descent and succession . . . property annexed itself to man [*homini conjunxit*] . . . and descends from man to man by succession, it infuses itself into each succeeding heir.[100]

The law, obligation or *iuris vinculum,* is a chain, a continuous link between father and son, an infusion of one in the other, of cause and effect. Yet to infuse is not only to permeate or know. Infusion is fluid and porous, it is to go within, to mix, to transmit. The principle of such transmission, the exchange of fluid, of sweat and of sperm, passes on not only according to an exterior principle but also by virtue of internal attributes, by reason, by nature and law.

There is no absolute interiority, there is no closure, there are simply processes, relations, motions—words and things. The moment of exchange, of fluidity or mixture between text and subject, body and environment or, most obviously, between public and private, is the moment of law. It is such because the exchange is not only a sign of mobility but also of reproduction, of inheritance and succession, of one law on the next. And the obverse of this law, its other side in doctrine, in the speech or dream of the institution, is a private exchange, "the first society . . . seminary or schoole, wherein are taught and learned the principles of authoritie [is] . . . oeconomical subjection."[101] Where Fortescue determined the pub-

100. Fortescue, *De Natura* at 291–292.

101. William Perkins, *Christian Oeconomie: Or a Short Survey of the Right Manner of Erecting and Ordering a Family, according to the Scripture* (Cambridge: Legge, 1609, 1618 ed.), Epistle.

lic incapacity of the woman in terms of a number of attributes drawn from theology and civil law, he borrowed also from a model of domestic exchange, of a curious interior government which was spelled out at great length not only in public law but in the ecclesiastical laws and treatises of domestic governance. Where lawyers such as Fortescue and, later, Thomas Smith borrowed from the other law to depict the unreal image, the feminine, as lacking in frame and reason, in heat and construction—in short, in masculinity, in reality—they speak to the institution of a being, to the constitution of femininity as a sign of deprivation, as an image of fear. At a superficial level, femininity is deficiency (*mas occasionatus*)[102] and according to the order of ownership spelled out above, woman is property, which is to say she is compensation for the loss or lack of bodily integrity that the male experiences in reproduction. There is something of the masculine in the feminine but other than that she is image: appearance but nothing more.

Woman, according to Thomas Smith's constitutional treatise, is "weake, fearefull, faire, curious of her bewtie and saving."[103] She is custodian of the "oikonomia," of the icon or image, of its reproduction and its circulation, but she is herself no more than an instrument of custody and transmission. She is defined by incapacity, by fluidity and fear. In that she is a member and not a head or *princeps,* she lacks essence and so should accept her own subjection to her principal without reason or question. Her subjection was spelled out doctrinally as both necessary, in that she was inferior in the order of being, and voluntary, in that she assumed internally a fear or "awful respect" of her father or husband.[104] Subjection is thus not merely a physical or external obedience, it is a duty of the soul "a convincement of the spirit in the woman" that requires humility both within and without, in speech and in actions for "subjection stands chiefly in the spirit of the wife, and nextly in her demeanour."[105] The woman should live in a certain fear and should express that internal negation through manifest and hidden signs. Where, for example, it is a question of chastity, then

---

Further examples of the genre include: John Dod and Robert Clever, *A Godlie Forme of Householde Government: For the Ordering of Private Families, according to the Direction of Gods Word* (London: Thomas Man, 1612); William Gouge, *Of Domesticall Duties Eight Treatises* (London: William Bladen, 1622); D. Rogers, *Matrimoniall Honour or the Mutual Crowne and Comfort of Godly, Loyall, and Chaste Marriage* (London: P. Nevil, 1642).

102. Usually translated as "mulcted male" or "deficient male," but is more accurately "one fallen from the male sex" or "without the force of the male"; see Fortescue, *De Natura* at 257; see also Alciatus, *De Notitia Dignitatem* at 195: "Quid est mulier? Hominis confusio, insaturabilis bestia, continua sollicitudo."

103. Smith, *De Republica Anglorum* at 12.

104. Gouge, *Of Domesticall Duties* at 274.

105. Rogers, *Matrimoniall Honour* at 259.

the injunction is that "they express the inward chastity of their minds; which chastity must be seated in the countenance as well as in the heart."[106] The world, in one description, is a snare, and the woman, as a member, or an element of the external world, also constantly threatens to trap or mislead or distract: "If the thoughts be impure, they will betray the body to the eye . . . and company of the unclean."[107] The law must constantly struggle to direct or avert the lure of the image or the betrayal of the eye. Beauty is no great pleasure but rather "a provocative to much evil" whereas "in the minde consist the true lineaments and properties of fairness, which entice and provoke spiritual and heavenly love."[108] In short, it is the concern of the law to control an internal femininity, to prevent passion and to restrict imagination through the denial of the value or worth of the surface, of the image or face of things, and also of any thought that follows a surface or dwells upon face, imagery, or appearance. To control the woman, to subject the femininity of thought through a prosaic law, was to determine as much as anything else what it was *not* to be a woman, to outline the positivity against which her nothingness could be if not measured at least demarcated. She was the site of disappearance, a pool, a mirror, a fascination in which reality (or masculinity) would be all too quickly lost.

The laws of the household and of its various forms of subjection can be interpreted not only as the mechanism of internal governance, of the application of law to being, but also and more rigorously as the specification of the laws of thought. To spell out in great detail the laws of "iconomic" subjection, of control and indeed banishment of the woman and of the image, of the woman as the image, is to specify at length and in detail the protocols, the rules or laws not simply of virtue but equally of the subjection of thought. Thus if the governance of femininity is read as a legislation of masculine imagination, simultaneously as its expression and as its suppression, the significance of the image and of gender reappears in the interstices of thought. A few instances will suffice to illustrate—as if we could see—the specific character of these legal thoughts. First, there is the word, and "it is the duty of the householder to administer the word" for only through the "ingrafted word" can the prosaic principles of subjection, of fear, obedience, and faith be properly inculcated and implanted.[109] More than that, "man is a word," and it is as a word, as law, that he "clasps together bodily and spiritual, visible and invisible, mortal and immortal

106. Griffith, *Bethel* at 120. Cf. Rogers, *Matrimoniall Honour* at 172: "The centre of chastity is the mind and spirit. If that be pure there needs be no keepers . . . if that be unclean, no keepers will serve the turn, unbridled lust will soon mount over the wall."

107. Rogers, *Matrimoniall Honour* at 172–173.

108. Dod and Clever, *A Godlie Form of Householde Government* at 142.

109. Ibid. at 20.

substances, conjoining in one person both an earthly and a heavenly nature." Even more strikingly, "Man is Gods Text; and all the creatures are but so many commentaries upon him; Heaven resembles his soul, Earth his heart."[110] The text has its subject, its real image, and no challenge or apparent image, no idol or woman can be allowed to threaten the security of his textuality or the propriety of his interpretations or thoughts.

As if an image might lead us astray or take us beyond the text, the next rule of "iconomy" is that a woman is defined not intrinsically but extrinsically; she is a place, she is the *gynaeceum,* the mother, the inner household. To this the law adds a second and correlative duty: "the woman is not to take liberty of wanderings and straying abroad from her owne house," she is to stay rather at home "in the mans knowledge" and within his walls.[111] She is not to stray or wander, flit or depart or elope with any new cause or novel interpretation. She is rather to tend the immortality of the husband, the continuance of the word, through the nurture of the children to a comparable obedience to the father. While the wife must follow the husband where he so requires from place to place, she must otherwise keep to her place or remain at home indefinitely while he wanders abroad. The law states her place as ancillary or secondary; the woman waits, she remains, she gestates or otherwise registers an external imperative. The worst of all feminine crimes, a kind of madness, is that of the woman who takes off or leaves the home, and whether adulterous or singular, such departure from her place, her guardian or lord, deprives a woman of all rights and benefits, of dower and inheritance.[112] To leave would be to abandon her place, to forsake her authorities, to think for herself, to think for oneself: *domus* and *dominus,* house and lord, home and subjection are cognate terms and constitute analogues of private and mental spaces.

A final example and the third duty of feminine subjection is instituted as silence: "Finally let her learn for herself alone and her young children . . . for it neither becomes a woman to rule a school, nor to live among men, to speak abroad."[113] The history of feminine speech, as Fox reminds his readers, begins with Eve's seduction of Adam, with feminine speech as deceit, as betrayal and fall. It must be recollected, therefore, that subjection to the word is also and literally subjection to a specific order and *telos* of speech which will compensate for or strive to recover that which was lost through the dispersion and confusion of the fall and of Babel. What is required is a language that will transcend the failure of

110. Griffith, *Bethel* at 145.

111. Perkins, *Christian Oeconomie* at 692 v.

112. See Anonymous, *The Lawes Resolutions* at 144.

113. Vives, *De Institutione* at fol. D i a–b. See, for a lengthier study, G. Fox, *The Woman Learning in Silence or, the Mysterie of Womans Subjection to her Husband* (London: T. Simmonds, 1655), especially at 1–3.

speech or at least direct the inward eye toward a truth beyond mere language, beyond both figuration and visibility, to a sublime and ineffable form. It is thus intrinsic to the order of discourse that femininity be subjected to a prosaic form of textuality, a rhetoric that refuses the flowers or ornaments of feminine speech, the figures or images of eloquence or of verbal seduction. The law, however ill such an assertion may sit with the history of legal language, is represented in doctrine as plain speaking, it is "straight" in style, its word is its singular bond. The model of teaching and of treatise set out by Dod and Clever is reasonably exemplary: "This treatise is not garnished with eloquence; nor full of great cunning, nor beautified with flowers of wisdom, neither yet does it discourse or treat of high or dark things, neither is it stuffed with subtle questions, and arguments, nor indicted with Rhetoricall and eloquent style . . . but it is plain and without any gayness." Having so comprehensively and figuratively denounced rhetoric and the other virtues of an emotive persuasion, our authors stoop metaphorically to conjure the following: "And undoubtedly it may be said, that unto true Christians, good and holy books are as ladders to climb unto heaven."[114] The metaphor that denounces metaphor bespeaks a certain fluidity or uncertainty within the law, it denotes an internal threat or simply a fear of a language that may escape the confines of the institution, a poetry that may speak of woman as *logos* or word or temptation to a disparate thought. For what is at stake in language is thought, to which it should be added that suppression has increasingly become its law.

The denunciation of rhetoric within doctrine has certain consistencies of style. The attributes of rhetorical eloquence or linguistic persuasion appeal to the eye and the ear, the figures are variously beguiling, heretical, and clamorous, they break the law and they do so in the manner of the feminine. If woman is to be excluded from the public sphere, if she is neither to govern, judge, hold office or teach, then she is left without speech and cannot be other than an image. In a sense, the law could be said explicitly to institute woman as an image so as to denounce her nonbeing. Similarly in linguistic terms, law defines rhetoric as falsehood, as the opposite of "evident words," so as to challenge an idolatry that was always deemed to deceive the eye, to be both feminine and unclean.[115] Her learning in silence in this sense represents the confinement of any thought that would claim a reality exterior to or competitive with the plain and morose, the unseen or transparent, words of law. To be silent is to appear without presence, it is to be an image without reference, it is to be nothing other than the visual, a sign that vanishes without trace because it was

114. Dod and Clever, *A Godlie Forme of Householde Government* at fol. A 5 b.

115. Thomas Harding, *A Confutation* at fol. 96 b.

never the mark of anything external to itself—it was simply what it was, a contingency, a woman. In this respect the feminine veils nothing; at best she seduces by pretending a substance which she lacks, a veiled absence, air. The destiny of femininity within ecclesiastical and civil law, within the mixed and impossible governance of the soul, was to abandon the accidents of femininity, to alienate herself without inheritance or succession to the family of another (*in alienam familiam*) in the civil death of marriage.[116] The mystery of marriage and correlatively of the household was that of the sacrifice of a woman: she became "covert," *nupta* or veiled, hidden in both a literal and an allegorical sense. The woman alienated to another family was a woman without desire, without speech or public role, a woman in subjection. Subjection was inward as well as outward, and its sign even within the Christian tradition was that of denial, of loss of will, name and personality *sub potestate viri*. In addition to silence, the "noblest ornament of a woman,"[117] she was also to be veiled against the eyes and fascination of men, thus corresponding in visual terms to her verbal absence. Whether veiled by clothes or by downcast eyes, by shamefacedness or some other modesty of the face, her image too transpires to be illusion, a veil over the "idol of the face," a screen of both desire and sensuality.

That the face was covered against desire betrayed a fear of fascination and a terror of the power of the eye.[118] The veil or shamed face signaled subjection, modesty, and obedience to an exterior principle which was only to be seen through the distance or screen of a covert status. There is of course a heavy irony and a deep repression to the image of a woman stripped bare of her rhetoric and hidden from view. She learns in silence and she sees darkly, she lacks both the flowers of speech and the ornaments of beauty. More than that, however, the veil is itself a most powerful metaphor of seduction, of a desire or truth that cannot be seen, of a void or nonbeing that woman might almost represent were it not that "women are not concerned with Truth, they are profoundly skeptical; they know perfectly well that there is no such thing as 'truth,' that behind their veils there is yet another veil, and try as one may to remove them, one after another, truth in its 'nudity,' like a goddess, will never appear."[119] To which

116. Anonymous, *Lawes Resolutions* at 6: "All women are understood either married or to be married and their desires subject to their husband. . . . The common law here shakes hands with the divinity."

117. Vives, *Instruction of a Christen Woman* at fol. M iii a. The patristic phrase is *mulier taceat de muliere.*

118. See Tertullian, *De Virginibus Velandis,* in A. Roberts and J. Donaldson (eds.), *Ante-Nicene Christian Library* (Edinburgh: T & T Clark, 1870), Vol. 18 at 177. For a recent and interesting commentary, see Joyce E. Salisbury, *Church Fathers, Independent Virgins* (London: Verso Books, 1991).

119. Sarah Kofman, *The Enigma of Woman: Woman in Freud's Writings* (Ithaca: Cornell Uni-

precarious or unstable state it can be added that the veil of the feminine is an inverse image, a negative sensibility whose motile quality is the threat of a truth that the law does not know, the threat or virtue of another law, and equally the possibility of the collapse of the order of truth through the unveiling of its indistinction.[120] The veil is a mark of absence, a metaphor or substitute, which takes the place of speech and of the face. It is also a fetish or illusion, an extravagant sign of *aporia*, of doubt, indeterminacy, and loss.

VIRTUE AND EXCESS

A relatively early defense of the virtues of women, *A Woman's Woorth*, translated into English in 1599, concludes by commending "women's singularities both in body and mind, [which] do far outgo whatsoever perfections in men."[121] Among the singular women referred to were recluses and authors, as well as women of charitable renown and of good works, whose singularity lay in their ability to depart from custom or to exceed the law. Singularity was the form of difference, it was singular because it exceeded the bounds of masculine custom, but more than that, singularity was that which differed from the norm or lay outside or beyond the (common) law and its contemporary repetitions. The feminine, as enigma or singularity, as show or excess, was thus also a sign of plurality, of a difference that escaped the unity or standard and sequence of law. Such plurality intimated the possibilities of thought outside the law for such was the genius and the madness of the feminine, that of challenging the norm, of replacing the habitual body of legal personality with the lived body—the singularity—of a feminine erudition, that of images, contingencies, surfaces, and their various bodies or inscriptions.

From the point of view of the law, singularity is precisely that which escapes the line or the term of judgment. The singular dissolves beyond the boundaries of the rule, it deconstructs the rule by doubting the relevance of its normativity and by challenging its abstraction, its method. For the law such a challenge is dangerous. While the feminine may represent virtue, it also intimates a constant dissipation or dissolution of doctrine and its unities. A woman weeps, a woman escapes definition in passion:

---

versity Press, 1985) at 105. The other famous instance of this argument is Derrida, *Spurs* at 51: "Out of the depths, endless and unfathomable, she engulfs and distorts all vestige of essentiality, of identity, of property. . . . There is no such thing as the truth of woman."

120. Irigaray, *Speculum of the Other Woman*, especially at 82–90.

121. Anthony Gibson (trans.), *A Womans Woorth, defended against all the men in the world: Prooving them to be more perfect, excellent and absolute in all vertuous actions, then any man of what qualitie soever* (London: John Wolfe, 1599) at sig. 63r.

"The best kinds of beasts are those which most use to weep; if it be so, there is nothing more facile in a woman than tears, nay it is a thing naturally given unto them."[122] Again the metaphor of tears offers an image of the fearful fluidity of the feminine, of an ever-present absence, a dissolution as extravagant as it is inexorable, as ecstatic as it is illegal. To weep, it might be said, is to adopt another veil, it masks precisely by collapsing, by decomposition, or by waves. None of which is to say anything more than that the singular, as idol, as face or as woman, as rhetoric or eloquence, is a representation of difference, of indefinition or plurality within and without the law. The image, contingency or that which dissolves in tears, resists the abstract machine, the construction of faces in the principle of totality or of *Haec Imago* in which territory the face is a unitary power, a cipher:

> The reason is simple. The face is not universal. It is not even that of the white man; it is White Man himself, with his broad white cheeks and the black hole of his eyes. The face is Christ. The face is the typical European, what Ezra Pound called the average sensual man, in short the ordinary everyday Erotomaniac . . . not universal, but *facies totius universi.*[123]

The weeping face loses that definition, even if "I have noted many ladies not to loose one jot their perfection thereby."[124]

To follow the eye of the law is to follow the direction of a vision normatively lodged upon the surface of things so as to discover their depths; in Bacon's aphorism "the law looks upon the proximate cause and not upon the distant [*in jure non remota causa, sed proxima spectatur*]."[125] In textual terms, such a visual hermeneutic or specular reading addresses the word but ignores the figure, claiming that the figure, the other body or face, the feminine motility of language, can be subjected to and defined by the art of interpretation. The image is secondary to the norm, and where it escapes definition it must exist outside the sphere or territory of legitimacy. In the immediate subsequent history of the question of feminine status at common law, the tradition which follows Fortescue and his elaborate rendering of the *querelle des femmes* in common law tends to revolve around specific issues and does not directly rely upon any genuine reopening of the question or place of image or woman. The Janus face of common law is

122. Ibid. at sig. 40r. The theme of fluidity is an important one in contemporary feminist theory and its jurisprudence. See Luce Irigaray, *This Sex Which Is Not One* (Ithaca: Cornell University Press, 1985) at 106–118; Drucilla Cornell, *Beyond Accommodation: Ethical Feminism, Deconstruction and the Law* (New York: Routledge, 1990) at 7–17.

123. Gilles Deleuze and Félix Guattari, *A Thousand Plateaus: Capitalism and Schizophrenia* (Minneapolis: University of Minnesota Press, 1987) at 176. Jardine, *Gynesis* at 70–87, usefully discusses the genderization of the face and the figure. It is a theme to which the next chapter returns in greater detail.

124. Gibson (trans.), *A Womans Woorth* at fol. 40 a.

125. Bacon, *Elements of the Common Lawes* at 1.

turned elsewhere. Thus in John Perkins, *A Profitable Book Treating of the Lawes of England,* first published in 1532, women are not a legal category but rather a series of statuses spelled out in relation to specific property rights and transactions. The married woman is compared to the monk, friar, servant, or canon as one without right and incapable of either livery or seisin.[126] A grant made by a *feme covert* during the absence of her husband, "notwithstanding the husband were abroad or out of the country, wandering at the time of such grant . . . so that it was not known whether he were alive or dead . . . is void if he be living."[127] Nor can the wife make a testament in the absence or without the consent of the husband. The rules may be multiplied and on occasion Courts of Equity would recognize certain rights in the wife who would be treated for such purposes under the fiction that she was a *feme sole,* for example with respect to property granted specifically for her separate use or with regard to certain devices used by the husband to enfeoff the wife.[128] In conceptual terms, Sir Thomas Smith in the influential *De Republica Anglorum* simply reasserts the Aristotelian limitations upon the role of women and adds as a flourish that the civil law on the issue of succession should govern in England, "on which consideration also we do reject women."[129] Yet neither in Rastell's *The Expocision of the Termes of the Lawes of Englande,* nor for that matter in Cowell's *The Interpreter or Booke Containing the Signification of Words,* is "woman"—either *mulier* or *feme* or *foemina*—an entry in its own right.[130] It is tempting to think that as suddenly as it appeared in common law, the category of woman would seem to have disappeared in a literature of abridgments, formbooks, entries, breviaries, year books, and rolls that had as yet made no attempt at systematic or conceptual classification.

In a sense that corresponds quite directly to the lack of a legal classification of woman or of a feminine *persona,* the appearance of woman was her disappearance. Woman, like the image, should hide herself or be discrete: "The long hair of a woman is the ornament of her sex, and bashful shamfastenesse her chiefe honour."[131] Both *indicia* of femininity marked her sex

126. J. Perkins, *A Profitable Book Treating of the Lawes of England* (London: R. Totel, 1532, 1555 ed.) at s. 86–87.

127. Ibid. at s. 6.

128. Ibid. at s. 8. See further, Swinburne, *A Brief Treatise*; Godolphin, *The Orphan's Legacy.*

129. Thomas Smith, *De Republica Anglorum* at 19.

130. John Rastell, *An Exposition of Certaine Difficult and Obscure Words, and Termes of the Lawes of this Realme* (London: T. Wright, 1526, 1602 ed.); Cowell, *The Interpreter.* Both authors list *mulier* in a technical meaning, as lawfully born rather than bastard: *ex muliere* as opposed to *ex concubina.* Both dictionaries nonetheless provide definitions of relevant legal statuses such as *patria postestas, coverture,* or *maritagium.*

131. Anonymous, *Hic Mulier, or The Man-Woman* (London: Christ Church Gate, 1620) at fol. B 3 a.

through nondisclosure. Long hair and downcast eyes or veils displayed a sex that lacked being, that was *genus* without *species*, a class without individuality or singularity. The legal and political invisibility of women was thus staged in terms of a curious indifference or concealment of the very femininity that might mark a body or a person as a woman:

> O hide them (these inticing tongues, bared breasts seducing, and naked armes imbracing) for shame hide them in closest prisons of your strictest government: shroud them with modest and comely garments . . . that no unchaste eye may come neare and assayle them, no lascivious tongue woo a forbidden passage, nor no prophane hand touch reliques so pure and religious. Guard them about with counter-scarfes of Innocence, Trenches of humane reason, and impregnable walles of sacred divinitie.[132]

The legal problem of woman did not concern personality or legal definition, it was rather a problem of indifferentiation or innocence which was most frequently encountered in the negative form of legislation directed against excess and the visual imagination. Early in the sixteenth century, an *Act for the Reform of Apparell* (1509) was directed at "the better repressing of the inordinate excess of apparel by some moderation, and for a reasonable order like to be observed and performed in the wearing thereof."[133] The ostensive aim of this statute and its numerous later epigones was to prevent dress beyond the status, dignity, or sex of the wearer. The classification of colors, cuts, styles, and sources of cloth were legislated for all ranks, including doctors of the law, King's Counsel, Justices, Barons of the Kings Exchequer, Serjeants at Law, and Masters of the Chancery. As to the nature of excessive dress it might also be noted that the topic of dress and status is also regularly addressed in relation to dower, and in particular to the widow's right to paraphernalia, namely that, in common law, *bona paraphernalia* does not refer to the wife's "Apparel, bed, jewels, ornaments" but rather to her "*convenient* Apparel, and only such things as are agreeable to her degree."[134] It was decided thus in *Harwel's Case* that the wife can have necessary apparel "for her body" upon the death of her husband, but she shall not have "excessive apparel."[135] If she takes more than is deemed appropriate to her status she loses all—not even her wardrobe is her own.

It seems reasonable to suppose that the concern with apparel is with the maintenance of a variety of orders of distinction, of which gender is

132. Ibid. at fol. B 5 a.

133. Rastall, *A Collection in English*.

134. The source of this rule is D.9.5.2 but the immediate reference is to Dyer; see Godolphin, *Orphan's Legacy* at 130.

135. Anonymous, *Baron and Feme: A Treatise of the Common Law Concerning Husbands and Wives* (London: Walthoe, 1700) at 65–66.

but one. To legislate the appropriate colors and qualities of cloth by rank, office, and degree suggests that there is considerable or at least growing uncertainty as to the other criteria demarcating the hierarchy. Such is certainly evident in the legislation of the Inns of Court governing dress and deportment. William Dugdale[136] details numerous such regulations at the same time that John Ferne,[137] Sir George Buc,[138] and others indicate that the forgery of heraldic arms and the false assertion of "coat armour," gentility (*generosity*), and nobility was common at the Inns. The most devastating condemnation of dress comes, however, from the chronicles of William Harrison, who deals at length with "the phantasticall folly of our Nation, even from the courtier to the carter. . . . For my part I can tell better how to inveigh against [its] enormity, than to describe with any certainty of our attire." He proceeds to list the flow of fashion from Spanish guise to French toys, Turkish manner to German high fashion, Moroccan gowns to Barbarian sleeves, all of which simply indicates excess and vanity, pomp and bravery, change and variety, "and finally the sickness and the folly that is in all degrees." Yet it is more than simple extravagance, it is a confusion of body and soul, of costume and custom, which sees its worst disgrace in the wearing of gold rings, stones, or pearls in the ears: "Thus it is now come to pass, that women are become men, and men transformed into monsters."[139]

The offense of extravagant or excessive dress is economic in both senses of the word, it confuses and so offends the eye while also costing more than the husband would wish to spend. The manner of offense is depicted as plurality, and in a sense the woman that becomes image, that lives as image, that takes the law at its word, is condemned for excess: "Our women's excess in this kind [of apparel] is no less ridiculous than various, some of them never thinking themselves in the fashions complete, till they have put off their sex, country, conscience and etcetera."[140] Clothes, which hide the figure and augment the image, are a sign of substance, "a woman's attire shows what she is. . . . By her habit you may give a near guess at her heart."[141] By being an image, the woman resists or claims a space and

136. Dugdale, *Origines Juridiciales* at fol. s. 98a–99b, 191b–192b, 196b–199a.

137. Ferne, *Blazon of Gentrie* at 92–93, deploring the fraudulent assumption of gentility and coats of arms by ignoble entrants to the Inns of Court. The "ungentle legists" are inflated in their numbers and not worth their rent. Thomas Wilson, *The State of England, A.D. 1600* (London: Camden Miscellany, 1601, 1936 ed.); and Powell, *The Attourney's Academy*, make similar complaints.

138. Buc, *The Third Universitie of England* at 968–969. More generally on the status of barristers see W. Prest, *Rise of the Barristers: A Social History of the English Bar 1590–1640* (Oxford: Oxford University Press, 1986) at 127–184.

139. Harrison, *An Historicall Description* at 172a–b.

140. Griffith, *Bethel* at 122.

141. Ibid. at 261.

difference of her own, a difference undeterred by plurality and indifferent to the claim of confusion of genders, orders, and laws:

> These painted faces, which they weare,
> can any tell from whence they came
> (Don Sathan) Lord of fained lies,
> All these new fangles did devise
> These glittering caules, of golden plate
> wherewith their heads are nihlie dect
> makes them to seeme an Angels mate,
> in judgment of the simple sect.
> To peacockes I compare them right
> that glorieth in their features bright.[142]

The imagery denouncing the images assumed by women, their dress and painted faces, is evidently theological. Satan inspires the image, the woman, to distract or tempt, and doctrine denounces the gold and glitter of appearance as being for the hidden purposes of misdirection or evil, deceit, or betrayal. The woman is again singular and many, her image will confuse and her body will destroy. The woman is no more than appearance, her being is her representation and should therefore be shunned outside the realm of her legitimate circulation, that of the "oeconomie" or domesticity. The woman as image and as singularity, however, clearly threatens and allures, attracts and repels. What then if the image speaks? The ensuing chapter will pursue that possibility under the title of *gynaetopia,* or woman's place.

142. Anonymous, *A Glasse to view the Pride of Vainglorious Women* at fol. A 4–b.

SIX

Gynaetopia

Feminine Genealogies of Common Law

The Aegyptian hieroglyphics figured the Heavens by a woman, having her eyes covered, and laden with many mountains on her back: making hereby, that these divine creatures saw all things, even they which were to come, as then present, and withall supported the misdeeds of men with a forgetful remission; signified by the burdens so far removed from their regard, as all mens defects whatsoever, were cast behind their backs.[1]

The destruction of images, the privileging of the word against the figures of discourse, marks a certain repression which is itself figured in the blindness of justice, in the all-seeing yet masked eyes of a woman burdened by measure and men. This chapter will trace the backface of that repression, that parasite, and indicate some of the possibilities of justice as an image and as a woman. The theme is as old as the *querelle des femmes,* the criticism of law and of the legal profession from feminine perspectives being an essential theme in all criticism or resistance to the misogyny or tyranny of the institution. Positive law was satirized as an expression of masculinity that ignored nature and justice alike:

> These prophane men would bind the feminine sex to such laws as themselves are not able to observe, laws drawn from their own jealousy, their suspicion, their weakness, their avarice, their depraved conscience, their pride, thinking it good to prohibit others, such things as themselves could never effect: wherein they have regard to their own particular imperfection, and not the law of nature.[2]

It would seriously embarrass lawyers, remarked Poulain de la Barre somewhat later, "if they were forced to explain what they meant by nature . . . and to explain how nature distinguishes the two sexes in the ways they imagine."[3]

In many respects lawyers were a privileged object of feminine critique while law itself represented the essential reason, antagonism, and distance

1. Gibson (trans.), *A Womans Woorth* at sig. 33v.

2. Ibid. at sig. 30r.

3. François Poulain de la Barre, *Discours physique et moral de l'égalité des deux sexes, où l'on voit l'importance de se défaire des préjugez* (Paris: Fayard, 1673, 1984 ed.) at 77.

ALIUD.

DUm tuus ambiguâ *Janus*, facieque biformi
Reſpicit antiqua, & poſteriora videt:
Archivos Themidis canos, monumentaque legum
Vindicat à veteri ſemi-ſopita ſitu.
Hinc duplex te *Jane* manet veterane corona,
Gratia canitie, poſteritate decus.

Gulielmus Bakerus Oxon.

ASTRÆÆ

Figure 1. Laudation of Selden as Janus.

that characterized the masculine domination of the polity. The correspondence of women married to barristers of the Elizabethan Bar indicate that it was emotionally unfortunate and domestically undesirable to attach oneself to men of law. Lawyers, it was said, married for venal motives, namely money, social advancement, and political influence; they were married first and exclusively to their profession; they were mean-spirited, caviling, and much absent; the law consumed them and left them spent, deprived of civility, humor, and emotion.[4] A slightly later tract, *In Defence of the Female Sex,* summarized the failings of lawyers in terms of "eager and disputative" men whose undoubted wit and judgment was expended in "thwarting and opposing one another" to the effect that they became "impatient, sour . . . morose" and incapable of conversation. The evidence explicitly offered for this observation was the training that lawyers received at the Inns of Court, where students "lead a recluse and monastic life, and converse little with our sex. They want neither wit nor learning . . . yet when they come into gay, though ingenious company, are either damped and silent

4. Prest, *The Rise of the Barristers* at 115–126. For a comparable study of the lower branch of the profession, see Brooks, *Pettyfoggers and Vipers* at 132–151.

or unseasonably frolicsome and free, so that they appear either dull or ridiculous."[5]

It is not the purpose of this chapter to rehearse directly the perennial and frequently barren terrain of the social incompetence, subjective estrangement, or emotional ineptitude of lawyers. The criticism of the male character of the early modern and modern legal professions can be juxtaposed more interestingly with a series of constitutional texts that not only argue the political and legal preeminence of women but also suggest the possible presence of a feminine genealogy repressed within the ancient constitution, a feminine unconscious to the doctrines of common law. At a popular level the misogyny of English law and the "dissembling practice" of its lawyers was countered explicitly in terms of female courts, women's law, and feminine justice. The anonymous theatrical polemic *Swetnam the Woman-Hater arraigned by Women* places the misogynist author of a tract published in 1615, titled *The Arraignment of lewde, idle, froward and unconstant Women,* on trial before a specially constituted women's court presided over by a "Ladie Chiefe Justice."[6] The sentence passed by this "Female Court" upon the misogynist was (ironically) that he be silenced, that is, deprived of speech, and exiled.[7] The pseudonymous Ester Sowernam responded to the same misogynist pamphlet by presenting a striking defense of women in terms of a genealogy of the feminine extracted from the Bible and ancient histories. Her argument listed the achievements of great women, the lineage of feminine rulers, and the virtues of the feminine more generally understood in terms of the attributes of specific women rather than in terms of any essential or homogeneous class character.[8]

The focus of this chapter will be on the popular and learned invoca-

5. Drake, *An Essay in Defence of the Female Sex* at 140–141. See also Astell, *A Serious Proposal* at 132–151.

6. Anonymous, *Swetnam the Woman-Hater Arraigned by Women* (London: Meighen, 1620). J. Swetnam, *The Arraignment of lewde, idle, froward, and unconstant Women* (London: T. Archer, 1615). For commentary, see Joan Kelly, *Women, History and Theory: The Essays of Joan Kelly* (Chicago: Chicago University Press, 1984): Denise Riley, *Am I That Name? Feminism and the Category of "Women" in History* (London: Macmillan, 1988); Maclean, *Woman Triumphant*; Jordan, *Renaissance Feminism*; Maureen Quilligan, *The Allegory of Female Authority: Christine de Pisan's Cité des Dames* (Ithaca: Cornell University Press, 1991); Mary Anne Case, "From the Mirror of Reason to the Measure of Justice" (1993) 5 *Yale Journal of Law and the Humanities* 115.

7. Anonymous, *Swetnam the Woman-Hater* at fol. K i b. The irony is simply that silence was in theological terms at least the duty or fate of women, as explicated, for example, in Fox, *The Woman Learning in Silence.*

8. Ester Sowernam, *Ester hath hang'd Haman: Or an answere to a lewde Pamphlet* (London: N. Bourne, 1617). Also of interest are Rachel Speght, *A Mouzell for Melastomus . . . or an apologeticall answere to that pamphlet made by J. Swetnam* (London: T. Archer, 1617); Constantia Munda (pseud.), *The Worming of a Mad Dogge: Or, a soppe for Cerberus the Iaylor of Hell* (London: L. Hayes, 1617).

tions of feminine courts, female justices, and a separate and superior law originating from and administered by women under the feminine sign of fate or justice, fortune or phronesis. It will be argued that such texts—and I will analyze two in particular detail, John Selden's *Jani Anglorum Facies Altera* (1610) and the anonymous *Lawes Resolutions of Women's Rights* (1632)[9]—form part of a repressed tradition of constitutional writings that traced a feminine genealogy of common law, an origin and a telos of legal judgment, in a lost or future gynocratic polity. In both method and substance, object and subject, such a retracing or going back deconstructs doctrine and recollects in place of the *universalia* of legal historicism the plural identities, the folds and dispersions, the heterogeneity of common law. In this respect the analysis takes up the challenge of repression and of the return of the repressed within juristic texts and specifically within constitutional doctrine.[10] Genealogical method, in short, is forced by its consideration of the repressed, by the exigencies of a symptomatic reading to take the surfaces of law's history, its images and signs, its material body, as the site of its meanings, as the source of its interpretations, as its law of law. There will be, as there always is, an element of polemic in the reconstruction of other laws and alternative histories, and for that reason certain elements of the polemic should be indicated in advance.

First, the genealogy of a common law and custom unrecognized by men and unreported by Coke's sages of the doctrinal tradition[11] involves the analysis of certain elements of the antirrhetic. It places one tradition, custom, and ethic against that of a singular law, one past in place of another, one temporality to the side of the Christian ethos, its economy, and its law. As Judith Drake percipiently remarked in her *Defence of the Female Sex*,

> I cannot prove all this from Ancient records; for if any Histories were anciently written by women, time and the malice of men have effectually conspired to suppress them, and it is not reasonable to think that men should transmit, or suffer to be transmitted to posterity, any thing that might show the weakness and illegality of their title to a power they still exercise so arbitrarily, and are so fond of.[12]

9. Selden, *Jani Anglorum;* Anonymous, *Lawes Resolutions.*

10. I have attempted to outline the exigencies of such a method in Peter Goodrich, "A Short History of Failure: Law and Criticism 1460–1620," in Goodrich, *Languages of Law* (London: Weidenfeld and Nicolson, 1990); and also in Goodrich, "Critical Legal Studies in England." See further, Marianne Constable, *The Law of the Other: The Mixed Jury and Changing Conceptions of Citizenship, Law and Knowledge* (Chicago: Chicago University Press, 1994).

11. For general accounts of that tradition and its mentality, see Pocock, *The Ancient Constitution and the Feudal Law*; Baker, *The Reports of John Spelman*; Goodrich, "Ars Bablativa"; also Goodrich, "Poor Illiterate Reason."

12. Drake, *An Essay,* at 23. For contemporary discussions of this issue, see P. Labalme (ed.). *Beyond Their Sex: Learned Women of the European Past* (New York: New York University

Other authors consistently make a comparable point in antirrhetical terms, as Edward Gosynhill, for example, who in a work titled *In Prayse of all Women* in 1542 writes of

> histories many I could forth lay
> that maketh well with the feminine
> of like sentence I dare well say
> and grounded on good authority
> howbeit because that poetry
> is taken now in such despite
> of other reasons I well you write.[13]

A history of feminine practice is necessarily a psychoanalytic encounter: "Thus much remembered for women's constancy. . . . For men (maliciously jealous of women's honour) have buried (as much as in them lay) the most commendable deeds of such, to whom themselves were not more than Apes, nay worse imitators, if worse may be."[14] In short, the historical evidence, in terms of gender, is negative and oppositional or dissonant with what was historically the exclusively male status and environment of the legal profession: "One must assume that those who made the laws, being men, discriminated in favour of their own sex."[15] Finally, the intimacy of history and law ensures feminine genealogy can only be reconstructed through allusions culled either from the extralegal writings of women or through the analysis of the "other face" or repressed text of constitutional doctrine.[16]

Second, as already remarked, the genealogical form of historical argument is somewhat allusive and its method correspondingly symptomatic. Its concern is not with an origin or continuity of descent but rather with

---

Press, 1980) at ch. 8; Michelle Perrot (ed.), *Writing Women's History* (Oxford: Blackwell, 1982); P. Dronke, *Women Writers of the Middle Ages* (Cambridge: Cambridge University Press, 1984). Specifically on the politics of feminine history, see C. Pateman, *The Sexual Contract* (Cambridge: Polity Press, 1988); R. Coward, *Patriarchal Precedents* (London: Routledge, 1983); and in philosophical terms see le Doeuff, *The Philosophical Imaginary*.

13. Edward Gosynhill, *The Prayse of all Women called Mulierum Pean: Very fruytful and delectable unto all the reders* (London: Ihones, 1542) at fol. B iii b. Gosynhill was most well known for another work, *Here Begynneth a Lytle Boke Named the Scholhouse of Women: Wherein every man may rede a goodly pryse of the condicyons of women* (London: Thomas Petyt, 1541).

14. Gibson (trans.). *A Womans Woorth* at sig. 15v. Cf. Hélène Cixous and C. Clement, *The Newly Born Woman* (Minneapolis: University of Minnesota Press, 1986).

15. Poulain de la Barre, *Discours* at 78.

16. The intimacy of history and law is a singular theme of Hotman, *Anti-Tribonian*, a work that was extremely influential among the antiquaries of the Elizabethan Bar. On the broader correlation, see Donald Kelley, *Foundations of Modern Historical Scholarship*; and philosophically, Derrida, *Of Grammatology*.

the "accidents, the minute deviations—or conversely the complete reversals—the errors, the false appraisals, and the faulty calculations that gave birth to those things that continue to exist and have value for us."[17] Genealogy suggests the study of the dispersed traditions and other customs of common law, its disparate sources, its several languages, its incorporation of many jurisdictions. At one level, the law is based upon what Selden terms "dulling custom,"[18] upon legally discovered precedent and the transmission of narrow repetitions which Mary Astell somewhat later designated as the "foundation of vice . . . a merciless torrent that carries all before it," including prudence and virtue.[19] In this sense the basis of law in custom is a species of ignorance or of forgetting. A feminine genealogy suggests that custom must face at least a double challenge. On the one hand it should be subjected to the criteria and criticism of reason and the virtue of its plural principles; on the other hand, it should be confronted by other forms of historical narrative, including those that predate or otherwise circumvent the doctrinally accepted progressions of legal custom, the self-evident and false truths of the common law tradition.

In both cases, the classical form of argument is to resort to a mythology of origins or of the "origins" of common law which are mystical precisely because the human source of law can never be directly represented. While it may be noted that common law has always resorted to mythical and often transparently feminine categories of origin in "time immemorial" or some other indistinct *corpus mysticum* at the dawn or border of law, the explicit invocation of female origins tends to take the rhetorical form of an opposition of history and tradition, past and precedent, as primary or first sources of law.[20] That origin and reproduction are best figured by the image of woman or of femininity should occasion no great surprise, since "the definition of law can unfold only in relation to the question of the origin of law" and the question of origin or creativity is always at some level a question of femininity.[21] The significance of the image of reproduction is indicative also of the need to recognize that the opposition between different species of historical narrative is a principal stake in the politics of

17. Foucault, *Language, Counter-Memory* at 146.

18. Selden, *Historie of Tithes* at vi.

19. Astell, *A Serious Proposal* at 30, 49, 81–82.

20. For a recent general discussion of the mystical origin, in which the mystical comes to designate that which has become separate from the institution, see de Certeau, *The Mystic Fable* at 79–121. On the concept of antiquity and origin see, for legal examples, Spelman, *Original of the Four Law Termes*; Dugdale, *Origines Juridiciales*. For a fascinating series of theological arguments, see Favour, *Antiquitie Triumphing over Noveltie.*

21. Hélène Cixous, *Readings: The Poetics of Blanchot, Joyce, Kafka, Kleist, Lispector, and Tsvetayva* (Minneapolis: University of Minnesota Press, 1991) at 19.

constitutional history.[22] The play of history and of myth, of text and interpretation, is as much a feature of common law doctrine and its theory of sources as it is of the repressed genealogies of feminine jurisdictions.

Following the image or nothing, idol or woman, in the texts of law takes its place within an extensive history of repression and of failure, a history of texts and traditions that were interpreted out of existence by the ascendant doctrinal writers. The recuperation of repressed traditions, of abandoned customs, of the positive unconscious of legal science, can serve finally to remind the contemporary legal institution and profession of the more extensive and varied scholarly and popular traditions whose repression both accompanies and undermines the positivistic or scientific conception of law. It is a criticism of the margins predicated upon a truth lost within an interior space of legal history. It is a criticism that traces, in this instance, a feminine genealogy and practice of law so as to establish a lineage and possibility of difference that has been specified usefully by Luce Irigaray in terms of both history and myth. She argues first that "in order to make an ethics of sexual difference possible, it is necessary to retrace the ties of feminine genealogies . . . at the levels of law, religion, language, truth and wisdom. . . . [I]t is necessary to introduce into the history of reason an interpretation of the forgetting of feminine genealogies and thereby re-establish their economy."[23] A genealogy of the feminine gender of common law, of its representation as a woman and its expression through the history of feminine lawgivers, as also of illustrious and erudite women, is also a form of political critique. An ethics of legal difference is developed so as to indicate the dispersed basis of common law, the plurality that exists within the constitution and prevents it ever claiming a unitary identity, a face that is purely its own: "A return to the origins of our culture reveals that it was once otherwise, that there was an epoch when it was the woman who initiated the rites of love. In that time, the woman was goddess and not servant, she guarded both the carnal and the spiritual dimensions of love."[24] Whatever the legal implications of such an alternative mythology, the elaboration or the patient recollection of the diverse forms of myth, of other histories and practices, is indicative of both philosophical and cul-

22. On which theme see Rossi Braidotti, *Patterns of Dissonance* (Oxford: Polity Press, 1991) at ch. 6; and addressed in terms of race, see Peter Fitzpatrick, *The Mythology of Modern Law* (London: Routledge, 1992).

23. Luce Irigaray, "Le Mystere oublié des généalogies féminines," in Luce Irigaray, *Le Temps de la différence* (Paris: Livre de Poche, 1989) at 120–121.

24. Irigaray, *J'aime à toi* at 210. In a secondary although related sense a genealogical form of historical narrative is one committed to the study of the plural and dispersed roots of identity: "If genealogy in its own right gives rise to questions concerning our native land, native language, or the laws that govern us, its intention is to reveal the heterogeneous systems which, masked by the self, inhibit the formation of any form of identity." Foucault, *Language, Counter-Memory, Practice* at 162. See also Irigaray, *Marine Lover of Friedrich Nietzsche.*

tural possibilities. Its concern is with an ethics or practice that includes the possibility of a positive construction of alterity and with it a remission or better pluralization of the antirrhetic through its dispersion. There is, it will be argued, a certain politics to the use of history as a means of thinking difference.

The past is an extension of the present and it is salutary to recollect the implications of temporal horizons. It is salutary to reconsider the currently outmoded dialectical premise that the past thinks through us just as much as we think the past. The question which genealogy poses in this perspective is that of attentiveness and of the opportunities made available through psychoanalytic method of being thought differently, of thinking for oneself.[25] More specifically in terms of the history of women in law, genealogy may contribute to what has been termed a "historicization of feminist jurisprudence,"[26] to the analysis of the plural, disparate, and mutable statuses of women in law over the *longue durée* of the Anglican legal tradition. In a stronger political sense, however, the jurisprudence of difference is a jurisprudence concerned to recognize and advocate the specific and separate status or space of women in law. Its aim is to specify in legal terms the thought of difference, to engender a legal protection of sexual identity, speech, writing, and relationship.[27] Legal recognition of an ethic of sexual difference, it will be argued here, depends upon a concept and practice of justice capable of recognizing a separate and plural status for the genres of the "other," the stranger, the nomad, alien, feminine, and animal.[28] As part of a jurisprudence of difference the legal recognition of the separate status of the feminine genre can borrow significantly from the feminine genealogies of law implicit in early constitutional texts and in the histories of women that are here spelled out under the name of *gynaetopia*. In contemporary terms the question is not simply that of

25. Michel Pêcheux, *Language, Semantics and Ideology* (London: Macmillan, 1982) at 220: "Nobody can think in anybody else's place: the practical primacy of the unconscious, which means that one must put up with what comes to be thought, i.e., one must 'dare to think for oneself.'"

26. See particularly Jeanne Schroeder, "Feminism Historicized: Medieval Misogynist Stereotypes in Contemporary Feminist Jurisprudence" (1990) 75 *Iowa Law Review* 1135; for a substantive example of such analysis see Jane Larson, "Women Understand So Little, They Call My Good Nature Deceit: A Feminist Rethinking of Seduction" (1993) 93 *Columbia Law Review* 374.

27. On justice and difference, see Iris Marion Young, *Justice and the Politics of Difference* (Princeton: Princeton University Press, 1990), particularly at 226–241. For further and disparate discussion see Irigaray, *Speculum of the Other Woman* at 227–242; Cornell, *Beyond Accommodation* at 1–20.

28. On the stranger and the feminine, see Julia Kristeva, *Strangers to Ourselves* (New York: Columbia University Press, 1990), especially at 42–46: "It is noteworthy that the first foreigners to emerge at the dawn of our civilization are foreign women—the Danaides."

recovering feminine genealogies, of remembering the imaginary zone of all that which the institution has excluded, it is also that of comprehending the extent of the legal repression of the feminine, not simply in terms of legal doctrine but equally in terms of legal method and conceptions of justice: "To claim a right to subjectivity and to freedom for women, without defining the objective rights of the feminine genre, appears to be an illusory solution to the historical hierarchy between the sexes and risks subjecting women to the power of an empty affirmation."[29] The specification of the legal spaces, languages or sites of genre and of difference, of corporeality, subjectivity, and sexuality takes jurisprudence both forward and back to the feminine as the structural principle of difference.

JANUS, OR THE BACKFACE OF COMMON LAW

The reference to Janus as the deity that emblematized the feminine virtues in and of history is a standard trope within the *querelle des femmes.* Janus looked both forward and back, to the people and to the Gods, but also, as historiography, Janus represented a feminine principle, the mixture of memory and foresight, evidence and faith.[30] There is a sense in which Janus could represent betrayal, in the contemporary idiom of the "two-faced" or of deception, and one history of women, Heywood's *Tunaikeion,* offers such betrayal by a woman as the source of the Salic prohibition upon feminine succession.[31] More usually, however, Janus was the sign of a history of feminine virtue and fame, a history of the power of women and of the deceit or neglect that veiled such histories from public view. Janus was in many respects the emblem of histories of feminine alterity in opposition to the laws and historiographies of dogma and doctrine. Such genealogies, for they were inevitably plural accounts of virtues, powers, archetypes, and myths, belonged to the tradition of laudation of famous women, but they were not merely formulaic exercises, and on occasion their political impetus would be made quite explicit, as where Agrippa observes that "had women but the power of making laws, and writing histories, what tragedies might they not have published of men's unparalleled villainy?"[32]

The correlation of history and law was no accident. The genealogical challenge to the history of famous men as universal history was necessarily a defensive or apologetic exercise and it was equally necessarily an attack upon law, upon the rules of inheritance, succession, and transmission. In a

29. Irigaray, *J'aime à toi* at 18.

30. For one example, in the context of ecclesiastical governance, see Griffith, *Bethel* at 5, depicting the household economy as being "Janus-like, it hath two faces: it looks backward, and forward."

31. Heywood, *Tunaikeion* at 123.

32. Agrippa, *De Nobilitate* at 51.

sense only Janus could mark the history of famous women and feminine virtues as a history of difference or of women *within* the polity and mark such discourse as a political and legal polemic. The assertion of a feminine reason within history was of itself a challenge to law, to written reason, to its history and inheritance. Feminine genealogies challenged doctrine by refuting the claims of natural law and its imagined differentiation of the sexes, and they equally challenged the authorities, the texts upon which doctrine was founded. Sir Thomas Elyot's *Defence of Good Women* builds upon the apologetic tradition by directly refuting the scholastic subordination of women drawn from Aristotle's *De Generatione Animalium.* The response to Aristotle's claim that woman is an imperfect work of nature (an infertile male) is that "the said words so spitefully spoken, proceeded only of cankered malice, whereunto he was of his own nature disposed." That Aristotle was dissolute and also inconstant could be proved by the stories of his idolization of Hermia, his concubine to whom he would apparently make sacrifices and sing hymns, to which information it is added that "this great philosopher was a blasphemer."[33] Elyot's dialogue then proceeds to list the virtues of the feminine within the polity and specifically refutes the scholastic claim that masculinity and rationality are cognate terms. Feminine attributes of "discretion, election and prudence" are the soul of reason and "do make that wisdom, which pertains to governments."[34] It is also pointed out that reason is unconnected with strength or bodily power, to which it is added that the bulk of the arts pertaining to the polity were invented by women and are best signaled by femininity, by the Muses but also by Minerva, Diotima, Aspasia, Theophraste, Leconcium, Carmentis, and all the other erudite and eloquent women of classical history.[35]

The history of alterity, and specifically of the feminine figures of the arts and the virtues, suggests that there might be another history of reason, an unconscious or repressed narrative of law. The possibility that there might be an alternative eloquence and disparate forms of reasoning and of their transmission was already a significant challenge to law. The literary and iconographic histories of women suggested the preexistence of an imaginary within the polity, of images within custom, fantasms within law. Time and again the stake of history is the questioning of the doctrinal

33. Sir Thomas Elyot, *The Defence of Good Women* (London: T. Berthelet, 1534, 1545 ed.) at fol. B v b.

34. Ibid. at fol. C vi a.

35. Ibid. at fol. C vi b–C vii a. For various lists of such erudite and artistic women, see also John Leslie, *De Illustrium Foeminarum in Republica Administrandi, ac Ferandis Legibus Authoritate* (Rheims: Fognaeus, 1580) at sig. 15v–23v. Gibson (trans.), *A Womans Woorth* at sig. 4r–14v; Gilles Ménage, *Historia Mulierum Philosopharum* (1690), translated as *The History of Women Philosophers* (Latham: University Press of America, 1984).

notion that there is only one reason and so only one law. More than that, the histories of "noble learned women" are predicated upon the historical character of all law and so opposed to the very notion of a law of nature which transcendentally predetermines the status of women. Law, for John Leslie in his protracted *Defence of Princesse Marie Queene of Scotland,* was the product of human history: "The law of nature or *ius gentium* is and ever was *after* the time that there were any nations or people and ever shall be."[36] If history, as custom, practice, and precedent, was the basis of common law, then the significance of the depiction and the telling of histories of feminine governance, of women lawgivers and other illustrious or erudite figures, had the direct status of political and legal evidence of women's suffrage. History could play the law: "For time to Laws themselves gives Law full oft."[37]

The enfolding of orders, of genres and genders, is in many respects the signal theme of *Jani Anglorum Facies Altera,* a work that is explicitly dedicated to "the Janus face of English law . . . [so that] its noble origin does not lie hidden, but light attending makes it far more clear and bright."[38] The emblem of common law was explicitly "the Reverse or Back-Face of the English Janus,"[39] which was taken to mean the stories, fictions, and legends of common law, "which I offer up in sacrifice . . . these scraps and fragments of collection, relating entirely, what they are, and as far as the present age may be supposed to be concerned in ancient stories and customs to the English-British state and Government."[40] The two faces (*facieque biformi*) of English law, "for thou canst hardly choose but own him having two faces,"[41] are variously British and Norman, preconquest and postconquest, native and foreign, saturnine and mercurial, antique and contemporary, before and behind, and finally, and most significantly, both male and female. It is a law that is marked, in other words, like Janus by ambiguity and a certain indistinction. Where Janus was the god of doors and gates and presided over the beginning or origin of things, the Janus of English law similarly guarded the origin or entry into law, the indistinct, preinstitutional, and indefinite time of customary or unwritten law. Its history, Selden argues, is not only two-faced but also effaced by antiquity and

36. Leslie, *A Defence* at sig. 129r. See Jordan, *Renaissance Feminism* at 243–246, for discussion of this point. See also another Scot, David Chambers, *Discours de la légitime succession des femmes aux possessions de leur parens et du gouvernment des princessess aux empires et royaumes* (Paris, 1577, n.p.). More broadly, see Gerda Lerner, *The Creation of Feminist Consciousness* (New York: Oxford University Press, 1993), ch. 11.

37. Selden, *Jani Anglorum* at 4.

38. Ibid., Preface.

39. Ibid. at fol. A 2 a.

40. Ibid. at fol. A 2 a.

41. Ibid. at fol. A 4 a.

marred by neglect, by lack of regard and "the injury of time" such that its past and its records are as close to myth as to historical narrative. From the remains of record and history Selden endeavors to describe the legal constitution of "Pananglium, that is, All England,"[42] a realm that in one view, that of Marcianus Heracleotes, has in it thirty-three nations.[43] And behind the legends of origin, of the various nations and languages of Albion and so of common law, behind the narratives of its diverse temporal beginnings, the representation or image of common law, its symbolic descent, is consistently portrayed as being from a variety of feminine images and female figures, the forgotten faces of a law that was never one.

The metaphor of *prosographia,* used by Fortescue and others, of a feminine face of justice returns most forcefully in Selden. To represent the backface or underside of the constitution, the institutional unconscious, myth, or image, leads to a return to the legal *querelle des femmes.* It leads in particular to a tabulation of famous or illustrious women, legislators, lawgivers, and sovereigns from antiquity to contemporaneity. In the time of the laws, old heroes went by the names of gods and in the druidical Celtic colony of Britain, the *semnaitheia* or "venerable Goddesses" ruled. These were the goddesses of justice, the Furies, "also called Themis," who sat "upon the skirts of the wicked" and, as (by *antiphrasis*) the Eumenides, rewarded the good and "such as are blameless and faultless."[44] They are the first judges of the Celtic common law, the *Deis Matribus* or mother goddesses to whom altars were inscribed and before whose dreadful justice the populace would tremble and shake. To this description Selden adds: "Nor let it be any hindrance, that so splendid and so manly a name is taken from the weaker sex, to wit, the Goddesses."[45] It is in honor of these Goddesses of the night that the terms of the law and indeed the divisions of the calendar—"the spaces or intervals of all time"—are defined not by the number of days, but that of nights.[46]

As to the historical face of the common law, it was frequently female. Thus, for example, the histories relay the government of Martia, from whom the Britains got the term Martian law or Merchenlage, which became one of the three local systems of law to be merged by Edward the

42. Ibid. at 94.

43. Ibid. at fol. A 3 b.

44. Ibid. at 4–5. For a further and contrary discussion of the three Furies—Alecto (or Luctificia), Tesiphone, and Megaera—see Heywood, *Tunaikeion* at 47–50, where they are listed as "infernal Goddesses." See also Selden, *De Diis Syris Syntagmata II.*

45. Selden, *Jani Anglorum* at 5.

46. Ibid. at 6. (As, for example, in "fortnight.") The gender of night, of course, has many further significant connotations, some of which can be pursued in Schiesari, *The Gendering of Melancholia.* See also Kristeva, *Black Sun.*

Confessor into a law common to the three kingdoms of Britain.[47] While Selden admits a certain "poetick licence and rhetorical figure" to the pre-Roman stories, his own account, which starts with the druids, the severe and melancholic figures reported by Caesar, Strabo, and Tacitus, is even more explicitly feministic. Taking the side of Tacitus, who reported that the Germanic tribes held their women in almost mystical awe, Selden savages the antifeminine sentiments of Bodin, of the Salic lawyers, and of Aristotle himself. Women in Britain participated in counsels of war and in military duties, indeed "Britons were want to war under the conduct of women, and to make no difference of sexes in places of government and command."[48] In one aspect the argument is specific to Britain and to the regency of English Queens, particularly those most illustrious of monarchs, Boadicea and Elizabeth. Women monarchs had often been the most successful and, as Serjeant Lodowick Lloyd, in an equally feministic passage, argued slightly earlier, "if men govern like women, then women should govern."[49]

Selden's view was both descriptive and prescriptive, it being his belief that women had governed and that they should govern. In terms of the various pasts that Selden depicts, all are witness to feminine rule. In mythology there were "more She-Gods than He-Gods," while "virtue herself . . . is female in dress (*cultu*) and in name."[50] Indeed Selden states that "I will not declaim female excellency here: the thing speaks for itself more than I can, and the subject is its own best orator." What follows this rhetorical gesture is a denunciation of Bodin's *De Republica* and an even more polemical assertion that Aristotle would admit women to government "whatever the foolish interpreters of the *Politics* say."[51] Such an argument is a commonplace drawn fairly directly from the antinomic or polarized form of the *querelle des femmes*.[52] There can be no natural law prohibiting women from government because historical counterexamples indicate that male rule, far from being universal and unchanging, is quite frequently the historical exception. Against Bodin, Selden thus lists the instances of matriarchy at the level both of cultures, such as Egypt and Israel, and at that of individual monarchs, such as Deborah or Artemis.[53] At an ontological level he

47. On which see, particularly, Dugdale, *Origines Juridiciales* at sig. 5r–v.

48. Selden, *Jani Anglorum* at 18–19.

49. Lodowick Lloyd, *A Briefe Conference of Divers Lawes: Divided into Certaine Regiments* (London: Creede, 1600, 1602 ed.) at 90. (The source of argument, ironically, is Aristotle, *Politics*, ch. 7.)

50. Selden, *Jani Anglorum* at 18.

51. Ibid. at 21.

52. See Maclean, *Woman Triumphant* at 29–31, 38–39; the polarities of argument are also analyzed in Maclean, *Renaissance Notion of Women* at 2–5.

53. Selden, *Jani Anglorum* at 19–21. Lloyd, *Conference of Divers Lawes* at 91–92, offers a similar list.

aligns women to the other face of reason, to the virtues of "sanctity and foresight," on the strength of which the arguments against women can only be taken for "mad rude expressions . . . not unfit for a professor in Bedlam College. . . . Virtue shuts no door against anybody, any sex, but freely admits all."[54]

In one aspect, Selden's argument is explicitly that femininity is the other face of law, which face he links directly to mythology, to fragmentary records, to a feminine imaginary and figures of virtue. Elsewhere, in a study of the genealogy of the gods, Selden depicts the plastic symbolism of justice in terms of a left-handed God, blind and beautiful, pure and untouched; she was nature in culture, wisdom in law.[55] The metaphor (*prosopopoeia*) of another face of law may indeed be taken in many different senses. By analogy with Janus, the female face of law is not only the face that looks to the gods, but also that which looks back, that remembers the historical succession of feminine rulers and also and more profoundly the experience or generation of habits and customs that are "antique, buried in rubbish, old and musty." In other words the history of law had covered over or failed to disinter the signs of a sex "equally divine as the male."[56] To understand custom one must look at law, but that law is never simply one. In this instance the law of custom was "other" to law or, more accurately, an other law in that in and through custom, laws were to be "discovered" or "found" or "declared" or otherwise born. Femininity would here be the hidden face of the source of tradition, and women would be both the custodians of the unwritten and the symbols of its transmission. Here, in the iconography of justice, Justitia would be blindfolded to indicate eyes that looked back as well as to suggest the sightless vision of interiority, of foresight, and so of the future. The innocence of law, its iconic representation as a system in the image of Justitia, thus signals a deep irony. It can be formulated best in terms of the dissemblance that presents the emblem of the legal system as a whole to be justice as a woman, in the context of a substantive discipline of law that denied personality, inheritance, and public office to women. Such, however, is the logic of the icon: it can never be present, it represents that which cannot appear for itself. Thus, as the representation of the rule of law, of pure governance or totality, Justitia can never be present as the content of the system. That justice is represented as a woman and that the reality of her feminine form, her body, exists precisely outside the legal institution as its image, connotes further ironies. One such irony must be the reemergence in the sixteenth century of the symbolization of justice as a blindfolded woman. How better to represent

54. Selden, *Jani Anglorum* at 20.
55. Selden, *De Diis Syris Syntagmata II* at 124–125.
56. Selden, *Jani Anglorum* at Preface.

an inaugural and mathematically repeated justice than as blind to the world? How better to repress the body than by closing its eyes and forcing it into an internal and dark world of the spirit? How better to figure the control or subjection of a woman and of her passion than by hiding her eyes—theologically and, poetically, her soul—from the vision of law? In the last instance could it not be argued that through blindfolding a woman, through erasing her face, the representation of the purity of law was only possible though the practice of injustice? The men who burden the back of the feminine deity in the Egyptian hieroglyphic could perhaps be read as having established a timeless metaphor of innocence parasitic upon blinding their host.

Janus and Justitia are alike ambiguous figures and both connote a savage or at least extreme power of the feminine. The icon of Justitia in this sense institutes a space both of potential and of danger within which the femininity of virtue is a paradox against established law.[57] Virtue is a feature of the soul, and although the soul has no sex, "the formal understanding of things that are, or may be, is signified to us by the feminine virtues." The same treatise later adds that in relation to government "the virtues feminine hath been of greater efficacy than men . . . it consists much more of debating cases, and the faculty imaginative, which are indeed the functions of the soul."[58] A further paradox is that despite such attributions of power, wisdom, and foresight to the feminine soul, the woman is also the figure of a radical evil, of idolatry, and of image-service. The foresight that Selden attributes to femininity is not only a sign of the transcendental quality of legality itself. Foresight is connotative also of soothsaying and divining, of the powers of the divine which belong either within or without the law, dependent upon the tasks or the purposes to which these powers are put. A law that borrowed substantially from the Anglican conception of a dual polity could not avoid confronting the power of such feminine reason, either to confirm or to banish its art and practice. For in the end, the principle of reason upon which law was founded was neither male nor female. It had a sex only in its embodiment (*in corporibus est sexum*), in its materialization, in the intuition, discrimination, memory, or choice through which it becomes law for us: the reason of judgment, of the application of law, is deemed the law of the second Venus, the copulation of norm and fact, general and particular, rule and circumstance.[59]

57. Gibson (trans.), *A Womans Woorth* at fol. A 10 a: "I might call it a paradoxe, because some men (vainly transported) no doubt will tearme it so."

58. Ibid. at fol. 4 a.

59. Selden, *Jani Anglorum* at 11. Cf. Elyot, *Defence of Good Women* at fol. C iii a–C iv b, who particularly stressed this point. Not only is reason, as an aspect of the soul, by nature both

WOMEN'S LAW

In concluding his argument as to the right of women to govern, Selden states, "nor could I forbear out of conscience with my suffrage, to assist as far as I could, that sex, which is so great and comfortable an importance to mankind."[60] The question which will now be posed is that of the significance and legal context of this self-confessed desire to alter the constitutional, political, and legal boundaries of female personality. It is not a desire that appears to have greatly affected Selden's other works, and in his *Titles of Honour* and in his *Table Talk,* to take the two most obvious examples, the place of women is not visibly altered. In the former work, "oeconomic rule" is described in scholastic manner as the basis of community and civil society—as itself the first form of *societas*—and is said to have "in its state, the Husband, father and master, as *King.*"[61] Where Selden's legal community was historicist and civilian and so only generically concerned with the personality of women, the feminine regency of the latter portion of the sixteenth century, and certain theological debates around that issue, had a far more direct and practical effect on common law.

As is appropriate for a discussion that stems in part from the English Janus, the most significant contribution to the debate arguably comes from, or is responsive to, Scottish writers. Selden had challenged some aspects of the Renaissance interpretation of Aristotle, and in this regard he builds upon a political tradition that saw Elizabeth's sovereignty as an occasion to reassert the argument for feminine office and rule. John Case, in *Sphaera Civitatis* of 1588, had attacked the assumption that the domestic duties and subjugation of women should be interpreted as extending to the public sphere. "Experience makes her wise. What, therefore, prevents women from playing a full part in public affairs? If one is born free, why should she obey? If one is heiress to a kingdom, why should she not reign?"[62] At one level this argument simply recognizes female regency as historical reality and suggests that constitutional doctrine recognize this accomplished fact. More interesting, however, than the political assertion of a challenge to scholasticism is the desire to develop and interpret this

male and female, but *prudence,* the feminine quality of *prudentia* or foresight by which the exercise of judgment is made possible, is a female art.

60. Selden, *Jani Anglorum* at 21.

61. Selden, *Titles of Honour* at 2–3. Selden, *Table Talk* at 20–22. Mention should also be made of one of Selden's most extraordinary works, *De Diis Syris Syntagmata II,* which lists fabulous idols and other illicit gods mentioned in the Bible. It also includes, at 151–165, a genealogy of the gods (*De Genealogia Deorum*) which lists justice and law under the heading *De Diis Moralibus.*

62. John Case, *Sphaera Civitatis* (Oxford: n.p., 1588) at 40–41, cited and discussed in Maclean, *Renaissance Notion of Women* at 60–61.

argument on the strength not of the classics but of common law. Thus, in debating the more complex issue of Mary Queen of Scots, it is John Knox, attacking the "monstriferous empire," the enormity, vanity, odor, and "pestiferous policies" of this idol, this "cursed Jezebel," who, ironically, relies most comprehensively upon Roman law and patristic interpretations.[63] The Anglican apologists for women turn to the vernacular English jurisdiction and the maternal common law.

The most indicative and proleptic feature of Bishop Aylmer's response to Knox is that, after listing the fallacies of the traditional attack upon women, he specifically turns from theology to jurisprudence and directly addresses the question of which law should govern and determine this debate:

> I say therefore that this matter belongs not to the civil law, but to the municipal law of England, for like as every field brings forth not all fruits: so is not one law meet for all countries. I grant that the civil law is the best, the perfectest and the largest, that ever was made: yet comprehends it not all things in all countries . . . wherefore in appointing us to be ordered by civil law you offend *in iustitia distributiva* . . . our law must direct us, because it best agrees with our country.[64]

Civil law would smother England and extinguish those customary rules that were the distinctive inheritance of common law, its ancient stories, "the witness of time, the candle of truth, the life of memory . . . and the register of antiquity."[65] The civil law, in its universality and abstraction, in its size and its strength, would destroy the feminine virtues of the local and particular experience of common law. Like a woman, the common law is represented as being inessential and particular when compared to its parent or its Continental competitor; it has either to mimic the stronger and prior law or differentiate itself by defining itself against it. But whichever is the case, the rule of the parent civil law is a trauma for a common law which seeks its own identity through separation, antirrhetic, and polemic. For Aylmer it is thus our "own weights" that should weigh in the scales of justice, and by those measures women are to be more liberally treated and their right to succession and office allowed.

Even more striking for its assertion of the vernacular law is the work of John Leslie in defence of Mary Queen of Scot's claim to the English Crown: neither civil law nor Salic law have any place in England where the law is unwritten and "grounded onlie upon a common and generall custome throughe owte the whole realme . . . as apperethe by the treatise of the aunciente and famous writter upon the lawes of the realme named

63. Knox, *First Blast of the Trumpet* at 40 and 58.
64. Aylmer, *Harborowe* at fol. K 4 b–L i a.
65. Ibid. at fol. E 4 b.

Ranulphus de Glanvilla."[66] Leslie's account of the law ostensibly builds upon a detailed knowledge of uniquely English rules. The question of succession, concerning as it does the royal prerogative and powers, must be decided by rules that uniquely govern the sovereign. To this effect he cites the "maxime of lawe" that "no maxime or rule in the lawe can extende to binde the kinge or crowne, unless the same be speciallie mentioned therein."[67] On the strength of this principle of interpretation, Leslie admonishes those who had taken legislation of 1350, *An Act Touching such as be born beyond the Seas,* confirmed in 1368, as applying to the Crown, which was not specifically named. The legislation was taken, though only by implication, to deny the right of inheritance in England to those who were born out of England, out of the "ligeance of the King," and whose parents were not "of the obedience of the Kinge of Englande."[68] To apply such law to the Crown not only ignored the principles of statutory interpretation but also ignored constitutional history and the law on strangers recollected from English cases whose records no longer survived.

The distinction and idiosyncracy of English law is a theme common to Aylmer and to Leslie. It is this concern to argue a question of natural and biblical law in terms of local custom and the specific character or constitution of Britain to which later feministic legal texts return. Aylmer has a marginal note which states laconically that "God is English," while Leslie revives an antique aphorism, "*Regnum Angli[a]e est regnum Dei* . . . and that God hathe ever had a special care of yt."[69] Although Leslie returns to refute the traditional arguments of the *querelle* against women, namely that the Bible, nature, history, grammar, and common sense all exclude them from office, it is significant that his work ends in the manner of common law doctrine by citing English custom and English legislation: "By custom in England all manner of . . . jurisdictions and other prerogatives [are], and ought to be, as fully and wholly and absolutely in the Prince female as in the male, and so was it ever deemed, judged and accepted."[70] It is also noteworthy that in terms of historical examples of illustrious women (*illustrium foeminarum*) it is queens of England who are lauded all the way back to Noah, "whom prophane writers call Janus,"[71] the other emblem of English law. In short, the repressed genealogy of the feminine rulers of the Island Britannia is all that is needed to overturn foreign prescriptions and

66. Leslie, *A Defence* at sig. 57r–v. His other major statement on women was the more derivative *De Illustrium Foeminarum,* which lists erudite women (*eruditae mulieres*) and urges Queen Mary upon England.

67. Leslie, *A Defence* at sig. 59r.

68. Ibid. at 75r–v.

69. Aylmer, *Harborowe* at fol. P iv b; Leslie, *A Defence* at sig. 97v.

70. Leslie, *A Defence* at sig. 137v.

71. Ibid. at sig. 132r.

their "counterfeit law." It is enough, Leslie argues laconically, "to show and prove that women have from time to time born princely regiment in the most notable parts of the world and most famous commonwealths."[72]

It is upon the particular character and quality of Leslie's legal interests that attention should be focused. Subsequent texts that argue for female rights or simply attempt to protect or defend the status or the interests of women are most striking where they attach such concern to substantive legal issues. Thus, for example, there are texts such as Heale, *An Apologie for Women* of 1609, which endeavor to argue for change in the law on the basis of theological and moral prescriptions. The sole topic of Heale's *Apologie* is whether a husband has a legal right to beat his wife. In analyzing the civil law—which governs all aspects of spousals and marriage—Heale finds many rules that are archaic, ignorant, or simply morally objectionable. The catalog of laws in need of reform includes the dependence of the wife on the husband in terms of dignity (she takes his name and status), and the duty of the wife to follow the husband from city to city or even abroad. It includes the "strict and obdurate" rule that the wife lose her dowrie for giving a "lascivious kiss" and equally remarks the inequality that allows the husband to commit adultery but rules that if the wife "play the Adulteresse . . . the husband may then produce her into publike judgment, deprive her of her promised dowrie and expose her to perpetual divorcement."[73] Nowhere, however, in civil or canon law can Heale find any "positive sentence or verdict that it is lawful for a husband to beat his wife."[74] It is pure interpretation based upon the invective of "mysogynaes" and "cynickes" who have either the hate or the ignorance necessary to bend the law and to suggest that so indecorous, immoral, and ill-mannered a custom could possibly be English law. If it is, however, to be taken as law, nothing says that the wife is legally bound to endure or tolerate such beating. She may leave her husband and the husband must pay her an adequate maintenance during her absence.[75]

72. Ibid. at sig. 129v.

73. W. Heale, *An Apologie for Women* (Oxford: J. Barnes, 1609) at 25–26. (Citing *Code* 9.7.)

74. Ibid. at 28. Perkins, *Christian Oeconomie* at 688.1, indicates that a wife may leave her husband if he fails to protect her from a stranger or if the husband threatens harm. Ridley, *View of the Civille and Ecclesiasticall Law* at 82: "If any man beat his wife for any other cause, than for which he may be justly severed or divorced from her, he shall for such injury be punished."

75. Heale, *Apologie* at 46. Godolphin, *Repertorium Canonicum* at 507–508, cites *Sir Thomas Simmond's Case* as well as ecclesiastical doctrine to the effect that correction must be reasonable. Reasonable appeared to mean that the husband could use physical force to correct the wife but only where her offense was one for which the husband could sue for divorce. Interestingly, in light of the earlier discussion, Swinburne, *A Briefe Treatise of Testaments* at 300, exempts the Queen from the exclusion of women from making wills without the consent of their husbands.

Heale, whose text has generally been taken as an overextravagant praise of women, argues by extensive analogy and by reason of consistency. While his work certainly has its share of arguments drawn from the *querelle*—he praises famous women, he adopts the theological argument that Eve was made of man, but man was made of earth ("man by a strange kind of *metamorphosis* [was] converted into woman"[76])—the primary force of the argument is pragmatic and legalistic and does not go further than suggesting that male and female are equal in their qualities as in their failings. It is, for Heale, ultimately a constitutional question and so a question of manners, decency, and decorum in the estate of husband and wife. As decorum is the end or goal of the Anglican commonwealth, it is the task of the lawyer "as a laborious traveller [to go] through all estates, to bring all unto decency. He ordereth the estate of monarchs and princes; of peers and nobles; of magistrates and subjects; of parents and children; of husbands and wives; of masters and servants . . . so that an absolute *indecorum* is an absolute breach of the law."[77] Such a view may well seem to come close to the heart of the unwritten tradition: what is against the judicial perception of good manners or is "not without vice" is unlawful of itself as being *contra bonos mores,* indelicate and extreme.

The evidence of the *Repertorium Canonicum* and other abridgments and treatises would seem to suggest that in some areas the law does change to the end of greater protection of the separate rights of women. The rights or interests protected vary over time and are normally attendant upon, or secondary to, male interests. Nonetheless, fictions are developed to allow the husband to endow the wife;[78] the issue of duress in marriage is canvassed in relation to gifts and wills made by the wife either to the husband or to strangers to the marriage;[79] the wife is allowed a plea of *non est factum* in relation to debts;[80] the interest of the unmarried woman in her own reputation is protected rigorously by laws of defamation;[81] there is legislation on rape and the carrying away of unmarried women with property;[82] the law governing separation and rights of alimony is further

76. Heale, *Apologie* at 55–56.

77. Ibid. at 49–50. Compare Downing, *A Discourse* at 2–3: "Good manners cause obedience, and religion naturally begets good manners . . . for although ill manners are *per accidens* the cause, or rather the occasion of making good laws, yet they are better in the executing, best when they are obeyed."

78. On the development of fictions, see Perkins, *Profitable Book* at 196; Thomas Wood, *An Institute of the Laws of England* (Savoy: Sare, 1720) at 101–104.

79. See Swinburne, *A Brief Treatise of Testaments,* at 80–84; Godolphin, *Orphan's Legacy* at 31–35.

80. See Godolphin, *Repertorium Canonicum* at 507.

81. Ibid. at 515–519. See, for example, *Pollard v Armshaw* (1601) 75 ER 1073, or *Dorothy Brian v Cockman* 79 ER 881.

82. A line of legislation which begins with a statute of 1486 (3 H VII cap. 2) raising the penalties for carrying a woman away against her will "that hath lands of goods."

elaborated,[83] as are other rules designed to maintain the reputation and decorum of the feminine. Decorum, however, while it may be the oldest of legal criteria is hardly the most definite nor necessarily the most accessible in the eyes of lawyers. The greatest legal monument of the *querelle* is not Heale's impassioned defense, nor Selden's lucubrations on the English Janus, but rather a legal manual in the style of a work of self-help called *The Lawes Resolutions of Women's Rights,* anonymously published in 1632.[84] While the popularization of legal knowledge was a dimension of the vernacularization that accompanied print, and many law dictionaries and books of precedents and treatises were prefaced with remarks to the effect that every subject of the realm could now know the law,[85] a book devoted to women's law with a running title *Woman's Lawyer* was a remarkable event. What could "woman's law" be if the law knew no such category? The answer is that for the purposes of this new legal discipline, the author of the *Woman's Lawyer* replaces the first division of the law of persons—that between slave and free—with "a primary distribution" between masculine and feminine, for *masculum et foeminam fecit eos.*[86] Yet the category of woman includes no single designation or definition but rather lists every transaction in which femininity—the various categories of *feme, mulier, foeminam,* dowager, concubine, virgin, or ward—was an element.

The purpose of the treatise is twofold. It is first designed simply to extract from common law sources—from statutes, conjoining customs, cases, opinions, sayings, arguments, judgments, and points of learning—that part of English law "belonging to women" or that which "contains the immunities, advantages, interests and duties of women."[87] In this respect the work is ostensibly addressed generically to the illusory referent "women" and is designed to provide information not otherwise readily available "with as

83. See, for example, *Hyatt's Case* deciding the right of women to alimony, reported in Godolphin, *Repertorium Canonicum* at 493–504; also, Wood, *An Institute* at 105–109.

84. Anonymous, *The Lawes Resolutions.* Some have attempted to attribute the work to Sir John Doderidge, author inter alia of *The English Lawyer* of 1631, but there is no compelling evidence. The work is unique in its scope in English law, although it might be noted that there is one German legal treatise that goes some way to achieving the same end: J. Wolff, *Discursus: De Foeminarum in jure civili et canonico privilegiis, immunitatibus et praeeminenta* (Rostock: M. Saxo, 1615). In contemporary terms, the notion of "Women's Law" has been resurrected by T. Stang-Dahl, *Women's Law: An Introduction to Feminist Jurisprudence* (Oxford: Norwegian University Press, 1987), who defines the purpose of women's law as being "to examine and understand how women are considered in law and how the law corresponds to women's reality and needs" (12). See also and similarly, S. Atkins and B. Hoggett, *Women and the Law* (Oxford: Blackwell, 1985) at 1: "We seek to understand how the law has perceived women and responded to their lives."

85. See, for example, Swinburne, *A Brief Treatise of Testaments* at fol. B i b.

86. Anonymous, *Lawes Resolutions* at 2.

87. Ibid. at 403 and 3.

little tediousness as I can."[88] In this sense the work is an exhaustive catalog of points of law that mention, touch, or affect the different categories, statuses, or faces of the feminine. Such popular intent, however, has deeper roots, for as Selden found in *Jani Anglorum,* it is not possible to write a constitutional history, let alone list the laws that govern a majority of legal subjects, without becoming aware of the ambiguity or the ethical inconsistency of the tradition. To compile an extended account of the law touching women was to produce a document enfolded in several jurisdictions or laws and of itself a record of peculiar cultural and political significance. The constant theme of the advice offered throughout the treatise was that of the defense of women, the critique of common law, and the manipulation of hostile rules to the benefit of an oppressed class.

Wherever the law could be ameliorated or its application tempered by foresight of feminine need, the *Woman's Lawyer* offered the means of such fiction or improvement. Heale's example of the lawful right of the husband to beat the wife is confirmed, according to the author, by Brooke's *Abridgement,* which states that "if a man beat an outlaw, a traitor, a pagan, his villein, or his wife it is dispunishable, because by the law common these persons can have no action."[89] The reason at law for this disability is both specific, in the form of the precedent cited, and a consequence of the general status of the wife as being in the power of the husband, and so is without independent legal personality for most although not all purposes. It might be noted that by case law also cited in the *Woman's Lawyer,* a woman prisoner of the "Marshalsey" complained to the court that the "Marshalls man had ravished her in prison. Gascoigne commanded the Marshall to take his man to his custody, and his staff from him, and the Court told the woman, that alone she could not bring appeal, *sans son Baron,* but if her husband would come, and they two together prove the rape, the ravisher should be hanged."[90] There is thus no obvious legal solution to the problems of the woman whose husband is violent, either in precedent or in doctrine. The *Woman's Lawyer,* however, does not limit itself to remarking the woman's bad choice of company. A writ listed by Fitzherbert is cited which states that "she may sue out of Chancery to compell him to find surety of honest behaviour toward her, and that he shall neither do nor procure to be done to her (marke I pray you) any bodily damage, otherwise than appertains to the office of husband or lawful and reasonable correction."[91] The English Janus gave with one hand what it took away with the other. The *Woman's Lawyer* remarks that the scope of this power

88. Ibid. at 3.
89. Ibid. at 128.
90. Ibid. at 210 (citing 8 H 4, fol. 21).
91. Ibid. at 128.

of correction is uncertain, yet continues to observe that "the sex feminine is at no very great disadvantage. . . . Why may not the wife beat the husband . . . what action can he have if she do. . . . The actionless woman beaten by her husband, hath retaliation left to beat him again, if she dares."[92] The discussion of "lawfulness" is concluded by remarking that if the husband comes to Chancery to compel surety he is unlikely to be heard. While this may well have been good law, it is hard to imagine that it was good or feasible practice in a legal context in which a wife who killed her husband was guilty of the felony of treason, albeit petty treason against the prerogative of the husband.[93]

The advice offered in the above example would appear to be in part ironic, yet the fact that every section of the work contains similar advice for the woman suggests that in that instance it was more likely despair than flippancy that motivated the sentence. In other segments of the treatise the advice is of obvious purport, and the suggestion of fictions would genuinely change the law. Different transactions, relationships, and threats create different problems for the female "persona" in law and the *Woman's Lawyer* attempts no one solution or form of exchange for distinctive situations. Thus one chapter of the treatise is devoted to the law on loss of dower, the wife's entitlement in law should the husband die before her: "The rest of the fourth book shall consist most in warnings to widows and women tenants in particular estates, that they do nothing prejudicial to their warrant," namely to the writ of *quod ei deforciat* which allows a widow to recover dower.[94] The subsequent chapter lists the various ways in which a widow might lose dower, as by allowing buildings or woods to fall to waste and so threatening the interest of the reversioner, or, if she alienated or made a gift of lands held in dower, the heir could recover.

In respect of other transactions, the woman may or may not retain legal personality according to specific rules. In some instances the advice is trivial or humorous. The widow who takes more apparel than is convenient for her degree is made an executrix *de son tort demesne,* which is "a troublesome office."[95] A wife only becomes entitled to dower upon consummation of the marriage and so is advised to leave the wedding party early "and leave out the long measurles till you be in bed. . . . Get you there quickly, and pay the minstrels tomorrow."[96] More serious advice pertains to the presumption of duress in relation to contracts between husband and wife, the possibility of employing fictions to enfeoff the wife or the husband, and the circumstances under which the crimes of the husband will

92. Ibid. at 129.
93. Ibid. at 206.
94. Ibid. at 305.
95. Ibid. at 233.
96. Ibid. at 118.

be visited upon the wife, as when she loses her dower if her husband is outlawed or attainted of felony.[97] The status of the married woman is that of infant, she loses her property, is incapable of making contracts, cannot sue or bring a writ in her own right, and can neither inherit by nor make a will. At the same time, "in matters of criminal and capital causes, a *feme covert* shall answer without her husband" unless the crime was committed with the husband or by coercion of the husband, in which case the wife cannot be charged.[98]

The disabilities and incapacities as well as the rights of women are specific to occasions and transactions. The *Woman's Lawyer* attempts to situate particular legal relations with regard to their impact upon the female sex. The closest that the work comes to a general account or critique of the law governing women is in relation to the inequality of legal provision in circumstances where difference of sex—however defined—would not appear determinative. Thus the law governing elopement, whereby a woman forfeits her dower for adultery but the husband is immune and is allowed any number of adulterous relationships without forfeiture of land, is criticized. Redress for this inequality should be "by Parliament" and, in the meantime, one had the Christian solace of knowing that "liberty or impunity in doing evil by immodest life or lascivious gallops, is no freedom or happiness."[99] In suggesting reforms of the law or in berating aspects of specific legal conditions such as the loss of noble status in a woman who marries below her degree, it is not so much the unity "woman" as the fragmentary condition that is the object of critique. The feminine sex of legal subjects should not be "abstruded," smothered, concealed, or "scattered in corners of an uncouth language," but at the same time the *Woman's Lawyer* does not treat that sex in an undifferentiated way.[100] Thus, to take one final example, the *Woman's Lawyer* begins not by defining the classification of all persons into male or female, but rather by listing the seven ages that the woman has for legal purposes. The different legal states of femininity, as maiden, wife, widow, are crosscut by virginity and maternity, but also by age, as, for example, "woman is out of ward for her body [i.e., she can marry] before she is out of ward for her land."[101] If she marries a man under age, she remains in her father's ward. She may have dower at the age of nine, at twelve she may consent to marriage, at fourteen she may choose a guardian.[102]

97. Ibid. at 52, citing Stamford.

98. Ibid. at 206.

99. Ibid. at 146. See, for an earlier and equally powerful denunciation of this rule, Agrippa, *De Nobilitate* at 31.

100. Ibid. at 403.

101. Ibid. at 22–23, giving as the reason that she is quickly able *domui precesse, vivo subesse.*

102. Ibid. at 23. For further discussion, see, for example, Wood, *An Institute* at 19.

GYNAETOPIA, OR THE LEGAL PLACE OF THE FEMININE

The most strikingly contemporary feature of the *Woman's Lawyer* and of feminine genealogies of law more generally is the uncertainty of the category of women within early legal thought. In Selden's terms, the feminine was both the other face and the particularity of common law. At one level this ambiguity forced law to mix with other literatures and to search the languages of theology, nature, philosophy, medicine, politics, ethics, and the other occult sciences to find some way of characterizing an essentially inessential being. The feminine, however, escaped delimitation—it was both fecund and fluid, image and flesh, ignorant and erudite, illustrious and idolatrous, Justitia and Jezebel, matter and wonder. This sex which was not one, which was lost or "clean abstruded" in the law, was never successfully defined in advance as the *querelle des femmes* would have intended. Women were not a predicate of law but rather impermanent subjects of legal judgment. A woman was an expression of a legal event, of decisions and discretions, and so was constructed from the various realms of legal experience as opposed to being reflective either of some underlying juridical structure or of the schemata of being that popular sentiment and occult science together intended. For the law, after all, persons were divided between slave and free. Although many women were slaves, *in alieni iuris,* and *indigni,* not all slaves were women.

The common law *querelle des femmes* is symptomatic, in other words, of certain deeper shifts within the structure and reason of English law. Dedicating its political effort to the memory of that "most excellent lawgiver and renowned Queen Elizabeth," whose sovereignty had seen much reform of the law touching women, the *Woman's Lawyer* intended its minute description or *chorographica descriptio* of the particulars of English law to act as "a firm bulwark against all manner of injuries that possibly might oppress women."[103] If it could not embark upon such an endeavor equipped with a preexistent or agreed legal or political definition of women, then it had inevitably to resort either to an immanent description of femininity derived from the infinite particulars of common law or to the generic description of the figures or images of women in the surrounding literature of the *querelle.* Indeed, literature here came to play the law, and to the extent that it embraced the literary representation of femininity, it did so at times to the benefit of women: it was through figures, presumptions, fictions, and dreams, through the imaginary, the other, the aesthetic, through a certain novel *écriture* as well as ethical argument that legal change occurred.

Fortescue and Selden derive what may properly be described as an im-

103. Anonymous, *Lawes Resolutions* at 401.

age of women from a lost genealogy or historical memory of femininity. It is also, in terms of its representation, under the sign of *Polyhimnia,*[104] the femininity of memory as reminiscence, whereby "out of one thing remembered others are discovered."[105] *Jani Anglorum* maps the places of women in the repressed, neglected, or forgotten history of common law. It is possible that this narrative of the feminine in common law, of custody or custom as creativity and of tradition as generation, is to some large degree linked to the literary recollection of women, to *gynaetopia* and its illustrious women. In the *City of Ladies* it is after all Justice—defined as measure—who comes to the dreamer in 1404 and offers to people the City, the feminine commonwealth with women of reason, prerogative, and honor.[106] Justice is the third Lady but the chief virtue, and she represents a juridical history of illustrious women. In the ensuing tradition it is not only the task of literary feminism to chart the narrative of feminine excellence and erudition,[107] it also states the constitutional case for the right and sovereignty of women in the varied spheres of their political experience. In such terms Agrippa, for example, remarks that "the English nation were most ungrateful, should they ever forget their obligations to this sex," or allow "unjust laws, foolish customs, and an ill-mode of education" to continue to usurp their liberties.[108] For Agrippa, to continue with the same example, women's proximity to generation and reproduction granted them an ontological superiority as well as a mythological sovereignty, for "woman was formed miraculously . . . [and] was the end, and last work of God, and introduced into the world, not unlike a Queen into a royal palace. . . . Man seemed only her *harbinger* or attendant."[109] The feminine was here the telos of nature, just as for Selden, Justitia, a woman, was the telos of law.[110]

At one level it might be argued that this concern with justice as feminine, as an image and end of law, simply spells out in hyperbolic manner

104. Heywood, *Tunaikeion* at 313.

105. Doderidge, *English Lawyer* at 15 (defining *actus reminiscendi* as one part of memory intellective).

106. Christine de Pisan, *Cyte of Ladies* at fol. C c iii a. See further the prescriptions for *gynaetopia* in Astell, *A Serious Proposal* at 40–45; and also the Castle of Fortuna, depicted in Christine de Pisan, *Le Livre de la mutacion de fortune* (Paris: Picard, 1404, 1959 ed.). For Pisan, justice was anything but blind.

107. As in Leslie, *De Illustrium Foeminarum* at 23 ff.; see also Daniel Tuvil, *Asylum Veneris, or a Sanctuary for Ladies* (London: E. Griffin, 1616); and for a classic study of philosophical women, see Ménage, *Historia Mulierum Philosopharum.* Most influential in England were Agrippa, *De Nobilitate*; Vives, *De Institutione;* and Elyot, *Defence*; all of whom list women philosophers amongst other illustrious women.

108. Agrippa, *De Nobilitate,* respectively at 66, 76.

109. Ibid. at 10–13.

110. Selden, *Jani Anglorum* at 4–5. For contemporaneous examples, see Finch, *Law, or, A Discourse Therof* at 11; Fulbeck, *Direction or Preparative to the Study of Law* at 2–3.

the formulaic commonplaces of feminist and antifeminist rhetorics.[111] In this sense, feminist argument, its exaggeration, speculation, and apocryphal histories, would simply represent the externality of the feminine to the legal: the image that is chosen to represent the system of law, the legal totality, would necessarily come from outside it. In Fortscue's terms the likeness of law is not the law itself, and there perhaps is a further reason why in Renaissance iconography the face of justice was blindfolded, self-consciously following a classical tradition of mutilated representations of virtue in which justice would not see the face of the litigants nor they the face of Justitia.[112] If, as contemporary philosophy suggests, "the face is presence" and command, and so neither metaphor nor figure, a feminine representation that is blindfolded would thereby be disallowed full presence, just as a woman could not command, except by way of exception.[113] Yet the argument made is that where law sought to be blind, the feminine face of justice looked back so as to see. To consider further the significance of the face to law it is necessary to return to the *querelle* and to postclassical rhetorics of gesture. In generic terms, "by the outward countenance we do judge of the qualities and disposition. . . . The most pliable part of virtue, is by greatest observance planted in the most proportionate feature."[114] The outward face is the "judgment of nature," for *vultus est index animi*, and the countenance and the eye are the signs of the soul. At the same time, as Fortescue and Selden made clear, the face is not without its ambiguities. The face was both likeness and the possibility of illusion, both image and mask or screen of the soul. Thus one critic remarked of the countenance of the common lawyer that "this face seems as intricate as the most winding cause": it was neither infallible as an index nor permanent as a sign of inward disposition.[115]

The face is also sexed. For the antifeminist literature of the *querelle*, it was man that was made in the image of God, and it was for this reason that men should neither cover their heads nor hide their faces. Women, however, were not in God's image and were consequently *nupta*, covert or veiled. For the other side of the debate, the opposite was true: "Shamefastness [i.e., shamefacedness] and soberness be the inseparable companions of chastity, in so much as that she cannot be chaste, that is not

111. A conclusion arrived at by Maclean, *Woman Triumphant* at 58.

112. See Lloyd, *Conference of Divers Lawes* at 130–131, for a direct expression of this view.

113. Of the many contemporary analyses of the face, see E. Levinas, *Otherwise than Being* (The Hague: Nijhoff, 1981) at 89–93; Derrida, *Writing and Difference* at 100ff.: Deleuze and Guattari, *A Thousand Plateaus* 167–192; Jardine, *Gynesis* at 76–79.

114. Angel Day, *The English Secretorie* at 121–122.

115. Head, *Proteus Redivivus*, respectively at 2 and 256. See also at 53: "The face is the index of the mind; yet experience tells us it is no infallible indicium of the nature or disposition of the person . . . [for] always to see, is not to know."

ashamed: for that is as a cover and a veil to her face."[116] Nature had, according to Vives, given the veil of shamefacedness so as to clothe and cover the face to the end of picturing virtue and saving those who might look upon its nakedness from lust and from the sin that comes of lust. Agrippa takes the argument further in viewing the female face as the sign of feminine superiority: its nakedness is its virtue to such an extent that the Laws of the Twelve Tables are even said to have provided that women should not shave their cheeks, "lest it might occasion the growth of beards and destroy their nature."[117] That Justitia was blindfolded might well have a residual connotation of impartiality, but it must also be recognized that in the eyes of contemporaries it would also be likely to be perceived as a veil that rendered a feminine representation of justice an inoperative element in the gaze of law. There could be no face to face of justice nor evidence nor experience of the particular without eyes to see. Indeed, in depicting the judge's decision in the case of succession to a kingdom in *De Natura,* Fortescue even begins by describing the eyes of the judge, who was also variously, it should be recollected, Justitia, Phronesis, Prudentia, and *viva vox iuris*: "The judge, keeping silence for no great interval, with downcast eyes (*vultu ad yma dismisso*) . . . at length raised his eyes by little and little, and thus in modest style began his discourse."[118]

The shamefacedness of women was designed to protect men from themselves and to protect them from sin. The blindfold on the face of justice seems plausibly to have also benefited men through the limitation, mutilation—it could also be a bandage—or sensory deprivation of women. The stake of such an effigie, shadow, or image is never innocent. In a secondary sense the blindness of justice can be taken to represent the peculiar folly of common law in its dependence upon the blind reason of precedent and the unseeing eye of an aural or auricular tradition. In common with other critiques of common law, particularly that contemporaneously associated with the English civilians,[119] the argument would be that without some vision of the peculiarities of parties and the particularities of circumstance and experience, the law has no connection with reality but simply and stupidly repeats past judgments as if they were both reason and law. Such repetition of judgment stipulates the present instance as a predicate of the past instance, without reason, foresight, or ethics. The *Woman's*

116. Vives, *De Institutione* at fol. K i a–b. See further Allestree, *The Ladies Calling* at 5–7 (discussing modesty and the face); Astell, *Reflections upon Marriage* at 32 (discussing those that "doat on a Face").

117. Agrippa, *De Nobilitate* at 21–22.

118. Fortescue, *De Natura* at 321.

119. See, for a particularly strong example, Wiseman, *The Law of Laws* at 38–45, discussing the failings of argument from precedent. More generally see Levack, *The Civil Lawyers in England.*

Lawyer challenges that predication and in constructing the law as it related to the various aspects of women, suggests that it is through the specific character, experience, and reason of judgment, through what the ancients termed *synderesis,*[120] that legal personality is formed and the plurality of faces of women are distributed through the institutions and relations that constitute the social world for us.

There is a final argument, one that develops the metaphor of the faces of law and of the legal past. The Baroque notion of retrospection multiplying the images of the past in the same way that a broken mirror proliferates our reflection suggests, as Fortescue and Selden in particular bear witness, a certain ambiguity if not crisis in the relation of the present to the past. Where humanism and historicism relied upon the value of the classical tradition and so adopted a custodial stance to the transmission of that tradition, the common law could not so easily assume a linear progression from antiquity to the legal present.[121] The pasts of the law were varied in national particulars and in their languages. The common law had no single identity, its polity was plurality and its history Janus-faced. In breaking away from Rome and from the civilian tradition, the common lawyers had to invent a unitary national law and find an image or representation of that unity that could affix an imagined tradition to disparate legal practices. The solution, in the form of an image, an emblem, or effigy of English common law, became that of an immanent, local, and particular tradition based upon precedent, practice, and popular rule. Even in the terms of those that argued most forcefully for the scientific status of English law, this science was based upon a law that was *lesbia regula,* or pliable rule,[122] that was made by the infinite uses of experience (*per varios usus artem legem experientia fecit*) and was connatural to the people.[123] This was English justice and it was supposed to express the genius of the people, that of an unbroken, uninterrupted, and unwritten tradition which was reasserted through throwing off the arrogance, abstraction, and indeed the novelty of the civil law. To represent the separate and local features of the common law ironically seemed to require that even the most misogynist of doctrinal writers emphasize the distinctive and particular character of common law in terms of what would then and now be perceived as feminine characteristics. The crisis of the national law, its rebirth in terms of specifically Anglican features, required that it abandon the paternal *regulae*

120. In terms of the period in question, see the influential St. German, *Doctor and Student* at 81.

121. On the plural and multilingual histories of common law, see, for example, Spelman, *Original of the Four Law Terms of the Year.*

122. Sir John Davies, *Le Primer Report des Cases & Matters en Ley Resolves et Adjudges in Les Courts del Roy en Ireland* (Dublin: Franckton, 1614, 1615 ed.) at sig. 4r.

123. Ibid. at sigs. 2v–3r.

or rules of Rome and represent instead the poetry and the fecundity, the experience and the antique *douceur* of common law. It had to turn, in other words, to the second face of the English Janus, which face was that of women: either Fate or Justice, Fortune, Nature, Prudence or Phronesis, as occasion might demand. The emblem of the feminine or at least the attribution of female characteristics allowed the reassertion or even the apparent rescue of common law from the harsh or at least foreign imposition of the civilian tradition. Humanism consistently argued by reference to the "great Ladie of Learning . . . true Philologie" and through her referred to ever earlier, older, or more pristine textual sources.[124] It was implicit in the philological form of humanistic argument not only that the most ancient source was the true source but also that time and diligence would constantly uncover new antiquities. In short, just as common law was shown to precede Roman law, so other insular laws were shown to antedate the common law. Prior to Edward the Confessor's unification of the kingdoms of Albion into one common law, the philologist could discover several other laws, the regencies of feminine monarchs and before them of venerable goddesses. The priority of antiquity forced the possibility of feminine governance upon the common law, if only as its other face or exceptional past. These were the stories, the feminine genealogies of the greatest antiquity, of an indefinite age of women which was original and so true: "That is truth which is first, that is adulterous which comes after."[125] It is not surprising in this context that certain common lawyers even went so far as to suggest the recognition of feminine difference in the positive form of political suffrage, civil and domestic rights. Insofar as elements of common law changed, it is not incorrect to say that legal events altered the "relative or civil" definitions of women.[126] It is also plain that such civil definitions of feminine status were relative to male governance and relative further to the loss or repression of the feminine genealogies that Renaissance lawyers had briefly recollected. To understand that failure, loss, or forgetting of a specific history and its texts it is necessary to return again to the question of difference.

CONCLUSION: THE JURISPRUDENCE OF DIFFERENCE

The simultaneous praise and denigration or assimilation of the feminine has traditionally been played out over a series of ambiguous and often

124. Selden, *Historie of Tithes* at xix.

125. Favour, *Antiquitie Triumphing over Noveltie* at 39–40. (Id est verum quodcumque primum, id est adulteram quodcumque posterius.)

126. Wood, *An Institute* at 17 advocates that the law of persons consider persons in "their *Natural*, and in their *Relative* and *Civil* capacities."

antagonistic metaphors. Women, in the theological language that underpinned the ecclesiastical law, were images, surfaces, or screens that lacked substance and depth. The feminine was empty and dissimulated or hid its emptiness through "sophistic reasoning and carnal pretence."[127] More than that, the feminine transgressed the orders of nature and like the plastic image polluted the spirit by confusing it with sense. In one respect this reference to sense was a mark of the contingency under which the feminine traveled. Contingency implied the realm of the inessential, of the aesthetic, the floral,[128] the inconstant, the gustatory, ornamental, and emotive, but also, by virtue of the particularity of the contingent, the feminine symbolized justice, the law of the event and of the parties to dispute. In this latter aspect, the feminine was a sign of *contingencia* or touch, of a materiality, historicity, locality, or relation that theology and ecclesiastical law often labeled unclean or polluted, of sense and flesh and earthly pleasure (*erato*).[129] The belief that "the feminine power prevailed in Heaven" was even listed in the *Repertorium Canonicum* as the heresy of the Sethiani.[130] Women, by having no fixed value, by virtue of their uncertainty and ephemerality as also by virtue of their worldliness or reproductive force, were a threat not simply to the temporal order of political sovereignty but also to the logic of a common law that inherited both Roman and ecclesiastical conceptions of *universalia* and with them the notion of lawful meaning as a transcendent or spiritual property of eternal decrees and the reign of a reason that moved from like to like within the inexorable realm of the same.[131] The belief in contingent values and in the arbitrary temporal power of fortune and fate, were pre-Christian elements of a Stoic philosophy which natural law had specifically replaced. "Experience," in the words of one influential lawyer "which is wholly gained by the observation of particular things is slow, blind, doubtful, and deceivable, and truly called the mistress of fools."[132] This mistress has an ambivalent and charged position in common law. As Fortescue had earlier remarked, it was experience—induction—which "by the assistance of the senses and the memory" discovered law.[133] It was the vernacular experience of the *leges terrae* which

127. Parker, *A Scholasticall Discourse against Symbolizing* at 10.

128. On the "misteries of *Flora*," see Lloyd, *A Briefe Conference of Divers Lawes* at 12; and more broadly on flowers, see Puttenham, *Arte of English Poesie.*

129. For striking theological examples, see particularly Parker, *A Scholasticall Discourse against Symbolizing* at 7–8, 14–17, 19–21; Sander, *A Treatise of the Images*; Hammond, *Of Idolatry* at 7–9, 12–13. This literature is discussed in greater detail in Goodrich, "Antirrhesis."

130. Godolphin, *Repertorium Canonicum* at 582.

131. On the *universalia* of law see J. Fortescue, *De Laudibus Legum Angliae* at 13–14; see also Ernst Kantorowicz, "The Sovereignty of the Artist: A Note on Legal Maxims and Renaissance Theories of Art," in Ernst Kantorowicz, *Selected Studies* (New York: J. Augustin, 1965).

132. Doderidge, *English Lawyer* at 240.

133. Fortescue, *De Laudibus Legum Angliae* at 13–14.

the Anglican judges had to apply and which differentiated common law from civil law, England from Rome.[134] The common law had to assert a certain femininity, a reliance at least upon the mistress of experience, to identify itself as a separate form of law. Common law was like a woman, but likeness was not essence, similarity was not identity, and so experience remained a medium but not a source of law. To experience, which is characterized doctrinally as a feminine vice and opposed to the speculations, *regulae,* and maxims[135] of the universal law, might be added contingency and materiality as such. The vice of femininity was precisely its nature, its plurality, both its diversity and its ability to reproduce, both its inconstancy over time and its production of difference.[136] As one study has recently detailed, the category of the feminine in law was not simply plural, its attributes changed with time and historical circumstance. The virtues of the feminine might later be the attributes of the masculine, the value of contingency might latterly be the criterion of reason or the source of law, for nothing was certain in the realm of experience nor was anything constant where a feminine reason threatened to play the role of law.[137]

The argument traced through the texts suggests that there was no singular category of woman, and as Sir Robert Filmer argued of the law in a rather different context, "there is great difficulty in discovering, *what* or *who* a [woman] is."[138] The plurality of concepts and usages of "woman" range from the female as an image or, worse, an idol in puritanical legal thought, the bearer of diabolical powers, soothsayer and magician, to the praise of illustrious women, female gods, muses, and lawmakers whose soul and reason is indistinguishable from or even superior to that of men.[139] There is no common essence to the various categories of women, nor indeed is there any common definition of women in law.[140] The "feme sole"

134. See Fortescue, *De Natura* at 205–206: "Even the judges are bound by their oaths not to render judgment against the laws of the land [*leges terrae*]," and similarly, see Selden, *Ad Fletam Dissertatio* at 173.

135. See, for example, Noy, *Grounds and Maxims of the English Law* at fol. D 3 b: "Every maxim is a sufficient authority to itself; and which is a maxim, and which is not, shall always be determined by the judges, because they are known to none but the learned." More broadly on this point, see Wiseman, *The Law of Laws.*

136. On which, in philosophical terms, see Irigaray, *Speculum of the Other Woman,* especially 227–240; Irigaray, *This Sex Which is Not One,* chs. 2 and 6.

137. Schroeder, "Feminism Historicised," particularly at 1143–1147, 1214–1217, indicating that at certain points in history, the values currently experienced as "uniquely female" were experienced as "uniquely male."

138. Filmer, *An Advertisement.*

139. See, particularly, in an English context, Agrippa, *De Nobilitate*; Elyot, *The Defence of Good Women*; Leslie, *De Illustrium Foeminarum.*

140. See Riley, *Am I That Name?*; Cornell, *Beyond Accommodation*; Judith Butler, *Gender Trouble: Feminism and the Subversion of Identity* (New York: Routledge, 1990); Suzanne Gibson, "The Structure of the Veil" (1989) 52 *Modern Law Review* 420.

may share certain attributes of the married woman or "feme covert." The concubine may be granted certain aspects of the legal recognition of the wife. Unmarried women may in certain respects resemble the dowager lady. But the differences between statuses, between having a will and the civil death of marriage, between being *sui iuris* and *alieni iuris,* namely between being in the *potestas* or power of the husband, or of the father and having independent status at common law, between the figure of women as *indigni* in the ecclesiastical law of succession, the *detior conditio* of civil law and the exclusion of women from office in a Salic law that many considered to apply also in England, are too great to allow for the construction of any single concept of the feminine. For the purposes of the ecclesiastical law on witchcraft it should be noted finally that even the civil law test of gender, as adopted by Bracton from the *Digest*[141] to distinguish the sex of the hermaphrodite, was inapplicable in that it was precisely the power of the witch to work wonders (*mirum*), to deceive the eye and so to appear in the form of the dead or the masculine or animals that constituted both an office and a proof of being a witch.[142]

The latter example indicates both the power and threat constituted by femininity and its difference. To recollect the texts of feminine genealogies is to recollect an order of difference, a separate terrain and time of feminine kinship and regency approximating in myth or historical narrative to early law. In terms of legal history the speech or mythology of female deities and women lawgivers had the status either of fabulous (and idolatrous) tales or, in Heywood's words, they were "a fantasme, or an apprehension of an imaginarie thing" whose essence could not lawfully be sought.[143] The negative connotations of difference linked the mythology of feminine genealogies to inconsequence or to heresy within the normative gaze of a common law that owed much to its ecclesiastical derivations. Under the category of difference were listed all the figures of exclusion, while the place of feminine difference was aligned with the *gynaeceum,* with the private, with the infantile, with impermanence and fantasy.[144] It remains to be argued that returning, as this text has endeavored, to the mythologies of femininity in the ancient customs of common law may yet

141. *Digest* 1.5.10: "With whom is a hermaphrodite comparable? I rather think that each one should be ascribed to that sex which is prevalent in his or her make up."

142. Perkins, *A Discourse on the Damnable Art of Witchcraft* at fols. 6 a–b, 22 a–27 b. For legislation and writs, see Coke, *Book of Entries.*

143. Respectively, Selden, *De Diis Syris* II at 140–146, and Heywood, *Tunaikeion* at 2–3.

144. For a legal definition of the *gynaeceum,* see Alciatus, *De Verborum Significatione* at 204 and 229. It should also be observed of the *gynaeceum* that it was there the duty of the woman to teach virtue, as indicated, for example, in S. Champier, *La Nef des dames: Vertueuses composée par Maistre Simphorien Champier* (Paris: n.p., 1515) at bk. II, ch. xix.

prove to be an important resource for feminist critiques of common law. Difference, or the uncertain surface, the image, subjectivity, contingency, and indeterminacy—the "inchaunting void"—of the diverse figures of femininity may prove to be a positive resource for the reform of law.

For early feminine critiques of law, the difference of the feminine was a powerful argument for a separate and positive status and law for women. *La Cité des dames* proposed a literal *gynaetopia,* a castle (*fortuna*) or a community of virtuous women kept separate from the world of men so as to pursue their virtue and their talents, to read, to learn, and to educate in female commonality free from the demands and the degradations imposed by the medieval world. In *A Serious Proposal to the Ladies,* Mary Astell later makes a similar suggestion. The proposal was to establish institutions for women, similar to religious houses, in which women could retreat from the world to a discipline, education, community, and charity of their own. The purpose of this *gynaetopia* was also political. It aimed to "amend the present and improve the future age."[145] The regime of the community was again to be scholarly and studious, it would endeavor through learning to expel the "cloud of ignorance which custom has involved us in . . . that the souls of women may no longer be the only unadorned and neglected things."[146] The proposal thus aimed to establish the value and the worth of women, to promote a philosophy of the feminine as well as a society dedicated to the furtherance of the education of its own sex. The regime of this collectivity was to reflect a society "whose soul is love" and whose kinship was friendship.[147] In a practical and political manner, the proposals of *gynaetopias* suggest a species of return to what Irigaray terms forgotten feminine genealogies or "to certain ancient but very advanced traditions in which it was the women who initiated the men into love" and into the relationships and subjectivities, the politics and the civilities of *eros.*[148]

In a series of recent texts contemporary feminists have suggested a return to the politics of difference. At one level the argument has been that it is essential to recognize and give space both to feminine difference and to differences within the feminine. Thus legal feminists have taken up the cause of a right to subjectivity, to care, and to relationship that emerged from a psychological study of the "different voice" of the feminine.[149] In

145. Astell, *A Serious Proposal* at 40.

146. Ibid. at 48.

147. Ibid. at 81 and 91.

148. Irigaray, *Le Temps de la différence* at 103–105. See also Irigaray, *J'aime à toi* at 210–222.

149. Particularly, C. Gilligan, *In a Different Voice* (Cambridge, Mass.: Harvard University Press, 1982). For criticism of that study, see Joan Williams, "Deconstructing Gender" (1989) 87 *Michigan Law Review* 797. See also Joan Williams, "Feminist Discourse, Moral Values and

a more sophisticated vein, feminist jurisprudence has asserted the need to allow a rhetoric or writing of the feminine, a speech authentic to feminine differences and so also a series of rights and legal protections for the sphere, space, time, or speech of femininity.[150] Utilizing the much frequented Sophoclean tragedy of *Antigone,* an argument is made for an "other" law of the feminine which respects nature and spirit, ecology and divinity, "for in that time of feminine legal right, civil order was tied to respect for the gods and the civil and religious powers were not yet dissociated."[151] The recourse to tragedy, to the dramatic representation of myth, is in effect a recourse to a series of political demands for respect for and guarantees of difference. In place of the demand for equality or for the legal right to be the same, Irigaray, for example, argues for an urgent and simple series of juridical reforms designed to establish a sphere of objective legal protections for feminine difference, namely for a separate legally protected identity and full civic personality for the feminine and for the plurality which the feminine represents. The domains of sexually engendered identities and rights would reconstitute the law of persons according to a primary difference, that of sex: "Out of fidelity to sexual liberation and to the changes in the political horizon which it provoked, and further to permit a cultural cohabitation between the sexes, it is necessary to endow both women and men with rights corresponding to their respective needs."[152]

The legal right to difference, to a juridically protected sphere of autonomous feminine differences, would require a considerable rewriting both of law and of legal method. In an immediate sense the right to a separate legally guaranteed civil identity ranges from protection of the physical, moral, and imagistic personalities of women, to genuine maternity rights free of economic, ideological (conjugal), or institutional constraints, and a right to a culture, to languages, religions, arts, and sciences appropriate to the autonomy of feminine identities.[153] In a broader sense it is ar-

---

the Law—A Conversation" (1985) 34 *Buffalo Law Review* 11. For a series of stronger arguments in relation to difference and law, see Angela Harris, "Race and Essentialism in Feminist Legal Theory" (1990) 42 *Stanford Law Review* 581; Patricia Cain, "Feminist Jurisprudence: Grounding the Theories" (1990) 4 *Berkeley Women's Law Journal* 191; K. Crenshaw, "A Black Feminist Critique of Antidiscrimination Law and Politics," in D. Karys (ed.). *The Politics of Law* (New York: Pantheon Books, 1990).

150. For philosophical discussion of such rights, see Julia Kristeva, "Women's Time" (1981) 7 *Signs* 13; Cixous and Clement, *Newly Born Woman;* Hélène Cixous, *Coming to Writing* (Cambridge, Mass.: Harvard University Press, 1991).

151. Irigaray, *Le Temps de la différence* at 83. For a more detailed discussion, see Luce Irigaray, *Éthique de la différence sexuelle* (Paris: Editions de Minuit, 1984) at 114–124.

152. Irigaray, *J'aime à toi* at 205.

153. On the latter right, see also Irigaray, *Marine Lover of Friedrich Nietzsche.* Also important in the discussion of cultural rights and literary styles was Jacques Derrida, *Spurs: Nietzsche's*

gued that civil law needs to be reformed so as to take account of the participation of two autonomous persons, two sexes, two genres, in love as also in the other relations of private and public life.[154] Essential to this transformation is a recognition of rights of speech, a recognition of the other as an irreducible source of meaning, a recognition that would entail a certain respect for the mythologies, the languages, the figures, and the fictions of feminine genealogies not only in the texts of law but equally in the law of texts. The argument that underpins much of this move to a jurisprudence of difference is one of a direct and politically compelling sense of the significance of law in the reconstruction of sexual ethics. It is the curious dialectic of the present analysis to suggest that the identity of the feminine and the "objective rights and laws" which are to guarantee its autonomy are also the sites of the disappearance of any singular identity or unitary essence of the feminine. What is left, at least in theory, is the right and speech of women identified with a lineage or genealogy of law and of meaning which transmits from mother to daughter as well as from father to son. In this context the forgotten history of feminine genealogies and of various *gynaetopias* can offer a juridical narrative of the feminine genre and a language of difference as a practical sign of reciprocal right. Without embarking upon details of legal substance, the model of one law faced by or in juxtaposition with another is one of the oldest and most interesting of the histories of common law. One law on the other was the history of *utrumque ius,* the relation of the ecclesiastical to the "profane" jurisdictions and of the spiritual to the secular laws. At various points in the history of the relation between jurisdictions, the same civil transaction, for example, would be tried before both spiritual and secular courts, either *pro laesione fidei* or upon a temporal contract, and would be decided according to two separate laws, according to faith and corporal penance and according to profane law and its monetary compensations. The two jurisdictions dealt with two significantly different realities and adopted quite separate procedures and forms of knowing.[155] There is no reason, either in history or in doctrine, why different laws cannot govern different genres, separate statuses, or the plural identities of legal persons.

Styles (Chicago: Chicago University Press, 1979). In terms of legal feminism, see the discussion in Mary-Joe Frug, "A Postmodern Feminist Legal Manifesto" (1992) 105 *Harvard Law Review* 1045.

154. Irigaray, *J'aime à toi* at 207.

155. For an excellent discussion of the ecclesiastical practice, see Cosin, *An Apologie* at 51–58. See further Stillingfleet, *Ecclesiastical Cases*; Consett, *Practice of the Spiritual or Ecclesiastical Courts.* In explicitly feminist terms, see Mary-Joe Frug, "Re-Reading Contracts: A Feminist Analysis of a Contracts Casebook" (1985) 34 *American University Law Review* 1065; also Mary-Joe Frug, "Rescuing Impossibility Doctrine: A Postmodern Feminist Analysis of Contract Law" (1992) 140 *University of Pennsylvania Law Review* 1029.

When the common lawyers greedily took exception to or challenged ecclesiastical causes in the name of the vernacular law, they nonetheless "pretended to ground themselves . . . not only on the laws of the realm but upon God's law also, the civil, the canon, or ecclesiastical law, and upon equity and reason."[156] The arrogation of the "ghostly power of the Church and of Ecclesiastical persons" to common lawyers occurred in practice over the course of somewhat more than a century and it did so within varied and most usually polemical contexts.[157] It was primarily important for the common law not to have its jurisdiction challenged by the Courts of Conscience, and it was from early on a "contempt" for ecclesiastical judges to deal with a matter appertaining to the temporal courts.[158] While certain parochial or institutional matters remained within the spiritual jurisdiction, the common law took over the governance of conscience, of attachments or affectivities, of the passions, of interiority and its development. Common law, however, had neither the imagination nor the procedures to deal with conscience or spiritual matters as anything other than accidents or effects of an arbitrary political expansion of royal power. While it would make little sense to invoke the ecclesiastical jurisdiction over interiority as anything other than a formal model of plurality of jurisdictions, procedures, and substantive rules, there are also a variety of jurisprudential significances to that plurality. It is salutary to recollect the diversity of jurisdictions as a repressed dimension of common law as a method of judgment and to recollect that within the tradition there already existed a court of conscience, a ghostly or spiritual jurisdiction in excess of the contemporary antipathy to anything but positivized legal rules. An early discussion of the dual jurisdiction, *Justice Vindicated,* observes laconically of the dual jurisdictions that "it is a miserable servitude, where the law is wandering or unknown [*misera servitus, ubi ius est vagum aut incognitum*]."[159] Adopting that metaphor, the next chapter, will utilize elements of the contemporary model of interpretation of that which has wandered or is unknown, namely psychoanalysis, to pursue the images within law's texts, the figures of a law within law. While the figure of unknowing itself belongs, at least in modern demarcations of the disciplines, to psychoanalysis, it will be argued that where it is a question of reading legal texts or interpreting judgments as the cultural work of the legal institution, then rhetoric is the older and more rigorous of the interpretative disciplines.

156. Cosin, *An Apologie* at fol. A 3 a; Consett, *Spiritual or Ecclesiastical Courts* at fol. A 2 b: "That our ecclesiastical laws professed in this land, have lain, and at this time, do lie under most unjust and severe imputations, I am very sensible."

157. Coke, *Justice Vindicated* at 21.

158. Cosin, *An Apologie* at 40.

159. Coke, *Justice Vindicated* at 42.

SEVEN

Oedipus Lex

Interpretation and the Unconscious of Law

We approve not of a stoical apathy . . . for passions are the feet of the soul.[1]

If the argument of the previous chapters has succeeded in any measure it will be in having outlined the displacement of the power of the image from plastic to textual forms. If the image is the sign or figure of a historically feminine difference within the textual tradition and culture of print which followed the Reformation, then literary theory, hermeneutics, and rhetoric are the appropriate disciplines for the analysis of that difference. Textual aesthetics as well as philology and its modern variations become the techniques through which to analyze the other body, the spirit, dignity, or *corpus mysticum* of legal judgment. The juridical word as text, as print, as *ratio scripta,* embodies the tokens or tropes of secular belonging, it marks out the spiritual territory, the meaning, and the mysticism within the positivities of judgment. While it will be argued in this chapter that an analysis that traces the images, figures, and women within the juristic text is a first gesture in the direction of a politics and writing of legal difference, of thinking law differently, the specific argument to be addressed devolves upon a certain discovery in relation to the tradition and politics of legal textual analysis. In unadorned terms, this discovery is that rhetoric is the premodern form of psychoanalysis, of a secular interpretation of conscience, emotion, and the passions. A jurisprudence that endeavors to offer a critical analysis of what has here been termed the institutional unconscious can thus begin its effort to trace, to analyze, and to activate law's creativity through the techniques and the procedures of forensic rhetoric and its theory of the legal emotions.

Forensic rhetoric was and is the premodern curricular form of analysis of legal speech acts or, more felicitously, of the force of law. In this regard

1. Allestree, *Funeral Handkerchief* at 7.

it is already a methodology of symptomatic reading or of interpretation of the unconscious of law. The specific analyses substantiating and exemplifying this argument will be developed through the rhetorical analysis of three legal anomalies, namely the rule allowing the recovery of damages in tort for psychiatric harm occasioned by damage to property, the postal or mailbox rule in contract, and the relative immunity of the Crown from actions for contempt of court. Legal anomalies, slips or symptoms, are here understood as points of condensation and are thus to be analyzed not only in terms of a rhetoric of persuasion or emotion but also as signs of discursive divergence in which more than one legal narrative plays against another, surface against surface, depth against depth, word against image.[2] The figure can here be termed a sign of repression; it masks the compression, displacement, or omission of other significations and other meanings. It is specifically, it will be argued, an indication of the imaginary, of difference within the text of law.[3] In each of the cases to be examined, the analysis of a specific trope or textual figure—*antonomasia, allegoria,* and *synecdoche*—will allow for the reconstruction of the genealogy of a substantive legal anomaly. The analysis of the rhetorical form, the elocution, or figuration of the legal rule will trigger a zone of affectivity within institutional memory and serve to indicate a repressed history at the source of the anomaly. In explicitly psychoanalytic terms, the tropes and figures of the texts analyzed all represent species of displacement or substitution which invite interpretation of the unconscious affect, the "dream thoughts" in Freud's terms, which organize or make sense, or make the other sense, of the text.

The argument builds upon classical rhetorical forms in which both the trope and the figure of speech are linked to memory and to desire, to emotion and to the images or places that recollect or reinvoke the passions

2. Freud, *Interpretation of Dreams,* especially at 312–319, elaborating the concept of condensation in terms of compression of thought in the content of the dream. Condensation is predicated upon omission, upon the unconscious process of thought within the dream.

3. On the specific issue of imagining difference in law and legal culture see the excellent introductory analysis in Cornell, "What Takes Place in the Dark," particularly at 51–52: "We cannot, in other words, know in advance what the ultimate meaning of our attempts to encounter difference will be, precisely because such attempts break the hold of common sense over our imaginations. . . . We have to be able to re-imagine the sensible, given to us by our own standards of making sense." Cornell draws much from Clifford Geertz, "The Uses of Diversity" (1986) 25 *Michigan Quarterly Review* 105. See also Patricia Williams, *The Alchemy of Race and Rights* (Cambridge, Mass.: Harvard University Press, 1991); and for liberal variations on that theme, see M. Minow, "Partial Justice: Law and Minorities" in A. Sarat and T. Kearns (eds.), *The Fate of Law* (Ann Arbor: University of Michigan Press, 1991); James Boyd White, *Justice as Translation.* For further anthropological analyses, see James Clifford and George Marcus (eds.), *Writing Culture: The Poetics and Politics of Ethnography* (Berkeley and Los Angeles: University of California Press, 1986).

that persuade or move to action.[4] Rhetoric studies language, or the forms of bodily and verbal enunciation, as the signs of the passions, as indexes of an invisible, unconscious, or oneiric logic of institutional speech. Rhetoric had always been perceived as the "artificer of persuasion," as will and word doing the work of imagination.[5] Law, which reasons explicitly by images, analogies, associations, and other narratives or metonymies, similarly represents or dissimulates the invisible affects or unconscious desires of legal custom, judicial intention, or sovereign will. It is possible to go further and to suggest that rhetoric studied the symptoms or signs of desire through which Freud and later Lacan mapped out the linguistic structure of oneiric or unconscious laws.[6] "Linguistic evolution," Freud remarked, "has made things very easy for dreams. For language has a whole number of words at its command which originally had a pictorial and concrete significance, but are used today in a colourless and abstract sense."[7] Without the theme of evolution, the remark still has a remarkable historical and theoretical force: language is already an archive of image and imagination, of law, of judgment, of interpretation. Rhetoric, which studies the tropes and figures of language simultaneously and necessarily, studies also the unconscious of the institution as the long-term significance of its figures and as the symptoms of the culture, work, and affect of law.

The analysis of unconscious aspects of legal decision making is not a new theme either within European or Anglo-American legal thought.[8]

4. On the rhetorical art of memory, see for example the forensic rhetorical manual of Wilson, *Arte of Rhetorique* at 413–430, on *memoria*; and on specifically legal memory, see Doderidge, *English Lawyer* at 12 and 200 ff., arguing that memory is the first legal art and record its most permanent practice. On the schemata of memory see Ramus, *The Logike* at 13–14 on memory and argument. For an excellent recent study see Carruthers, *Book of Memory*; on collective memory, see Paul Connerton, *How Societies Remember* (Cambridge: Cambridge University Press, 1990); on law's collective memory, see Goodrich, "Eating Law."

5. Plato, *Gorgias* at 453 a. For discussion see Thomas Cole, *The Origins of Rhetoric in Ancient Greece* (Baltimore: Johns Hopkins University Press, 1991).

6. The classic texts on language, symptom, and unconscious are Freud, *Interpretation of Dreams*; Sigmund Freud, *Psychopathology of Everyday Life* (Harmondsworth: Pelican, 1942); Jacques Lacan, "The Function and Field of Speech and Language in Psychoanalysis," in Jacques Lacan *Écrits: A Selection* (London: Tavistock, 1977). For discussion, see Jacques Lacan and A. Wilden, *Speech and Language in Psychoanalysis* (Baltimore: Johns Hopkins University Press, 1981).

7. Freud, *Interpretation of Dreams* at 442.

8. In an Anglo-American common law context, there exists a quite varied history of jurisprudential recourse to psychoanalysis. See J. Frank, *Law and the Modern Mind* (Garden City, N.Y.: Anchor, 1930, 1963 ed.); A. Ehrenzweig, *Psychoanalytic Jurisprudence: On Ethics, Aesthetics, and Law* (Leiden: Dordrecht, 1971); C. G. Schoenfeld, *Psychoanalysis and the Law* (Springfield, Ill.: Thomas, 1973); F. R. Beinfenfeld, "Prolegomena to a Psychoanalysis of Law and Justice" (1965) 53 *California Law Review* 957, 1254; P. Gabel, "The Phenomenology of Rights Consciousness and the Pact of the Withdrawn Selves" (1984) 62 *Texas Law Review* 1563. For a review of recent and critical works on psychoanalysis and law, see Caudill, "Freud and Critical

Jurisprudential analyses of legal language in terms of its metaphoric, symbolic, narrational, and ideological characteristics are a commonplace of critiques of law that range in their theoretical perspective from legal realism to feminism, from pragmatism to semiotics, and from existentialism to systems theory. That history of the conjunction of the two disciplines will not be rehearsed here, for the simple reason that metaphors of surface and depth, phenomenon and structure, appearance and reality, lack sufficient linguistic or, more properly, philological detail to allow for the development of a methodology of reading and so writing and practicing law. I will argue here that it was rhetoric which was the discipline that traditionally classified the forms of language use, of invention, topics, argumentative distribution, tropes, discursive (sentential) figures, elocution, and memory in terms of emotive effect. Psychoanalysis and jurisprudence can, therefore, draw historically upon a common language and certain shared themes. It may be briefly noted from the existing literature that both disciplines are concerned with authority and with prohibition, innocence, and guilt. The law of the father equiparates with that of the sovereign, and the private self is considered as juridical an institution as is public legal personality.[9] In a pragmatic sense, lawyers and analysts take cases and endeavor to resolve conflicts and, more broadly, to adapt the individual to the conditions of institutional existence.[10] In a more hermeneutic sense, both professions indulge in symptomatic readings of written and also often unwritten texts.[11] The surface is never an adequate explanation, but is rather to be interpreted in terms of gaps, symptoms, slips,

---

Legal Studies." In Continental terms, the most important work has been that of the Lacanian lawyer, Pierre Legendre. His first and in many ways most influential works on psychoanalysis and law were Legendre, *L'Amour du censeur*; Legendre, *Jouir du pouvoir*. See also Papageorgiou-Legendre, *Filiation*. For an introduction to Legendre's work, see my chapter "Law's Emotional Body" in Goodrich, *Languages of Law*; Alain Pottage, "The Paternity of Law," in Costas Douzinas et al. (eds.), *Politics, Postmodernity and Critical Legal Studies: The Legality of the Contingent* (London: Routledge, 1994).

9. This theme is central to Lacan, *Écrits*; see also Lacan, *Four Fundamental Concepts*. See further Jacques Lacan, *Le Seminaire IV: L'Ethique de la psychanalyse* (Paris: Seuil, 1990). For commentary and application of that model, see Legendre, *Le Crime du Caporal Lortie*; see also David Caudill, "Name of the Father and the Logic of Psychosis: Lacan's Law and Ours" (1993) 4 *Legal Studies Forum* 421. On the educational significance of this theme, see Peter Rush, "Killing Me Softly with His Words" (1990) 1 *Law and Critique* 21; Peter Goodrich, "Psychoanalysis in Legal Education: Notes on the Violence of the Sign," in R. Kevelson (ed.), *Law and Semiotics* (New York: Plenum Press, 1987). More broadly see P. Gabel and D. Kennedy, "Roll Over Beethoven" (1984) 36 *Stanford Law Review* 1.

10. On which theme see particularly Legendre, *Le Crime du Caporal Lortie*; Papageorgiou-Legendre, *Filiation*. For a discussion of the former work see Alain Pottage, "Crime and Culture: The Relevance of the Psychoanalytical" (1992) 55 *Modern Law Review* 421.

11. This theme is addressed directly in David Caudill, "Lacan and Legal Language: Meanings in the Gaps, Gaps in the Meaning" (1992) 3 *Law and Critique* 165.

repetitions, and other indications of repression or unconscious cause.[12] The list of coincidences, of themes or terms, doubts or desires that are shared by law and psychoanalysis could be proliferated, but to little purpose. The argument here will rather concentrate upon the linguistic and specifically rhetorical interest that the two disciplines share.

Rhetoric studies language use, particularly as argument, style, and memory, in terms of topics, tropes, and figures of speech. It studies flawed linguistic phenomena—the figures of enigma (*aenigma*), slip (*paracriasis*), lapse (*aposiopesis*), neologism (*soraismus*), ambiguity (*amphibologia*), paradox (*paradoxon*), repetition (*anaphora*), solecism, impropriety (*catachresis*), deceit (*ironia*) and error (*cacozelia*)—as well as decorous speech (analogical *decorum*) and felicitous use (*gnome*) so as to discover the underlying emotion or affective content of language use.[13] For the rhetorician, words are inevitably signs and should thus be read as symptoms of affective states. In its classical definition, a trope was not simply the use of a word in a changed or "non-proper signification" but was further defined as a linguistic shift either between species or between affections: thus metonymy, irony, metaphor, and synecdoche are the principal tropes of species, while *catachresis* (borrowing), *hyperbole* (exaggeration), *metalepsis* (cause for effect) and *litotes* (diminution) are the master tropes of the affections.[14] The figures of speech, the schemata, are defined as the linguistic forms of representation, as "the apparel and ornament of the body . . . of words and speech" which allow the speaker not only to represent but equally to fashion, to carry across, to feign, dissimulate, seduce, delight, and move.[15] The *gnome* or figures of sentence are thus defined by Smith as "pathetical, or such as move affection and passion."[16] The figures of speech are understood rhetorically as condensations of emotion, as the specific languages of particular passions. In rhetorical manuals the most powerful or effective of figures were thus those that carried the greatest emotional content or were deemed likely to have the greatest affective impact. Figures were therefore listed according to their potential use in different genres of speech. In most lists of figures, however, extremity of emotion was associated particularly with figures of antithesis (*oppositio*), exclamation (*ecphonesis*), emphasis (*auxesis*), recollection (*anamnesis*), or visual effect (*hypotyposis*).[17] The

12. See Freud, *Psychopathology of Everyday Life*; Obeyesekere, *Work of Culture*; Derrida, *Writing and Difference*; Ricouer, *Freud and Philosophy*.

13. These figures are drawn primarily from Puttenham, *Arte of English Poesie*; Peacham, *Garden of Eloquence*. Further useful lists and discussions can be found in Thomas Farnaby, *Index Rhetoricus*; Smith, *Mysterie of Rhetorique*.

14. See, for this particular classification, Smith, *Mysterie of Rhetorique* at fol. B 1 b.

15. See particularly Puttenham, *Arte of Poesie* at 155–161.

16. Smith, *Mysterie of Rhetorique* at fol. B 4 b.

17. Quintilian, *Institutio Oratoria* (on *enargeia*); Lamy, *Art of Speaking*; and more broadly, Derrida, "The White Mythology"; Goodrich, "We Orators."

classical art and practice of rhetoric was that of persuasion or at least of discovery of the means of persuasion; it sought to manipulate emotion, to advocate policies, plead causes, or praise civic offices by means of identification between audience and oratorical projection. The judicious use of the lexicon of tropes and other rhetorical and argumentative forms would institute a distinction, discrimination, or judgment between affect and antipathy, between identical and alien, like and unlike and, finally, in terms not dissimilar to Freud's basic drives of *eros* and *thanatos,*[18] between affirmation and negation, between life and death.

The rhetorician pursued the linguistic levers of passion. The orator was always an advocate in search of the continued oratorical play (*permutatio*) of irony or allegory, of things signified "by other words."[19] Rhetoric was a consistent pursuit of emotive force, of some movement of the mind "as of love, hatred, gladness or sorrow" under the general label of vehemence of affection (*pathopoeia* or *affectus expressio*).[20] This oratorical goal of affective dissimulation, of allegorical representation of the "other scene" of human motive, desire, and action, was subject to a further unconscious law. As the definition of affective expression suggests, the language of public speech, or institutional enunciation, which is to say the language of rhetorical genres, of law (forensic), politics (deliberative), and ceremony (panegyric), was antagonistically structured. What was represented earlier to be the antirrhetic character of dogmatic discourses may be found in detail in the figuration of dogmatic argumentation. In terms of law and the agonistic presentation of argument and judgment, doctrine and decision, it follows logically that its characteristic emotional force was and is to be found in figures of antithesis or opposition whereby the realm of affectivity may be identified and separated from that of the alien, unfamiliar, or other. In broader terms it can be argued further that all institutional speech is pleading in the context of some species of trial: the hearer is always a judge.[21] Whether the court is that of reason, taste, opinion, or law, all auditors are in some measure forensic actors and they play the role of both jury and judge.[22] A further explanation might project the juridical into the social so as to suggest that the antagonistic or properly *antirrhetic* structure of discourse was a consistent form of institutional self-representation. To have an effect, to persuade, threaten, or otherwise move its auditor, the legal speech or written judgment had to identify its audience or constituency

18. See Freud, *Beyond the Pleasure Principle.*

19. Puttenham, *Arte of Poesie* at 155–156; Smith, *Mysterie of Rhetorique* at fol. E 6 a.

20. Smith, *Mysterie of Rhetorique* at fol. S 5 b.

21. In most of the curricular manuals, hearer and judge are synonyms, as for example in Puttenham, *Arte of Poesie* at 189.

22. This Aristotelian *dictum* is discussed in Vickers, *In Defence of Rhetoric* at 77.

and provide that audience or those hearers with such symbols, images, icons, or figures as would allow communication in its classical or at least etymological sense of communion, of meaning as a transference that displaces the auditor from one realm to another, from opinion to reason, temporality to spirituality, visibility to invisibility. The audience of law will identify itself narcissistically with the legal institution, with the mirror of its projected images, and will simultaneously reject its competitors, neighbors, or simple alternatives, those whom the law has denounced or the judge admonished. Thus the rhetoric of affectivity is coupled with that of negation. The praise of the identical, the similar, the like or proportionate is accompanied by denunciation, denial, or negation of the strange, the unlike, disproportionate or heteroclite. It does so in the same historical and political sense in which it was argued earlier that the antirrhetic institutes orthodoxy as that which creates heterodoxy, and doctrine as that which defines heresy as its necessary or complementary and so also supplementary form.[23] A preliminary illustration from a collection of moralizing essays should suffice to indicate the nature of this correlation between affirmation and negation, praise and denunciation and, more broadly, between unconscious intent and the figures of speech. For where rhetoric maps the emotional body of the institutional audience, psychoanalysis will subsequently attend to the images, figures, and symbols whereby linguistic practice can be read symptomatically as representing past patterns of power, repressed emotive sources of action, and the residue more generally of unconscious desires.

In an exemplary essay directly concerned with persuasion through appeal to the affections, Daniel Tuvil represented the effective orator as speaking with the "tongue of the heart." To capture the affection of the auditor is the principal part of rhetorical success,

> and the reason hereof is not farre from hand. For passions are certain internal acts, and operations of our soul, which being joined and linked in a most inviolable, and long-continued league of friendship with the sensitive power, and facultie thereof, do conspire together like disobedient and rebellious subjects, to shake off the *yoake of reason,* and exempt themselves from her command and controllment, that they still exercise those disordered motions, in the contract world of our frail and human bodies.[24]

Borrowing in no little measure from the theological conception of the invocation of faith through appeal to and inscription upon the heart, Tuvil

23. This argument is made most forcefully by Foucault, "The Discourse on Language." For an interesting example of this thesis, see Godolphin, *Repertorium Canonicum,* especially ch. 40, "Of Blashphemy and Heresy."

24. Tuvil, *Essaies Politike and Morall* at sig. 15v–16r. For another striking example of this argument, see J-F. Senault, *De l'usage des passions* (Paris: Fayard, 1641, 1992 ed.) at 137–148.

argues for a practice of persuasion that takes hold of the body, which is ethical in the strong sense of determining habitual practice; the body, in short, is the unconscious. Rhetoric is here used to analyze, evoke and, on occasion, to unleash a dark and unconscious realm of vehement affection, sense, and corporeal volition or will. Whether it is depicted as deceitful, irrational, or simply subversive, the rhetoric of affection plainly depends upon or harbors either other reasons or the other of reason, which is in rhetoric variously termed the imagination, intensivity, violence or affection, image or idol.

Rhetoric and psychoanalysis converge in the analysis of the conflict or cause that relates the institutional to the individual, and in both disciplines law is the term used to depict the relation of the subject to patristic judgment, *patria, regia, iudex,* or *pater.* The common theme of cause, conflict, or disputation is most noticeable in the alignment of rhetoric with specific images of conflict, trial, demagogy, and verbal war. The telos of rhetorical speech is victory rather than any more direct cure, a metaphor that was lengthily elaborated in Bernard Lamy's *The Art of Speaking,* although other handbooks provide equally striking elaborations in terms of confutation, defeat, and overcoming, as well as the more obviously forensic forms of figuration such as demonstration, self-evidence, necessity, and disproof.[25] In Lamy's depiction our effect upon others is most typically a consequence of the figures of our speech, which include the bodily gestures, tears, and other physical signs that accompany oratory. The necessity of figures, however, lies in the hostility of institutional environments or the adversarial contexts of speaking. The rhetorician is always on trial or "before the law." Such trial dates back historically to an "original," which was trial by combat, by ordeal, or by physical omen,[26] and Lamy simply recollects this antagonistic and physically threatening history of pleading a cause by subsequently and lengthily comparing the orator and the pleader to a soldier fighting, suggesting if nothing else that the soul is constantly in conflict, both in directing its own passions and in defending itself from those of others. In broader rhetorical terms, the discourse of the institution manipulates figures of speech, dissimulates, cajoles, threatens, orders, and persuades because these are the forms of social action. The unconscious is a jurist pleading both innocence and guilt, torn between hedonism and pessimism, desire and law. The dogma or "delirium" of institutional speech, its insistence and its repetition, is simply a further level or reflection of the antinomy of affection and negation, praise and denuncia-

25. As, for example, in Fenner, *Artes of Logike and Rhetorike*; Sherry, *Treatise of Schemes and Tropes.*

26. See Sir John Davies, *Of the Antiquity of Lawful Combats in England* (1601) in R. Grosart (ed.), *The Works of Sir John Davies* (London: private circulation, 1869).

tion, approval and polemic, through which the soul, or in contemporary terminology, identity, is instituted and prolonged.

If autobiography provides both the lexicon and the narrative structure—the affections and the antagonisms of the individual unconscious—social history is the unconscious structure of institutions. To the extent that the institution survives, insofar as it is independent of any single generation of its custodians, access to its unconscious motivations, its repressions and its desires, must frequently be indirect. Access will not, for obvious reasons, be by means of the "royal road" to the science of the unconscious, the interpretation of dreams. The institution is delirious or uncontrolled only in its habitual procedures, standard forms, precedents, protocols, and other texts. It is in the slips or figures of the text that rhetoric may attend to, recover, or reconstruct certain of the antagonisms, fears, identities, and desires that over the long term motivate or cause institutional enunciations. In the ensuing analysis three examples of anomalous common law rule will be used to illustrate the potential uses of rhetoric in locating an institutional delirium or unconscious of law. The examples, which are all of contemporary legal anachronisms, will move from the analysis of textual figures to that of the emotions, conflicts, or repressed histories that may be used more or less persuasively to interpret them.

ANTONOMASIA: PSYCHIATRIC HARM AND THE ENGLISHMAN'S HOME

The first example is taken from the law of torts. It concerns the recoverability of damages for psychiatric harm caused by negligently occasioned nervous shock. The anomalous case is that of *Attia* v *British Gas plc*.[27] The plaintiff employed the defendants to install central heating in her house in Middlesex. "[R]eturning home at about 4 P.M. on 1 July 1981 she saw smoke coming from the loft of the house. She telephoned the fire brigade but, by the time the firemen arrived, the whole house was on fire. . . . Obviously the house and its contents were extensively damaged." The defendants admitted liability in negligence for the physical damage to the house, but the question remained whether the plaintiff could recover damages for "nervous shock," the psychiatric harm occasioned by seeing her "home and its contents ablaze" for a period of somewhat over four hours.[28] The Court of Appeal held unanimously that psychiatric damage occasioned by seeing "her home and possessions damaged and/or destroyed"

27. *Attia* v *British Gas plc* [1987] 2 AER 455.
28. Ibid. at 456 g–j.

was recoverable. The decision is in some respects an obvious one, and it could be argued that it simply extends the general criterion of foreseeability to a new situation. The categories of negligence, as Lord Macmillan once remarked, are never closed. The stronger argument, however, and one to which, fortuitously, I adhere, is that the decision is anomalous both in terms of lacking doctrinal justification and in terms of failure to accord with existing precedent.

The extant law on recoverability of damages for psychiatric harm at the time that *Attia* v *British Gas* was decided was the House of Lords decision in *McLoughlin* v *O'Brian.*[29] In terms of doctrinal development, the decision in *McLoughlin* explicitly established a multiple test of proximity as the basis for recoverability in actions for nervous shock. Lord Wilberforce, in a judgment that has more recently been annotated and affirmed by the House of Lords in *Alcock* v *Chief Constable of South Yorkshire,*[30] stated that three elements were inherent in any claim: "the class of persons whose claims should be recognized; the proximity of such persons to the accident; and the means by which the shock is caused."[31] It is clearly the first head of foreseeability that is here significant:

> As regards the class of persons, the possible range is between the closest family ties, of parent and child, or husband and wife, and the ordinary bystander. Existing law recognises the claims of the first; it denies that of the second, either on the basis that such persons must be assumed to be possessed of fortitude sufficient to enable them to endure the calamities of modern life or that defendants cannot be expected to compensate the world at large.[32]

The basis for drawing the line was the familiar policy ground of Anglo-American torts, namely that the admissibility of such actions would raise the specter of indefinite liability owed to an indeterminate class of potential plaintiff.

Without discussing whether British Gas plc was a recognized calamity of the modern world, Lord Wilberforce may finally be cited as authority for a methodological argument, namely that in situations of the type under discussion, "the courts have proceeded in the traditional manner of the common law from case to case, on a basis of logical necessity."[33] The figurative use of the term "logical necessity" deserves brief comment in terms precisely of figuration or condensation. To claim that reasoning by likeness,

29. *McLoughlin* v *O'Brian and others* [1982] 2 AER 298.
30. *Alcock and others* v *Chief Constable of the South Yorkshire Police* [1991] 4 AER 907.
31. *McLoughlin* v *O'Brian* at 304 f–g.
32. Ibid. at 304 f–h. Cited and approved in *Alcock* at 912–913.
33. Ibid. 302 f–g.

by metaphor or simile, by translation from one image to another, from one affection or experience to the next, is a procedure of logical necessity can only be understood as irony, *antiphrasis*, or the dissimulation of dream-work. It is no more possible to "deduce" a relation between one context and another than it is feasible to claim any strict identity between the legal reconstruction of different events occurring at different times and affecting different parties. The logical necessity of analogy is at most a subjective necessity imposed by custom and habit. Whereas Roman law long recognized the logical weakness of such arguments predicated upon similarity, the common law returns continuously to claim, somewhat mystically in the context of common law's avowed empiricism, that analogy is the "natural tendency of the human and legal mind."[34] The analogy then suggested by Lord Wilberforce is that of the different situations in which parents can recover for psychiatric harm caused by injury to their child. Lord Scarman added laconically that "I foresee social and financial problems if damages for 'nervous shock' should be made available to persons other than parents and children."[35] The Australian case of *Jaensch* v *Coffey*, which stipulated no specific kinship tie but a "close, constructive, and loving relation" between the parties probably hit upon a formulation that best describes the current law: the tie must be close and affectionate and while it need not necessarily fall within the conventional classifications of lineal or familial proximity it does require a human affection lodged between human partners.[36]

With the well canvassed exception of rescue cases and the unique example of a claim based upon fear of injury to a workmate,[37] legal doctrine has consistently maintained that proximity with regard to the class of persons that is to be allowed to recover means a tie of blood or of recognized relationship. Such a relationship has always been taken to mean a relationship between persons. Even taking account of judicial paternalism or the

34. For discussion of this issue, see W. T. Murphy and R. W. Rawlings, "After the Ancien Regime: The Writing of Judgments in the House of Lords 1979/1980" (1981) 44 *Modern Law Review* 617; Goodrich, *Reading the Law*, ch. 6. More broadly, see W. T. Murphy, "The Oldest Social Science? The Epistemic Properties of the Common Law Tradition" (1991) 54 *Modern Law Review* 182; and Goodrich, "Poor Illiterate Reason." For a discussion specifically relating to nervous shock, see Joanne Conaghan and Wade Mansell, *The Wrongs of Tort* (London: Pluto Press, 1993) at 28. "What is clear is that the nervous shock cases represent not a considered and logical extension to tortious rules of liability but rather an arbitrary and essentially non-logical extension to what we have argued is an illogical process."

35. Ibid. at 311 e.

36. *Jaensch* v *Coffey* [1984] 54 ALR 417 at 457 (per Deane J).

37. On rescue see *Chadwick* v *British Transport Commission* [1967] 2 AER 945, and also the American decision of *Wagner* v *International Railway Co.* (1921) 232 NY 176; on workmates see *Dooley* v *Cammell Laird. & Co. Ltd.* [1951] 1 Lloyd's Rep. 271, and for an Australian example see *Mount Isa Mines Ltd.* v *Pusey* [1970] 125 CLR 383.

doctrinal desire to keep the legal judgment separate from the sphere of domesticity, it is hard to see that it falls within the "natural tendency of the human and legal mind" to perceive a house either as or as being "like" a relative or "analogous to" a person. Nor does precedent provide any examples of "logical necessity" leading from person to property or from animate to inanimate. A person is not in ordinary speech nor in art nor in legal language like a house. The only precedent that could offer support of any kind for the Court of Appeal decision would be the somewhat obscure earlier decision of the Court of Appeal in the case of *Owens* v *Liverpool Corporation*.[38] In that case the plaintiff's dead relative, an inanimate person, was in a coffin that was dislodged by a tram-car operated by the defendants. Severe "mental shock" was occasioned to close relatives of the deceased who witnessed the accident and who feared the coffin would be ejected into the road. On the grounds that it is the dignity or office of the dead to be in repose, the disturbance to the coffin and the threat that it might at any moment slide out of the damaged hearse and fall to the street was sufficient ground for recovery. The court recognized that the threat of injury to the dead was a marginal if not tenuous analogy to earlier situations, but it suggested that what was significant was the proximity or strength of affection between the parties. MacKinnon L.J. went further at one point and suggested consideration of the moot case of mental damage caused by the death of a much loved pet dog.[39] The "beloved" dog, of course, is the Englishman's best, most trusted, and most loyal friend, and it is easy to imagine that the court might well have difficulties distinguishing the family dog from other members of the family. It remains the case, however, that the subjects of injury in precedent cases extended no further than a hypothetical living nonperson or a dead relative.

Returning to the decision in *Attia* it is evident rhetorically that more is at stake than a simple question of the foreseeable consequences of damage to property. There is indeed an immediate shift in the depiction of the facts of that case from the cognitive to the affective and from description to evaluation when the object of damage is renamed and becomes not a house but a home. The figure[40] in question is that of *antonomasia,* or change of name. It is described by Smith as a sentential figure (*figura sententiae*), which "is a figure . . . for the forcible moving of affections, which doth after a sort beautify the sense and very meaning of a sentence."[41] Its

38. *Owens* v *Liverpool Corporation* [1938] 4 AER 727.

39. Ibid. at 730 f–g.

40. It should be noted that for Peacham, *Garden of Eloquence* at fol. E iii b, *antonomasia* is listed under "tropes of words," while for Puttenham, *Arte of Poesie* at 168, it is listed under figures. While it is properly a trope, *antonomasia* can also be a figure of speech where it is used argumentatively rather than simply as an "improper" or "borrowed" sense of a word.

41. Smith, *Mysterie of Rhetorique* at fol. B 4 a.

rhetorical effect is depicted by Peacham as that of metonymically transferring the value of some "dignity, office, profession, science, or trade" from its proper referent to a novel *comparata*.[42] In its usual rhetorical manipulation, the substitution of name is metonymic in the sense of selecting a quality or essence that is representative of the whole: Cicero for eloquence, the philosopher for Aristotle, Blackstone for the law, and so on, where the substituted name elects to qualify the object or subject in either a positive or negative fashion. The attribution is the more powerful for being unmarked or tacit, its force and accuracy are simply assumed, and not only is the lauded or denigrated part taken for the whole but there is also a move from passive to active, from description to qualification and in sum, from object to *telos* or goal. Whether the term "house" or "home" is more properly descriptive of the structure that formed the subject matter of the decision, it is the shift or slippage from one term to the other, from species to species or from the descriptive to the evaluative, that should give occasion for rhetorical concern. The trope is an indicator of an affectivity or unconscious intent, it is a figure of a subtle argumentative shift, and it is precisely the hidden, oneiric, or repressed connotations of "home" that the rhetorical analyst should pursue. It will be claimed here that these connotations are institutional and largely unconscious. It is certainly the case that the legal status or meaning of a home is not addressed in the judgments, nor would it appear to have been raised by counsel in argument. The institutional connotations of the shift from one noun to another have in these circumstances to be reconstructed in terms of the particular judgment and also in the longer term context of the doctrinal text of which the decision in *Attia* is but a minor incidence.

In the course of a preliminary judgment in favor of the defendants, Sir Douglas Frank at first instance had noted that grief and sorrow were understandable responses to "the loss of all that is embodied in the word 'home' and of one's possessions."[43] In a statement that reversed the order of substitution, such that home became house, Sir Douglas Frank took the "modern" view that loss of possessions and of "one's own house" was not a foreseeable cause of mental illness. The Court of Appeal differed. It recognized that the claim broke new ground, indeed "that no analogous claim has ever . . . been upheld or even advanced."[44] Nonetheless the court managed to discover a duty of care and to deem it possible that as a matter of fact it was foreseeable that the plaintiff would suffer psychiatric harm. Bingham L.J. went so far as to list other objects of affection that might, if

42. Peacham, *Garden of Eloquence* at fol. E iii b. See also Smith, *Mysterie of Rhetorique* at fol. F 1 b; and Lamy, *Art of Speaking* at 215.

43. *Attia* at 461 c–d.

44. Ibid. at 464 c–d.

destroyed, so unsettle the seemingly restrained emotional world of their owner that recovery should probably be allowed: namely, a scholar's life's work of research or composition and a householder's "cherished possessions" or heirlooms.[45] In the present instance the damage was not simply to contents but to the structure and place of the home itself.

To "fall in love" with a house is ungrammatical in law and is also not recognized as a cause of action for mental distress in either contract or tort according to a recent decision of the Court of Appeal, with Bingham L.J. (unpromoted) again sitting.[46] In *Watts* v *Morrow*, the plaintiffs, a stockbroker and a solicitor, jointly purchased a second home, a country house, relying upon a negligently prepared survey. The summary of facts records that Mr. Watts "fell in love with the house" and that Mrs. Watts said that "it was very beautiful, a house with a heart and difficult to resist."[47] Nonetheless, the Court of Appeal had no difficulty in denying a claim for damages for distress or loss of peace of mind: "frustration, anxiety, displeasure, vexation, tension, or aggravation" occasioned by breach of contract were, for reasons of policy, irrecoverable.[48] It would be, it might be argued, somewhat promiscuous to allow recovery of damages for melancholia occasioned by witnessing harm to a second home, however much loved. To digress momentarily, the decision in *Attia* might be taken to suggest a concept of fidelity to a single home: monogamy might be matched by what could be termed *monoheimy*. In short, in the absence of any manifest legal reason, in doctrine or in precedent, for the extension of liability in psychiatric harm to cover damage occasioned by injury to things, it is necessary to follow the curious moral extensions and the rhetoric, symptom and trope, of the judgment in *Attia* and to inquire further into the legal significance of the home. The conscious surface of the decision is here of less importance than its unconscious longings and loves—what is proffered as immediate justification is of less moment than the longer term, structural causes of judgment. The apparent logic must face the delirium that is the law.

There are two important legal connotations associated with the home and traceable to the very dawn of the modern common law. First, both in case law and in doctrinal writing, the Englishman's home is his castle. As early at 1605, in *Semayne's Case*,[49] it was held that the home was a place of sanctity, of tranquility and peace. It was the safest of all refuges (*domus sua cuique est tutissimum refugium*). It was a hiding place, an escape, a castle, a

45. Ibid. at 464 e–f.
46. *Watts and another* v *Morrow* [1991] 4 AER 937.
47. Ibid. at 940.
48. Ibid. at 956.
49. *Semayne's Case* [1605] 5 Co Rep 91.

fortress, a site of repose and of defense. In Thomas Wood's *Institute of the Laws of England,*[50] *Semayne's Case* is discussed and cited as authority for the rule that whereas an assembly or meeting of three of more is an offense, it is not punishable if it is "for the safeguard of his *House,* and for the Defence of the possession thereof." It is permissible for a citizen to gather friends to prevent any unlawful entry into his own house "but he cannot assemble his friends for the defence of his *person* against those that threaten to beat him, while he is out of his house." The carapace of skin is obviously of less material significance and is of course—and not only by virtue of this legal rule—shorter lived than the edifice of bricks and mortar, the family home. Elsewhere in *An Institute,* a variety of definitions are provided of house (*domus*) and of mansion house (*domus mansionalis*), and the protection of these spaces and structures is spelled out at length. It is again not without significance that "a chamber in an Inn of Court, where one usually lodges, is a mansion-house" and so inviolate, a rule that no doubt did much to aid the longevity of members of the legal profession.[51]

In later case law the sanctity of the home and garden is reiterated and emphasized. The most famous statement of right comes in *Entick* v *Carrington,* where Lord Camden asserted the legal protection of the home to be an "extraordinary jurisdiction" coeval with the law itself and so without origin or evidence beyond its statement, save that "precedent supports it."[52] The Saxon concept of "house-peace" and the liberties spelled out in *Magna Carta* are likely sources of such precedent, although none is needed for so ancient a rule.[53] He subsequently remarks upon the ethical legitimation of the rule as being coincident with the end or *telos* of law and of society itself: "The great end, for which men entered society, was to secure their property. That right is preserved sacred and incommunicable in all instances, where it has not been taken away or abridged by some public law for the good of the whole." With a measure of hyperbole suitable to the occasion and the threat to this admittedly defeasible right, Lord Camden concludes with the celebrated defense of the English home and garden, stating that "no man can set foot upon my ground without my licence, but he is liable to an action, though the damage be nothing . . . [even for no more than] bruising the grass . . . or treading upon the soil." In later cases a similar exaggeration of an impermanent right is stated in terms of the protection of every single room in the house by separate writs

50. Wood, *An Institute* at 735–736.

51. Ibid. at 652.

52. *Entick* v *Carrington and three others,* 1765, in *State Trials* (London: Hansard, 1813), vol. 19 at 1066.

53. See Coke, *Magna Carta,* particularly fol. H iv b, K i a.

of trespass.[54] The house, of course, was many things in legal terms and was certainly not free of legal and ecclesiastical interference with regard, for example, to "good government"[55] or with respect to the proper forms of worship or the duties of husband and wife.[56] It was in an express sense a symbol, a condensation of numerous narratives of English identity, of political apathy and personal privacy, of freedom and domestic servitude.

Whether the common law protection of the house as home of the subject is viewed as successful or otherwise effective, the home is a legal term and an image invested with a remarkable significance. The home is autobiographically both domesticity and family, the site of an originary law, that of paternity, as also in its earliest stages it is the *gynaeceum,* or maternal domain. The home is connotative psychoanalytically of emotional security, of a second law of nurture, of the "nursing parent" and of the immemorial, of that which is—like common law—a record or testament *aere perennius.*[57] The home represents tradition in the precise sense that the home is external to and survives its occupation, it is the place of the ancestors and forefathers, of the graven image or *imago,* of all that, *in nuce,* to which we belong. The instant that the court in *Attia* v *British Gas plc* turned from house to home, categorizing the injury as being occasioned not simply by damage to property but, far more specifically, by damage that was caused by the burning of the home, it returned unconsciously to a category of legal tradition with an extraordinary, although heavily veiled, affective force. The description—by the figure of *prosographia*—of the burning home as the material cause of the harm suffered carries an unconscious sense of an absolute violation: to destroy a sacred place is by ecclesiastical law a sacrilege,[58] a transgression of the boundaries between species or profanation of the marks of an iconic space. In more secular terms, destruction of the home is disrespectful of tradition—contemptuous of lineage, of ancestral virtue, and of the "titles of antiquity" which honor and family pass on through the home. One can go further and suggest that destruction of the home connotes a challenge to the most basic law, not simply that of kinship but in legal terms that of the first *societas,* the family and its order of succession. To destroy the home is technically a "monstrous" act because

54. See *Bruce* v *Rawlins* [1770] 95 Eng. Rep. 934; *Ratcliffe* v *Burton* [1802] 27 Eng. Rep. 123.

55. See *An Act to retain the Queen's subjects in obedience,* 1593 (35 Eliz. cap. I).

56. See *Queen's Injunctions,* 1559, extracted in G. Prothero (ed.), *Select Statutes and other Constitutional Documents illustrative of the Reigns of Elizabeth and James I* (Oxford: Clarendon Press, 1894) at 185–187.

57. See Carl Jung, *Memories, Dreams, Reflections* (London: Collins and Routledge, 1963), especially 221 ff.

58. See Spelman, *History and Fate of Sacrilege* at 22–25.

it takes away from the support of the family and threatens a situation in which reproduction is no longer reproduction of the same, in which the child is a monster because it is unlike the father or the mother.[59]

It remains to be observed that the plaintiff was a woman. In *Owens* v *Liverpool Corporation,* the court remarked that "if real injury has genuinely been caused by shock from apprehension as to something less than human life (for example, the life of a beloved dog), can the sufferer recover no damages for the injury he, or perhaps oftener she, has sustained?"[60] It is not clear what weight this shift in gender would have in determining the factual outcome of either case, but it should undoubtedly be observed that in affective terms the home is a gendered category. In constitutional doctrine, the household, according to Sir Thomas Smith, here following Aristotle, is the internal domain of women while the external world is the sphere of men.[61] In terms of the ecclesiastical law of marriage contemporary with the earliest surviving statements of the privacy and sanctity of the home, it is clear that protection of the home is protection of the vulnerable, the women and children for whom the home is the world. In this respect the portrait of the facts in *Attia* again betrays an unconscious reservoir of institutional emotions or structures of value that persist over the *longue durée* of common law. The figure of *antonomasia* indicates a slip or unconscious motive, it allows for the reconstruction of "another scene" of legal judgment, that of affectivity and desire.[62] In terms, finally, of the structure of the legal unconscious, the case of *Attia* is representative of one dimension of the conflict that constitutes the dogma, dream order, or delirium of the institution. It opens up a zone of affectivity, an object among objects of identification and of love, a political desire toward which legal policy will inevitably be directed. It forms an inside, an identity against which must be compared the corresponding zone of exclusion, of alienity, foreignness, or otherness with which a later example will be concerned. In the next example, however, the question of identification is again central to the rhetorical recovery of a repressed memory of the objects and meanings of a specific legal anomaly, the treatment of contractual communications sent by post.

59. Selden, *Titles of Honour* at sig. b 4 a. For extensive discussion of this theme of genealogical legitimacy, see Legendre, *L'Inestimable objet de la transmission*; and more technically, see Legendre et al., *Le Dosier occidental de la parenté.*

60. *Owens* v *Liverpool Corporation* at 730.

61. Smith, *De Republica Anglorum* at 58–59: "The first sort or beginning of an House or Familie called Oikonomia."

62. On the use of this metaphor, see Pierre Legendre, "Analecta" in A. Papageorgiou Legendre, *Filiation* at 216–218 (on "Freud's concept of *l'autre scene*").

ALLEGORIA, OR THE ERASED FACE OF THE OFFEREE

The second example is taken from the law of contract. It concerns the much remarked anomaly that while contracts are the result of consensus and thus depend upon communication between the parties, an acceptance is binding once put in the post. The postal or mailbox rule is generally accredited in Anglo-American case law with an early nineteenth-century origin in the decision of the King's Bench in *Adams* v *Lindsell*.[63] In doctrinal terms, the rule in that case was justified by reference to the imposition of a necessarily arbitrary cutoff point in relation to communication. If such a point of no return were not imposed, then in the view of the court "no contract could ever be completed by post. For if the defendants were not bound by their offer when accepted by the plaintiffs till the answer was received, then the plaintiffs ought not to be bound till after they had received the notification that the defendants had received their answer and assented to it. And so it might go on *ad infinitum*."[64] Such an arbitrary drawing of the line, a version of what Bachelard would have termed *nemesis* complex,[65] the desire for finality, has been viewed by most commentators at best as an ill-conceived concession to the needs of business certainty and at worst as irrational by virtue of being inconsistent with the consensual principles of contract formation. Explanations for the rule are various and will be briefly reviewed. If nothing else, the absence of any plausible, let alone satisfactory, justification for the postal rule generates continued academic debate.[66] Most commentators accept that in its original terms, covering letters and subsequently the telegraph, the rule—with the exception of the *per incuriam* decision of the Massachusetts supreme court in *McCullough* v *Eagle Insurance* and the historically misconceived decision in *Rhode Island Tool Co.* v *United States*[67]—is here to stay.[68] Justifications for the rule become secondary and less consequential save in the area of the potential adoption or disavowal of the rule in relation to more recent technologies.

63. *Adams* v *Lindsell* [1818] 1 B. & Ald. 681; *Henthorn* v *Fraser* [1892] 2 Ch. 27; *Holwell Securities* v *Hughes* [1974] 1 WLR 155.

64. *Adams* v *Lindsell* at 683.

65. Gaston Bachelard, *The Psychoanalysis of Fire* (New York: Harper and Row, 1974) at 43–45.

66. Simon Gardiner, "Trashing with Trollope: A Deconstruction of the Postal Rules in Contract" (1992) 12 *Oxford Journal of Legal Studies* 170; also Goodrich, "Contractions"; Costas Douzinas and Ronnie Warrington, "Posting the Law: Social Contracts and the Postal Rule's Grammatology" (1991) 4 *International Journal for the Semiotics of Law* 115.

67. Respectively *McCullough* v *Eagle Insurance Co.* [1822] 18 Mass. (1 Pick.) 278; and *Rhode Island Tool Co.* v *United States*, 128 F. Supp. 417 (Ct. Cl. 1955).

68. G. Treitel, *The Law of Contract* (London: Sweet and Maxwell, 1991) at 24; P. S. Atiyah, *An Introduction to the Law of Contract* (Oxford: Clarendon Press, 1989) at 77; *Brinkibon Ltd.* v *Stahag Stahl und Stahlwarenhandelsgesellschaft mbH* [1983] 2 AC 34.

In brief doctrinal terms, the mailbox rule is an exception to the requirement that the formation of a contract conform to the voluntary assumption of obligations by the parties. For the contract to be adequately consensual, for there to be *consensus ad idem*, or a meeting of minds at the same time, it is necessary for the substance of both offer and agreement to be brought to the notice of the relevant party either by explicit words or by conduct or behavior that can be deemed to have the same communicative effect. What is required of both words or actions is that they come to the knowledge or notice of the other party.[69] That a posted acceptance escapes this rule is illogical, but it is presented in the case law as either an aspect of the law of agency or a feature of the fiction of continuing assent. With regard to the issue of agency, the principle is adapted from the Roman law of sale. Once the letter or message is placed in the hands of the authorized messenger, then the master or sender is deemed to have entrusted the messenger with the communication and it is reasonable to rely upon the message as communicated by the bare messenger or agent. Thus in the American case law, much has revolved around a line drawn at the point where the message leaves the control of the sender. In *Lucas* v *Western Union Telegraph Co.* in 1906, the American authority for viewing the moment of completion as being the moment that the acceptance takes effect is rehearsed as being because "thereafter the acceptor has no right to the letter and cannot withdraw it from the mails. Even if he should succeed in doing so the withdrawal will not invalidate the contract entered into."[70] In English case law a similar view, predicated upon a species of control compulsion, is also evident from early in the history of the rule: "The acceptor in posting the letter, has . . . put it out of his control and done an extraneous act which clenches the matter, and shows beyond all doubt that each side is bound. How then can a casualty in the post, whether resulting in delay, or in non-delivery unbind the parties or unmake the contract? . . . If he [the offeror] trusts to the post he trusts to a means of communication which, as a rule, does not fail."[71] The additional justification, adding conceptual legitimacy to the empirical observation of the general trustworthiness of the postal service, was derived from the earlier decision of *Cooke* v *Oxley* which designated a mailed offer as a continuing offer and found, upon the fiction that at each moment of transmission the offeror renewed his consent and that the assent of the offeree consequently constituted an irreversible meeting of minds.[72]

69. Thus, classically, *Dickinson* v *Dodds* [1876] 2 ChD 463.

70. 131 Iowa 669, 109 N.W. 191. Confirming, *inter alia, Tuttle* v *Iowa State Traveling Men's Association*, 132 Iowa 652, 104 N.W. 1131.

71. *Household Fire and Carriage Accident Insurance Co. Ltd.* v *Grant* [1879] 4 Ex. D. 216.

72. *Cooke* v *Oxley* [1790] Times Reports 653, discussed in *Morison* v *Thoelke*, 155 So.d 889 [1963]. This explanation of the rule is also rehearsed by Allan Farnsworth, "Meaning in the Law of Contracts" (1967) 76 *Yale Law Journal* 939.

The tenor of textbook explanations of the postal rule is either mutely resigned or straightforwardly cynical. For Corbin, to take an exemplary exposition, the explanation is empirical: "A better explanation of the existing rule seems to be that in such cases the mailing of a letter has long been a customary and expected way of accepting the offer. It is ordinary business usage," to which Corbin adds that while there may be inconvenience occasionally engendered, "we need a definite and uniform rule as to this."[73] For Llewellyn, the question of the justification of the anomalous rule was best addressed pragmatically: "The vital reason for throwing the hardship of an odd delayed or lost letter upon the offeror remains this: the offeree is already relying, with the best reason in the world, on the deal being on; the offeror is only holding things open; and, in view of the efficiency of communication facilities, we can protect the offeree in all these deals at the price of hardship on offerors in very few of them."[74] The judicial reiteration of these explanations adds little more than a sense of habitual caution or institutional faith. As recently as 1983, Lord Fraser summarized the view of the majority of the House of Lords on the distinction between telex and post in no more compelling logical terms than the observation that the rule "seems to have worked without leading to serious difficulty or complaint from the business community."[75] In *Holwell Securities Ltd.* v *Hughes* the arbitrariness of the rule or at least the apparent idiosyncracy of its continued usage was such as to prompt Lord Justice Lawton to assert a species of the indeterminacy thesis, a vague but doubtless deeply felt limitation to the rule, namely that it was not to be applied where its application would lead to absurdity: "The rule does not apply if, having regard to all the circumstances, including the nature of the subject matter under consideration, the negotiating parties cannot have intended that there should be a binding agreement until the party accepting the offer had in fact communicated acceptance."[76] Underlying such a view is most probably a simple sense of historical incomprehension: why continue to apply an archaic and anomalous rule when it seems to lack any logical necessity even at the time of its inception? As one court famously remarked, in the course of a failed attempt to overturn the rule, "to apply an outmoded formula is not only unjust, it runs counter to the whole stream of human experience. It is like insisting on an oxcart as the official means of transportation in the age of the automobile. The cart served a useful purpose in its day, but is now a museum piece. . . . The rea-

73. Arthur Linton Corbin, *Corbin on Contracts* (St. Paul: West Publishing, 1950), s. 78.

74. Llewellyn, "Our Case-Law of Contract: Offer and Acceptance," pt. 2 (1939) 48 *Yale Law Journal* 779, 795.

75. *Brinkibon Ltd.* at 39.

76. *Holwell Securities* at 159.

son for the rule [has] disappeared."[77] Both in the textbooks and in the courts, however, the balance of habit and reaction, of tradition and deference to precedent, tips the scales imperceptibly toward continued adherence to the rule, toward what Nusbaum, an American, termed "repetition compulsion."

Attempts to find some more rational explanation for the postal rule range from the historical through the literary to the psychoanalytic.[78] Starting with the latter, an article in the mid-1930s by Professor Nusbaum suggested that criticism of the postal rule and of the decision in *Adams v Lindsell* in particular had been extensive and was "sufficient" to discredit the rule. Nonetheless "they [the judges] stick to it in England as well as in this country. An attempt should be ventured to apply some 'psychoanalysis' to their actions and to look for the 'complex' behind them."[79] While Nusbaum offers neither diagnosis nor therapy for the Anglo-American judiciary, his suggestion has considerable merit. Why repeat a discredited decision, or at least a rule that even the judiciary has acknowledged to be arbitrary, if not for some other reason that is either repressed, forgotten, or inadmissible? Nusbaum concentrates on the idiosyncracy of the rule and adverts to its lack of historical or comparative justification. His purpose is in large measure simply to show (arguably inaccurately) that civil law systems historically have not had such a rule and that there is good reason for that absence.

A recent commentator, Simon Gardiner, elliptically takes up Nusbaum's challenge and offers a "deconstruction" of the postal rules in terms of their historical and social context of origin. The context, he argues rather unconvincingly, is that of the nineteenth-century reform of the post office: the post office monopoly, standardized rates, prepayment of postage, and the cutting of letter boxes in doors all merged in the public imagination to equate posting with the certainty of delivery: "The thesis, then, is that the decisions of the 1840s were influenced not so much by internal considerations about offer and acceptance in contract as by way of regarding

77. *Rhode Island Tool Co.*

78. See additionally A. Nusbaum, "Comparative Aspects of the Anglo-American Offer-and-Acceptance Doctrine" (1936) 33 *Columbia Law Review* 920; P. Winfield, "Some Aspects of Offer and Acceptance" (1939) 55 *Law Quarterly Review* 499: M. Sharp, "Reflections on Contract" (1966) 33 *University of Chicago Law Review* 211.

79. Nusbaum, "Offer-Acceptance Doctrine" at 922. That Nusbaum, in a paper that originated as a seminar presentation to Karl Llewellyn's contracts class, refers to psychoanalysis should not come as a surprise, granted the influence of Freud upon the realists in the 1930s. For a discussion of this point see particularly Neil Duxbury, "Jerome Frank and the Legacy of Legal Realism" (1991) 18 *Journal of Law and Society* 175. See also Caudill, "Freud and Critical Legal Studies" at 662–667. The major realist discussion of psychoanalysis and law is probably Frank, *Law and the Modern Mind.*

the phenomena of posting as such."[80] Using Trollope's novels as a literary pre-text for reformulating the logic of the postal rule, the deconstruction ends by confirming the repressed or at least lost external cause of the rule: "The postal acceptance . . . thus stands alone as an exception to a general requirement for full communication. . . . [The] rule may be regarded as something of a museum piece."[81] The fiction or "artificiality"[82] whereby the act of posting is treated by simulation "as if" it were communication of acceptance is here viewed as anomalous or as "compulsive," and so arbitrary if not necessarily evil. Gardiner also recognizes that like repression itself the postal rule is likely to return: "It is worth noticing, however, that there is a chance of history repeating itself."[83]

Where Gardiner introduces history and literature to provide an indication of the "real reason"[84] for the rule, it is arguable that his analysis of the rule does not take the logic of deconstruction—or Nusbaum's suggested psychoanalysis—far enough. As other contributors to the debate over the rule have pointed out, the postal exception may well be more significant than the standard rule.[85] While the rule of full communication suggests a linguistically unrealistic ideology of consensus, the postal rule introduces the objective possibility of the nonarrival of the letter and faces the consequences of that failure of delivery or noncommunication which constantly threatens to undermine the subjective theory of contracts. The narrative of the nonarriving letter would be similar to Poe's popular story of the purloined letter: the repetition or the "sticking" of the postal rule would serve to recollect or even to cure a general theory of contractual communication that represses the mechanisms, the grammatological but also linguistic means whereby the letter, the *ipsissima verba* of the contract, circulates or finds its destination.[86] The rule of full communication would be part of the blindness of law, the exception would be conceptually anterior and liberatory: "The exception comes before the rule in order to put the

80. Gardiner, "Trashing with Trollope" at 184. A more plausible version of this argument in relation to post and politics is made in Geoffrey Bennington, "Postal Politics and the Institution of the Nation," in Homi Bhabba (ed.), *Nation and Narration* (Routledge: London, 1989).

81. Gardiner, "Trashing with Trollope" at 192.

82. *Holwell Securities* at 157 (per Russell LJ).

83. Gardiner, "Trashing with Trollope" at 192.

84. Ibid. at 176.

85. See Douzinas and Warrington, "Posting the Law" at 123–125; Goodrich, *Languages of Law* at 150–152.

86. The "Purloined Letter" is much discussed within psychoanalysis and also increasingly within law: Jacques Lacan, "Seminar on the Purloined Letter" (1972) 48 *Yale French Studies* 39; Jacques Derrida, "Le Facteur de la Vérité," in Derrida, *The Post Card*; S. Felman, *Jacques Lacan and the Adventure of Insight* (Cambridge, Mass.: Harvard University Press, 1987), ch. 2; Caudill, "Lacan and Legal Language" at 200 ff.

rule into circulation. The post comes before the prior, the letter before the *phone,* endless circulation before the wealth of tradition, the postal relay before the fixity of meaning and the order of politics and law."[87] What one commentator views as being an inappropriate extension of the ideology of the metaphor of "meeting of minds," namely that the offer is made continuously as it travels to the offeree,[88] is represented deconstructively as the precondition for the possibility of contract as such. Where psychoanalysis would assert the priority of the postal rule because it privileged the signifier over the signified, deconstruction would support the postal rule on the basis of a similar inversion of the hierarchical opposition of writing to speech: the written is anterior to the spoken, the post thus represents the "destinal of Being," and the postal rule in consequence would be the emblem of the discipline of contract as a whole.[89]

There is support in the history of contract, and particularly in the early formbooks such as West's *Symbolaeography,* to support both the psychoanalytic and the deconstructive readings adverted to above.[90] The earliest forms of contract were written obligations adopted and adapted from precedent writings provided by means of "the [notarial] trade of the making of evidence, and terms thereof, which as they be most ancient, so without doubt are they the surest, and [of] most vailable effect, and a greater danger it is for those not exactly learned in the laws to alter or vary from the same."[91] The contract, *symbolon,* creed or record, is in legal principle immemorial and immutable: the language of law is in Coke's terms *vocabula artis,* an "unknown grammar,"[92] which circulates perpetually within its own professional genre. The language of legal record, as the "language of memorials" was destined more for posterity than for secular receipt.[93] The written obligation, *assumpsit,* or consensual bond circulated in the external language of durable legal forms. The contract is here a trace or vestige of a structure, of a prior and external agreement, of a code or language of law which precedes and survives its momentary intentional or temporal use. The postal rule, which recognizes precisely the priority of the signifier, of

87. Douzinas and Warrington, "Posting the Law" at 124. The argument comes directly from G. C. Cheshire and C. H. S. Fifoot, *Law of Contract* (London: Butterworth, 1945, 1991 ed.) at 53: "[The rule] is perhaps less surprising if we attend to the history of the matter. *Adams* v *Lindsell* was the first genuine offer and acceptance case in English law and, in 1818 there was no rule that acceptance must be communicated. As so often happens in English law, the exception is historically anterior to the rule."

88. This argument is suggested by Farnsworth, "Meaning in the Law of Contracts" at 945.

89. Derrida, *The Post Card* at 65.

90. West, *First Part of Symbolaeography,* particularly fol. A 8 a.

91. T. Phayr, *A New Boke of Presidentes, in manner of a Register* (London: Whytchurche, 1544) at fol. ii a.

92. Coke, *The First Part of the Institutes of the Laws of England* at fol. C 6 a.

93. Doderidge, *English Lawyer,* at 51.

the letter, over the sense or content, directly expresses the logic of common law history. It would be presumptuous in the extreme to suppose that there exists any single explanation—historical, literary, philosophical, or psychoanalytic—to this rule. Too much has condensed around the continued metaphor or, properly, allegory, of the post and the rule of posting. That the fiction continues to return, that letters bind without being read, that the law treats writing "as if" it were speech, in short the allegorical narrative of contract by letters, necessarily suggests an other scene or unconscious place of judgment.

In historical terms, the postal rule can be traced to the *Digest,* which in 18.1.1.2 rules that "sale is a contract of the law of nations and so is concluded by simple agreement; it can thus be contracted by parties not present together, through messengers, or by letters [*per nuntium et per literas*]." In the reception, as Gordley has shown, the glossatorial interpretation of this passage frequently addressed the question of when the contract by "bare messenger" or letter was complete. Accursius, in the *Glossa Ordinaria,* thus takes the view that if the offeree's letter or message of acceptance has been sent, an attempted revocation by the seller before receipt of the acceptance would not be effective:[94] "To Petrus, Cinus, and Bartolus the obvious difficulty with this position is that the seller becomes bound to a contract to which he did not consent at the moment it was formed. The issue in Accursius's mind, however, was not whether the seller had consented but the moment at which a communication is effective."[95] In terms of the postreception development of civil law, the issue raised by correspondence was that of the status of messengers or other agents in communication between absent parties. The question became that of whether a simple or bare messenger could represent a continuing condition or consent to the transaction. The letter, in Alciatus's definition, was a silent messenger (*tacitus nuntius*) and so out of the power of the sender it communicated in its own right. By this logic, the offeree was entitled to rely upon the continuing validity of the offer.[96] Gordley mentions one other significant circumstance in the *Corpus Iuris Civilis* in which letters are effective even if not received. It is that by *Code* 5 17 6 a marriage can be dissolved by a document that never reaches the other spouse.[97] This last example will prove to be of the utmost importance.

The glossatorial reception of the law of sale has an indirect impact upon

94. Gloss to D 18 1 1 2 (*et per literas*), discussed in James Gordley, *The Philosophical Origins of Modern Contract Doctrine* (Oxford: Clarendon Press, 1991) at 45–46.

95. Gordley, *Modern Contract Doctrine* at 46.

96. Alciatus, *De Notitia Dignitatem* at 190.

97. Gordley, *Modern Contract Doctrine* at 46.

English law.[98] Historical accounts of the development of modern contract doctrine make it clear that the elaboration of indigenous rules governing assumpsit and covenant was as significant as was the earlier inheritance of Roman law.[99] Although it is evident, not least from Gordley's discussion, that the common law of contract had significant Roman borrowings and further that nineteenth-century developments were borrowed almost entirely from civil law,[100] the most significant, yet least discussed, area of reception of contract doctrine was in the law on "spousals" or marriage contracts. In premodern English law, the use of the term "contract" was often synonymous with marriage, and it was in relation to the law of spousals that many of the doctrines later developed as part of the modern law of contract were first developed. In particular, rules relating to capacity, to duress, to consideration, to offer and acceptance *in praesentia* and *in absentia,* to present and future intent, and to the plea of *non est factum* all had their earliest development in relation to the law of marriage.[101] It should also be emphasized that the law of marriage was subject to the jurisdiction of ecclesiastical courts and judges trained in civil law, and it is that Roman inheritance that the common lawyers admitted subsequently into English law.

The specific point to be made is simple and surprising. The postal rule, the allegory of the privileged offeree, is the allegory of the law's somewhat limited protection of women in the formation of spousals contracts. Henry Swinburne provides the most succinct annotation of the law governing spousals contracted *inter absentes,* by messenger or by letter. His analysis begins with a relatively complicated discussion of the theory of the formation of spousals. The contract is to be inferred from words or from manifested intentions: "What are words but the messengers of men's minds? And wherefore serve tongues, but to express men's meanings?"[102] The word is already, in this analysis, a species of letter, a symbol of intent that can, however, be corrected or referred to its precedent cause, the intention of the author or sender, for if

98. On the position of Roman law in England during the early reception, see F. de Zulueta and P. Stein, *The Teaching of Roman Law in England around 1200* (London: Selden Society, 1990). Bracton, *De Legibus,* vol. II at 62–65 and 283–290, evidences a clear knowledge of glossatorial discussion of the *Digest,* on gifts, contracts, and obligations.

99. See particularly A. W. B. Simpson, *A History of the Common Law of Contract: The Rise of the Action of Assumpsit* (Oxford: Clarendon Press, 1987).

100. See particularly, A. W. B. Simpson, "Innovation in Nineteenth Century Contract Law" (1977) 91 *Law Quarterly Review* 247; Gordley, *Modern Contract Doctrine* at 161–214.

101. I shall concentrate here upon Henry Swinburne, *A Treatise of Spousals, or Matrimonial Contracts* (London: Browne, 1686, 1711 ed.); Godolphin, *Repertorium Canonicum*; Anonymous, *Baron and Feme*; Wood, *An Institute.*

102. Swinburne, *Treatise of Spousals* at 63.

> the Parties did *intend* to contract matrimony, then although the words import no more than spousals *de futuro* [i.e., engagement], the contract is no less matrimony; but when the meaning doth appear, then, howsoever the Rude and Vulgar sort do often abuse their terms, and speak improperly, we must be directed by the [rule which says] we must not otherwise depart from the signification of words, but in case it be manifest, that the speaker meant otherwise.[103]

With the stated exception of a manifest dissonance between word and intention, the meaning of the utterance and of its sending is to be construed by law and not by reference either to illocution or subjective states. The analysis of the contract made *inter absentes* thus begins by taking up the glossatorial distinction between proctor and messenger and, following Alciatus, defines the messenger as without warrant or authority but "imployed only about the expedition of a bare fact, as the delivery of a meer message, or a sole postage of a letter."[104] It is thus the instrument, the symbol, messenger, or letter that is the object of analysis: between whom can the letter legitimately circulate, who can send and who can receive these messages? The question concerns the circulation of the "deed," obligation, or fact, the movement of the signifier and not of the signified. It is a question initially of whether the woman has the capacity to utilize a particular form of acceptance. The question Swinburne addresses next is therefore that of "whether the woman may contract matrimony by a special messenger or letters, as well as the man?"[105] Deciding that by canon law she can in principle, Swinburne is then faced with the question, "what if the party to whom the message or letter importing consent of matrimony, being delivered, do immediately upon the receipt thereof express the like consent, whether is the contract hereby finished?"[106] The answer is that at the instant of responding to the messenger or letter, "there is mutual agreement at one instant . . . because the party which did first consent is still presumed to continue and persevere in the same mind, until the time of the others consent." In short, the contract is "perfect" or finished *the moment that the woman* to whom the offer of marriage was sent expresses consent. The offeror cannot, in other words, revoke the offer between the time of consent and the time of receipt of consent. The manifest fiction cited by Swinburne relates to the offerors' continued offer, *idem est non esse et non apparere,* which is to say that not to be and not to appear is all one in the construction of law: if the revocation has not been received it is taken not to exist. Underlying this figure of consent is the relation of man to

103. Ibid. at 63–64.
104. Ibid. at 178.
105. Ibid. at 180.
106. Ibid. at 181.

woman. It is the woman that benefits from the fiction of continued assent or continuing offer, it is the woman who is protected by the "artificial" or fictive operation of the postal rule. If in later common law it seems anomalous to protect the offeree, this is only because of the erasure of the face of the offeree—it has been forgotten that it was a woman who put a letter of acceptance in the post.

The question of the image and of gender lurks unrecognized in the background of the early development of the modern law of contract. They are certainly not the only unseen influences, but it should be noted that it is not only the postal rule that survives as a memory of contracting women. The bulk of rules governing what is now termed the "policing of the bargain" had their early operation developed around the regulation of marriage contracts. It is beyond the scope of the present argument to examine the rules of contract that develop around domestic relations and primarily concern the wife's lack of will and so of capacity,[107] but the unconscious memory of marriage contracts can be seen in the judicial use of hypotheticals drawn from the law of spousals to explain the rules of offer and acceptance. What if a soldier on leave from the front offers marriage by post just before returning to the front? What if a man shouts a proposal of marriage across a river and the offeree's answer is drowned out by a passing steamboat? Baron Barmwell, in *British and American Telegraph Co.* v *Colson,*[108] thus asks "if a man proposed to a woman and the woman was to consult her friends and let him know, would it be enough if she wrote and posted a letter which never reached him?" The answer that Lord Bramwell offers is of less significance than the continued presence of the female offeree.[109] The example is not insignificant nor merely hypothetical, it recollects an institutional history, an unconscious structure within which it would be ethically absurd to allow the man to escape his duties and dishonorable in the extreme to leave a woman in suspense or unprotected. The spiritual exemplar of contract had always been that of marriage. In ecclesiastical law the order of marriage ran from that of the church to Christ, that of the priest to the church, that of the Christian to the creed, that of woman to man. The hierarchical order of marriages was not only a symptom of the necessary permanence of the contracted institution, it was also a sign—a symbol or credo—of an order of communication, of the places of communication in a dialogue in which the sovereign, father, parent, priest, or male suitor or proposer would ask a question or make an offer to which

107. On which see Anonymous, *Baron and Feme* at 4–6, 214–217. Wood, *An Institute* at 96–103. For interesting discussion in the case law, see *Copland* v *Pyatt,* Trinity Term, 6 Car. 1 Roll 687, 79 ER 814. For discussion of the political implications of these rules, see C. Pateman, *The Sexual Contract* (Cambridge: Polity Press, 1988).

108. *British and American Telegraph Co.* v *Colson* [1871] LR 6 Exch 108 at 118.

109. The example is recited by Lawton LJ in *Holwell Securities.*

the offeree could only say yes or no. The offeree in this model of contract is powerless in the sense of being brought to speech in a formulaic place, in being subject to no more than an elective rite. If the law recognized the minimal duty of protecting the offeree's election, it should not be supposed that this granted the woman offeree any very great or very real right.

In place of the simple anomaly of the postal rule it is possible to offer an account and explanation of the rule that is both more poetic and more sensitive to its political circumstance. In place of the ideal speech situation, or indeed some variant theory of the rational discourse of law, the historical and analytic reconstruction of the postal rule tells a more complicated and less optimistic story. The postal rule always potentially binds the offeror to a contract of which they are not aware. It binds the parties objectively and imposes a fiction of consent upon what is always potentially a failed communication. At one level it can simply be observed that the rule is a historical residue, a relic whereby the law protects the feminine gender at the moment of its civil death, the point of its entry into an irreversible subjection to the husband. The postal rule, in protecting the feminine offeree, is itself ironically an exception to the general rule of law, which is that the married woman or "feme covert" has no contractual capacity whatsoever, for husband and wife are one person. In common law the married woman was *sub potestate viri,* under the control or in the law of the husband,[110] while the unmarried woman was for a considerable portion of time likely to be *in patria potestas,* or some form of guardianship or wardship.[111] The protection of the woman offered by the postal rule should thus serve to recollect the inequality of the contracting parties and the "civil death" that the marriage contract represented for the feminine offeree.[112]

The argument from the postal rule can be taken somewhat further. Far from simply evidencing the possible failure at the heart of all communication, the postal rule indicates the inequality of communication and offers one potential explanation of the failures of legal meaning. The legal recognition of the rights of the offeree should not hide the nature of the contract to which the offeree is destined to submit. While it is true that the law offered a minimal protection to the woman through recognizing and enforcing premarital contracts or spousals, such that, for example, in *Synge* v *Synge* the Queen's Bench enforced a premarital promise of disposition of property by the husband, the general rule was to the opposite effect.[113]

110. Bracton, *De Legibus* at 36.

111. Glanvill, *Tractatus de Legibus* at 59.

112. See Anonymous, *The Lawes Resolutions* at 2–4. It might also be added that the consent of the woman to the offer of marriage was only a minor aspect of a much broader network of legal relations. Ultimate consent to marriage lay with the father, whose consent also brought with it the property (*maritagium*) that would pass with the marriage itself.

113. *Synge* v *Synge* [1894] 1 QB 466. See, for a similar principle, *Hammersley* v *De Biel*

Mary Astell, writing in the late seventeenth century and considerably before the decision in *Balfour* v *Balfour*, confirmed the modern contractual incapacity of the wife[114] and cogently and proleptically observed that "covenants between husband and wife, like laws in an arbitrary government, are of little force, the will of the sovereign is all in all. . . . Thus men happily sign articles relating to property and goods but then retract them, because being absolute master, she and all the grants he makes her are in his power."[115] The model of communication offered by the postal rule and affirmed by the legal incapacity of the wife is one of an explicitly hierarchical and predetermined series of enunciative positions. The slave or the wife or the offeree can communicate, they have an *animus* or will (*voluntas*), but the law will only recognize their speech or writing within the preestablished terms of a licit hierarchy of transmission. While the postal rule can be used to indicate that there are indeed circumstances under which the woman or the subordinate can communicate and bind in law, it is equally indicative of the powerlessness of the feminine offeree after the contract has been made. It allows us to observe that the woman is granted a final request, but it does not fit easily into any model of communicative rationality. It offers rather a glimpse of the other scene of communication, a vision of speech and of writing by position, a bureaucracy of intentions, a repression rather than a poetics of transmission. In strict historical and doctrinal terms, it has to be reiterated that the model of legal communication to which the postal rule forms a limited exception is one that denies the validity of domestic contracts, that refuses to grant legal status to promises defined as belonging to the private sphere, and that frequently does not recognize the juridical personality of the woman in the context of the home. It should be reiterated also that the doctrinal context of the postal rule can only be reconstructed through the recognition of the unequal legal background of the parties communicating by post. The postal

(1845) XII Clark and Finlay 46; 8 ER 1312 at 1327: "If a party holds out inducements to another to celebrate a marriage, and holds them out deliberately and plainly, and the other party consents, and celebrates the marriage in consequence of them, if he had good reason to expect that it was intended that he should have the benefit of the proposal which was so held out, a Court of Equity will take care that he [sic] is not disappointed, and will give effect to the proposal." The decision is in many respects more liberal than that arrived at in current state law in New York, see *Morone* v *Morone*, 50 N.Y.2d. 481, 429 N.Y.S.2d. 592, 413 N.E.2d 1154 (1980).

114. *Balfour* v *Balfour* [1919] 2 KB 571, at 579: "In respect of these promises each house is a domain into which the King's writ does not seek to run, and to which his officers do not seek to be admitted." The reason is also, of course, that there would be a conflict of sovereigns and of prerogative rights. *Regia potestas* would vie with *patria potestas*.

115. Astell, *Some Reflections upon Marriage* at 38.

rule makes legal sense only if it is analyzed in terms of inequality of speech situations and, specifically, the difference and inequality of genders.

SYNECDOCHE: EGYPTIANS, ALIENS, OTHERS, AND THE CROWN

The example of the postal rule is again an instance of the image, of the long-term movement of law across considerable distances of institutional time. The trope, figure, or anomaly in the text in many senses contradicts the legal maxim that what does not appear does not exist. It is precisely through these figurations, through slips, lapses, or displacements from one institutional category to another, that the unconscious of law can be glimpsed and its reconstruction attempted. The examples argue persuasively that the survival of the institution is intimately linked to a dogmatics that appears arcane or obtuse in part by virtue of relying upon an unconscious reservoir of institutional connotations, metaphoric structures, and long-term deployments of meaning that develop in the indefinite time of precedent. As Fortescue once remarked, "we have several set forms which are held as law, and so held and used for good reason, though we cannot at present remember that reason."[116] Rhetoric was explicitly the art of memory, of reconstructing the forgotten or repressed, as well as that of civil speech.[117] Like psychoanalysis is sought not only to classify the places or *topoi* of memory but also to map the dialectic of memory and its erasure, of repetition and forgetting, and to provide some significance both to that which surfaces in memory or dream and to that which is conspicuous or marked by its absence.

The two examples so far given of the law relating to a woman and her home and to the anomaly of the postal rule, to a woman contracting *in absentia,* both imply a certain legal politics of the sexes or of gender. There is more at stake in these legal examples than is immediately apparent. In the example of the home, it should be recollected that the anomalous ruling reverts to a history in which the woman is in several legal contexts treated as property while the home and garden, the spheres of domesticity, are treated as persons. With regard to the postal rule, the example of the law's patronage of women offerees should be placed in the context of a law of marriage in which the marriage contract is often the last contract that the

116. Fortescue J. in *Anon* [1458] YB 36 Hen VI 25–26.

117. Stanley Fish, a great contemporary forensic rhetorician, inadvertently forgets this aspect of rhetoric in repeatedly arguing that the practice of judgment requires forgetfulness as the condition of deciding. See Fish, "The Law Wishes to have a Formal Existence" at 204–205. See also Stanley Fish, *Doing What Comes Naturally* (Durham, N.C.: Duke University Press, 1989) at 397.

married woman ever makes. She is subsequently incapable either of contracting or of making a will because she is *plene in potestate viri*—in the complete power of the husband[118] or, in Bracton's phrase, not simply *alieni iuris* but *sub virga,* or under the rod.[119] It may not be inappropriate to recollect in this context that the primary and "simplest" division of the law of persons is not between male and female but between slave and free.[120] It is that stake, the distinction between freedom and slavery, which is the subject matter of the final example to be canvassed here, namely the law of contempt of court and the prerogative of the Crown as opposed to the right of aliens, asylum seekers, and others belonging to the category of *peregrinus* or foreigner. By way of link to the previous examples, it may first be noted incidentally that the earliest foreigners to emerge within the Western tradition were the Danaides, who were female and Egyptian.[121]

The distinction between slave and free is crosscut in classical Roman law by that between citizen and foreigner. Similarly, one of the oldest and most venerable of rules of common law relates to the distinction between members of the community and strangers. If we start with the commonality of lawyers itself, it is not insignificant that one of the first rules learned by those that joined the archetypical community of the Inns of Court was that they were prohibited from inviting "forraigners, discontinuers . . . [and] strangers" into the Inn.[122] Other legislation of the Inns was concerned directly and unremittingly with maintaining the specific physical appearance of community. Not only were foreigners and strangers excluded from the ironically titled Inns of Court, but it was forbidden to look like a foreigner, to dress like a foreigner, or to behave like a foreigner.[123] While it is true that the rules governing the exclusion of foreign fashions and Continental mores had a peculiar and distinctive urgency in the Reformation, the principles of patriotism and xenophobia involved are of much longer standing.

Commencing with Bracton, the legal term "Englishry" (*Englecerie*) refers generically to being an Englishman and also to certain consequences

118. The rule is elaborated in Glanvill, *Tractatus de Legibus* at 59. See further, Anonymous, *Baron and Feme* at 4–7. On testaments, see further Swinburne, *A Briefe Treatise*; Godolphin, *The Orphan's Legacy*.

119. Bracton, *De Legibus* at 35.

120. This classification derives from Gaius. See de Zulueta (ed.), *The Institutes of Gaius* at 4: "Omnes homines aut liberi sunt aut servi." Bracton, *De Legibus* at 29, repeats the definition.

121. On which point see Kristeva, *Strangers to Ourselves* at 42: "It is noteworthy to observe that the first foreigners to emerge at the dawn of our civilisation are foreign women—the Danaides."

122. Dugdale, *Origines Juridiciales* at sig. 192r–v, referring to legislation of the Middle Temple of 1631 and 1635. This literature is commented on in Goodrich, "Eating Law."

123. See Dugdale, *Origines Juridiciales* at sigs. 148–155; 191–195.

of such a designation in cases of murder. The antithesis of Englishry was *Francingena,* or being a Frenchman, which term was taken to include all foreigners or aliens, "all outlandish men and women and especially Danes."[124] To be a foreigner was a synonym of being outlandish, uncouth, or simply dangerous. So too by the earliest common law, again reported in Bracton, to be a stranger (*extraneum*) was equally opprobrious and suspicious, and "it was because of this suspicion that it was established that no one receive a stranger into his house or permit him to depart except in broad daylight."[125] The legal image of the foreigner is already quite precise: he was alien, other, outlandish, extraneous, and suspect. The condition was also infectious: those that traveled with foreigners or Egyptians were likely to become not simply like them but of them.[126] In later legislation the foreigner is linked both to the stranger and to the Egyptian. An Act of 1540, *An Act Concerning Strangers,* simply expelled foreigners, whereas legislation as early as 1350, *An Act Touching such as be born beyond the Seas,* specifically defined the rights of succession and of property of those born outside the "faith and ligeance" of the English Crown.[127] It is in relation particularly to the break with Rome and with the principles of a universal church that the fear of foreigners became most extreme during the post-Reformation period.

Rastall's *Collection in English of the Statutes in Force* in its 1603 edition lists five Acts of the Realm in force specifically concerning Egyptians, foreigners, and vagabonds. The associations of the stranger are insidious in the extreme, and the definitions of foreignness and its consequences are multiple. Thus Egyptians are defined as "divers and outlandish people . . . using no craft nor seal of merchandise . . . [and who] use great subtlety and crafty means to deceive the people . . . of their money."[128] The foreigner would take away fortune and wealth by deceit. The Egyptian was however an amorphous or spreading category and not simply an economic and ethical threat. Later legislation defined Egyptians further as "foreigners—come from abroad" and continued to include "vagabonds" who were inhabitants of England who had fallen into the ways or company of Egyptians. "Be it enacted . . . that every person and persons, which . . . shall within this realm of England or Wales, in any company or fellowship of vagabonds, commonly called, or calling themselves Egyptians, or

124. Bracton, *De Legibus* at vol. II, 381–383. See also Cowell, *The Interpreter.*

125. Bracton, *De Legibus* at vol. II, 387.

126. For an excellent analysis of this metaphor of the alien as viral, drawing upon Baudrillard, *La Transparence du mal,* see P. Minkkinen, "Otherness and Difference: On the Cultural Logic of Racial Intolerance" (1992) 3 *Law and Critique* 147.

127. Respectively, 1540 32 H. VIII cap. 16, and 1350 25 Ed. III cap. 2, which was confirmed in 1368 in 42 Ed. III cap. 10.

128. Rastall, *A Collection in English* at sigs. 144v–145v.

counterfeiting, transporting, or disguising themselves by their apparell, speech, or other behaviour, like unto such vagabonds . . . and shall or continue to do so . . . for the space of one month . . . shall be deemed a felon."[129] The extent of the legislative drive against the stranger, foreigner, nomad, Egyptian, or vagabond suggests an extreme fear not simply of external danger but of internal decay. Even at the level of self-representation or appearance, any suggestion of foreignness had to be abhored, and legislation too frequent to tabulate governing "apparrell" was concerned as much as anything else with the avoidance of foreign cloths, cuts, fashions, and colors of dress, in the interest both of recognizability but also for the avoiding of foreign vices, namely that "inordinate excess of apparel" associated with strangers who neither knew their place nor their degree.[130]

The fear of the strange, outlandish, Egyptian, or foreign repeats itself historically through differing institutional forms that range across Jew, barbarian, intellectual, witch, colored, unclean, heretic, poor, ill, communist, hedonist, homeless, woman, idolater, and nomad. While qualities or properties of strangeness become conflated with the terroristic exclusion of the specter of the other as such, it is possible to trace an institutional delirium concerned with the imaginary essence of the immigrant, the alien, and the foreign. Such a chorography or, in rhetorical terms, *topothesia*,[131] the feigned description or illusory mapping of the threat of foreignness against which community defines itself, has been attempted in various forms by political theory. Attempts also have been made to trace the concept of the foreign in common law, the antirrhetic or antiportrait of those outside the "ligeance" of social legitimacy, kinship, or common identity.[132] The final example borrows from that obscure or repressed history of exclusion and examines the figure of *synecdoche* in the law of the land. It is by means of this metonymy, by means of a tellurian contiguity or contagion that makes the law of England the law of the land or *lex terrae*, by means of proximity (*Englecerie*) and insularity, inhabitation and domicile, that alienity, foreignness, and nomadism more broadly can be both defined and by definition excluded. The contemporary law, in other words, still manipulates

129. Ibid. at sig. 145v.

130. Ibid. at sigs. 12r–14v. For a contemporaneous discussion of wanton excess of dress and of the insidious character of appearing like a foreigner or a woman, see Harrison, *An Historicall Description* at fols. 172r–173r, stating that "nothing is more constant in England than inconstancy of attire. Oh how much cost is bestowed nowadays upon our bodies and how little upon our souls."

131. Peacham, *Garden of Eloquence* at fol. U iii a.

132. For an interesting discussion of this theme, see Costas Douzinas and Ronnie Warrington, "A Well-Founded Fear of Justice: Law and Ethics in Postmodernity" (1991) 2 *Law and Critique* 115, and in a more extended form, in Douzinas and Warrington, *Justice MisCarried*; Drucilla Cornell, *The Philosophy of the Limit* (New York: Routledge, 1992).

antithetical affections. It nurtures identity and sacrifices those beyond the pale or geography of common law.

The case in question stems from an application for asylum in the United Kingdom. In *M.* v *Home Office,*[133] the letter M. marks an omission and, on its facts, an exclusion, the place where the applicant would have stood. It concerns again the circulation of a letter, an alphabetical character, M., between Zaire, Paris, and London, in a case concerning a refugee from political persecution. It ends with the return of the letter and the revocation of a possible (social) contract. The letter is the letter M., a terrifying textual metonymy, a *synecdoche,* a minimalist monument for an asylum seeker who died so as not to confuse the cartographic fictions or heraldic symbols of common law. The letter M. is all that remains, it is the trace of a being; M.—perhaps for murder, the stop mark after the letter by convention noting that additional letters are missing. For the narrative purposes of the case, we pick up in September of 1990 when the applicant originally sought political asylum in Britain. The applicant was a union organizer in Zaire, where he had participated in organizing antigovernment strike action. He had been arrested and had escaped from Zaire to Nigeria and from there to Britain. M. applied for asylum in Britain under the Geneva Convention relating to the Status of Refugees and was refused by the Home Office. The Home Office did not regard M.'s story as credible, and the letter of 16 November informing M. of the decision concludes by stating the all-encompassing discretionary power of the Home Office in such cases: "The Secretary of State recognises that a person fleeing persecution may not be able to provide documentary or other proof to support his statements . . . however, allowance for such a lack of evidence does not oblige the Secretary of State to accept unsupported evidence as necessarily being true."[134] Although the conclusion lacks logical force—its two propositions are not connected—the issue of writing, of text and body, reemerges in the subsequent stages of the case.

M., through his lawyers, sought leave to apply for judicial review of the decision to refuse him asylum and his application was refused on 25 March 1991. He promptly sought to renew his application and while that application was pending he was examined by a doctor provided by the Medical Foundation for the Care of Victims of Torture. The doctor reported that "[t]he scars he bears are entirely compatible with the causes he ascribes to them. He is suffering a degree of deafness and spinal trouble quite likely to have arisen from his mistreatment. Psychologically he describes symptoms very likely to arise from the experiences he

133. In the Court of Appeal [1992] 2 WLR 73 and in the House of Lords [1993] 3 AER 537.

134. Ibid. at 81.

describes."[135] The skin was and is the first site of writing: not only was the letter (M.) a brand on the forehead of the slave, but inscription upon the body and the pain of mutilation were the archetypes of a memory that later became attached to writing. In the instant case the bearer of this writing was about to depart the jurisdiction: his text was about to circulate elsewhere in the direct sense that pending further appeal M. was to be repatriated on 1 May.

At 5:30 P.M. on 1 May, a further application for review was made to Mr. Justice Garland, who was apprised also of the fact that M.'s plane was due to leave Britain at 6:00 P.M. for Paris and from there he would be transferred, still in custody, to an aircraft bound for Kinasha, Zaire. Mr. Justice Garland "did what any judge would have done in these circumstances. Having concluded that the application was not frivolous, he sought to obtain an undertaking from Mr. Gordon on behalf of the Home Office that M. would not be flown out of the jurisdiction and *thus the protection* of the courts of this country"[136] until after the application had been heard. The Home Office was informed of this request but for reasons that are unclear, failed to respond in time to prevent M.'s departure to Paris, from where he was flown to Zaire. Solicitors for M. contacted Mr. Justice Garland later that night and informed him of M.'s plight. Garland J. responded by issuing a mandatory order for the return of M. to the jurisdiction of the court and secondly ordering that pending M.'s return he be kept in the custody of servants or agents of the Crown in Zaire. This order was communicated to the Home Office, and the British embassy in Zaire was informed that M. should be placed in protective custody and returned to Britain.

M. arrived in Zaire at 7:30 A.M. and was taken to the British embassy pending return to Britain. In the meantime the Home Office considered the case. At a meeting later that day, the Home Secretary took advice and decided to revoke the order to return M. to the jurisdiction on the grounds firstly that the underlying decision to refuse M. refugee status was correct and would be affirmed and secondly that Mr. Justice Garland had exceeded his powers in making an order against the Crown: a mandatory order against the Crown was outside the jurisdiction of the courts. The consequence of this decision was that M. was informed that his appearance in London was no longer required, and he was released from the custody of the embassy. M. was never heard from again. The question before the court, on this set of facts, was whether the Home Secretary, a Minister of the Crown, was in contempt of court in refusing to comply with the mandatory order issued by Mr. Justice Garland.

At first instance, before Mr. Justice Brown, it was held that the court

135. Ibid.
136. Ibid. at 84. (Emphasis added)

had no power to issue a prerogative order (mandamus) against the Crown. The reason given was that the relationship between government and judiciary is one based upon "trust"[137] and has no greater status than that of a request. It may be noted, somewhat ironically, that the word "trust," coming from the old Norse *traust* meaning "strong," is a perhaps unwittingly appropriate description of the *de facto* relation between Crown and law, but it is hardly an appropriate depiction of a legal value. On appeal, on the specific issue of contempt, the Court of Appeal found no reason to deny the court's power to issue a prerogative order such as mandamus or habeas corpus against the Crown. While the word of the Crown "is its bond,"[138] and such orders are to be viewed as largely unnecessary, the High Court is nonetheless in principle a court of unlimited jurisdiction and so is capable of issuing any orders it wishes so long as they are not illegal.

The ensuing question, whether the Crown could be held liable for contempt of court, has not only a symbolic significance as a form of atonement for the treatment of M. but a more considerable importance for the fate of all those that subsequently seek remedy or justice in matters of asylum. Can the Crown be made to listen to the alien, the other, or the refugee? It is, after all, an age-old principle stemming from Roman law, that *in fictione juris semper est aequitas.*[139] The Court of Appeal made no reference to such a principle but rather argued that actions in contempt could only be taken against "a person or body with sufficient legal personality. As neither the Crown nor the Home Office has any legal personality, no such proceedings can be brought against them."[140] The logic of this decision requires careful reconstruction. The Crown, Rex or Regina, is a legal fiction without personality; it is a metaphor, and as a "symbol of royalty, 'the Crown' was no doubt [historically] a convenient way of denoting and distinguishing the monarch when doing acts of government in his political capacity from the monarch when doing private acts in his personal capacity."[141] In this context neither "the Crown" nor its equally fictitious substitute "the Government" can be imbued with either natural or juridical personality. Thus while the Home Secretary, as a Minister of the Crown, was in honor and in trust obliged to comply with the order of mandamus, no action for contempt of court could lie if he did not. Further, it would be absurd to attempt to enforce contempt proceedings, its sanctions being *in personam,* against the Crown or government. The three remedies avail-

137. Ibid. at 80.

138. Ibid. at 92.

139. (Fiction in law is always toward just ends.) See, for example, *Wilkes* v *The Earl of Halifax* [1769] 2 Wils. KB 256 (95 ER 797).

140. *M.* v *Home Office* at 94.

141. *Town Investments Ltd. and others* v *Dept. of Environment* [1978] AC 359, at 380, per Lord Diplock.

able, imprisonment, fine, or sequestration of assets, would be each and alike ineffective. It would be impossible to imprison "some body or thing which, whatever else it may be, is not a natural person. It would be largely futile to fine a department . . . it would be impossible to sequestrate all the Government's financial assets."[142]

What chance then does an alien or foreign natural body have against such an icon of social presence? How can a single letter be the means of holding an office and dignity in contempt and so bound to act? The "deliberate decision"[143] to ignore an order of the court had as its consequence the probable death of M., the sacrifice of a natural body, a refugee, a person, to the cause of preserving the symbol—the icon—of an imaginary unity and community, the mystic body of the realm, this England. As in any act of sacrifice, the symbolic was held to have priority over the real. Further, the imaginary here determined that the symbolic, the "political body," the realm as represented in the Crown, was beyond the law. There could be no retribution against nor legal accountability for the acts of fictitious persons, nonnatural bodies or imaginary juridical beings. The life of one implied the death of the other. The silence of one was the speech of the other. The incivility or alienity of one was the propriety of the other. The court proceeded latterly to distinguish "contempt" from more serious offenses and cited approvingly the following elaboration, "the phrase contempt does not in the least describe the true nature of the class of offense with which we are here concerned. . . . It is not the dignity of the court which is offended—it is the fundamental supremacy of the law which is challenged."[144] The Secretary of State for the Home Department, as a Minister of the Crown and as one "mutually recognised" element in the "unwritten constitution," could not be said to be in contempt either of the supremacy of law or of the dignity of its administration.[145]

At one level the example of *M.* v *The Home Office* is a simple, although important, instance of the ultimate stake of legal fiction. The representation of legal acts and more specifically the figures of the legal text have striking and violent consequences. This is not to differentiate legal interpretation from other species of interpretation and enforcement, nor the community of law from other political or social forms. The issue is rather that of reading the rhetorical figure, the *synecdoche,* the letter M., the diminutive or vanished part for the whole, the disappearing sign of a deeply embedded and dramatically implemented unconscious form and conflict, that of antirrhesis or here antinomy, in the production and life of the legal

142. *M.* v *Home Office* at 95.
143. Ibid. at 98.
144. Ibid., citing *Johnson* v *Grant* [1923] S.C. 789, 790.
145. Ibid. at 99.

text. The singular letter, the lone syntagma, the "undocumented" stranger or outsider comes before the law and is made to wait. His testimony is disbelieved by the Home Office, yet no attempt is made to verify or falsify his narrative. He is expelled contrary to an express order of the court, yet it is held that this defiance of the law is not contempt and is not punishable, at least insofar as such an action would have to lie against the other *synecdoche* in the case, the symbol of our unity, the icon of our presence, the Crown.[146] On one side of the conflict in this particular case, the affectivity of law holds to an image of inviolate unity, of fictive presence, and of imaginary trust or honor. This affectivity constitutes that most significant of images, that of the body of the realm, of the constitution and the jurisdiction of law. On the other side of this affectivity lies a relatively silent antiportrait, a refusal to listen, a void or absence of speech in which the other is characterized not simply as without jurisdiction but as mendacious, demanding, inconsistent, and without credibility or right to any further appeal. This was an Egyptian or "outlandish" person, *Francingena* or vagabond, not merely potentially a felon but unconsciously always already fated to being disbelieved, unknown, untruthful, and eventually silent.

On appeal to the House of Lords the decision was affirmed although the distinction which the Court of Appeal had drawn between the two personalities of the Home Secretary, namely that of officeholder and that of private person or "Mr. Baker personally," was deemed to be "unduly technical."[147] It was perhaps an element of what Lord Woolf termed earlier "the theory which clouds this subject."[148] It was therefore held, and not without a certain unconscious historical sensibility, that the Crown did have juridical personality: "It can be appropriately described as a corporation sole or a corporation aggregate."[149] The crowning irony of the final decision was that while no explicit distinction was to be drawn between person and dignity, subject and office, the corporation sole or aggregate is nonetheless a collective *corpus,* an invisible or notional personality, a mystic body or fiction whose "relationship with the courts does not depend on coercion."[150] Lord Woolf thus admitted without apparent qualm or conscience that "contempt proceedings against a government department or a minister in an official capacity would not be either personal or punitive"

146. The majority in the case held that an action could lie against the Home Secretary, Mr. Kenneth Baker, in person. In person, however, while Mr. Baker could in principle be held in contempt, he would not be regarded as being in any great measure culpable and in consequence the action would have no significant effect, nor would the then Home Secretary be personally liable for any fine consequent upon a ruling of contempt.

147. *M.* v *Home Office* [1993] 3 AER 537 at 568.

148. Ibid. at 544.

149. Ibid. at 566.

150. Ibid. at 567.

and that "it would clearly not be appropriate to fine or sequest the assets of the Crown or a government department or an officer of the Crown acting in his official capacity."[151] In short, there would be no law between the Crown and Her Majesty's Judges who, after all, exercise their function as lawyers *sub prerogativa regis,* with both majesty and power (*maiestatem vel potestatem*).[152] The same contradiction, therefore, still holds and the fiction of the Crown binding one body with the other would connote too directly the attempt to engender presence in the word of the law; it would connote the impossible circularity of the presence of spirituality and temporality in the same body and was thus to be fictionalized again in terms of a finding of contempt that was explicitly without legal force or enforcement. To punish the corporation sole of Her Majesty's Government would be too narcissistic an act, it would require self-mutilation, in that one member of the body would have to punish another. The *synecdoches* of Crown for custom and country, and of M. for applicant, both suggest a contiguity, however protracted, between part and whole. For the Crown to sanction itself would have to be a fiction, and such was the solution at which the House of Lords arrived in intimating that a finding of contempt was all that was needed to bring law to government or to force compliance with an injunction. In any event, as a practical matter it was a decision arrived at far too late, in the wrong place, and without any significant legal effect: a justice miscarried or a law displaced.

The only other judge to offer an opinion in the House of Lords was his honor Lord Templeman, who again made appropriate historical references, this time to the principle that what pleases the prince has the force of law—"the judges cannot enforce the law against the Crown as monarch because the Crown as monarch can do no wrong"—but then proceeded to claim that enforcement may be against the Crown as executive. The ground for that decision was that any other decision would "establish the proposition that the executive obey the law as a matter of grace and not as a matter of necessity, a proposition that would reverse the result of the civil war."[153] The rhetoric of the case thus returns again to the bellicose and agonistic. The civil war established parliamentary supremacy and subjected the judiciary to the supremacy of legislation. In the case of M., a case that was deemed by Lord Donaldson to be remarkable for "the chapter of accidents, mistakes and misunderstandings" which occurred, the judiciary fell very far short of challenging the legality or the justice of ministerial actions.[154] What the courts variously required was that the grace by

151. Ibid. at 566.
152. The definition of legal function comes from Cowell, *The Interpreter.*
153. *M.* v *Home Office* [1993] 3 AER at 541.
154. *M.* v *Home Office* [1992] 2 WLR at 96.

which parliament related to the law be an invisible grace, the apparent relation an apparent subjection. For all its metaphysical complexities of corporate and individual subjects, the transmission of interior grace—of the meaning or spirit of law, of unwritten tradition or knowledge (*subauditio* or *subintellectio*)—was a matter of convention, of manners or of proper form. It was transmission of an image, of a law prior to law in which necessity was the figure of grace and law an allegory, as it always is, of the legitimacy, the domesticity of power: it is in this image that we see ourselves, in this effigy that necessity speaks and law is honored as decorum and *patria*. Lord Donaldson, again in a case of contempt, remarked a few years earlier of a journalist's refusal to disclose his sources, that the rule of law and specifically its provisions relating to contempt of court are "society's answer given through the mouth of Parliament, and who are journalists, victims or judges to set themselves up as knowing better? . . . Personal and professional honour surely equates with the acceptance of, and obedience to, the rule of law."[155] There is always, in short, the face of the law as an attribute of social presence and as an element in the iconic representation of the self-presence of the polity, of the unity of plurality.

ENVOI

The ornaments, symbols, and images of law, in this instance the figures of the legal text, indicate those slips or unconscious motives that allow for the reconstruction of an "other scene" of legal judgment. The other scene is that of the unconscious, of repressed desires and internalized prohibitions, of the affects and identifications that constitute reason and institute law, as visibility, as affect, and as text. The example of *M.* v *The Home Office* is in this context a striking instance not only of the latent violence of textual interpretation but also of the rhetorical forms that constitute the *indicia* or signs of structure in the surface figurations of legal texts. The analysis of the rhetoric of the antirrhetic, of the polemical or agonistic structure of the legal unconscious, indicates a series of oppositions, antitheses, or simple contradictions in the organization and force of legal thought and its corresponding forms of textuality. The legal text constitutes a visible material surface, a "terranean" screen, a body of law whose figurative function is that of representing in the *imago* or *effegie*, mask or face of a corporation sole or aggregate, an invisible order, a spiritual coherence, a dogma, fiction, or unity which will identify and direct the thought or the vision of the subject of law to its licit mythic image or source. The text is only ever a sign of apparent juridical community, of a mixture of visual and epistemic

155. *X Ltd.* v *Morgan-Grampian (Publishers) Ltd. and others* [1990] 1 AER 616 at 622.

control, of the combination of image and word. It is the visible surface or icon of a more complex source and belief, order and unity. The unity and identity of law experienced in and through the figures of the text are pitched against—and mark the boundaries of—an outside or externality that is both heteroclite and dispersed, confused and dissembling. The incidence and continuance of such an oppositional or antinomic argumentative structure, the explicit study of law as an instance of the dogmatic genre of an unconscious antirrhetical structure, deserves a final comment.

It might be said that the case of *M.* v *The Home Office* represents an instance of empty speech, of a speech that has lost its subject yet cannot mourn. The text erases a letter and kills a person; it removes one possible and existent gloss and thereby it blots out a child of the text. It negates—denies, rejects, or annihilates—that which is excluded from the text, yet it simultaneously represses and so incorporates an other of the law. Repression drives within. Negation accepts or at least takes account of that which is repressed and repression thereby is paradoxically symptomatic of the persistence of that which doctrine or orthodoxy would seek to exclude.[156] In the literal sense of negation it is easy to observe that the antirrhetic establishes over time an imaginary—or indeed a bestiary—of lost objects, exiled subjects, illicit images, condemned words, and failed memories. It peoples the text with orthodoxies, the *iuris vincula,* of dogma and faith while establishing an unconscious lexicon of the voiceless, the silent, the exiled, and the excommunicated. The jurisdiction is the sphere of legal affectivity as well as the site or institutionally authorized place of its enunciation. Yet a speech that has lost its subject, a speech that represses its "other scene" or unconscious bonds, cannot mourn its losses and so cannot recognize either the death of the subject or the unconscious of the text implicit in the violence that legal discourse does to things. A final brief narrative of the contemporary symbolization of legal violence will serve as a conclusion.

It is ironic that at a time when the legal profession and judiciary have had to face considerable criticism by virtue of miscarriages of justice, as also by virtue of the age, inflexibility, archaism, and elitism of the law, that the Lord Chancellor comes upon the idea of a review of Court Dress, with a specific reference to the abolition of the wig. The wig, the coif, rings, robes, and dinners are all significant symbols of an internal community or affective "brotherhood" of the law. The wig and its more elaborate forerunners are mentioned in many descriptions of investiture ceremonies for

156. See Sigmund Freud, "Negation," in Sigmund Freud, *General Psychological Theory* (New York: Collier Macmillan, 1963). For further discussion of negation, see Julia Kristeva, *Revolution in Poetic Language* (New York: Columbia University Press, 1984); on "empty speech," see Lacan, *Écrits* at ch. 3; M. Borch-Jacobsen, *The Freudian Subject* (London: Macmillan, 1989).

Serjeants at Law.[157] "Hoods and Coyfes" were placed on the heads of new Serjeants. The question is why, and it is answered in terms of the "Quoyff" being a symbol of two things: "*Videlicet,* it is a Helmet or Sallet, that they should not feare having that on to speake bowldly the Law, and *est sicut vestis candida et immaculata,* and they might weare it in [the] place of justice before the King's presens; and their partye garment and hoodd betokeneth prudence and temperancye."[158] Again, the emblem or symbol can be reconstructed according to a historical genealogy. The original headdress of the lawyer was in certain French jurisdictions a metal helmet that would guard the lawyer from attack by irate clients. The helmet was soon replaced, however, by the coif, which became in less aggressive circumstances the wig or *perruque,* a symbolic helmet, a memory of the need to protect the learned head from attack in times when that attack would be verbal or political rather than physical. Consciously, or more probably unconsciously, the legal institution no longer wishes to recollect the sudden and surprising criticism that was formerly meted out to the sagacious cerebellum. The Lord Chancellor's consultation document has been interpreted as asking whether the time has come to abolish the wig. I am tempted to suggest that the better question would have been that of whether current circumstances have made it advisable for the profession to return to the use of the helmet.

157. See Dugdale, *Origines Juridiciales* at fols. 118 a–122 b. See also J. H. Baker, *The Order of Serjeants at Law* (London: Selden Society, 1984).

158. The source is Sir Christopher Wraye Lord Chief Justice, cited in Dugdale, *Origines Juridiciales* at fol. 120 a.

EIGHT

Conclusion

A Legality of the Contingent

The order of Western law has traditionally been founded both upon and against the image. The image may be defined for institutional purposes as the emblem or mask that covers the absence of the source of law. This denial of legal sources is also a denial of law's creativity, of its femininity, and so also of the gender of its concealment. In classical terms, the image as law took the form of the icon, that of the authoritative and singular sign of a faceless origin. The image in this sense masked the absence, the invisible order and unknowable form, of the divine cause of both nature and law. The iconic image in early law could never show the face of the living, nor could it represent the appearance of divinity; it was an image of power that could not claim to represent but only to disguise the cause, contingency, and femininity of human forms. As an idol, the image was the mask of the plurality of absent causes. In psychoanalytic terms, the idol remained to represent the real cause, the motive or desire which was repressed or was only ever indirectly expressed in law. The idol was the illicit or feminine face of institutional creativity. It was no accident that in its earliest representation in the decalogue, the icon of law as commandment inscribed in stone was instituted, or founded, upon the destruction of an idol. The idol, the golden calf, has been variously interpreted as representing Egypt, polytheism, and feminine cults of creativity. In each instance the idolatrous image represented an other law, a face or emblem of that which legality must exclude so as to remain law. The idolatrous image is thus a sign of difference. In the example of the decalogue, which the tradition has endlessly repeated, the law excludes difference in the name of semblance. Under the sign of written reason or encoded law, the dogmatic tradition excludes difference in its various imaginary forms. First, it excludes the Egyptian, the foreigner or stranger. Second, it excludes the veneration of other gods, the plurality of sources and of meanings as well as the possibilities of other rhetorics or forms of writing law. Finally, it excludes the feminine, the image that would represent directly the plurality and contingency of creativity, the materiality and judgment of law.

In each instance of law, the icon represented the exclusion of a difference that the image threatened to express. The image, as appearance, as matter, and as presence threatened to expose the invisible order of causes to human or profane view. The illicit or idolatrous image attached meaning to the surface, to the contingent, material and feminine. The idol reunited law and desire in the surface or materiality of things, and in this union it acted sacrilegiously, it took the image for what it was, a woman and a form of inscription or writing. In terms both of the history of law and of the *ius imaginum*, it is thus important to recollect that the classical juristic definition of the idol was of *nihil* or nothing.[1] The idol was a feigned image, it was *rei mortua*, the image of a dead thing, and its very death, or better repression, allowed the direct opposition of the idol to the icon. It was the icon which lived both in faith and in reference, as pure consciousness, as spirit or universality without gender or face.[2] The danger and the power of the theory of images lie precisely in this distinction between two separate and opposed orders of imagination. The icon is law as negation. The icon nihilates the idol and all other forms of writing law. Such annihilation is its purpose and form of being. It opposes presence to absence, law to desire, becoming to completion, and masculine to feminine. Such is the most basic scission, mirroring, or splitting within the order of classification, and it is also the separation that founds law, both as identity and as institution, or in psychoanalytic terms, as misrecognition and deceit.

The genealogy of laws and images attempted in this study is played out over the history of the relation between two laws, spiritual and secular, divine and human.[3] The essential feature of that genealogy lies in the hierarchy and the conflict between the two procedures and jurisdictions of law. The relation of conscience to positive law, which the Renaissance termed that between Salem and Bizance, is central to the understanding of the history and critique of law. Law was never a merely temporal or secular

1. On the idol as *rei mortua*, see Sander, *Treatise of the Images* at 111. For a sophisticated development of this theme in relation to the decalogue, see Jacobson, "The Idolatry of Rules."

2. It is significant to note in relation to this point that one of the first rules of iconography was the biblically derived prohibition upon the graphic representation of the face. See, for example, A. Amboise, *Discours ou traicte des devises ou est mise la raison et difference des emblemes, enigmes, sentences et autres* (Paris: R. Boutonne, 1621) at fol. A v a.

3. The classical definition of jurisprudence was, of course, that of the "knowledge of things divine and human, and the science of what is just and unjust" (Iuris Prudentia est divinarum atque humanarum rerum notitia, iusti atque iniusti scientia) *Digest* 1.1.10.2 (Ulpian).

study nor was the substance of law ever to be conceived as divorced from its spiritual essence. The positive forms of law, in short, were inevitably and inexorably bound to the methods of an art and the criteria of justice and truth. Far from being "pure" or based upon the exclusion or repression of other disciplines, the classical tradition incorporated law into a complex and plural epistemological frame in which the diverse disciplines of particular courts and laws were subject ultimately to the dictates or criteria of an absolute knowledge only in part accessible to humanity and its fragile perspectives of reason and faith. In which sense it might be noted finally that in hermeneutic terms the truth of law or of judgment was in each instance to be determined ultimately by reference to ontological rather than epistemological criteria. A text, a tradition, or a reported rule might provide access to some aspect of nature or truth, but the criteria and methods of human law were only ever forms of return to, or of partial apprehension of, a truth that belonged in its entirety to another order and to the being or essence of the divinity. The text was thus secondary to the meaning (*mens legis*), the word to the spirit (*anima legis*), the language of law to the force, power, or virtue that underlies its enunciation.[4]

THE MAN WHO MISTOOK THE LAW FOR A HAT

The conflict of jurisdictions and more specifically the relation between canon, civil, and common law was an integral theme of the earliest common law treatises although it gained its most vehement expressions during the Reformation. Rather than review the polemical and apologetic literature in any detail, an indicative sense of the levels and the issues of the division between the different laws can be gained through reconstructing an example from an era somewhat after the reestablishment of the Anglican constitution. It is taken from an exchange between the Anglican bishop Dr. Edward Stillingfleet and the recusant divine Thomas Godden. In *A Discourse Concerning the Idolatry practised in the Church of Rome,* Stillingfleet had defended the Anglican prohibition on the worship (*latria*) of images, but he distinguished civil worship and gave as an instance of permissible civil reverence the example of honor given to the chair of state.[5] It is against this example of civil worship that Godden reacts, and toward the end of his treatise, titled *Catholicks no Idolaters or a full Refutation of Dr. Stillingfleet's Unjust Charge of Idolatry against the Church of Rome,* he inverts the Anglican

4. See, classically, D 1.3.17 (Celsus); D 1.3.29 (Paulus); D 50.16.6.1 (Ulpian). For a discussion of these texts in their Renaissance context, see Maclean, *Interpretation and Meaning* at 142–158.

5. Stillingfleet, *A Discourse* at 91–92. The same position and example can be found in Perkins, *A Warning* at 96–97. For discussion of the latter text and its context, see Aston, *England's Iconoclasts* at 408 ff.

arguments against images by using them to ridicule those engaged in accepted forms of civil reverence.

Godden tells an anecdote of a countryman or peasant before the law. A gentleman passing the Royal Court observes a countryman being apprehended at the entrance to the court by the "yeoman guards" because "the clown, it seems, would have gone into the Presence covered. They pulled him back, and told him when he went into that room he must pull off his Hat."[6] He challenged that demand on the ground that he saw nothing in the court but a chair and a canopy. On being informed that it was the king's chair of state and that "he must do it to the Chair out of respect for the King" the countryman demands to know "whether any worship at all were due to the Chair or no?" Mimicking the scholastic argument against St. Basil,[7] the peasant reasons that the reverence or worship shown to the chair has either to be the same as that given to the king or distinct from it. If the same, proper regal worship would be given to something beside the king, "which were treason." If distinct, the chair would be worshiped "with regal honour for itself, and not relatively, which were for a man to submit himself to a piece of wood."

Aside from more general arguments as to the inconsistency of the Anglican position, for example that it allowed people to bow at the name of Jesus or to kneel at the altar, Godden's argument is that the countryman's objections arise from a peculiarly English empiricism or, indeed, stupidity. The argument that a chair is a chair is a chair and no more denies all sense of aesthetics, of history, and of the symbolic. It also indicates an extreme inability to distinguish, or radical resistance to, the division between the visible world or "spectacle of things" and the invisibility or force of which it is the spectacle.[8] The Protestant position against the image is presented by Godden both as repressive and as denigrating the subject that worships: civil worship simply implies, as does the use of images, an ability or intelligence capable of distinguishing "like proportionable reverence" from the honor due divinity. In scholastic terms, *honor est in honorante,* honor resides in the mind that gives it. More than that, the image is simply writing, a mark of memory, a trace that can touch or depict or reflect the colors of the soul:

> If one thing hath connexion with, or analogy to another, although invisible, when the former is represented to a person that understands the analogy or connexion there is between them, it is apt to bring to his remembrance the

6. Godden, *Catholicks no Idolaters* at 179.

7. The often cited iconophilic *topos* attributed to St. Basil is the maxim *honos qui eis exhibetur, refertur ad prototypa.*

8. Calfhill, *An Answere* at 169v: "The world itself is a certain spectacle of things invisible, for that the order and frame of it, is a glass to behold the secret working and hidden grace of God."

> latter. Hence it is, that although the soul of man cannot be drawn in colours, yet when the body to which it is united, is represented in picture, the representation serves as a means to bring to our minds the perfections or graces of the soul which informs it; and not to draw them down to the figure and lineaments of a body drawn upon a Table, or carved in an image.[9]

Within this perspective, *latria* and *dulia* can be distinguished by virtue of the difference of their object, one ending in or terminated upon the divine substance, the other relative to the signs or marks of divine governance or dominion.[10] The idol, upon the same principle of reference, is distinct by virtue of transparency: *idolum nihil representat,* it is nothing, a simulation, *rei mortua.*

For the sake of completeness, Stillingfleet's response to Godden requires brief advertisement. The original claim had simply been that there was a category distinction to be made between divine worship and civil worship, and that "bowing towards the Chair of State" or the king's picture or garments was "of the same nature with putting off of our Hats" while in court or church; it was a relative or inferior honor and should be conceived as a natural act of reverence, similar to "that way which the ancient Christians did use to direct their worship."[11] At a more fundamental doctrinal level, the argument in relation to the chair of state was linked to a distinction between two forms of law. Divine worship was to proceed without the use of either external or "inward images" for the reason that God had so prescribed: the law, the second commandment, dictated that it was forbidden to worship by means of images. In the case of the reverence shown the chair of state, a separate and more secular source of law operated: "All expressions of respect depend on custom and the Prince's pleasure, or the Rules of the Court, the only question a man is to ask, is, whether it be custom of the Court, or the will of the Prince to have men uncovered."[12] It is the law of custom or the common practice of the court which determines the material or secular issue of reverence, and while it entails an element of symbolism and of indirect representation, the knowledge of civil matters and common laws was, at least for Stillingfleet, distinct from those images that purported to relate to a God whose essence was invisibility and whose substance was a self-presence that denied the possibility of any further representation: divinity could neither be painted, nor through any "creature, nor phantasm of God in our minds" be portrayed.[13]

The references to different orders of knowledge and to separate species

9. Godden, *Catholicks no Idolaters* at 84.

10. For discussion of the distinction between *latria* and *dulia,* see, for example, Sander, *A Treatise of the Images* at 78–90.

11. Stillingfleet, *A Discourse* at 91–94.

12. Stillingfleet, *A Defence of the Discourse* at 849–850.

13. Stillingfleet, *A Discourse* at 79.

of law are not unconnected. The various visibilities that the two laws jointly yet distinctly endeavor to regulate belong to separate epistemic fields and constitute distinct positivities. The object of perception, either external or internal, only exists by virtue of a law that defines not only its visibility but also the scopic regime within which the subject's gaze (*honorariam adorationem*) terminates upon an object that is neither present nor visible to the naked eye. The joint orders of visibility and of law, of icon and idol, have their own histories or discursive archaeologies which will here be ignored. It is my intention rather to reread Godden's story of the peasant before the law in more legalistic terms. What is at stake in this story is also a question of a juridical transition and closure, of an unacknowledged transmission or succession from one law to another. It is a question of inheritance that might be termed an enfolding of laws, and it is within that enfolding that a specific jurisdiction and imaginary unity of law, a fictively distinct juridical reason is constituted and elaborated for the modern tradition of common or Anglican law. The repression of the image is but one instance of a much wider order and regime of antagonism and repression that this study has endeavored to trace.

GHOSTLY POWERS

The brief relation of the story of the peasant before the law can be reconstructed in detail as a dispute over the concept of presence within two separate orders or jurisdictions of law. What is significant about the debate, however, is not the distinction between the respective theological positions but rather their similarity. The most forceful feature of the Anglican defense of civil honor as being in accordance with custom or local law (*ius commune*) is not the distinctiveness of the locality or institution but rather its adaptation, its borrowing or reception, of the principle of interior law or inward court, from the very position which it apparently excluded. There is, in short, an identity forged through negation, an identity that takes up what has been denied in the form of repression or, at the very least, in the form of displacement. It is this curious transmission of the spiritual into the secular law which I will now address directly.

The rhetoric of common law, of an Anglican constitution and English custom has always paid a certain respect toward higher orders or sources of justice and law. Such recognition, however, has tended to be in terms of the very specific and direct relation of common law or indigenous custom (*leges terrae*) to some art, divinity, justice, or other "higher" source of law. Thus, in its classic formulation, *regnum Angliae est regnum Dei,* to which it is immediately added that common law is the appropriate measure of all issues tried in England and should be kept free of canon and civil law which are "but beggarly baggage, and arguments of brawling braines."[14] Even in a late and moderate institutional treatise the point is made at some length that "the law of England in particular, is an Art to know what is Justice in England" and concludes that "the common law is the absolute perfection of reason."[15] What is important about such statements or, more accurately, denials, is not the formulaic exaggeration of a tenuous identity but rather the repression of the genealogy or more simply the diversity of knowledges and practices that make up the common law. The anecdote of the countryman refusing to show reverence in the Royal Court is to be understood initially precisely as a narrative of the plurality of laws and of practices. It is to be interpreted in this sense as a struggle over jurisdiction and correlatively over the site of enunciation of law. It is a question of geography to be sure, but this resistance which the peasant showed toward the site and the pretention of secular law can be taken further and understood as a species of irreverence or nascent critique of law's presence as such. In this respect the solid and simple peasant is an emblem not only of skepticism as to the place of law but also a figure or omen of the future positivization of the secular form and institution of law.

The peasant, in ridiculing the claim of the Royal Court to be honored in precisely the same terms as the Protestants had used to debunk the Roman Catholic defense of the image, provides an interesting clue as to a further feature of the debate between the two laws. The attack on the image and the correlative movement toward a law without images was predicated upon the power and hence the danger of the image and of circumscription. In refusing the claim of the image to represent truth or inward virtue, the reform of the law had simultaneously to replace the image, the terrain of nothing and nonrepresentation, with licit figures of law and of direction of perception. The result was, on the surface at least, an order of vision predicated upon the text and hostile to both plastic figures and textual images. The figures of truth and the rules of law were to have an identical and unitary expression in demonstrable and literal forms. One order of figuration was to be succeeded by another, but this succession was also a denial of what was inherited, acquired, or taken on with the form and the power of law itself. It inherited the jurisdiction of the spirituality but in the form of negation. It instituted an internal law but in the form of repression. It established an order, constitution, and reason, but it did so in the form of passivity.

In synoptic style a contrast may be drawn between two separate but

14. Leslie, *A Defence of the Honour* at 97v and 120r. The other exemplary expression of this argument is to be found in Aylmer, *Harborowe* at fol. P i b–P iv a.

15. Wood, *An Institute* at 6–7.

comparable laws. On one side of the transition from spiritual to temporal supremacy lay the shattered and increasingly subordinate jurisdiction of spiritual law. The distinction is signaled most powerfully in the debate between Sir Thomas More and Christopher St. German in the early sixteenth century, and it is the barrister St. German who first opposes Salem and Bizance, spiritual and temporal law. As against the Lord Chancellor Thomas More, St. German argued strenuously for the restriction of the powers of the Ordinaries (the spiritual judges) and for increasing the use of writs of prohibition which would take temporal matters out of the discretionary *arbitrium* of the church courts. The argument against the spiritual jurisdiction was against the excessive authority of the ecclesiastical courts and against the illiberal character of its procedures. Actions *ex officio* for heresy under the statute *De Haeretico Comburendo* were exemplary of all that was wrong in the process and the substance of the spirituality, and St. German lists lengthily the details of such excess of power and the forms of its abuse.[16] The significant issue, however, is not the tabling of abuses nor the justification of the increasingly absolutist jurisdiction of the common law courts but rather the subsistence of the spiritual jurisdiction in ever-new places and forms. With regard to St. German, the polemic against the spirituality is reformist in the precise sense that he believed that the common law was a safer guardian of the nation's soul than arbitrary and excessive Roman legal practices. In particular, it may be noted that the principal effect of his arguments was to insist upon the right of the common law to incorporate or to subsume the spirituality. It is not that the spiritual jurisdiction should be removed or abandoned but rather that it be transferred so as better to reflect the "true state of English law."[17] In his classic dialogue on the virtue of common law, *Doctor and Student,* it is plain in the extreme that St. German supports fully the spiritual power of law and the divine character of all judgment. The law is always subject to equity and to conscience, a point that can be elaborated through St. German's complex explanation of knowledge and judgment:

> Conscience, which derives from *cum scientia,* with knowledge, imports both knowledge of itself and knowledge with another thing. As knowledge by itself it is a natural act and is both cognitive and also motive and inclines the soul to pursue good and eschew evil. Thus its place is superior to reason and

16. See St. German, *A Treatise Concerning the Division*; and St. German, *Salem and Bizance.* For Thomas More's responses, see Sir Thomas More, *The Apologye* (London: W. Rastall, 1533), and More, *Debellacyon of Salem and Bizance.*

17. Thus, St. German, *A Treatise* at 28v: "Another cause of the division has been by reason of divers laws and constitutions which have been made by the church . . . wherein they have many times exceeded their authority, and attempted in many things against the laws of the realm."

> is conjoined with that higher light of reason called sinderesis. As knowledge with another thing it imports knowledge with some particular act.[18]

In this lesser form it subordinates the application of knowledge or law to the equity or desire that governs the function of judgment. The spiritual, in short, is and was always a part of the temporal law, it was its source and its authority,[19] and if any should doubt that conjunction of source and spirit, Sir John Fortescue early on had observed that the very word law (*ius*) was but an abbreviation of the figure and term of justice (*iustitia*).[20]

The complaint of the canon lawyers and the polemical virulence of recusants and Catholics had little to do with the substance of the jurisdiction nor did it relate directly to the application of law but rather to the politics of institutional place. Robert Cosin, in an important defense of the ecclesiastical courts, argues that the "mean spirited and unchristian" gibes and attacks upon ecclesiastical courts were both unnecessary and self-contradictory. In terms of self-contradiction, he points precisely to the irony that "these professed dealers for an innovation in the Church doe most greedily take holde of these exceptions from the common lawe, against jurisdiction ecclesiastical, and doe alledge also sundry others, yet pretending to ground themselves for both, not alonely upon the lawes of the realme . . . but upon Gods lawe also, the civill, the Canon, or Ecclesiasticall law, and upon equitie and reason."[21] The issue was not therefore the abandonment or loss of a jurisdiction or type of action but simply a question of its transmission to new institutional sites. Thus, somewhat later, John Godolphin in a classic compilation of ecclesiastical law remarks by way of preface to the abridgment that "all that follows would be but insignificant and disfigured cyphers" without an understanding of the implications of the Act of Supremacy, for "[w]hen Henry VIII was both Parliamentarily and Synodically invested herewith, although it were with all the privileges and preheminences incident thereto, yet no more accrues to the Crown thereby, than was legally inherent in it before."[22]

Where canon and civilian lawyers argued in favor of a plurality of laws,

18. St. German, *Doctor and Student* at 87–89.

19. See, for example, John Poynet, *A Short Treatise of Politike power, and of the obedience which subjectes owe to kynges and other civile Governours* (London: n.p., 1556) at B iii b: "Rulers in the world have sometimes wished to be taken for Gods, that is, the ministers and images of God here on earth, the examples and mirrors of all godliness, justice, equity and other virtues, and claim and exercise an absolute power . . . with *sic volo, sic iubeo*. . . . Such power is laughable. God instituted civil and political power to maintain justice."

20. Fortescue, *De Natura* at 231.

21. Cosin, *An Apologie for Sundrie Proceedings* at fol. A 2 a.

22. Godolphin, *Repertorium Canonicum* at 1–2. This argument was a common one. See, for further examples, Fulke, *T. Stapleton and Martiall*; Favour, *Antiquitie Triumphing.*

not least on the ground that the "exorbitant licentiousness"[23] of the age would justify any number of laws however manifold in source and procedure, the Anglican defense of the English constitution asserted both the priority and the particularity of common law. This defense of an imaginary past, of an immemorial law tied indissolubly to the body politic of England in spite of all foreign incursions, was no more than a thinly veiled transposition of Catholic arguments into the new polity. Hooker's "love of things ancient" and belief in the "ripeness of understanding . . . and virtue of old age" referred to principles of establishment, of tradition and conservation, with which the Romans would have been equally at home.[24] It is indeed tradition as unwritten law and as perfected knowledge that Stillingfleet praises as the genuine source of common law and its various constitutions. Turning to the discussion of the obligatory force of ecclesiastical law and canons within the constitution, he therefore propounds the view that time and uninterrupted usage are the real foundations of the force of law; *longa possessio parit ius possindendi,* long possession transfers dominion. Custom gains the authority of law by virtue of the affirmation of time and the consent, the practice, and the reception of the populace.[25] Antiquity was foundation, and tradition was the form of its legitimacy, its approval, and also the means of its transmission.

The notion that time would write the law and further that uninterrupted usage took the form of prescription are both broadly phenomenological conceptions of legality. What distinguishes the Anglican Catholic sense of tradition and customary law from later and less artistic or less dynamic forms of legal positivization is precisely the sense of interiority that accompanies tradition as law. The classical conception of ecclesiastical jurisdiction was a law that regulated the manifestations or manners and good order of the public sphere, but as incidents and expressions of interior states. The authority of the ordinary was a ghostly power, it was determined as a control of the spirit and as an ordering of inward sense because it was subjectivity, the soul, which was the object or termination of law's rule. The constitution was that of both an ecclesiastical and a civil polity, and the person was likewise an impossible duality, substance and soul alike. The struggle over images and the correlative growth in the power and extent of common law was not a dispute over the object of law's power but rather over the means or institutions through which to achieve an appropriate discipline. The natural image, in one apologetic definition, was an "inward image, an inward imagination. An image is of past tidings and affections, it repeats and calls to remembrance . . . [for] the

23. Consett, *The Practice of the Spiritual or Ecclesiastical Courts* at fol. A 2 b.
24. Hooker, *Ecclesiastical Politie* at 195–196.
25. Stillingfleet, *Ecclesiastical Cases* at 329 and 349.

mind reads backwards, as it were in its inward book, the whole order of its history."[26] In an exemplary polemic against the image, the same relationship of reference is referred to but in disparaging terms, the fantasm or inward imagination distracts, it is *esse vestitum imagine,* being clothed with an image.[27]

The position of a secular law that was founded in the midst of the war over images and that was nominally iconomachal and for a time quite actively iconoclastic was somewhat ambivalent and frequently less than explicit. For the principal authors of the settlement and the modern discourse of constitution and law, the interplay of tradition and text, of ghostly power and positive law, of unwritten truth and visible word, in short, of spirit and meaning, was a complex inheritance of a law of images and their inward sense, of spiritual laws and their pastoral implementation. The ecclesiastical eye or *speculum pastoralis,*[28] the watchtower that surveyed the soul, became an element in a combined or dual polity in which common law was to take on the full custody of the *corpus mysticum* of the state. As Stillingfleet made clear in justifying the civil honor to be shown to the chair of state, the mystical antiquity of common law custom, the essential legality of the unwritten tradition as expressive of the soul of the people and the spirit of the land, was never to be understood as the only source of law. It was to be joined with the sacral character of the sovereign and its legislation and, indeed, whether a specific custom or practice was to be observed at any instance was in the end a matter of legislation, the question being, did it please the prince and so take on the force of law?

The relation between these sources of law, custom, and sovereignty need not be rehearsed here save to observe that in its own particular way the common law accepted in a somewhat interpolated form the Roman principle that all the laws were inscribed in the sovereign's breast.[29] As early as Glanvill and Fleta, common law had also observed the principle of absolute royal power and simply transferred the domain of its application and the extent of its jurisdiction in recognizing the common lawyers as the principal directors and interpreters of this pleasure or volition, which would always have the power or *potestas* of father and law.[30] In unifying polity and law, the sovereign and everything which such sovereignty implied in terms of custom, constitution, and law was taken into or enfolded

26. Sander, *A Treatise of the Images* at 159.

27. Parker, *A Scholasticall Discourse* at 2r.

28. Stapleton, *A Returne of Untruthes upon M. Jewell* at sig. 57r: "*Specula pastoralis*—the pastoral watchtower is common to all that bear the office of Bishop."

29. The classical maxim is usually given as *omnia iura habet in scrinio pectoris sui.* For commentary on this theme see Legendre, *Le Désir politique de Dieu* at 221–235.

30. See H. G. Richardson and G. O. Sayles (eds.), *Fleta* (London: Selden Society, 1955) at 36: "*Quod principi placuit legis habet vigorem.*" All right belonged to the Crown—*sui iura est.*

within the positivity of common law. In becoming a science, common law became mystical. Sir Edward Coke's *vocabula artis* and professional knowledge, his self-evident antiquity and permanent tradition, was beyond record as connatural to the people and in need of no proof, an initiate science whose trauma of inauguration instituted a pattern of repetition which is arguably still repeated today.[31] The law embraced both *patria potestas* and *regia potestas,* it instituted an incommunicable and supreme power (*iura sublimia*), a law which joined in one jurisdiction both *iure positivo pontificio* and *iure divino Apostolico.*[32]

The Crown, in one peculiarly striking definition, was a "Nursing Father," whose ghostly power was to be used to the end of nurturing the inner subjection or spiritual obedience of both institutions and individuals within the commonwealth.[33] The function of law, deriving from this seizure or paternity and dominion over all subjects, was to order the external laws of the commonwealth so as to abide by and contribute toward both knowledge and its spiritual objects, for *misera servitus, ubi jus est vagum aut incognitum*; it is a miserable servitude where law is both wandering and unknown.[34] The final end or *ratio finalis* of law was not that of maintaining external security but an internal cause, that of establishing "peace inwardly" and governing *in ordine ad bonum spirituale.*[35] Human laws, concerned as they are with the external positivities of the public sphere, were mere accidents or effects of a superior and anterior cause, of that essence or being that formed the inner nature and supreme law of the subject. Human law was simply indicative. It pointed to causes and virtues that would bind the conscience, it was no more than the image or legitimate representation of an invisible nature and its divine cause, and in that sense or role common law was in substance and effect an aspect of the law of nature and a reflection of an atemporal and inalterable essence, given *ex institutione naturae.* Subjection was thus similarly derived from the law, and virtue of nature and the regulation of such subjectivity was in the same sense a feature of bonds or obligations that belonged to conscience and to the order of nature and of causes and not only or simply to that of positive law.

AN ENGLISH UNCONSCIOUS

The order of sources of law reflected a hierarchy of forms of subjection. One law depended on the other and took its meaning and its justification

31. See Coke, *Institutes,* I at 6r. See, for comparable analysis, Davies, *A Discourse.* See Goodrich, "Critical Legal Studies in England."

32. Downing, *A Discourse of the State Ecclesiasticall* at 66–68.

33. Coke, *Justice Vindicated* at 98–99.

34. Ibid. at 42.

35. Ibid. at 33–34.

from its higher source. In practical terms it would thus be possible to trace the orders of subjection in direct parallel to the historical hierarchy of sources of law. While the orders and jurisdictions were soon fused in a unitary concept of a system of law, a genealogical reading of one law in the other, of *utrumque ius,* can offer considerable insight into the past and possibilities of plural legal jurisdictions and the various implications and residues of a diversity of laws.[36] In the first instance it is important to trace again the subject of spiritual law and to indicate the features of a law that addressed directly the inner sense, the conscience and imagination of the hidden citizen or invisible subject, nursed although not always directly acknowledged by state, sovereign, and law.

The most direct expression of the role of law within the ecclesiastical constitution can be found in some of the earliest defenses of the Anglican polity. The subject of law was not external obedience, nor was it a mere conformity to the text, but rather an internalization of the word and a "keeping of the tradition" in its unwritten and lived form. The order of governance is in a sense unexceptionable: "Carry not images but the law in your heart," to which it is added that such law, transmitted by print and by speech, is no mere text or apostolic preaching but rather "those things which are spoken . . . are images of their souls" and should be heard and incorporated as such.[37] In Bishop Jewel's words, even literal interpretation of the law by the text was a species of "ostentation and sophistry" to which it was necessary to oppose an unwritten law "graven not in stone but in the heart," or, in a classical maxim, *corde creditur ad iustitiam,* he who believes with the heart will do justice.[38] The law was to be understood as an allegory for the direction and protection of conscience, its basis being virtue and an ethics of custom that would lead the internal subject of the realm, the undying body or *corpus mysticum* of state and subject, to truth.

The logic of internalization is spelled out through metaphors of the mouth and the eye. The law can neither be seen nor read in itself, it is not touched with the body nor seen with the eye, but rather "there is a spiritual mouth of the inner man which is nourished by receiving the word of life (*verbum vitae*)" as also there are eyes of the spirit (*oculi spiritus*) "which are able to see things that are not seen, and have no being . . . for *oculi anima,* the eyes of the soul, will pass through all obstacles whereas *oculi corporales,* that see visible things, cannot do so much."[39] The inward spiritual eyes saw through imagining and through mystery, through substance and faith, and not through any merely apparent phenomena or manifest forms. Thus for St. German, "man received of God a double eye, that is to say, an

36. On the concept of *utrumque ius,* see Legendre, "Le Droit romain, modèle et langage."

37. Calfhill, *An Answere* at 65v.

38. Jewel, *An Apologie* at A viii b. For the maxim, see Stapleton, *A Fortresse of the Faith* at 162r.

39. Jewel, *A Defence of the Apologie* at 272–273.

outward and an inward eye . . . that is the eye of reason, whereby he knows things invisible and divine."[40] It is in this inventive sense that the reference to ethics and to conscience should be understood, they are references to the substance of subjectivity, to an unconscious discipline or juristic soul. It is indeed equally in this sense that the division of laws and of courts should also be comprehended. The positive law existed to adjudicate and rule *in foro exteriori et contentioso,* in the forum of external conflicts, but such conflict and its resolution was only a living metaphor or allegory for the courts of conscience and of the spirit, wherein outward obligation was subjected to interior substance. The cure of the soul belonged not only to that authority and law which adjudicated *in foro exteriori,* but equally and also to judgment *in foro interiori,* and on occasion to both, *in utroque simul.*[41]

Such a concept of the depth of law may be contemporarily opaque, as also is the language of ethics and of laws of the soul, but the order of progression or enfolding of exterior law and interior subjection, the movement from one visibility to another, spells out much of the power that is at stake in law. It is a question again of the potentially dynamic or creative character of law, a question well understood in certain of the more incidental debates over the law of images. In one such, adverted to earlier, the relation between the different courts and their corresponding regimes of visibility is beautifully elaborated in terms of vanishing or "aereall signs." The debate in question concerned whether an "aereall" sign, which is "transient and presently vanishing," such as the sign of the cross made in air or with water on the forehead, should be deemed idolatry at law. The response was that "the image is, and always was, a vanishing aereall shadow, like the ghost or shade [*umbra*] of one dead, which being true, the vanishing ayrenes [airiness] of the cross furthereth and stayeth not the idolizing of it. The cross aereall is if anything more dangerous [than the material] because *in similitudinem umbrarum, transeunt et intereunt,* they vanish and pass away like shadows."[42] In a stronger formulation, the danger of the transient or vanishing sign is precisely the inversion of the relation between, and significance of, this transience and the substance to which it refers. The danger of the contingent or impermanent sign was its fluidity, its momentary and uncircumscribed excitation of the mind: the less material the sign, so much the quicker is the passage *ab imagine ad rem significatam,* from the image to the thing signified.[43]

The vanishing sign is not least threatening by virtue of its recollection of the immateriality of law and the transience of the text or *litera* of regulation. The fluidity of the discipline and the contingency of the art of law is

40. St. German, *Doctor and Student* at 83.
41. Stillingfleet, *Ecclesiastical Cases* at 24–25.
42. Parker, *Scholasticall Discourse* at 17–18.
43. Ibid. at 48.

evidenced quite clearly in the sign which disappears in the moment of its signification. More than that, however, the transience of the sign diminishes the status of positive law or recollects an order and plurality of jurisdictions which directly challenge the shallow and conformist belief in the unity of the system of positive law. Common law, as Selden most vividly pronounced it, was two-faced, its emblem being Janus and its sign that of Mercury. The Janus face of common law was a reference not only to the repressed history of the spiritual jurisdiction but, more than that, it was a recollection of the plurality of laws that subsisted within the tradition and which, in their fragmentary and partial forms, made up the commonality of English law.[44] It was justice, in Selden's argument, that lay hidden by the positivization of law, and it was against that very local, contemporary, and oblivious sense of legal rule that he counterposed the "reverse or back face" of English law. The other face was of plural histories, of fragments or scraps of forgotten rule, of the lost customs, myths, and other remainders of neglected laws and injured subjectivities that convention, desuetude, and blindness had obscured from view. The other faces of English law were, for Selden, those of plurality and of the diversity of its legal jurisdictions, times and peoples. His work indeed constantly returned to the history of laws that had been excluded or ignored by the unscholarly breed of lawyers at the Inns of Court.[45] In the broader and more synoptic terms of the present argument, the Janus face of English law may be taken to refer quite simply to its dual character and to the repression or duplicity whereby it shows only one face and simulates a science of dogmatics pertaining to a singular law.

The brief recapitulation of a jurisdiction and method historically and substantively hidden or lost within the common law offers a number of lessons or at least allows certain observations of contemporary forms of legal governance. The first is simply topographic. To the side or on the margins of common law there subsists the jurisdiction, the residue, and certain vestiges of the spiritual jurisdiction and the functions of conscience. The art of judgment, in other words, might be deemed to include, if only in the most displaced of forms, the inward court or imaginary *regulae* of ethical subjection. The discipline that governed the soul or tutored and bound the citizen of the ecclesiastical polity *iure divino* as well as by positive law taught the subject a species of fatalism. Providence dictated the order of law and it also marked the place and purpose, the fate or destiny of the subject. It was against this background of the Christian version of *amor fati* or of fortune's decree that the order of spiritual law and the ruling of the spiritual courts had their place.

44. Selden, *Jani Anglorum,* Preface.
45. See, most particularly, Selden, *The Historie of Tithes.*

The courts of conscience bound in conscience alone and so took their place and their rule through the word and through the spirit. This dependence upon conscience did not preclude causes nor did it divorce the reason of spirituality from the practice of law. Although the spiritual courts gradually lost their powers of enforcement to the expansive jurisdiction of common law, the scope of this speculative justice should not be underestimated. The spiritual courts not only preceded the common law in ethical and hierarchical terms but also had the power to take cognizance of a wide range of speculative and institutional causes. Many such actions, as for example for perjury, blasphemy, sacrilege, apostasy, heresy and schism, simony, tithes, excommunication, and commutation of penance, were public forms of offense against the establishment, whereas rules governing slander, spousals, matrimony, divorce, bastardy, testaments, incests, fornications (incontinencies), adulteries, solicitation of chastity, drunkenness, and filthy talking came much closer to the application of rules governing personal ethics and care of the self. Much more so were the rules of "christian oeconomy" or domestic governance which spelled out the duties of the members of the smallest Christian community or polity, the family.[46] What is genuinely interesting about the application of rules within the domain of conscience, or within the internal sphere of the "other kingdom," the scene of a judgment that did not belong to this world, is not the detail of actual application but rather the rules and procedures of a distinct form of law.

The court of conscience would archetypically proceed according to rules of conscience and would apply the norms of a justice that transcended the temporal law and its positive procedures. More than that, however, the courts of spiritual justice existed alongside the community and process of common law not simply to apply a separate law to the community of the ecclesiastical estate in its institutional sense, the clerics and all who could plead the privilege of the clergy, but also to provide a parallel set of rules for those who would seek some other justice than that available at common law. A simple although perhaps slightly technical example could be taken from the judgment of contractual obligations in the spiritual courts. To prove a contract at common law required not simply evidence of a promise but also proof of a temporal bargain in the sense of consideration for the promise made. Without such proof, the exchange of bare promises created no obligation but was and indeed is viewed as *nudum pactum.* The Christian court, however, would hear any action based upon a "faith" or promise and would try an action for breach of faith or *pro laesione fidei* according to spiritual rules and spiritual punishments. A voluntary oath was a matter of conscience and upon a suit before the ec-

46. See Perkins, *Christian Oeconomie.*

clesiastical judges the breach of the promise would be followed by injunction to corporal penance without prejudice to any action for recovery of debt at common law.[47]

In more technical terms, parties to a contract would often, for greater security, make faith or oath of performance in private or before ordinaries. In either case the promise was termed *fidei praestatio,* and if either party failed to perform they would be called by ecclesiastical process before the ordinary and made to answer. If proved against them, "the offender was enjoined grievous penance, and compelled by censures to keep his faith or oath, by satisfying the other party. . . . The observation of an oath is *praeceptum iuris divini* and therefore indispensable."[48] In later law, the secular courts made various attempts to recognize these types of spiritual duty in the form of what were termed moral obligations or simply through the equitable diversion of positive norms. Increasingly, however, the source, the logic, and the domain of spiritual rules and their application were lost through an increasingly insular, positivized, and closed conception of common law system. The tie between law and a knowledge of things divine and human, the repressed and so merely residual and intellectually passive jurisdiction over the spirituality of the subject as well as the subordination of all rules of positive law to the criteria of an artistic justice, recollect a fecund set of possibilities for the deconstruction of the positivity of common law.

The Anglican law required the peasant, whose story began this chapter, to remove his hat before entering the court. That norm of civil honor or secular reverence was not an accident of custom or of local practice, it was a recognition, although perhaps only a partial one, of the historical transmission of spirituality and of "ghostly power" from natural to positive law. It was a recognition or an acting out of the displacement of social paternity or of *regia potestas* from ecclesiastical to civil sources, a displacement which was self-conciously represented as a continuity of the *longue durée* of common law: "We have overthrown no kingdom, we have decayed no men's power or right, we have disordered no commonwealth. There continue in their own accustomed state and ancient dignity the Kings of our country England."[49] Among the jurisdictions and the courts that were so transmitted must be included not only the residues of divine or natural justice, the rules of conscience and of spiritual action, but also the manners and norms of domestic relation, bodily function, and moral integrity. Both language and desire, belief and subjective place were subject now to

47. Cosin, *An Apologie for Sundrie Proceedings* at 25–26.

48. Ibid. at 51.

49. Jewel, *An Apologie* at fol. G i b. See also Cosin, *An Apologie for Sundrie Proceedings* at 40: "All jurisdiction Ecclesiastical being now in fact and Lawe united to the Crowne and from thence derived."

the governance of common law. What had to be assumed and passed on within this other unwritten tradition was what Fortescue had much earlier termed a "filial fear of God" and of the law.[50] In short, the institution had always to nurture and the law to nurse the subjects, the children which governance created. As "nursing father" the secular law took over the governance of conduct, and it entered a jurisdiction which included the specification and regulation of subjective space not only as "oikonomia," or domesticity and relation, but also as the site of education, ethics, conduct, and civic virtue. Where the contemporary legal form has endeavored to present law as an autonomous domain of positivized and merely written texts, the repression of the unwritten jurisdiction and of the invisible subject and its ghostly powers has merely rendered the subject of judgment and the governance of the soul unconscious. It is in that darkness, in that unlit territory of attachment to and dissemination of law, that the irrationality of the legal form and the injustice of legal decision have come to be most strikingly felt as the legality of a contingency that law can neither fully know nor directly address.

CRITICAL LEGAL STUDIES, OR *IUS INTERRUPTUS*

It has been the practical argument of the present work that a critical reading of law starts with its images, figures, and tropes and does so for the reason that these features or this face of law, its accidents, ornaments, or incidents, represent that which cannot be said directly, that which cannot be proved or seen, but must be taken on faith or not at all. In less metaphysical terms these symptoms of an "other scene" or unconscious of law are also the signs of the divisions or differences that constitute *this* place, *this* subjectification, *this* law, or the beauty and the devastation of *this* objectivity, this particular order of social being. In endeavoring to expose the role of the image and the specific *antirrhetic* in which early doctrine wrote of the identity of common law, the present study has concentrated upon a limited number of foundational images, particularly those of citizenship, place, and gender. Each substantive division or differentiation was shown to be instituted antithetically and to mirror the *antirrhetic* which founds the subject itself. Where positivized conceptions of law are concerned to use concepts of logic and system to mask or deny the difference, the power that founds law, a psychoanalytic critique of law is attentive precisely to the differences or others enfolded in law. It seeks to give voice or objectivity to those subjectivities, genres, places, or ethnicities that positive law denies or negates. In political terms this suggests, as Irigaray in particular has argued, a recognition, at the level of the social system and most fundamen-

50. Fortescue, *De Laudibus Legum Angliae* at 3.

tally at that of the legal system, of the identity, the existence of repressed subjects, of images, strangers, and women: "There is as yet no civil law (*code civil*) concerning real persons, and specifically men and women."[51] Ethics, in her terms, should be founded upon difference and most specifically upon sexual difference, upon the legal recognition of two sexes, rather than upon one sex as law for the other. To take up an ethic of difference is to oppose precedent, unity, establishment, and law precisely because of what it represents and precisely because of how it represents, how in *antirrhesis* it denies its fragmentations, how in establishing the same, as norm, as precedent, as law, it negates its others.[52]

The unconscious, the "discourse of the other," is that which has not yet been thought; it is the strangeness or ignorance of the subject, the confusion of identity, the dispersion of will. In institutional terms it has been suggested that whatever the possibilities of the other, and Irigaray for one suggests many such possibilities,[53] the initial problem for jurisprudence, and for justice, is to recognize and lay out a space of the other within the law. It is a question of identifying the conditions of difference, the places, occasions, energies, and institutional focuses within which difference, as difference, can appear or the other speak. Again using Irigaray's terms of sexual difference, it is a matter of establishing the possibilities or other places of the future: "Anything that once offered a possible future must be abandoned, turned back, like a limited horizon: a veil that imperceptibly conceals the world facing us."[54] While this new poetics inevitably appears both too transgressive and too speculative to the doctrines or horizons of positive law, that difficulty, awkwardness, or irreverence is precisely the expression and the threat of difference. It indicates an internal otherness, "a foreignness [which] does not even start at the skin's edge,"[55] a zone of repression laid out within the social subject, an interiority that can only be expressed as a species of abnormality or paradox against established custom, common sense, subjection, and its laws. It is possible to formulate this strangeness as radical political change in that sense of radicalism that is not only rooted in a deep doubt, an indeterminacy at the basis of "the wisdom of received ideas," but which also seeks to incorporate or live the *aporia*, the incomprehension, indeterminacy, or uncertainty of intellection

51. Irigaray, *J'aime à toi* at 43.

52. See particularly Luce Irigaray, *Sexes and Genealogies* (New York: Columbia University Press, 1993) at 25–53; and, most recently, Irigaray, *J'aime à toi.*

53. Irigaray, *Sexes and Genealogies* at 52; "The way to this strange adventure is found in the renunciation of any path that has already been proposed." See also Irigaray, *Marine Lover of Friedrich Nietzsche* at 69: "In the other, you are changed. Become other and without recurrence." See also Irigaray, *Le Temps de la différence.*

54. Irigaray, *Sexes and Genealogies* at 52. In *J'aime à toi* at 26, Irigaray makes a similar point in terms of "a militant politics of the impossible."

55. Cornell, "What Takes Place in the Dark" at 49.

and of writing. The diverse features of such change or becoming may serve as a tentative conclusion or epigraph to the present work.

The genealogy of the image is predicated upon a recounting of the histories of the undecidability of law. Its narratives are of a life that wavers, its subject the attempt to account those bodies or texts that escaped institutional representation, that were mystical, heretical, or poetic simply because unattached to the symbols of genre or the rules of bureaucratic prose. The genealogy of the image is predicated also upon a sense of the conceptual value of history, upon the power of the past. The most radical, although by no means necessarily the most successful, attempts at formulating a feminist jurisprudence as an instance of a law of the other have taken the histories of the image as an intrinsic element and resource in the critique of the institution. In a sense well captured by Lacan's remark that the idol "gives pleasure to other gods,"[56] the reconstruction or interpretation of myth, allegory, figuration, image, and poetic is an exercise in a plural interpretation of text and institution. It engages with the histories of the image so as to institute a certain plurality, or at least so as to raise the specter of other subjectivities, of difference as such.

Law, despite its imagery of justice, its feminine symbols, its plural and pagan rites, its polyglot texts, is in this respect the last universal, the emblem of the same in an era of encroaching difference, the symbolization of a formal unity in the face of substantive fragmentation. The genealogy of the law of images and specifically of the doctrinal images of text and of law is indicative not least of the contingency and the power of those images that constitute the presence or surface of the institution of subjectivity. The histories of the image are indicative also of that literal repression upon which common law doctrine was founded. It was not incidental that the denunciation of idols and of image-service, of ceremony, vestment, and rites, was also an attack upon the two Romes, those of the papacy and of civilian laws. Here and elsewhere the jurisdiction of the common law was predicated upon the radical suppression of other jurisdictions. Its unity was built upon the sacrifice, the devouring of other laws, not least those of conscience, of spirituality, and of the soul. The incorporation of the spiritual laws also included the repression of the ethical or interior discourses, the conscience, the subjective practices of the parent law. While the substance of those ethical or inner practices was often itself dramatically repressive, the secular repetition of practices that do not know their subjectivity or deny the relevance of interior space is probably a regressive movement.

The use of history and its images is not however simply nostalgic or corrective. Certainly it is possible to use history politically to think difference

56. Lacan, *Four Fundamental Concepts of Psychoanalysis* at 113.

and to find in an "older" history, in allegory, in myth, or in other poetic or repressed sources a variety of resources for a politics of difference. It is further possible to recognize the sense in which history thinks the political and to use that understanding of tradition, of repetition, or of compulsion to access or activate the other scene of law. More than that, however, the genealogy of the plurality of laws suggests the contingency of law's inscriptions. The histories of the image indicate both the power and the subjection, the indeterminacy that founds law, that founds each discipline upon subjection, upon a series of repressions. In other words, the image provides access to those spaces or discourses of law that modernity repressed. It suggests a contingency of law that may be used to formulate a positive construction of alterity and so to institute in new forms the creativity of law through the recognition of its failures, its repressed desires, its misrecognitions of its own identity.

Returning again to the foundational discourses of the Western legal tradition, and this time to its foundation in the reception of Roman and canon law in the twelfth century, it is salutary to recall that alongside the glossatorial tradition and its reverence for the text there was also a tradition of resistance. The present work has endeavored to inscribe the history of the law of images within that forgotten tradition and subjectivity of resistance. It is a tradition within which the image signals the mobility of thought and the transience of texts, a tradition of peripatetic scholarship, of excluded figures and solitary teachers of "undesirable texts," of passionate and delirious speeches, of discourses that waver in reflection of a life which is not without its share of contingencies and uncertainties. The genre of critique which I will here invoke, as a final gesture, is that of legal satire and the poetics of a certain cynicism directed at the science of law. It belongs to what Pierre Legendre has termed the "twelfth century revolution in interpretation" and it endeavors to develop a jurisprudence that offers a certain "danger" of poetry, of speaking one's mind, as the method of comprehending and teaching or, equally productively, of failing to understand the love and the power of the text. It offers the obscure notion of a life lived in or, more properly, as a commentary upon the text.

At one level the psychoanalytic critique of law simply recollects the necessary internality of legal rules. There is no legal subject without an obedient soul, no letter of the law without the *anima legis* of its interpreter, no text without its bearer, no exterior court without its predicate in an interior judgment or court of conscience. The stake of a psychoanalytic reading of the history and practice of law is well known to the tradition in the history, briefly rehearsed here, of the combination of two laws and two courts, those of spirit and of sense, body and soul, and also in spiritual and temporal, external and internal species of law. The second function of the psychoanalytic critique of law is thus to attend to the voice or text of the other law. In historical terms the project suggests a radical revision of the history of legal thought and specifically a history that seeks to recollect and release the originary resistances, the poetics and play, the hedonisms of style and mixtures of genre that the earliest satires of the reception threw in the face of the glossatorial tradition. The tradition of written law, of scripture and text as well as of scriveners, chirographers, and tablers of rolls and fines always had its internal critics, its oracles, seers, madmen, artists, women, and poets who would not submit to the mere authority of texts or who dissented from the dogmas of their repetition. I will offer one example, that of a twelfth-century text that was for long unattributed and of uncertain authenticity, the *Sermo de legibus* or poetical sermon on the laws. In 1943 Herman Kantorowicz located the author of this work as the twelfth-century jurist Placentinus and published a definitive version compiled from the various surviving manuscripts.[57]

For Placentinus, law was writing and writing was a woman, or a woman was writing. The *Sermo de legibus,* an address to commencing law students, is an attempt in verse to spell out the conditions and specifically the interior space of law. At one level one might say that law binds through indetermination, through the image and through rhetoric and its uses of the *ars praedicandi.* For Placentinus, the law can only be addressed initially through a forcible and emotional appeal to the spirit or what the medievals termed the "ghostly power" of divine rule. The sermon is also a prayer, a song, an invocation of divinity or *rerum divinarum,* and as such the study and interpretation of law necessarily addressed an interior space or *foro interiori.* The subject of law was first conscience—*insitum cordibus nostris*—and its practice was the practice of virtue while its science was that of ethics or of the *Ethica vetus.*[58] The images that Placentinus chooses to represent this ethics or ancient virtue are those of *aurora* and most specifically that of *Jurisprudentia,* a goddess, a woman.[59] It is as a woman, as a virtue, and as justice that the poetical sermon can take the form of a satire which variously and vigorously castigates the inherited tradition, the *ager vetus* of Justinian's *Digest,* and the science of law or *legalis scientia* of the glossators, the sophists of the *literae* or dead letters of the text.

The dramatic form of the satire, of genre that combines vehemence, conceit, and polemic is entirely appropriate and historically exemplary of the critique of law. Placentinus writes against custom (*contra morem*) and against the ascetic and interminable character of legal study in the irreverent and fictive form of an encounter between our mistress ignorance—

57. Herman Kantorowicz, "The Poetical Sermon of a Mediaeval Jurist: Placentinus and his 'Sermo de Legibus'" (1943) 2 *Journal of the Warburg and Courtauld Institute* 22.

58. The reference is to Aristotle, *Nicomachean Ethics.* See Kantorowicz, "Poetical Sermon" at 34.

59. Ibid. at 26.

domina Ignorantia—a rudely healthy, high-spirited, and rustic girl, and legal science, an old, deformed, ugly, and disfigured woman.[60] Legal science, in Ignorantia's critique, dissembles the pedagogy of morals and of virtue while in truth it kills its subject with too much study, having first confused it with fantasms and disfigured it through privation. The science of legality, the scribal and sophistic observances of a glossatorial practice which merely relays and repeats the authorities not only is dismissed as a stultifying science (*stulta scientia*) but is further condemned as a murderous and self-nihilating undertaking:

> Dum corpus tuum afficis
> Tu te ipsam interficis
> Tu es homicida!
>
> [While you use your body in this way
> you are destroying yourself
> you are a murderer][61]

The glossatorial tradition offered affectation rather than authenticity: law was against life through being proprietary, jealous, and without desire. It offered tears, confusion, starvation, and a death in the midst of life: "Tu morieris in vivendo / Atque vivis moriendo."[62]

The satirical poem or *prosimetrum* belonged to the foundational discourses of law, even if only through antithesis, loss, or repression. It argued against the weary and dessicated texts of the exegetes with an image of vitality, youth, and creativity in the form of a woman and in the form of a savage and satirical ignorance, a pre-stoic cynicism. Here the scene of public life was the stage upon which to act out the great themes of the soul, of fate, fortune, and desire as the laws of an interior prescience. The law thus always sought an interior attachment or juridical soul, and Placentinus is remarkable only for the satirical and extreme version of the argument which he presents. It is that satire or cynicism which I intend to invoke as the flaw or failure through which the rewriting of the legal arts can take hold. It is that project to which contemporary critique can also be attached in the disparate figures of the immoralist, the satirist, polemicist, poet, and interior peripatetic.

It can be noted in even the briefest of terms that the work of Placentinus in many respects was emblematic of the forms of difference most feared by the legal tradition in its Christian form. The *Sermo de legibus* is a vituperative medley of prose and verse and is a genre which, through the

60. *Sermo de legibus* at line 80 ff.

61. Ibid. at lines 104–106. *Interficio* also has the meaning of cutting up, of dissecting into small pieces, of cutting up with law's pedantry, sophistry or "chop-logic."

62. Ibid. lines 99–100: "You are dying in the midst of life / and you live while deserving to die."

Palestinian Menippos of Gadara, probably came in the third century B.C. from the Orient. It is certainly taken up by Placentinus in the taunting and cynically hedonistic spirit of an internal Orient, a conscience at odds with its place, an outsider to its peers. Let us go further: although Placentinus was popular as a teacher, he was villified by the other doctors of law. His peripatetic lifestyle indeed began, we are told, when he ridiculed another Bolognese doctor, Henricus de Bayla, "and this man, who was at the same time a powerful knight, made a nocturnal assault on Placentinus, who fled in terror."[63] He taught law, so to speak, while on the run from its doctors, casuists, and other assiduous savants. He was not afraid to warn of the death of law or of the decay of tradition while equally flouting its laws and mixing its genres. Placentinus practised what Lacan would have termed that "ignorance which puts knowledge to work." More than that, there is a further nascent radicality to his style, most directly that of the cynic and satirist whose work is gauged to offend the institution, to mock the "sophisticated imbecillity" of the academy. It is a work addressed not to the academy but to its students, to those not yet seized in the ascetic yet nonetheless delirious apprenticeship to the science of law. The space of legal science is a space of silence, of rules and not of speech: "The institution confines within a linguistic prison (*prison langagière*), a mystic prison which we ignore as such . . . convinced that poetry, mad or delirious words have no place there, in the space we call power."[64] The poetical sermon of the medieval jurist expresses an interior difference and is designed to align writing—the art of the lawyer—with the gentle incomprehension of those whose discourse has the poetic strength to waver, to give up its certainties, its pretention to science, and so to engage instead in the hedonistic and living theater of interpretation.

This precursor represented, not least etymologically, a nascent art of legal poetics. The issue is a broad one. While some are keen to label the critical enterprise as nostalgic, pessimistic, and obsessive, the stronger interpretation would trace the undecidability, the indefinition, or the fluidity of the poetical sermon to an originary flaw in writing itself. The critic professes (and practices) a love of the text and that love costs her dear. It still has to be asked, however, what threat this affection and this writing represent. At one level it could be said that the poetical sermon threatens by evidencing the identity of law and writing, of surface and substance, in the same text. In another sense it displays the historicity of law and threatens through indicating the contingency of the norm. The more expansive point, however, is that the work of criticism traces the great absence within

63. Kantorowicz, "Poetical Sermon" at 25.
64. Legendre, *Paroles poétiques* at 58–59.

contemporary legal science. It is the absence of interpretation in its most technical and so also most poetic sense.

The poetical sermon of the medieval jurist makes no effort to persuade and is quite indifferent to communication. It is satirical in style, it is figurative and in many respects hedonistic, but its rests, as does all writing, upon a sense of the history and fate of its genre. The work of critique has endlessly labored the history of legal interpretation. It has done so by way of tracing the fate of the two laws, spiritual and secular, external and internal. One law is enfolded in the other and neither can be understood alone. The history of *utrumque ius* is also a history of the negation of the spiritual power, its denial and incorporation within the temporal law. The concern of critique is here to recollect the spiritual power of law and the discourses that expressed and contained that power in a written form: "The lesson of Baldus was again the following: the great lucubrations of power, which is to say those which make the body walk with the soul, those which move the unconscious to death, can only be expressed poetically, because power is organised around images and fictions."[65] It is the poetic art of law alone that can mobilize an *amor fati* long lost to a positivized tradition of law in a soulless modernity. It is the history of the two laws that gives its peculiar force to the work of critique, suggesting as it does not only the mystic body of the state but also the essential correlation of exterior and interior courts. *Amor fati*, to which theme modernity must increasingly return, translates as a coming to terms with the unconscious, and this in turn suggests the prescient ability to think for oneself and so to live, if not poetically, at least with a certain degree of art. The poetical sermon suggests in the genre of satire and in the hedonistic style of *amor fati* a certain resistance or, more properly, interruption to the laws of writing.

65. Ibid. at 212.

BIBLIOGRAPHY

WORKS PRINTED BEFORE 1750

Agrippa, Henry Cornelius. 1530. *De Incertitudine et vanitate omnium scientiarum et artium.* Translated as *Of the Vanitie and Uncertaintie of Artes and Sciences.* London: H. Bynneman, 1575 ed.

———. 1529. *De Nobilitate et Precellentia Foeminei Sexus.* Translated as *Female Pre-eminence or the Dignity and Excellency of that Sex, above the Male.* London: Million, 1670 ed.

Alberti, Leon, Battista. 1436. *On Painting.* New Haven: Yale University Press, 1956 ed.

Alciatus, A. 1651. *De Notitia Dignitatem.* Paris: Cramoisy.

———. 1550. *Emblemata.* Lug.: M. Bonhomme.

———. 1530. *De Verborum Significatione libri quatuor.* Luguduni: Gryphius.

Allestree, Richard. 1677. *The Ladies Calling.* London: no publisher.

———. 1694. *The Whole Duty of Mourning and the great concern of preparing ourselves for death practically considered.* London: J. Black.

Allestree, Thomas. 1671. *A Funeral Handkerchief.* London: for the author.

Amboise, A. 1621. *Discours ou traicte des devises ou est mise la raison et difference des emblemes, enigmes, sentences et autres.* Paris: R. Boutonne.

Ambrose, Saint. *De Viduis.* In *The Principal Works of St. Ambrose.* Select Library of Nicene and Post-Nicene Fathers, Vol. 10. Oxford: Parker and Co., 1896 ed.

An Act Against Conjurations, Enchantment and Witchcraft. 1562 (5 Eliz 16).

Anonymous. 1595. *A Glasse to view the Pride of Vainglorious Women: Containing: A pleasant invective against the fantastical foreigne Toyes, daylie used in Womens Apparell.* London: Richard Ihones.

Anonymous. 1598. "Of the Variety and Antiquity of Tombes and Monuments of Persons Deceased in Englande." In *A Collection of Curious Discourses,* ed. Thomas Hearne. London: J. Richardson, 1771 ed.

Anonymous. 1620. *Hic Mulier, or the Man-Woman.* London: Christ Church Gate.

Anonymous. 1620. *Swetnam the Woman-Hater Arraigned by Women.* London: Meighen.

Anonymous. 1700. *Baron and Feme: A Treatise of the Common Law Concerning Husbands and Wives*. London: Walthoe.

Anonymous. 1595. *Disputatio nova contra Mulieres qua probatur eas hominas non esse*. Hague: Burchornius, 1641 ed.

Anonymous. 1632. *The Lawes Resolutions of Women's Rights, or the Lawes Provision for Woemen*. London: J. More.

Aristotle. *De Memoria et Reminiscentia*. Translated and edited by R. Sorabji as *On Memory*. London: Duckworth, 1970.

———. 1886. *Rhetoric*. London: Macmillan.

Astell, Mary. 1694. *A Serious Proposal to the Ladies for the Advancement of their True and Greatest Interest*. London: R. Wilkin, 1698 ed.

———. 1700. *Some Reflections upon Marriage Occasioned by the Duke and Dutchess of Mazarine's Case*. London: J. Nutt.

Aylmer, Bishop. 1559. *An Harborowe for Faithfull and Trewe Subjectes against all the late blowne blaste, concerning the government of women, wherein be confuted all such reasons as a stranger of alte made in that behalf, with a brief exhortation to obedience*. Strasborowe: no publisher.

Bacon, Francis. 1620. *Novum Organum*. In *Works*, ed. T. Spedding. London: Longman, 1859 ed.

———. 1630. *The Elements of the Common Lawes of England*. London: J. More.

Bartolus de Saxoferrato. 1358. *Tractatus de Insigniis et Armis*. Published as *Consilia*. Venice: no publisher, 1485 ed.

Bede. 1565. *The History of the Church of England*. Translated and introduced in *A Fortresse of the Faith*, ed. T. Stapleton. Antwerp: I Laet.

Bird, William. 1642. *A Treatise of the Nobilitie of the Realme collected out of the body of the Common Law*. London: Walbanke.

Bodin, Jean. 1580. *De Republica*. Translated as *The Six Books of the Commonweale*. London: Knollers, 1606 ed.

Bossewell, J. 1572. *Workes of Armorie*. London: Totell.

Bossuet, J-B. 1709. *Politique tirée des propres paroles de l'écriture sainte*. Paris: Cot.

Bracton. *De Legibus et Consuetudinibus Angliae*. 1256. Translated as *On the Laws and Customs of England*, ed. S. Thorne. Cambridge, Mass.: Harvard University Press, 1968.

Breton, Nicholas. 1600. *Melancholike Humours*. London: Scholartis Press, 1929 ed.

Bright, T. 1586. *A Treatise of Melancholy*. London: Vautrollier.

Buc, Sir George. 1615. *The Third Universitie of England*. In *The Annales or General Chronicles of England*, ed. J. Stow. London: Society of Stationers.

Burton, Robert. 1628. *The Anatomie of Melancholy: What it is, with all the kinds, causes, symptomes, prognosticks, and severall cures of it by Democritus Junior*. Oxford: H. Cripps.

Calfhill, James. 1565. *An Answere to the Treatise of the Cross*. London: H. Denham.

Camden, William. 1586. *Britannia sive florentissimorum regnorum, Angliae, Scotiae, Hiberniae chorographica descriptio*. London: Collins, 1695 ed.

Case, John. 1588. *Sphaera Civitatis*. Oxford: n.p.

Casiglione, Baldesar. 1527. *The Book of the Courtier*. Harmondsworth: Penguin, 1967 ed.

Chambers, David. 1577. *Discours de la légitime succession des femmes aux possessions de leur parens et du gouvernment des princessess aux empires et royaumes.* Paris: no publisher.

Champier, S. 1515. *La Nef des dames: Vertueuses composée par Maistre Simphorien Champier.* Paris: no publisher.

Coke, Sir Edward. 1610. *A Book of Entries containing perfect and approved presidents of Courts, Declarations . . . and all other matters and proceedings (in effect) concerning the pratick part of the laws of England.* London: Streeter, 1671 ed.

———. 1611. *The Reports.* London: J. Rivington, 1777 ed.

———. 1629. *The First Part of the Institutes of the Laws of England; or, A Commentary upon Littleton, not the name of a Lawyer only, but of the Law it selfe.* London: I. More.

———. 1680. *Magna Carta with short but necessary observations by Lord Chief Justice Coke.* London: Atkins.

Coke, Roger. 1660. *Justice Vindicated, from the False Fucus put upon it, by Thomas White Gent, Mr Thomas Hobbes, and Hugo Grotius: As also Elements of Power and Subjection; wherein is demonstrated the Cause of all Humane, Christian and Legal Society.* London: T. Newcomb.

Consett, Henry. 1685. *The Practice of the Spiritual or Ecclesiastical Courts.* London: T. Bassett.

Cosin, Robert. 1604. "Ecclesiae Anglicanae Politeia." In Cosin, R. *Tabulas Digesta.* London: no publisher.

———. 1591. *An Apologie for Sundrie Proceedings by Jurisdiction Ecclesiastical, of late times by some challenged.* London: no publisher.

Cotton, Sir Robert. 1601. "Of the Antiquity, Use and Ceremony of Lawfull Combats in England." In *A Collection of Curious Discourses written by Eminent Antiquaries upon several Heads in our English Antiquities,* ed. Thomas Hearne. London: J. Richardson, 1771.

Cowell, Dr. John. 1605. *The Institutes of the Lawes of England, Digested into the Method of the Civill or Imperiall Institutions.* London: Roycroft, 1651 ed.

———. 1607. *The Interpreter or Booke containing the Signification of Words.* Cambridge: Legat.

Cujas, Jacques. 1567. *Opera Omnia.* Lyons: no publisher, 1606 ed.

Davies, Sir John. 1601. *Of the Antiquity of Lawful Combats in England.* In *The Works of Sir John Davies,* ed. R. Grosart. London: private circulation, 1869 ed.

———. 1614. *A Discourse of Law and Lawyers.* In *Le Primer Report des Cases and Matters en Ley Resolves et Adjudges in Les Courts del Roy en Ireland.* Dublin: Franckton, 1615 ed.

Day, Angel. 1586. *The English Secretorie or Methode of Writing of Epistles and Letters with a Declaration of such Tropes, Figures and Schemes, as either usually or for ornament sake are therein required.* London: Cuthbert Burby, 1607 ed.

Day, John. 1608. *Law Tricks.* Oxford: Malone Society Reprints, 1950 ed.

de Fredericis, Stephanus. 1574. *De iuris interpretatione.* In *Tractatus iuris universis.* Venice, n.p.

de Pisan, Christine. 1404. *Le Livre de la mutacion de fortune.* Paris: Picard, 1959 ed.

———. 1521. *The Boke of the Citye of Ladys.* London: H. Pepwell.

Dod, John, and Clever, Robert. 1612. *A Godlie Forme of Householde Government: For the Ordering of Private Families, according to the Direction of Gods Word.* London: Thomas Man.

Doderidge, Sir John. 1629. *The English Lawyer: Describing a Method for the Managing of the Lawes of this Land.* London: I. More, 1631 ed.

Downing, Calybute. 1586. *A Discourse of the State Ecclesiasticall of this Kingdome, in relation to the Civill.* Oxford: W. Turner, 1632 ed.

Drake, Judith. 1696. *An Essay in Defence of the Female Sex.* London: Roper.

Duck, Dr. A. 1679. *De Usu et Autoritate Juris Civilis Romanorum in Dominiis Principum Christianorum.* London: no publisher.

Dugdale, William. 1666. *Origines Juridiciales or Historical Memorials of the English Laws, Courts of Justice, Forms of Tryal.* Savoy: T. Newcomb, 1671 ed.

Elyot, Sir Thomas. 1534. *The Defence of Good Women.* London: T. Berthelet, 1545 ed.

Farnaby, Thomas. 1633. *Index Rhetoricus scholis et institutioni tenerioris aetatis accomodatus.* London: R. Allot.

Favour, John. 1619. *Antiquitie Triumphing over Noveltie: Whereby it is proved that Antiquity is a true and certaine note of the Christian Catholicke Church.* London: Richard Field.

Fenner, Dudley. 1584. *The Artes of Logike and Rhetorike, plainly set forth in the English Tongue, easie to be taught and remembered.* Middleburg: no publisher.

Ferne, Sir John. 1586. *The Blazon of Gentrie.* London: J. Winder.

Ficino, Marsilio. 1480. *De Vita.* Translated by C. Boer as *Book of Life.* Dallas: Spring Publications, 1980.

Filmer, Sir Robert. 1653. *An Advertisement to the Jury-Man of England Touching Witches.* London: Royston.

———. 1680. *Patriarcha or the Natural Power of Kings.* London: W. Davis.

Finch, Sir Henry. 1627. *Law or a Discourse thereof in Foure Bookes.* London: Society of Stationers.

Fleta. Ed. H. G. Richardson and G. O. Sayles. London: Selden Society, 1955 ed.

Fortescue, Sir John. 1466. *De Natura Legis Naturae et de eius censura in successione regnorum suprema.* In *The Works of Sir John Fortescue, Knight.* London: private distribution, 1869 ed.

———. 1468–70. *De Laudibus Legum Angliae.* London: Gosling, 1737 ed.

———. 1475. *The Difference between an Absolute and a Limited Monarchy, as it more particularly regards the English Constitution.* London: private distribution, 1714 ed.

Fortescue-Aland, J., 1714. "Preface." In Sir John Fortescue, *The Difference between an Absolute and a Limited Monarchy, as it more particularly regards the English Constitution.* London: private distribution, 1714.

Fox, G. 1655. *The Woman Learning in Silence or, the Mysterie of Womans Subjection to her Husband.* London: T. Simmonds.

Fraunce, Abraham. 1588. *The Lawiers Logike, exemplifying the praecepts of logike by the practice of the common lawe.* London: W. How.

Fulbecke, William. 1599. *Direction or Preparative to the Study of Law; Wherein it is shewed what things ought to be observed and used of them that are addicted to the study of law.* London: J & WT Clarke, 1829 ed.

———. 1602. *A Parallele or Conference of the Civil Law, the Canon Law and the Common Law of this Realme of Englande.* London: Society of Stationers, 1618 ed.

Fulke, Dr. W. 1580. *A Rejoinder to John Martials Reply against the Answere of Maister Calfhill.* London: H. Middleton.

———. 1580. *T. Stapleton and Martiall (two popish heretics) confuted and their particular Heresies Detected.* London: Middleton.

Gibson, Anthony, trans. 1599. *A Womans Woorth, defended against all the men in the world: Prooving them to be more perfect, excellent and absolute in all vertuous actions, then any man of what qualitie soever.* London: John Wolfe.

Glanvill. 1187. *Tractatus de Legibus et Consuetudinibus Regni Angliae qui Glanvilla Vocatur.* London: T. Nelson, 1965 ed.

Goddaeus. 1569. *Commentarius repetitae praelectionis in titulum xvi libri 1 Pandectarum de verborum et rerum significatione.* Nassau: no publisher, 1614 ed.

Godden, Thomas. 1672. *Catholicks no Idolaters or a full Refutation of Dr. Stillingfleet's Unjust Charge of Idolatry against the Church of Rome.* London: no publisher.

Godolphin, John. 1677. *The Orphan's Legacy or A Testementary Abridgement in three Parts.* London: C. Wilkinson.

———. 1678. *Reportorium Canonicum or, an Abridgement of the Ecclesiastical Laws of this Realm consistent with the Temporal.* London: R. Atkins, 1687 ed.

Gosynhill, Edward. 1541. *Here Begynneth a Lytle Boke Named the Scholhouse of Women: Wherein every man may rede a goodly pryse of the condicyons of women.* London: Thomas Petyt.

———. 1542. *The Prayse of all Women called Mulierum Pean: Very fruytful and delectable unto all the reders.* London: Ihones.

Gouge, William. 1622. *Of Domesticall Duties Eight Treatises.* London: William Bladen.

Gournay, Marie de. 1622. *Égalité des hommes et des femmes.* In *Fragments d'un discours féminin,* ed. E. Dezon-Jones. Paris: Corti, 1988.

Gratian. 1140. *Decretum.* In *Corpus iuris canonici.* ed. Emil Friedberg. Leipzig: B. Tauchnitz.

Griffith, Matthew. 1633. *Bethel or, a Forme for Families: In which all sorts, of both sexes, are so squared, and framed by the word of God, as they may best serve in their several places, for usefull pieces in God's Building.* London: Jacob Bloome.

Hale, Sir Matthew. 1650. *The Analysis of the Law: Being a Scheme, or Abstract of the Several Titles and Partitions of the Law of England, Digested into Method.* Chicago: Chicago University Press, 1971 ed.

Hammond, Henry. 1644. *Of Conscience, Scandall, Will-Worship and Superstition.* Oxford: H. Hall.

———. 1646. *Of Idolatry.* Oxford: H. Hall.

Harding, Thomas. 1565. *An Answere to Mr. Jewells Challenge.* Antwerp: Ihon Laet.

———. 1565. *A Confutation of a Booke Intituled an Apologie of the Church of England.* Antwerp: Ihon Laet.

Harrison, William. 1586. *An Historicall Description of the Island of Britaine, with a brief rehersall of the nature and qualities of the people of England.* London: no publisher.

Hayward, Sir John. 1624. *Of Supremacie in Affairs of Religion.* London: J. Bilt.

Head, Richard. 1675. *Proteus Redivivus or the Art of Wheedling or Insinuation.* London: W.D.

Heale, W. 1609. *An Apologie for Women.* Oxford: J. Barnes.

Hermogenes. circa 181. *On Types of Style.* Chapel Hill: University of North Carolina Press. Trans Cecil Wooten, 1987 ed.

Heywood, Thomas. 1624. *Tunaikeion or Nine Bookes of Various History concerninge Women.* London: Adam Islip.

Hobbes, Thomas. 1637. *A Briefe of the Arte of Rhetorique: Containing in Substance all the Aristotle hath written in his three bookes of that Subject.* London: A. Crook.

Hooker, Richard. 1593. *Of the Lawes of Ecclesiastical Politie.* London: R. Scott, 1676 ed.

Hotman, Antoine. 1611. *Traité de la Loy Salique.* In *Opuscules Francoises des Hotmans.* Paris: Mathieu Guilleme.

Hotman, François. 1567. *Anti-Tribonian ou discours d'un grand et renommé jurisconsulte de nostre temps sur l'estude des loix.* Paris: J. Perrier, 1603 ed.

———. 1574. *Franco-Gallia or, an Account of the Ancient Free State of France.* London: Goodwin, 1711 ed.

Jewel, John. 1562. *Apologia Ecclesiae Anglicanae.* Translated as *An Apologie or Answere in Defence of the Churche of Englande.* London: no publisher, 1564 ed.

———. 1567. *A Defence of the Apologie of the Churche of England.* London: Fleetstreet.

Johnson, Samuel. 1687. *The Absolute Impossibility of Transubstantiation Demonstrated.* London: William Rogers.

Justinian's Institutes. 536. Trans. Peter Birks and Grant Mcleod. London: Duckworth, 1987 ed.

Knox, John. 1558. *The First Blast of the Trumpet against the Monstrous Regiment of Women.* In *The Political Writings of John Knox.* Washington, D.C.: Associated University Press of America, 1985.

Lambard, William. 1591. *Archeion or Discourse upon the High Courts of Justice in England.* London: H. Seile, 1635 ed.

Lamy, Bernard. 1676. *The Art of Speaking.* London: M. Pitt.

Legh, Gerard. 1562. *The Accedens of Armory.* London: Tottill.

Leslie, John. 1569. *A Defence of the Honour of the Right Highe, Mightye and Noble Princesse Marie Queene of Scotlande and Dowager of France, with a declaration as well of her right, title and interest to the succession of the Crowne of Englande, as that the regimente of women ys conformable to the lawe of God and nature.* London: Eusebius Dicaeophile.

———. 1580. *De Illustrium Foeminarum in Republica Administrandi, ac Ferandis Legibus Authoritate.* Rheims: Fognaeus.

Lever, R. 1573. *The Arte of Reason, Rightly termed Witcraft, Teaching a Perfect way to Argue and Dispute.* London: Brynemman.

Lloyd, Lodowick. 1600. *A Briefe Conference of Divers Lawes: Divided into Certaine Regiments.* London: Creede, 1602 ed.

Logan, John. 1677. *Analogia Honorum.* London: Thomas Roycroft.

Martiall, John. 1564. *A Treatyse of the Crosse gathred out of the Scriptures, Councelles and Auncient Fathers of the Primitive Church, by John Martiall Bachelor of Lawe and Student in Divinitie.* Antwerp: I. Latius.

Ménage, Gilles. 1690. *Historia Mulierum Philosopharum.* Translated as *The History of Women Philosophers.* Latham: University Press of America, 1984 ed.

More, Sir Thomas. 1533. *The Apologye.* London: W. Rastell.

———. 1533. *The Debellacyon of Salem and Bizance.* London: W. Rastell.

———. 1534. *The Confutacyon of Tyndales Answere made by Syr Thomas More Knyght lorde Chancellour of England.* In *Complete Works of Thomas More.* New Haven: Yale University Press, 1973.

Mulcaster, Richard. 1582. *The First Part of the Elementary.* Menston: Scolar Press, 1970 ed.
Munda, Constantia (pseud.). 1617. *The Worming of a Mad Dogge: Or, a soppe for Cerberus the Iaylor of Hell.* London: L. Hayes.
Munday, A. 1593. *The Defence of Contraries: Paradoxes against common opinion, debated in forme of declarations in place of publike censure: Only to exercise yong wittes in difficult matters.* London: J. Winder.
North, Sir Roger. 1650. *A Discourse on the Study of the Laws.* London: T. White, 1824 ed.
Noy, William. 1634. *A Treatise of the Rights of the Crown.* London: Lintoth, 1715 ed.
———. 1641. *The Grounds and Maxims of the English Law.* London: H. Linoth, 1757 ed.
Parker, Robert. 1607. *A Scholasticall Discourse against Symbolizing with Antichrist in Ceremonies: Especially in the sign of the Crosse.* London: no publisher.
Peacham, Henry. 1593. *The Garden of Eloquence conteining the most excellent Ornaments, Exornations, Lightes, Flowers and formes of Speech commonly called the figures of rhetorike.* London: H. Jackson.
Perkins, J. 1532. *A Profitable Book Treating of the Lawes of England.* London: R. Totel, 1555 ed.
Perkins, William. 1601. *A Warning against the Idolatrie of the last times.* Cambridge: Legat.
———. 1603. *Art of Prophesying.* In William Perkins, *Work of William Perkins.* Abingdon: Sutton Courtenay Press, 1970 ed.
———. 1609. *Christian Oeconomie: Or a Short Survey of the Right Manner of Erecting and Ordering a Family, according to the Scripture.* Cambridge: Cantrell Legge, 1618 ed.
———. 1610. *A Discourse on the Damnable Art of Witchcraft; so farre forth as it is revealed in the Scripture, and manifest by true experience.* Cambridge: Legge.
Phayr, T. 1544. *A New Boke of Presidentes, in manner of a Register.* London: Whytchurche.
Phillips, W. 1667. *Studii Legalis Ratio or Direction for the Study of the Laws.* London: F. Kirkman.
Plato. 1971. *Gorgias.* Trans. Walter Hamilton. Harmondsworth: Penguin.
———. 1987. *Theaetetus.* Trans. Robin A. H. Waterfield. Harmondsworth: Penguin.
Polybius. 1977. *Histories.* Harmondsworth: Penguin.
Poulain de la Barre, François. 1673. *Discours physique et moral de l'galité des deux sexes, où l'on voit l'Importance de se défaire des préjugez.* Paris: Fayard, 1984 ed.
Powell, Thomas. 1610. *The Attourney's Academy.* London: Fisher.
Poynet, John. 1556. *A Short Treatise of Politike power, and of the obedience which subjectes owe to kynges and other civile Governours.* London: n.p.
Prothero, G. W. 1894. *Select Statutes and Other Constitutional Documents Illustrative of the Reigns of Elizabeth and James I.* Oxford: The Clarendon Press.
Puttenham, George. 1589. *The Arte of English Poesie.* London: Richard Field.
Quintilian. 1920–22. *The Institutio Oratoria of Quintilian.* Trans. H. E. Butler. Cambridge: Harvard University Press.
Ramus, Petrus. 1574. *The Logike.* London: Vautroullier.

Rastall, William. 1566. *A Collection in English, of the Statutes now in Force, continued from the beginning of Magna Charta . . . untill the end of the Parliament holden in the three and fortieth yere of the reigne of our late soveraigne lady Queene Elizabeth.* London: T. Wright, 1603 ed.

Rastell, John. 1526. *An Exposition of Certaine Difficult and Obscure Words, and Termes of the Lawes of this Realme.* London: T. Wright, 1602 ed.

Ridley, Sir Thomas. 1607. *A View of the Civille and Ecclesiasticall Law.* Oxford: H. Hall, 1676 ed.

Rogers, D. 1642. *Matrimoniall Honour or the Mutual Crowne and Comfort of Godly, Loyall, and Chaste Marriage.* London: P. Nevil.

Sander, N. 1624. *A Treatise of the Images of Christ and of his Saints: And that it is unlawful to breake them, and lawfull to honour them.* Omers: J. Heigham.

Sapcote, Jerome. 1579. *Ad primas leges Digestorum de verborum et rerum significatione.* Venice: n.p.

Selden, John. 1599. *Table Talk.* London: E. Smith, 1689 ed.

———. 1610. *The Duello or Single Combat: From antiquitie derived into this kingdome of England with several kindes, and ceremonious formes thereof from good authority described.* London: I. Helme.

———. 1610. *Jani Anglorum Facies Altera.* London: T. Bassett, 1683 ed.

———. 1614. *Titles of Honour.* London: W. Stansby.

———. 1617. *De Diis Syris Syntagmata II.* Lipsiae: L.S. Corneri, 1672, ed.

———. 1618. *The Historie of Tithes.* London: private circulation.

———. 1647. *Ad Fletam Dissertatio.* Cambridge: Cambridge University Press, 1925 ed.

Senault, J-F. 1641. *De l'usage des passions.* Paris: Fayard, 1992 ed.

Scot, Reginald. 1586. *Scots Discovery of Witchcraft: Proving the Common Opinions of Witches Contracting with Devils, Spirits, or Familiars . . . to be but erronious conceptions and novelties.* London: E. Cotes, 1654 ed.

Sherry, Richard. 1550. *A Treatise of Schemes and Tropes very profytable for the better understanding of good authors, gathered out of the best Grammarians and Orators.* London: J. Day.

Smith, John. 1657. *The Mysterie of Rhetorique Unveil'd.* London: E. Cotes.

Smith, Thomas. 1565. *De Republica Anglorum.* London: H. Middleton, 1583 ed.

Smyth, John. 1609. "Paralleles: Censures: Observations." In John Smyth, *The Works of John Smyth,* ed. W. T. Whitely. Cambridge: Cambridge University Press, 1915.

Sowernam, Ester. 1617. *Ester hath hang'd Haman: Or an answere to a lewed Pamphlet.* London: N. Bourne.

Speght, Rachel. 1617. *A Mouzell for Melastomus . . . or an apologeticall answere to that pamphlet made by J. Swetnam.* London: T. Archer.

Spelman, Sir Henry. 1610. *Aspilogia.* London: Martin and Allestry, 1654 ed.

———. 1614. *The Original of the Four Law Terms of the Year.* London: Gillyflower.

———. 1632. *The History and Fate of Sacrilege.* London: Hartley, 1698 ed.

St. German, Christopher. 1528. *Doctor and Student.* London: Selden Society, 1974 ed.

———. 1533. *Salem and Bizance.* London: Berthelti.

———. 1534. *A Treatise Concerning the Division between the Spirituality and Temporality.* London: R. Redman.

Stapleton, Thomas. 1566. *A Returne of Untruthes upon M. Jewell.* Antwerp: J. Latius.

———. 1565. *A Fortresse of the Faith first planted amonge us englishmen, and continued by the Universal Church of Christ.* Antwerp: Ihon Laet.

Starkey, Thomas, ed. 1535. *A Dialogue between Reginald Pole and Thomas Lupset.* London: Chatto & Windus, 1948 ed.

Staunford, W. 1607. *An Exposition of the King's Prerogative.* London: Society of Stationers.

Stillingfleet, Edward. 1671. *A Discourse Concerning the Idolatry practised in the Church of Rome.* London: H. Mortlock.

———. 1676. *A Defence of the Discourse concerning the idolatry practised in the Church of Rome, in answer to a book entituled, Catholicks no idolaters.* London: Robert White.

———. 1698. *Ecclesiastical Cases Relating to the Duties and Rights of the Parochial Clergy, Stated and Resolved according to principles of conscience and law.* London: Henry Mortlock.

Susenbrotus, Johannes. 1562. *Epitome Troporum ac Schematum et Grammaticorum & Rhetorum.* London: G. Dewes.

Swetnam, J. 1615. *The Arraignment of lewde, idle, froward, and unconstant Women.* London: T. Archer.

Swinburne, Henry. 1590. *A Brief Treatise of Testaments and Last Wills, very profitable to be understood of all the Subjects of the Realme of England.* London: Society of Stationers, 1711 ed.

———. 1686. *A Treatise of Spousals, or Matrimonial Contracts.* London: Browne, 1711 ed.

Tacitus. 1911. *Dialogue of Orators.* London: Loeb Classical Library.

Tertullian. 1869. *Apologeticus.* In *Ante-Nicene Christian Library,* Vol. 10, ed. A. Roberts and J. Donaldson. Edinburgh: T & T Clark.

———. 1869. *De Cultu Feminarum.* In *Ante-Nicene Library,* Vol. 11, ed. A. Roberts and J. Donaldson. Edinburgh: T&T Clark.

———. 1869. *De Idolatria.* In *Ante-Nicene Library,* Vol. 11, ed. A. Roberts and J. Donaldson. Edinburgh: T&T Clark.

———. 1869. *De Spectaculis.* In *Ante-Nicene Christian Library,* Vol. 11, ed. A. Roberts and J. Donaldson. Edinburgh: T & T Clark.

———. 1870. *De Virginibus Velandis* In *Ante-Nicene Christian Library,* Vol. 18, ed. A. Roberts and J. Donaldson. Edinburgh: T & T Clark.

Tourneur, Cyril. 1607. *The Revenger's Tragedy.* London: Eld.

Tribonian et al. 535. *The Digest of Justinian.* Ed. Alan Watson. Philadelphia: University of Pennsylvania Press, 1985 ed.

Tuvil, Daniel. 1608. *Essaies Politike and Morall.* London: M. Lownes.

———. 1616. *Asylum Veneris, or a Sanctuary for Ladies.* London: E. Griffin.

Tyndale, William. 1530. *An Answer unto Thomas Mores Dialogue made by William Tyndale.* London: n.p.

Verstegan, Richard (pseud.). 1605. *A Restitution of Decayed Intelligence in Antiquities: Concerning the most Noble and renowned English nation.* Antwerp: Robert Bruney.

Vives, Juan Luis. 1523. *De Institutione Foeminae Christianae.* Translated as *A Very Fruteful and Pleasant Boke Called the Instruction of a Christen Woman.* London: H. Wykes, 1557 ed.

Wake, William. 1685. *A Discourse Concerning the Nature of Idolatry.* London: W. Rogers.

Warr, John. 1649. *The Corruption and Deficiency of the Laws of England.* London: R. Dutton.

West, William. 1590. *The First Part of Symbolaeography, which may be termed the art, or description, of Instruments and Presidents, or the Notary or Scrivener.* London: T. Wright, 1603 ed.

Whitlocke, James. 1601. "Of the Antiquity of Lawful Combat in England." In *A Collection of Curious Discourses written by Eminent Antiquaries upon several Heads in our English Antiquities,* ed. Thomas Hearne. London: J. Richardson, 1771 ed.

Wilson, Thomas. 1553. *The Arte of Rhetorique.* London: Garland, 1982 ed.

———. 1584. *The Rule of Reason, conteyning the Arte of Logique.* London: John Kingston.

———. 1601. *The State of England, A.D. 1600.* London: Camden Miscellany, 1936 ed.

Wiseman, Sir Robert. 1656. *The Law of Laws or the Excellency of the Civil Law above all other humane laws.* London: Royston, 1666 ed.

Wolff, J. 1615. *Discursus: De Foeminarum in jure civili et canonico privilegiis, immunitatibus et praeeminenta.* Rostock: M. Saxo.

Wood, Thomas. 1720. *An Institute of the Laws of England.* Savoy: Sare.

———. 1727. *Some Thoughts Concerning the Study of the Laws of England.* London: J. Stagg.

Wryley, William. 1592. *The True Use of Armorie.* London: I. Jackson.

WORKS PRINTED AFTER 1750

Allott, P. 1979. "The Courts and Parliament: Who Whom?" 38 *Cambridge Law Journal* 79.

Agamben, Giorgio. 1993. *The Coming Community.* Minneapolis: Minnesota University Press.

Aston, Margaret. 1988. *England's Iconoclasts I: Laws Against Images.* Oxford: Clarendon Press.

Atiyah, P. S. 1987. "Correspondence," 50 *Modern Law Review* 227.

Atiyah, P. S. 1989. *An Introduction to the Law of Contract.* Oxford: Clarendon Press.

Atkins, S., and Hoggett, B. 1985. *Women and the Law.* Oxford: Blackwell.

Auerbach, Erich. 1984. "Figura." In *Scenes from the Drama of European Literature,* ed. Erich Auerbach. Minneapolis: University of Minnesota Press.

Bachelard, Gaston. 1974. *The Psychoanalysis of Fire.* New York: Harper and Row.

Baker, J. H., ed. 1978. *The Reports of John Spelman.* London: Selden Society.

———. 1978. "Introduction." In *The Reports of John Spelman,* ed. J. H. Baker. London: Selden Society.

———. 1984. *The Order of Serjeants at Law.* London: Selden Society.

Barron, Anne. 1993. "The Illusions of the 'I': Citizenship and the Politics of Identity." In *Closure and Critique in Contemporary Legal Theory,* ed. Alan Norrie. Edinburgh: Edinburgh University Press.

Barthes, Roland. 1970. "L'Ancienne rhetorique," 16 *Communications* 172.

Bataille, G. 1988. *The Accursed Share.* New York: Zone Books.

Baudinet, M-J. 1989. "The Face of Christ, the Form of the Church." In *Fragments for a History of the Human Body: Part One*, ed. M. Feher. New York: Zone Books.

Baudrillard, Jean. 1983. *Simulations*. New York: Semiotexte.

———. 1987. *The Evil Demon of Images*. Sydney: Power Institute.

———. 1990. *La Transparence du mal*. Paris: Galilée.

Beinfenfeld, F. R. 1965. "Prolegomena to a Psychoanalysis of Law and Justice," 53 *California Law Review* 957, 1254.

Benjamin, Walter. 1976. *The Origin of German Tragic Drama*. London: New Left Books.

Bennington, Geoffrey. 1989. "Postal Politics and the Institution of the Nation." In *Nation and Narration*, ed. Homi Bhabba. Routledge: London.

Berman, Harold. 1983. *Law and Revolution: The Formation of the Western Legal Tradition*. Cambridge, Mass.: Harvard University Press.

Blackstone, William. 1765. *Commentaries on the Laws of England*. Oxford: Clarendon Press.

Blamires, A., ed. 1992. *Woman Defamed and Woman Defended*. Oxford: Oxford University Press.

Borch-Jacobsen, M. 1989. *The Freudian Subject*. London: Macmillan.

Boreau, Alain. 1987. "Les Livres d'emblèmes sur la scène publique." In *Les Usages de l'imprimerie*, ed. R. Chartrier. Paris: Fayard.

Boyd White, James. 1985. *Heracles' Bow*. Madison: Wisconsin University Press.

———. 1990. *Justice as Translation*. Chicago: Chicago University Press.

Braidotti, Rossi. 1991. *Patterns of Dissonance*. Oxford: Polity Press.

Braudel, Fernand. 1980. *On History*. Chicago: Chicago University Press.

Brooks, C. W. 1986. *Pettyfoggers and Vipers of the Commonwealth: The Lower Branch of the Legal Profession in Early Modern England*. Cambridge: Cambridge University Press.

Brundage, James A. 1987. *Law, Sex, and Christian Society in Medieval Europe*. Chicago: Chicago University Press.

Buci-Glucksmann, Christine. 1984. *La Raison baroque: De Baudelaire à Benjamin*. Paris: Galilée.

———. 1986. *La Folie du voir: De l'esthétique baroque*. Paris: Galilée.

Buck-Morss, Susan. 1989. *The Dialectics of Seeing: Walter Benjamin and the Arcades Project*. Boston: MIT.

Butler, Judith. 1990. *Gender Trouble: Feminism and the Subversion of Identity*. New York: Routledge.

———. 1992. "The Lesbian Phallus and the Morphological Imaginary," 4.1 *differences: A Journal of Feminist Cultural Studies* 133.

———. 1993. *Bodies that Matter: On the Discursive Limits of Sex*. New York: Routledge.

Cain, Patricia. 1990. "Feminist Jurisprudence: Grounding the Theories," 4 *Berkeley Women's Law Journal* 191.

Camille, Michael. 1989. *The Gothic Idol: Ideology and Image Making in Medieval Art*. Cambridge: Cambridge University Press.

Carrington, P. 1984. "Of Law and the River," 34 *Journal of Legal Education* 222.

Carruthers, Mary. 1990. *The Book of Memory: A Study of Memory in Medieval Culture*. Cambridge: Cambridge University Press.

Case, Mary Anne. 1993. "From the Mirror of Reason to the Measure of Justice," 5 *Yale Journal of Law and the Humanities* 115.

Caudill, David. 1991. "Freud and Critical Legal Studies: Contours of a Radical Socio-Legal Psychoanalysis," 66 *Indiana Law Review* 651.

———. 1992. "Lacan and Legal Language: Meanings in the Gaps, Gaps in the Meaning," 3 *Law and Critique* 165.

———. 1993. "Name of the Father and the Logic of Psychosis: Lacan's Law and Ours," 4 *Legal Studies Forum* 421.

Chartrier, R., and Martin, H-J., eds. 1989. *Histoire de l'edition Francais.* Paris: Fayard.

Cheshire, G. C., and Fifoot, C. H. S. 1945. *Law of Contract.* London: Butterworth, 1991 ed.

Cixous, Hélène, and Clement, C. 1986. *The Newly Born Woman.* Minneapolis: University of Minnesota Press.

Cixous, Hélène. 1991. *Coming to Writing*. Cambridge, Mass.: Harvard University Press.

———. 1991. *Readings: The Poetics of Blanchot, Joyce, Kafka, Kleist, Lispector, and Tsvetayva.* Minneapolis: University of Minnesota Press.

———. 1993. *Three Steps on the Ladder of Writing.* New York: Columbia University Press.

Clanchy, M. T. 1979. *From Memory to Written Record.* Oxford: Blackwell, 1992.

Clifford, James, and Marcus, George, eds. 1986. *Writing Culture: The Poetics and Politics of Ethnography.* Berkeley and Los Angeles: University of California Press.

Cole, Thomas. 1991. *The Origins of Rhetoric in Ancient Greece.* Baltimore: Johns Hopkins University Press.

Collins, Stephen. 1992. *From Divine Cosmos to Sovereign State.* New York: Oxford University Press.

Conaghan, Joanne, and Mansell, Wade. 1993. *The Wrongs of Tort.* London: Pluto Press.

Connerton, Paul. 1990. *How Societies Remember.* Cambridge: Cambridge University Press.

Constable, Marianne. *The Law of the Other: The Mixed Jury and Changing Conceptions of Citizenship, Law and Knowledge* (Chicago: Chicago University Press, 1994).

Corbin, Arthur Linton. 1950. *Corbin on Contracts.* St. Paul: West Publishing.

Cornell, Drucilla. 1990. *Beyond Accommodation: Ethical Feminism, Deconstruction and the Law.* New York: Routledge.

———. 1992. *The Philosophy of the Limit.* New York: Routledge.

———. 1992. "What Takes Place in the Dark," 4.2 *differences: A Journal of Feminist Cultural Studies* 45.

Cousins, Mark. 1987. "The Practice of Historical Investigation." In *Poststructuralism and the Question of History,* ed. D. Attridge et al. Cambridge: Cambridge University Press.

Coward, R. 1983. *Patriarchal Precedents.* London: Routledge.

Crenshaw. K. 1990. "A Black Feminist Critique of Antidiscrimination Law and Politics." In *The Politics of Law,* ed. D. Kaiys. New York: Pantheon Books.

Curtis, D., and Resnik, J. 1986. "Images of Justice," 96 *Yale Law Journal* 1727.

Damisch, Hubert. 1972. *Théorie du nuage: Pour une histoire de la peinture.* Paris: Seuil.

Debray, Régis. 1983. *Critique of Political Reason.* London: Verso.

———. 1991. *Cours de mediologie generale.* Paris: Gallimard.
———. 1992. *Vie et mort de l'image: Une histoire du regard en occident.* Paris: Gallimard.
de Certeau, Michel. 1988. *The Writing of History.* New York: Columbia University Press.
———. 1992. *The Mystic Fable, Volume One: The Sixteenth and Seventeenth Centuries.* Chicago: Chicago University Press.
Deleuze, Gilles. 1968. *Différence et répétition.* Paris: Presses Universitaires de France.
———. 1993. *The Fold: Liebniz and the Baroque.* Minneapolis: University of Minnesota Press.
Deleuze, Gilles, and Guattari, Félix. 1987. *A Thousand Plateaus: Capitalism and Schizophrenia.* Minneapolis: University of Minnesota Press.
———. 1988. *A Thousand Plateaus.* London: Athlone.
Derrida, Jacques. 1976. *Of Grammatology.* Baltimore: Johns Hopkins University Press.
———. 1978. *Writing and Difference.* London: Routledge.
———. 1979. *Spurs: Nietzsche's Styles.* Chicago: Chicago University Press.
———. 1982. "The White Mythology." In Jacques Derrida, *Margins of Philosophy.* Brighton: Harvester Press.
———. 1986. "Mnemosyne." In Jacques Derrida, *Memoires: For Paul de Man.* New York: Columbia University Press.
———. 1987. "Des Tours de Babel." In Jacques Derrida, *Psyché.* Paris: Galilée.
———. 1987. *The Post Card: From Socrates to Freud and Beyond.* Chicago: Chicago University Press.
———. 1990. "Force of Law: The 'Mystical Foundation of Authority,'" 11 *Cardozo Law Review* 919.
de Zulueta, F., ed. 1946. *The Institutes of Gaius, Part I.* Oxford: Clarendon Press.
de Zulueta, F., and Stein, P. 1990. *The Teaching of Roman Law in England around 1200.* London: Selden Society.
Didi-Huberman, Georges. 1987. "La Couleur de chair ou le paradoxe de Tertullien," 35 *Nouvelle Revue de Psychanalyse* 9.
———. 1990. *Devant l'image: Question posée aux fins d'une histoire de l'art.* Paris: Éditions de Minuit.
Douzinas, Costas, and Warrington, Ronnie. 1991. "A Well-Founded Fear of Justice: Law and Ethics in Postmodernity," 2 *Law and Critique* 115.
———. 1991. "Posting the Law: Social Contracts and the Postal Rule's Grammatology," 4 *International Journal for the Semiotics of Law* 115.
———. 1994. *Justice MisCarried: Ethics and Aesthetics in Law.* Hemel Hempstead: Harvester.
Douzinas, Costas, et al. 1990. *Postmodern Jurisprudence: The Law of Text in the Texts of Law.* London: Routledge.
———. 1994. *Politics, Postmodernity and Critical Legal Studies: A Legality of the Contingent.* London: Routledge.
Dronke, P. 1984. *Women Writers of the Middle Ages.* Cambridge: Cambridge University Press.
Dupont, Florence. 1989. "The Emperor God's Other Body." In *Fragments for a History of the Human Body, Part Three,* ed. M. Feher. New York: Zone Books.

Duxbury, Neil. 1990. "Some Radicalism about Realism?" 10 *Oxford Journal of Legal Studies* 11.

———. 1991. "Jerome Frank and the Legacy of Legal Realism," 18 *Journal of Law and Society* 175.

Ehrenzweig, A. 1971. *Psychoanalytic Jurisprudence: On Ethics, Aesthetics, and Law*. Leiden: Dordrecht.

Eire, Carlos. 1986. *War Against the Idols: The Reformation of Worship from Erasmus to Calvin*. Cambridge: Cambridge University Press.

Eisenstein, Elizabeth. 1980. *The Printing Press as an Agent of Change*. Cambridge: Cambridge University Press.

Evans, David. 1993. "The Inns of Court: Speculations on the Body of Law," 1 *Arch-Text* 5.

Farnsworth, Allan. 1967. "Meaning in the Law of Contracts," 76 *Yale Law Journal* 939.

Farrell-Krell, D. 1990. *Of Memory, Reminiscence, and Writing*. Indianapolis: Indiana University Press.

Febvre, F. 1978. *A New Kind of History*. Princeton: Princeton University Press.

Felman, S. 1987. *Jacques Lacan and the Adventure of Insight*. Cambridge, Mass.: Harvard University Press.

Ferry, Luc. 1990. *Homo aestheticus: L'Invention du gout à l'age démocratique*. Paris: Grasset.

Fish, Stanley, 1989. *Doing What Comes Naturally*. Durham: Duke University Press.

———. 1991. "The Law Wishes to Have a Formal Existence." In *The Fate of Law*, ed. A. Sarat and T. Kearns. Ann Arbor: Michigan University Press.

Fitzpatrick, Peter. 1992. *The Mythology of Modern Law*. London: Routledge.

Florovsky, G. 1950. "Origen, Eusebius and the Iconoclastic Controversy," 19 *Church History* 77.

Foucault, Michel. 1973. *The Order of Things: An Archaeology of the Human Sciences*. New York: Vintage Books.

———. 1977. *Language, Counter-Memory, Practice*. Ed. D. F. Bouchard. Ithaca: Cornell University Press.

———. 1982. "The Discourse on Language." Reprinted as an appendix to Michel Foucault, *The Archaeology of Knowledge*. New York: Pantheon.

———. 1991. "La Vérité et les formes juridiques," 10 *Chimères* 9.

Frank, J. 1930. *Law and the Modern Mind*. Garden City, N.Y.: Anchor, 1963.

Freedberg, David. 1990. *The Power of Images*. Chicago: Chicago University Press.

Freud, Sigmund. 1914. *The Psychopathology of Everyday Life*. Harmondsworth: Pelican, 1942 ed.

———. 1919. *Totem and Taboo: Resemblances between the Psychic Lives of Savages and Neurotics*. Harmondsworth: Penguin Books.

———. 1939. *Moses and Monotheism*. London: Hogarth Press.

———. 1948. "Mourning and Melancholia." In Sigmund Freud, *Collected Papers, IV*. London: Hogarth Press.

———. 1961. *Beyond the Pleasure Principle*. London: Hogarth Press.

———. 1963. "Negation." In Sigmund Freud, *General Psychological Theory*. New York: Collier Macmillan.

———. 1965. *The Interpretation of Dreams*. New York: Avon Books.

———. 1975. *Civilization and its Discontents.* London: Hogarth Press.
Fried, C. 1988. "Jurisprudential Responses to Realism," 73 *Cornell Law Review* 331.
Frug, Gerry, 1988. "Argument as Character," 40 *Stanford Law Review* 869.
Frug, Mary-Joe. 1985. "Re-Reading Contracts: A Feminist Analysis of a Contracts Casebook," 34 *American University Law Review* 1065.
———. 1992. "A Postmodern Feminist Legal Manifesto," 105 *Harvard Law Review* 1045.
———. 1992. "Rescuing Impossibility Doctrine: A Postmodern Feminist Analysis of Contract Law," 140 *University of Pennsylvania Law Review* 1029.
Gabel, P. 1984. "The Phenomenology of Rights Consciousness and the Pact of the Withdrawn Selves," 62 *Texas Law Review* 1563.
Gabel, P., and Kennedy, D. 1984. "Roll Over Beethoven," 36 *Stanford Law Review* 1.
Gardiner, Simon. 1992. "Trashing with Trollope: A Deconstruction of the Postal Rules in Contract," 12 *Oxford Journal of Legal Studies* 170.
Gardner, Jane. 1986. *Women in Roman Law and Society.* London: Croom Helm.
Geertz, Clifford. 1986. "The Uses of Diversity," 25 *Michigan Quarterly Review* 105.
Genette, G. 1970. "La Rhetorique restreinte," 16 *Communications* 158.
Gibson, Suzanne. 1989. "The Structure of the Veil," 52 *Modern Law Review* 420.
Gilligan, C. 1982. *In a Different Voice.* Cambridge, Mass.: Harvard University Press.
Ginsburg, Carlo. 1990. "Clues: Roots of an Evidential Paradigm." In Carlo Ginsburg, *Myths, Emblems and Clues.* London: Radius.
Goodrich, Peter. 1984. "Rhetoric as Jurisprudence: An Introduction to the Politics of Legal Language," 4 *Oxford Journal of Legal Studies* 122.
———. 1986. *Reading the Law.* Oxford: Blackwell.
———. 1987. "Literacy and the Languages of the Early Common Law," 14 *Journal of Law and Society* 422.
———. 1987. "Psychoanalysis in Legal Education: Notes on the Violence of the Sign." In *Law and Semiotics,* ed. R. Kevelson. New York: Plenum Press.
———. 1990. "Contractions." In *Post-Modern Law,* ed. Anthony Carty. Edinburgh: Edinburgh University Press.
———. 1990. *Languages of Law: From Logics of Memory to Nomadic Masks.* London: Weidenfeld and Nicholson.
———. 1990. "We Orators," 53 *Modern Law Review* 546.
———. 1991. "Eating Law: Commons, Common Land and Common Law," 12 *Journal of Legal History* 246.
———. 1991. "Specula Laws: Image, Aesthetic and Common Law," 2 *Law and Critique* 233.
———. 1992. "Ars Bablativa: Ramism, Rhetoric and the Genealogy of English Jurisprudence." In *Law and Hermeneutics: History, Theory, Practice,* ed. G. Leyh. Berkeley and Los Angeles: University of California Press.
———. 1992. "Poor Illiterate Reason: History, Nationalism and Common Law," 1 *Social and Legal Studies* 7.
———. 1992. "The Continuance of the Antirrhetic," 4 *Cardozo Studies in Law and Literature* 207.
———. 1992. "Critical Legal Studies in England: Prospective Histories," 12 *Oxford Journal of Legal Studies* 196.
———. 1993. "Fate as Seduction: The Other Scene of Legal Judgment." In *Closure*

and Critique in Contemporary Legal Theory, ed. Alan Norrie. Edinburgh: Edinburgh University Press.

———. 1993. "Sleeping with the Enemy: An Essay on the Politics of Critical Legal Studies in America," 68 *New York University Law Review* 389.

———. 1993. "Writing Legal Difference," 6 *Women: A Cultural Journal* 173.

———. 1994. "Antirrhesis: Polemical Structures of Common Law Thought." In *Rhetoric and Law*, ed. A. Sarat and T. Kearns. Ann Arbor: Michigan University Press.

Gordley, James. 1991. *The Philosophical Origins of Modern Contract Doctrine*. Oxford: Clarendon Press.

Goux, Jean-Joseph. 1976. *Les Iconoclastes*. Paris: Éditions du Seuil.

———. 1990. *Oedipe Philosophe*. Paris: Éditions Aubier.

Grabar, André. 1968. *Christian Iconography: A Study of its Origins*. Princeton: Princeton University Press.

Gruzinski, Serge. 1990. *La Guerre des images*. Paris: Fayard.

Hachamovitch, Yifat. 1990. "One Law on the Other," 3 *International Journal for the Semiotics of Law* 187.

———. 1991. "The Ideal Object of Transmission: An Essay on the Faith which Attaches to Instruments," 2 *Law and Critique* 85.

———. 1994. "In Emulation of the Clouds: An Essay on the Obscure Object of Judgement." In *Politics, Postmodernity and Critical Legal Studies: The Legality of the Contingent*, ed. Costas Douzinas, Peter Goodrich, and Yifat Hachamovitch. London: Routledge.

Haldar, Piyel. 1991. "The Evidencer's Eye: Representations of Truth in the Laws of Evidence," 2 *Law and Critique* 171.

Harris, Angela. 1990. "Race and Essentialism in Feminist Legal Theory," 42 *Stanford Law Review* 581.

Hermogenes. 1987. *On Types of Style*. Chapel Hill: University of North Carolina Press.

Houlbrooke, Ralph. 1979. *Church Courts and the People during the English Reformation, 1520–1570*. Oxford: Oxford University Press.

Ingram, M. 1987. *Church and Courts, Sex and Marriage in England, 1570–1640*. Cambridge: Cambridge University Press.

Irigaray, Luce. 1984. *Éthique de la différence sexuelle*. Paris: Editions de Minuit.

———. 1985. *Speculum of the Other Woman*. Ithaca: Cornell University Press.

———. 1985. *This Sex Which Is Not One*. Ithaca: Cornell University Press.

———. 1989. *Le Temps de la différence*. Paris: Livre de Poche.

———. 1991. *Marine Lover of Friedrich Nietzsche*. New York: Columbia University Press.

———. 1992. *J'aime à toi: Equisse d'une félicité dans l'histoire*. Paris: Grasset.

———. 1993. *Sexes and Genealogies*. New York: Columbia University Press.

Jacobson, Arthur. 1990. "The Idolatry of Rules: Writing Law According to Moses, with Reference to Other Jurisprudences," 11 *Cardozo Law Review* 1079.

Jardine, Alice. 1985. *Gynesis: Configurations of Women and Modernity*. Ithaca: Cornell University Press.

Jay, Martin. 1993. *Downcast Eyes: The Denigration of Vision in Twentieth-Century French Thought*. Los Angeles and Berkeley: University of California Press.

Jordan, Constance. 1990. *Renaissance Feminism: Literary Texts and Political Models.* Ithaca: Cornell University Press.

Jung, Carl. 1963. *Memories, Dreams, Reflections.* London: Collins and Routledge.

Juranville, Anne. 1993. *La Femme et la mélancholie.* Paris: Presses Universitaires de France.

Kantorowicz, Ernst. 1957. *The King's Two Bodies.* Princeton: Princeton University Press.

———. 1965. "The Sovereignty of the Artist: A Note on Legal Maxims and Renaissance Theories of Art." In Ernst Kantorowicz, *Selected Studies.* New York: J. Augustin.

Kantorowicz, Herman. 1943. "The Poetical Sermon of a Mediaeval Jurist: Placentinus and his 'Sermo de Legibus.'" 2 *Journal of the Warburg and Courtauld Institute* 22.

Kelley, Donald. 1970. *Foundations of Modern Historical Scholarship: Language, Law, and History in the French Renaissance.* New York: Columbia University Press.

———. 1990. *The Human Measure: Social Thought in the Western Legal Tradition.* Cambridge, Mass.: Harvard University Press.

Kelly, Joan. 1984. *Women, History, and Theory: The Essays of Joan Kelly.* Chicago: University of Chicago Press.

Kitzinger, E. 1988. "The Cult of Images in the Age before Iconoclasm," 8 *Dumbarton Oaks Papers* 112–115.

Kofman, Sarah. 1985. *The Enigma of Woman: Woman in Freud's Writings.* Ithaca: Cornell University Press.

Kramer, Matthew H. 1991. *Legal Theory, Political Theory, and Deconstruction: Against Rhadamanthus.* Bloomington: Indiana University Press.

Kristeva, Julia. 1981. "Women's Time," 7 *Signs* 13.

———. 1983. "Psychoanalysis and the Polis." In *The Politics of Interpretation,* ed. W. J. T. Mitchell. Chicago: Chicago University Press.

———. 1984. *Revolution in Poetic Language.* New York: Columbia University Press.

———. 1989. *Black Sun: Depression and Melancholia.* New York: Columbia University Press.

———. 1990. *Strangers to Ourselves.* New York: Columbia University Press.

Labalme, P., ed. 1980. *Beyond Their Sex: Learned Women of the European Past.* New York: New York University Press.

Lacan, Jacques. 1972. "Seminar on the Purloined Letter," 48 *Yale French Studies* 39.

———. 1977. *Écrits: A Selection.* London: Tavistock.

———. 1978. *The Four Fundamental Concepts of Psychoanalysis.* London: Pelican.

———. 1988. *The Seminar of Jacques Lacan, Book II: The Ego in Freud's Theory and in the Technique of Psychoanalysis, 1954–55.* New York: Norton.

———. 1990. *Le Seminaire IV: L'Ethique de la psychanalyse.* Paris: Seuil.

Lacan, Jacques, and Wilden, A. 1981. *Speech and Language in Psychoanalysis.* Baltimore: Johns Hopkins University Press.

Ladner, G. 1983. "The Origin and Significance of the Byzantine Iconoclastic Controversy." In G. Ladner, *Images and Ideas in the Middle Ages: Selected Studies in History and Art I.* Rome: Edizioni di Storia e Letteratura.

Laplanche, Jean. 1992. *Seduction, Translation, Drives.* London: ICA.

Larson, Jane. 1993. "Women Understand So Little, They Call My Good Nature Deceit: A Feminist Rethinking of Seduction," 93 *Columbia Law Review* 374.

Lazard, Madeleine. 1985. *Images littéraries de la femme à la renaissance.* Paris: Presses Universitaires de France.

le Doeuf, Michèle. 1989. *The Philosophical Imaginary.* Stanford: Stanford University Press.

Legendre, A. Papageorgiou. 1990. *Filiation: Fondement généalogique du psychanalyse.* Paris: Fayard.

Legendre, Pierre. 1964. *La Pénétration du droit romain dans le droit canonique classique de Gratien à Innocent IV.* Paris: Imprimerie Jouve.

———. 1974. *L'Amour du censeur: Essai sur l'ordre dogmatique.* Paris: Éditions du Seuil.

———. 1976. *Jouir du pouvoir: Traité sur le bureaucratie patriote.* Paris: Éditions de Minuit.

———. 1982. *Paroles poétiques échapées du texte.* Paris: Éditions du Seuil.

———. 1983. *L'Empire de la vérité.* Paris: Fayard.

———. 1985. *L'Inestimable objet de la transmission: Étude sur le principe généalogique en occident.* Paris: Fayard.

———. 1988. "Le Droit romain, modèle et langage: De la signification de l'Utrumque Ius." In Pierre Legendre, *Écrits juridiques du Moyen Age occidental.* London: Valiorum.

———. 1989. *Le Crime du Caporal Lortie: Traité sur le père.* Paris: Fayard.

———. 1989. *Le Désir politique de Dieu: Étude sur les montages de l'état et du droit.* Paris: Fayard.

———. 1992. *Les Enfants du texte: Étude sur la fonction parentale des états.* Paris: Fayard.

———. 1994. *Dieu au mirroir.* Paris: Fayard.

Legendre, Pierre, et al. eds. 1988. *Le Dossier occidental de la parenté: Textes juridiques indésirables sur la généalogie.* Paris: Fayard.

Lerner, Gerda. 1993. *The Creation of Feminist Consciousness.* New York: Oxford University Press.

Levack, Brian. 1973. *The Civil Lawyers in England, 1603–1641.* Oxford: Oxford University Press.

Levinas, E. 1981. *Otherwise than Being.* The Hague: Nijhoff.

Llewellyn, K. N. 1939. "Our Case-Law of Contract: Offer and Acceptance" 48 *Yale Law Journal* 779, 795.

Llewellyn, Nigel. 1991. *The Art of Death: Visual Culture in the English Death Ritual c. 1500–c. 1800.* London: Reaktion Books.

MacCormick, D. N. 1990. "Reconstruction after Deconstruction: A Response to CLS," 10 *Oxford Journal of Legal Studies* 539.

Maclean, Ian. 1977. *Woman Triumphant: Feminism in French Literature 1610–1652.* Oxford: Clarendon Press.

———. 1980. *The Renaissance Notion of Women.* Cambridge: Cambridge University Press.

———. 1992. *Interpretation and Meaning in the Renaissance: The Case of Law.* Cambridge: Cambridge University Press.

Maravall, J. A. 1986. *Culture of the Baroque: Analysis of a Historical Structure.* Minneapolis: Minnesota University Press.

Marin, Louis. 1988. *Portrait of the King.* London: Macmillan.

———. 1993. *Des pouvoirs de l'image.* Paris: Éditions du Seuil.

Martin, E. J. 1930. *A History of the Iconoclastic Controversy.* London: SPCK.

Martin, H-J. 1988. *Histoire et pouvoirs de l'écrit.* Paris: Perrin.

Metz, Christian. 1982. *Psychoanalysis and Cinema: The Imaginary Signifier.* London: Macmillan.

Milner, Jean-Claude. 1990. *For the Love of Language.* London: Macmillan.

Minkkinen, P. 1992. "Otherness and Difference: On the Cultural Logic of Racial Intolerance," 3 *Law and Critique* 147.

Minow, M. 1991. "Partial Justice: Law and Minorities." In *The Fate of Law,* ed. A. Sarat and T. Kearns. Ann Arbor: University of Michigan Press.

Mondzain-Baudinet, M-J., ed. 1982. *Du visage.* Lille: Presse Universitaire de Lille.

———. 1989. *Nicephorus, discours contre les iconoclastes.* Paris: Klincksieck.

Murphy, W. T. 1989. "Memorising Politics of Ancient History," 50 *Modern Law Review* 384.

———. 1991. "The Oldest Social Science? The Epistemic Properties of the Common Law Tradition," 54 *Modern Law Review* 182.

Murphy, W. T., and Rawlings, R. W. 1981. "After the Ancien Regime: The Writing of Judgments in the House of Lords 1979/1980," 44 *Modern Law Review* 617.

Nietzsche, Friedrich. 1873. *On Language and Rhetoric.* Oxford: Oxford University Press, 1989.

———. 1909. "Homer and Classical Philology." In Friedrich Nietzsche, *On the Future of Our Educational Institutions.* Edinburgh: Foulis.

———. 1911. "We Philologists." In Friedrich Nietzsche, *The Case of Wagner.* Edinburgh: T. N. Foulis.

Norrie, Alan., ed. 1993. *Closure and Critique in Contemporary Legal Theory.* Edinburgh: Edinburgh University Press.

Nusbaum, A. 1936. "Comparative Aspects of the Anglo-American Offer-and-Acceptance Doctrine," 33 *Columbia Law Review* 920.

Obeyesekere, Gananath. 1990. *The Work of Culture: Symbolic Transformation in Psychoanalysis and Anthropology.* Chicago: Chicago University Press.

Ong, W. 1958. *Ramus: Method and the Decay of Dialogue.* Cambridge: Harvard University Press.

Pateman, C. 1988. *The Sexual Contract.* Cambridge: Polity Press.

Pêcheux, Michel. 1982. *Language, Semantics and Ideology.* London: Macmillan.

Perelman, Chaim. 1976. *Logique juridique, nouvelle rhetorique.* Paris: Dalloz.

Perelman, Chaim, and Tyteca, Obrechts. 1969. *The New Rhetoric: A Treatise on Argumentation.* Notre Dame: Notre Dame University Press.

Perrot, Michelle, ed. 1982. *Writing Women's History.* Oxford: Blackwell.

Pocock, J. G. A. 1987. *The Ancient Constitution and the Feudal Law.* Cambridge: Cambridge University Press.

Post, Gaines. 1964. *Studies in Medieval Legal Thought.* Princeton: Princeton University Press.

Post, R. 1991. "Post-Modernism and the Law," *London Review of Books,* February.

Postema, Gerald. 1989. *Bentham and the Common Law Tradition.* Oxford: Clarendon Press.

Pottage, Alain. 1992. "Crime and Culture: The Relevance of the Psychoanalytical," 55 *Modern Law Review* 421.

———. 1994. "The Paternity of Law." In *Politics, Postmodernity and Critical Legal Studies: The Legality of the Contingent,* ed. Costas Douzinas et al. London: Routledge.

Prest, Wilfred. 1986. *The Rise of the Barristers: A Social History of the English Bar 1590–1640.* Oxford: Oxford University Press.

———. "Law and Women's Rights in Early Modern Europe" (1991) VI.2 *The Seventeenth Century* 169.

Quilligan, Maureen. 1991. *The Allegory of Female Authority: Christine de Pisan's Cité des Dames.* Ithaca: Cornell University Press.

Ricouer, Paul. 1977. *Freud and Philosophy: An Essay on Interpretation.* New Haven: Yale University Press.

Riley, Denise. 1988. *Am I That Name? Feminism and the Category of "Women" in History.* London: Macmillan.

Robinson, Olivia. 1988. "The Historical Background." In *The Legal Relevance of Gender,* ed. S. McLean and N. Burrows. London: Macmillan.

Rose, Gillian. 1984. *Dialectic of Nihilism: Post-Structuralism and Law.* Oxford: Blackwell.

Rotman, Brian. 1987. *Signifying Nothing: The Semiotics of Zero.* London: Macmillan.

Rush, Peter. 1990. "Killing Me Softly with His Words," 1 *Law and Critique* 21.

Salecl, Renata. 1993. "Crime as a Mode of Subjectivization: Lacan and the Law," 4 *Law and Critique* 3.

Salisbury, Joyce E. 1991. *Church Fathers, Independent Virgins.* London: Verso Books.

Sartre, Jean-Paul. 1976. *Critique of Dialectical Reason I, Theory of Practical Ensembles.* London: New Left Books.

Schiesari, Juliana. 1992. *The Gendering of Melancholia: Feminism, Psychoanalysis, and the Symbolics of Loss in Renaissance Literature.* Ithaca: Cornell University Press.

Schoenfeld, C. G. 1973. *Psychoanalysis and the Law.* Springfield, Ill.: Thomas.

Schroeder, Jeanne. 1990. "Feminism Historicised: Medieval Misogynist Stereotypes in Contemporary Feminist Jurisprudence," 75 *Iowa Law Review* 1135.

Setton, Kenneth M. 1941. *Christian Attitudes Towards the Emperor in the Fourth Century.* New York: Columbia University Press.

Sharp, M. 1966. "Reflections on Contract," 33 *University of Chicago Law Review* 211.

Simpson, A. W. B. 1977. "Innovation in Nineteenth Century Contract Law," 91 *Law Quarterly Review* 247.

———. 1987. *A History of the Common Law of Contract: The Rise of the Action of Assumpsit.* Oxford: Clarendon Press.

Sloterdijk, Peter. 1987. *Critique of Cynical Reason.* Minneapolis: Minnesota University Press.

Stang-Dahl, T. 1987. *Women's Law: An Introduction to Feminist Jurisprudence.* Oxford: Norwegian University Press.

Thomas, Yan. 1991. "L'Institution de la majesté," 112 *Revue de synthèse* 331.

———. 1992. "The Division of the Sexes in Roman Law." In *A History of Women in the West I,* ed. P. S. Pantel. Cambridge, Mass.: Harvard University Press.

Todorov, T. 1982. *Theories of the Symbol.* Oxford: Basil Blackwell.
Treitel, G. 1991. *The Law of Contract.* London: Sweet and Maxwell.
Turkle, Sherry. 1978. *Psychoanalytic Politics.* New York: Basic Books.
Vickers, Brian. 1988. *In Defence of Rhetoric.* Oxford: Oxford University Press.
Virilio, Paul. 1991. *The Aesthetics of Disappearance.* New York: Semiotexte.
Watkin, T. G. 1984. "Tabula Picta: Images and Icons," 50 *Studia et Documenta Historiae et Iuris* 383.
Weber, Samuel. 1991. *Return to Freud: Jacques Lacan's Dislocation of Psychoanalysis.* Cambridge: Cambridge University Press.
White, James Boyd. 1985. *Heracles' Bow.* Madison: Wisconsin University Press.
———. 1990. *Justice as Translation: An Essay in Cultural and Legal Criticism.* Chicago: University of Chicago Press.
Williams, Joan. 1985. "Feminist Discourse, Moral Values and the Law—A Conversation," 34 *Buffalo Law Review* 11.
———. 1989. "Deconstructing Gender," 87 *Michigan Law Review* 797.
Williams, Patricia. 1991. *The Alchemy of Race and Rights.* Cambridge, Mass.: Harvard University Press.
Winfield, P. 1939. "Some Aspects of Offer and Acceptance," 55 *Law Quarterly Review* 499.
Wirth, Jean. 1989. *L'Image médiévale.* Paris: Méridiens Klincksieck.
Yates, Frances. 1966. *The Art of Memory.* London: Routledge and Kegan Paul.
Young, Iris Marion. 1990. *Justice and the Politics of Difference.* Princeton: Princeton University Press.

TABLE OF CASES

Adams v *Lindsell* [1818] 1 B & Ald 681.
Alcock and others v *Chief Constable of the South Yorkshire Police* [1991] 4 AER 907.
Attia v *British Gas plc* [1987] 2 AER 455.
Balfour v *Balfour* [1919] 2 KB 571.
Brinkibon Ltd. v *Stahag Stahl und Stahlwarenhandelsgesellschaft mbH* [1983] 2 AC 34.
British and American Telegraph Co. v *Colson* [1871] LR 6 Exch 108 at 118.
Bruce v *Rawlins* [1770] 95 Eng Rep 934.
Chadwick v *British Transport Commission* [1967] 2 AER 945.
Copland v *Pyatt,* Trinity Term, 6 Car. 1 Roll 687, 79 ER 814.
Darnel's Case [1627] 3 St. Tr. 1.
Dickinson v *Dodds* [1876] 2 ChD 463.
Dooley v *Cammell Laird. & Co. Ltd.* [1951] 1 Lloyd's Rep 271.
Dorothy Brian v *Cockman* 79 ER 881.
Entick v *Carrington and three others,* 1765. In *State Trials.* London: Hansard, 1813.
Hammersley v *De Biel* [1845] XII Clark and Finlay 46; 8 ER 1312.
Henry of Naburn v *Walter le Flemyng, Richard of Duffield and others* (1316) 74 Selden Society 72.
Henthorn v *Fraser* [1892] 2 Ch. 27.
Holwell Securities v *Hughes* [1974] 1 WLR 155.
Household Fire and Carriage Accident Insurance Co. Ltd. v *Grant* [1879] 4 Ex. D. 216.
Jaensch v *Coffey* [1984] 54 ALR 417 (per Deane J).

Johnson v *Grant* [1923] S.C. 789, 790.
M. v *Home Office* [1992] 2 WLR.
M. v *Home Office* [1993] 3 AER 537.
McCullough v *Eagle Insurance Co.* [1822] 18 Mass. (1 Pick.) 278.
McLoughlin v *O'Brian and others* [1982] 2 AER 298.
Morison v *Thoelke,* 155 So.d 889 [1963].
Morone v *Morone,* 50 N.Y.2d. 481, 429 N.Y.S.2d. 592, 413 N.E.2d 1154 (1980).
Mount Isa Mines Ltd. v *Pusey* [1970] 125 CLR 383.
Owens v *Liverpool Corporation* [1938] 4 AER 727.
Pollard v *Armshaw* (1601) 75 ER 1073.
Ratcliffe v *Burton* [1802] 27 Eng Rep 123.
Rhode Island Tool Co. v *United States,* 128 F. Supp. 417 [Ct. Cl. 1955].
Semayne's Case [1605] 5 Co Rep 91.
Synge v *Synge* [1894] 1 QB 466.
Town Investments Ltd. and Others v *Dept. of Environment* [1978] AC 359.
Tuttle v *Iowa State Traveling Men's Association,* 132 Iowa 652, 104 N.W. 1131 (1888).
Wagner v *International Railway Co.* (1921) 232 NY 176.
X Ltd. v *Morgan-Grampian (Publishers) Ltd. and others* [1990] 1 AER 616.
Watts and another v *Morrow* [1991] 4 AER 937.
Wilkes v *The Earl of Halifax* [1769] 2 Wils. KB 256 (95 ER 797).
William de Thorp v *Mackerel and another* (1318) Coram Rege Roll no 233, in Sayles ed. (1955) 74 Selden Society 79.

INDEX

Designer: U.C. Press Staff
Compositor: Prestige Typography
Text: 10/12 Baskerville
Display: Baskerville
Printer: Braun-Brumfield, Inc.
Binder: Braun-Brumfield, Inc.